ROCK&ICE
GEAR

EQUIPMENT FOR THE VERTICAL WORLD

ROCK&ICE

GEAR

EQUIPMENT FOR THE VERTICAL WORLD

by Clyde Soles

THE
MOUNTAINEERS
BOOKS

Published by
The Mountaineers Books
1001 SW Klickitat Way, Suite 201
Seattle, WA 98134

First edition, 2000

Published simultaneously in Great Britain by Cordee, 3a DeMontfort Street, Leicester, England, LE1 7HD

Manufactured in the United States of America

Project Editor: Christine Ummel Hosler
Editor: Paula Thurman
All photographs by the author
Cover and Book Designer: Ani Rucki
Layout Artist: Margarite Hargrave

Cover photograph: *Rock Climbing in Tuolumne in Yosemite* © Brian Bailey/Adventure Photo & Film
Frontispiece: *White core strands are brought together at a 48-bobbin sheath braider.*

Library of Congress Cataloging-in-Publication Data
Soles, Clyde, 1959-
  Rock & ice gear : equipment for the vertical world / by Clyde Soles.—1st ed.
   p. cm.
  Includes index.
  ISBN 0-89886-695-2
  1. Rock climbing—Equipment and supplies. 2. Snow and ice climbing—Equipment and supplies. I. Title: Rock and ice gear. II. Rock & ice. III. Title.
GV200.15 .S64 2000
796.52'2'0284—dc21
                      00-008988
                      CIP

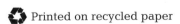

CONTENTS

INTRODUCTION

When I started climbing nearly thirty years ago, the equipment was easy to understand and gear selection was simple—there wasn't much to choose from. Ropes were twisted nylon. Wind shells were cotton blends. Insulated clothing was wool. Boots were leather. Ice-ax shafts and skis were wooden.

Now the market is flooded with products and you practically need degrees in chemistry, metallurgy, and physics just to decipher all the marketing hype. Unfortunately, the buzzwords often confuse consumers rather than educate them.

For the past six years, as the gear editor for *Rock & Ice* magazine, I have waded through stacks of claims, counterclaims, and test reports. I have visited twenty companies in the United States and Europe to see how gear is produced and tested. I, and many other climbers, have field-tested numerous products on mountains and cliffs all over the planet.

Longtime readers of our magazine will recognize that each chapter is based on one or more of my reviews, although they are substantially updated. You won't find the actual product reviews here—such a book would be obsolete before it went to press. Instead, you will find the background information that you need to make smart buying decisions. While the products often change (typically a new name, new colors, and a few minor tweaks), the underlying principles remain the same.

This book will help all climbers get the most for their money—without compromising safety. Though not an instruction manual, this book presents a lot of information on the proper use of gear, as well as tips on caring for your equipment.

While not meant to be read from beginning to end, this book is organized with information in the front that may be relevant to later discussions. The first twelve chapters cover the technical gear used for rock, snow, and ice climbing. The remaining thirteen chapters discuss the equipment that makes survival possible, even enjoyable, in the high mountain environment.

New climbers will find answers to basic gear questions that how-to books, and even guides or schools, rarely provide. I have tried to not overwhelm you with trivia but do believe that historical context and basic physics are important to understanding why gear is designed the way it is.

Veteran climbers possibly have the most to gain from this book. Whether you started four or forty years ago, much has changed since then and there is a lot that you never learned . . . or were taught incorrectly. Here you will find many straight answers given and myths dispelled.

Non-climbers can also learn a lot within these pages. For example, the chapters on clothing, sleeping bags, packs, and tents contain a great deal of information that is also relevant for backpacking. However, please understand that I am writing this from the perspective of an alpinist—staying alive in severe weather conditions, without possibility of shelter or retreat, requires far greater performance from equipment. Thus you may not need all the features described, but you will know what you are, or are not, getting when you make a purchase.

Although this is a book about climbing gear, I must emphasize that *gear does not make the climber!* Many of the great ascents of history were made with far less technology—just boldness, skill, and determination. To be a successful (read: living) climber, you must train your body and exercise your brain. Never stop learning, evaluating, and thinking! Remember, this *is* a dangerous game we play, but it *can* be safer than many other activities.

In a volume of this scope, much of which is about technology, some information will soon become outdated. Please send corrections, suggestions, and new information to Gear Editor, *Rock & Ice* magazine, 603 South Broadway, Suite A, Boulder, Colorado, 80305.

A NOTE ABOUT SAFETY

Safety is an important concern in all outdoor activities. No book can alert you to every hazard or anticipate the limitations of every reader. The descriptions of gear, techniques, and procedures in this book are intended to provide general information. This is not a complete text on climbing technique. Nothing substitutes for formal instruction, routine practice, and plenty of experience. When you follow any of the procedures described here, you assume responsibility for your own safety. Use this book as a general guide to further information. Under normal conditions, excursions into the backcountry require attention to traffic, road and trail conditions, weather, terrain, the capabilities of your party, and other factors. Keeping informed on current conditions and exercising common sense are the keys to a safe, enjoyable outing.

The Mountaineers Books

ACKNOWLEDGMENTS

This book would not be possible without the contributions and experience of many people and companies. It's impossible to name them all, but here are just a few to whom I owe thanks: Conrad Anker (The North Face), George Brackseick (*Rock & Ice*), Loui Clem (PMI), Ken Cline, Malcolm Daly (Trango), Bill Griggers (Omega Pacific), Chris Harmston (Black Diamond), Helmut Microys, Hal Murray, Steve Nagode (REI), Gary Neptune (Neptune Mountaineering), Emanuelle Pellizari, Mike Scherer (Kelty), Stevie Sidener, Randy Veneers (Marmot), and Russ Walling (Fish).

Also thanks to the crew at Neptune Mountaineering in Boulder, Colorado. I set up my photo studio in their store and spent 4 days borrowing products to shoot most of the images for this book.

Special thanks to Dougald MacDonald, publisher of *Rock & Ice* and *Trail Runner*, who lent his vast climbing experience and editing skills to this project.

And, of course, Tom and Brenda Soles, who encouraged my passion for the outdoors and photography. Sorry about all the worries my adventures have caused you!

CHAPTER 1

ROPES

FAALLLLLIIIING! IN ONLY 1.6 SECONDS, you will fall 40 ft. and reach 35 mph. In another 1.6 seconds you will fall an additional 130 ft. and reach 70 mph. And knowing that you can go only about 155 mph—terminal velocity—is somehow not very reassuring.

No piece of equipment is more important to climbers than the rope. For many aspects of climbing, a skinny nylon line connects us to terra firma and separates us from eternity.

Yet climbing ropes are among the least understood of the gear on which our lives depend. Most climbers have only a vague concept of the testing process and what the numbers on hangtags actually mean. Choosing the best rope should be based on more than just color and price, but that's often what it comes down to for climbers overwhelmed by technical trivia.

EARLY ROPES

Since early times, mountaineers have been tying together with ropes for security on climbs. The first climbing ropes were made from natural fibers—usually hemp, manila, or sisal—bundled into three or four strands and twisted or laid around one another (hence the term "laid construction"). Another less-common construction method was a solid braid that offered better handling at the expense of poor abrasion resistance and problems with rot. During the first half of this century, most climbing ropes came from the maritime world, as did some of our terms, such as "belay."

Not only were these old ropes static (they had minimal stretch) and relatively weak, but the principles of belaying had not really been worked out. At the alpine museum in Zermatt, Switzerland, it's scary just looking at the thin, roughly 7 mm braided rope used by the ill-fated Whymper party on the first ascent of the Matterhorn. Little wonder the creed of the day was "the leader must not fall!"

Though it was developed earlier, it was not until the 1930s that the Sierra Club refined the dynamic belay. By allowing controlled slipping of the rope through the belayer's hands, impact forces were considerably reduced. This radical development heralded the age of modern rock climbing, because climbers could push the limits and take falls with a reasonable chance of survival.

After the onset of World War II, when natural fibers were in short supply, Dupont introduced ropes made of its new polyamide synthetic fiber called nylon. (A German version of polyamide was called Perlon, though the term is seldom used anymore.) This laid-construction rope was lightweight and very strong, and stretched a great deal to absorb the impact of a fall. Commonly known as mountain lay Goldline (or Mountainline), this became the standard climbing rope for generations of climbers.

The twisted construction had problems, however. When dangling in midair, the climber would spin around nauseatingly. For jumaring, the ropes were excessively stretchy, akin to rubber bands. Because of the design, each fiber of the rope came to the surface every few inches, which made the rope prone to fuzzing from abrasion. Furthermore, Goldline ropes were stiff, handled poorly, created excessive rope drag, and tended to freeze easily.

In 1951, Edelrid introduced the first kernmantle-construction climbing ropes. These featured an inner load-bearing core *(kern)* protected by an outer sheath *(mantle)*. Kernmantle ropes solved most of the problems associated with laid ropes and eventually became the industry standard (laid ropes cannot be certified for climbing).

Since then, ropes have received many minor enhancements in handling, strength, and durability. There have also been some failed innovations—such as a rope with a plastic sheath between the core and mantle, a rope that was thicker on the ends than in the middle, and a rope with a radio cable inside. However, despite lots of hype, there have been no revolutionary improvements in climbing ropes in the past thirty years.

WHICH ROPE TYPE?

The terminology used to designate ropes and rope techniques is a source of confusion for many climbers. According to the *Union Internationale des Associations d'Alpinisme* (UIAA) and the *Comité Européen de Normalisation* (CEN), there are only three designations allowed for dynamic ropes: single (marked by 1 inside a circle), half (½ inside a circle), and twin (two overlapping circles) [Illustration 1.1]. "Half ropes" and "double ropes" are the same thing, although the former is the official designation.

Each type of rope requires a somewhat different technique for climbing—each with its own pros and cons. No one rope or technique is right for all climbing situations, so you need to choose appropriately.

SINGLE ROPE

Unquestionably the most popular type, single ropes generally have a diameter between 9.4 and 11 mm and weigh between 60 and 80 grams per meter.

Most climbers start out using single-rope technique because it is the easiest to learn and use. Using one medium- to large-diameter rope gives a good combination of simplicity, durability, and performance.

HALF ROPE

Half ropes usually are between 8.1 mm and 9.1 mm in diameter and have a mass of 47 to 54 grams per meter.

One of the biggest benefits of half-rope technique is extra security in the event of rope damage from ice tools, rockfall, or sharp edges. Proper half-rope technique can reduce rope drag on meandering pitches. Two ropes can provide better protection for both the leader and the second on traverses. When the protection is particularly dicey, impact forces can be lower and the length of a fall greatly reduced. A pair of ropes can significantly speed a party of three since the leader can belay both followers at the same time. Full-length rappels are possible, allowing faster retreats.

On the downside, two ropes can be more difficult for belaying a leader—there are times when you may be simultaneously taking in on one rope

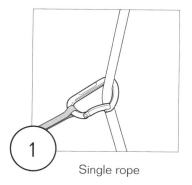
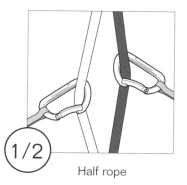
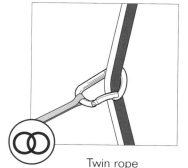

Single rope   Half rope   Twin rope

Illustration 1.1   Dynamic climbing-rope designations

while letting out on the other. Snarled ropes are fairly common unless you are well organized at the belay station. And the combined weight and bulk of a pair of half ropes is greater than that of a single rope (though less than a single and a haul line).

The use of double-rope technique is widely accepted throughout the world by alpine and ice climbers. Double-rope technique was once common at many traditional crags in Europe. However, it's relatively rare to see rock climbers in the United States using half ropes.

For roping up a climbing team on a glacier, a half rope is the best choice. Single ropes are too heavy and the forces of a fall into a crevasse do not warrant them, while skinny twin ropes don't work well with ascenders or prusiks.

TWIN ROPE

The ultrathin twin ropes typically have diameters between 7.4 and 8 mm and weigh only 41 to 43 grams per meter. Alone, they don't inspire much confidence. But together as intended, twins offer more nylon to protect you than other rope types.

Twins are used together as if they were a single rope. This technique is almost as convenient as single-rope technique and gives extra protection from cutting. So far, twins have not caught on, but this is partly because they are relatively new to the climbing world (a testing standard was only developed in 1991).

Never use a pair of single ropes as if they were twins, and it is a bad idea for half ropes as well. Your protection will be subjected to much more stress than when the ropes are clipped singly as intended. This could prove to be a critical difference with dicey rock pro and on ice climbs.

STATIC ROPE

Dynamic ropes are designed to absorb the impact of a fall and handle easily. A consequence of this ability is a great deal of stretch and less than maximum durability. For applications such as fixing lines, hauling loads on big walls, caving, and canyoneering, it is desirable to use more rugged ropes that have minimal stretch.

Commonly called static ropes, they are more properly termed low-elongation ropes, since they do stretch about 2 percent under body weight. These typically have thicker, coarser sheaths for added abrasion protection. The core strands and fibers have fewer twists and plies, so they do not have a tremendous ability to absorb impacts.

Static ropes usually come in 9 mm (⅜ in.) and 11 mm (⁷⁄₁₆ in.) diameters, so they are compatible with most ascenders, descenders, and pulleys. The narrower ropes are best reserved for alpine climbs where weight is the primary consideration.

Some expedition climbers use laid-construction polypropylene rope for fixed lines because it is lightweight and very cheap. My experience with the nasty stuff is that it abrades quickly and kinks horribly, plus ascenders sometimes grip poorly on it.

Recently, the CEN passed a standard for static ropes. The most notable requirement is that ropes must be 80 percent of one color and must have no more than two contrasting colors that spiral up the rope. Dynamic ropes are multicolored and have colored strands crossing each other.

Static ropes *can* be used for top-roping, but it's not a good idea because of the extra forces placed on body and anchors. Now that durable, low-impact-force ropes for climbing gyms are available, there is no point in using a static rope for top-rope climbing.

BUILDING A ROPE

Today, all climbing ropes are built from essentially the same materials and in the same way. That is not to say they are all alike—far from it—for there are large differences in the final products. Although a great deal of science is involved, the art of making a dynamic rope is in balancing many often-contradictory factors.

MATERIALS

Two types of polyamide are commonly used in ropes. Nylon 6 is primarily used for dynamic ropes, due to a molecular structure that has greater flexibility and elongation. Nylon 6,6 is often used in static ropes, where a slightly higher melting temperature and strength are prime considerations.

The raw nylon fibers come from numerous suppliers throughout the world, each with their own manufacturing and treatment process. The rope companies specify the denier (diameter) of the nylon and how much the fibers are stretched, which determines its elasticity.

Raw nylon is white, so fibers that will be used in the sheath are typically sent to a dye house for application of a surface dye. An alternative to using dyes is to extrude the color with the nylon, a less-expensive method that can yield a weaker fiber.

The energy-absorption capability of a dynamic rope comes mostly from its core. Imagine a steel wire with a tensile strength of 100 lbs. If the wire is pulled with greater force than that, it will snap. However, if the wire is first spiraled into a coil and heat set, it becomes a spring that will give and then recover. The more spirals in the spring, the more it will stretch before breaking. After a severe stress, the spring becomes stretched out and can no longer recoil.

Although nylon fibers have a greater ability to stretch and recover than steel, they still need help to reduce impact forces. Hence, the yarns are twisted (plied) together so that when subjected to a large impact, the mechanical unwinding absorbs energy and converts it to heat. When a rope finally fails in the CEN drop test, many of the core strands are actually melted together (nylon 6 melts at 428°F). By contrast, static ropes frequently have continuous parallel fibers to reduce stretch.

CONSTRUCTION

The nylon fibers are supplied on a giant spool (3½ ft. diameter and 8 ft. long) called a beam [Photo 1.1]. This contains numerous fibers that run its entire length. The rope maker collects the desired number of fibers together and runs them through a room-sized machine called a ring twister [Photo 1.2]. This twists the individual fibers into a yarn (known as the first ply) that is wound onto spools; some yarns have a clockwise Z-twist, others have a counterclockwise S-twist.

From three to six of these spools are then moved onto a much smaller egg-shaped twisting machine that combines the yarns into bundles—the second ply—that also have either an S- or Z-twist. The yarn bundles for the sheath are rewound onto bobbins that will go on the braider.

The twist rate at each stage is adjusted depending on whether the yarn or strand is going to the sheath or the core. The number of twists in the strands will largely determine how much the rope can stretch to absorb a fall, as well as its static elongation. Manufacturers can also vary the thickness of the plies, the number of plies per strand, and the number of strands within the core, depending upon the results they are trying to achieve.

Core Construction

There are two basic methods of making a dynamic rope's core: twisting and braiding. Most manufacturers use a twisted (cable) core construction. From six to fourteen strands are bundled parallel to one another for the length of the rope [Photo 1.3]. With the proper balance of S- and Z-twist strands, the rope will be neutral (i.e., have no tendency to spin and kink) and easy to handle.

Braided cores are made by plaiting large strands into either a single thick bundle or three smaller bundles. Although no twist is needed in the strands to make them dynamic, these cores take longer to produce.

Sheath Construction

While much of the strength and shock absorption come from the core, the majority of the rope's handling characteristics and durability come from the sheath. Once the core is made, it runs through a braiding machine that weaves the sheath around it [Photo 1.4]. Although you can't examine the guts of a rope, a close look at the sheath can give you a good idea about overall quality.

The thickness and number of plies and strands in the sheath play a significant factor in its abrasion resistance and durability. Lightweight ropes necessarily trade off something, and for many it is sheath thickness.

Some ropes have a low twist rate in the sheath plies; these tend to fuzz fairly quickly, while those with a high twist rate retain their "new look" much longer. The low twist rate means that individual yarns reach the surface only every few inches as opposed to every ¼ inch. When cut by abrasion, the shorter strands are shed (that pile of fluff you see after a rappel) while the longer strands are held in place. The argument goes that the fuzz helps

Photo 1.1 Fibers from the "beam" are made into yarn on the "ring twister."

protect the underlying fibers from further abrasion. So just because a rope fuzzes quickly doesn't necessarily mean it is less durable.

The type of braider that is used also plays a part in the sheath's thickness and feel. The more bobbins that dance about the core, like children playing maypole, the smoother the finish. Today the standard is a 48-carrier machine for single dynamic ropes.

These machines can be set up to weave different patterns, which are referred to by the number of times the bundles go over and under one another. A "2-over-2" sheath is the most common. Depending on the pattern that is used, the resulting rope has either a single- [Photo 1.5] or double-pic sheath [Photo 1.6] (a "pic" is an exposed bundle of fibers).

Photo 1.2   A ring twister plies the yarn into core strands.

Photo 1.3 Detail of a dynamic rope showing the core strands and a control tape (sticking up center) that indicates when the rope was made.

Single-pic sheaths are smoother, for reduced friction and a nice hand, and generally are used on narrower-diameter ropes. Double-pic sheaths are used on ropes where durability is a greater concern.

During the braiding process, the amount of tension that is used greatly affects the handling characteristics and durability of the sheath as well. A loose sheath makes the rope very supple, giving a nice hand, but the rope flattens in use and lacks durability. A very tightly woven sheath exhibits minimal slippage and helps keep out dirt and water but tends to be stiff and difficult to handle. Some ropes are made on variable-speed braiders, so the sheaths are soft and firm in different areas.

A bi-pattern rope is made by stopping the braider and rearranging the bobbins to change the pattern halfway through the sheath. This provides a permanent method for determining how much rope is remaining. They cost more, but the convenience makes up for it.

Stabilization

At some point during the rope's assembly, it needs to be stabilized with heat. This balances the movement of the sheath and the core, minimizes shrinkage, and increases the nylon's elasticity and strength. Following heat treatment, the fresh rope needs to rest for several days prior to being cut, to allow for continued shrinkage.

DRY TREATMENTS

As many climbers have discovered, nylon is hygroscopic, which means it can readily absorb water. A wet rope is heavier, about 30 percent weaker, stretches more, and is less abrasion-resistant. To make matters worse, a wet rope can freeze into a stiff, unmanageable cable.

Therefore, manufacturers attempt to make their ropes water repellent. The application of dry treatments can occur to the individual fibers prior to production of the rope (though some wears off during the twisting and braiding processes), after the rope is constructed, or both.

Photo 1.4   The white core strands are brought together at a 48-bobbin sheath braider.

Photo 1.5   Single-pic sheath

Many older ropes were treated with paraffin-based compounds (wax) that quickly wore off, turning the rope and our hands black with dirt and aluminum oxide from carabiners. Silicon treatments are cheap but don't last either.

Most companies now impregnate the entire rope with a fluoropolymer-based solution that bonds to the fibers rather than merely coating them. The rope is basically submerged in a bathtub until the trapped air stops bubbling, then removed and dried. Of course, each company has its own secret concoction and method of setting it.

Companies often claim that a test proved their new fancy-name treatment is the best. The reality is that no industry standard exists for comparison, and none of the tests I have seen translate to the real world. Don't buy the hype.

Some declare that dry treatments increase rope life by reducing friction of the rope over the rock and through carabiners. This may be true, at first, but the treatment on the surface abrades off relatively quickly. It is doubtful you will get the extra 15 to 20 percent (the percentage extra you pay) of rope life.

Ultimately, you should choose a rope for its other characteristics and then decide whether you need a dry treatment. Crag rats can save their money, but alpine and ice climbers will greatly benefit.

ROPE TESTING

The first standard for climbing ropes was created by the British Alpine Club in 1864. Based on this, Buckingham produced the "Alpine Club" rope from pure manila hemp, which was considered the best for over three decades (it weighed 74.4 grams per meter and had a tensile strength of 10 kilonewtons).

Photo 1.6   Double-pic sheath

Many climbers are somewhat familiar with the UIAA/CEN rope tests. Developed in the 1950s by Professor Dodéro in France, and updated several times since then, these standards are designed to ensure that climbers can have a high degree of confidence in their ropes. Considering that no modern rope in good condition has ever failed in the field, without first being cut or weakened by chemicals, the testing has been effective.

The UIAA/CEN standards also give a useful means for comparing ropes—*if* you understand the tests' limitations. However, relatively few climbers truly understand what the numbers mean.

The UIAA/CEN tests themselves are merely performance standards. They are carried out on a limited sample set (40 m of each rope model) selected by the manufacturer, every two years. And the results are pass/fail (except for measurement of diameter and mass).

Ropes cannot be sold in Europe without certification from the CEN (for which the UIAA is an advisory body)—there is no such legal requirement in North America.

DROP TESTS

In the drop test for single ropes, an 80-kg (176-lb.) weight is dropped 4.8 m (15.7 ft.) onto a 2.8-m (9.2-ft.) section of rope—a factor 1.71 fall. The rope is held statically (three wraps around a 30 mm bar and clamped) and passes over a 10 mm radius edge (approximating a carabiner) that is 30 cm (1 ft.) from the bar [Illustration 1.2]. Prior to the test, the ropes are conditioned for 4 days to ensure consistent temperature and humidity.

This is a very severe test—having watched it, I wouldn't want to take one of these falls. To pass, five rope samples from the same production batch must hold at least five consecutive falls (5 minutes apart with the weight removed from the rope within 1 minute), and the impact force at the "climber" on the first drop must not exceed 12 kilonewtons (kN) (2698 lbs. of force, or lbf). This maximum impact force was derived from military studies that showed the human body could briefly withstand

fifteen times its weight without injury when a parachute opens.

The same mass and maximum force requirements are used for pairs of twin ropes; however, they must withstand at least twelve of the falls.

Since half ropes are typically used in pairs yet clipped alternately into protection, the requirements of the drop test are changed. The falling weight is reduced to 55 kg (121 lbs.) and the permitted force on the "climber" is also reduced to 8 kN (1798 lbf). The half-rope samples must withstand five of these lighter drops. When I had an

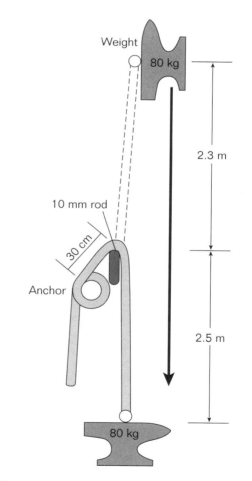

Illustration 1.2   The UIAA drop test

8-fall half rope tested with an 80 kg weight, the rope broke on the second fall—make sure your other rope is well-anchored!

ELONGATION

When jumaring and rappelling, you want a rope that stretches very little. The UIAA/CEN requires that single ropes and pairs of twins must not stretch more than 8 percent with a load of 80 kg. Using the same 80 kg weight, the static elongation for a half

---

ROPE STRETCH

One serious consequence of rope stretch is the high potential for decking during short falls right off the ground. To prevent a ground fall when the leader slips while about to make the next clip (worst-case, but plausible, scenario), use the following guidelines. If the first piece of protection is 13 ft. (4 m) off the ground, the next cannot be more than 4.2 ft. (1.3 m) above that and the third no more than 7.2 ft. (2.2 m) above the second. If the first anchor is 16 ft. (4.9 m) off the ground, the next cannot be more than 6.2 ft. (1.9 m) above that and the third no more than 9.8 ft. (3 m) above the second.

Very low-impact forces are often accomplished by designing the rope to stretch more. In a long, hard fall, that soft catch could mean an extra 10 ft. of dropping—hopefully no ledges are in the way. And a rope can stretch a great deal in a long, hard fall. One series of tests showed that with a 66-ft. (20-m), factor 1 fall—66 ft. out, 33 ft. (10 m) above the last piece, which is 33 ft. above the belayer—an 11 mm rope stretches over 26 ft. (8 m), roughly 40 percent. Remember that that stretch will be significantly longer as rope masses decrease. So with a lighter rope, what starts out as a 66-ft. fall (grim) could turn into a 100-ft. (30-m) fall (very grim)!

---

rope cannot be more than 10 percent. In fact, most single ropes stretch about 6 percent. Currently, there is no standard for dynamic elongation, although one has been proposed.

SHEATH SLIPPAGE

The UIAA/CEN also checks sheath slippage by pulling 1.93 m of rope four times through a device that squeezes the rope. Ideally, you don't want any slippage (40 mm is the maximum allowed) and few of us experience it in most climbing situations. Unless the rope is used for an exceptional amount of jumaring, rappelling, or lowering, this is a minor concern and few manufacturers specify it.

KNOTABILITY

This measure of rope stiffness has recently been discontinued. It was only a pass/fail test that modern ropes had no trouble passing.

COMPARING ROPES

The hangtags on climbing ropes provide a lot of information, but climbers often focus on the wrong numbers. Mass, rather than diameter, and impact force, rather than falls, give you the most useful information.

DIAMETER AND MASS

The diameter of a single rope is determined by weighting a section with 10 kg (22 lbs.), taking six measurements, and then averaging them. Half-rope diameters are determined by using a 6 kg (13.2 lb.) weight, while twins use a 5 kg (11 lb.) weight.

Thus an unweighted rope will be thicker than what is on the label, while the same rope will be thinner under body weight. This variability, plus the fact that all ropes are slightly oval-shaped, makes diameter a poor method of comparing ropes.

The mass of a rope indicates how much nylon

is in the rope. Given current technology, reducing rope mass also decreases cut resistance and durability while increasing stretch. Be suspicious of a rope that claims to have a high fall rating or superb durability yet has a low mass.

While diameter and mass allow differentiation between ropes, neither is actually specified in the standards. Theoretically, it may someday be possible to build a 5 mm single dynamic rope, although it would not inspire much confidence.

IMPACT FORCE

When looking at rope specifications, among the most important numbers to consider are impact forces—in general, lower is better. Using a lower-impact rope means that the falling leader receives a softer catch and the belayer has an easier task holding the fall. There will also be less force exerted on your anchors, and the chance of the rope cutting over an edge is reduced.

The UIAA/CEN standards require only that the first drop be below their threshold—the number on the hangtag is the average of the three tests (the highest and lowest are discarded). There are no impact force requirements on subsequent drops. Since the forces in some ropes climb faster than in others, the force on the later drops would be most enlightening. Tests of single ropes showed that the impact force from the first drop to the fourth ranged between 28 and 59 percent. Some companies claim their ropes have lower impact forces on subsequent drops, but there is currently no independent verification.

FALL RATING

The fall rating gives a rough approximation of a rope's durability, but so many other factors come into play that you should not use this number alone for selection. More falls does not necessarily mean a longer-lasting rope. But a high-fall rope *may* be less likely to cut over an edge than a rope that holds fewer falls.

All manufacturers recommend that any rope,

even a "12-fall" model, be retired after a long, hard fall. This is because the rope is subjected to the force for a much longer period of time. In other words, a short fall is less bad than a long fall—even if the fall factor is the same.

CUT RESISTANCE

In the standard drop test, the rope survives five falls over a "carabiner" with a radius of 10 mm. However, if the rope runs over a 90-degree corner with a radius of 0.5 mm, virtually all ropes will break on the first drop.

When the edge radius is increased to 0.75 mm, some standard 11 mm ropes can survive but look badly chewed. Several companies now offer cut-resistant ropes that are reinforced with monofilament. These are the only 10.5 mm ropes that can pass the unofficial "edge test."

The trade-off for greater safety is stiffer handling and higher price. While not needed for everyday cragging, cut-resistant ropes are the way to go for some alpine and big wall endeavors where rockfall or sharp edges are a concern.

Currently, there is no UIAA/CEN performance standard for cut resistance. However, it is likely to become a requirement in the future.

DURABILITY

The big question about any rope is durability. At first glance, a test of abrasion resistance would seem to answer the question. However, there is no consensus on how to design an abrasion test or interpret the results. There are many methods of testing, each of which favors one rope over another.

Furthermore, abrasion of the sheath is but one factor that determines a rope's durability. Because of the large number of falls sport climbers take, their ropes experience heavy wear between 5 and 10 ft. from the ends. Many sheaths blow out about 6 to 7 ft. from the end of the rope.

Accumulated impacts also take their toll. In one test, a 10.5 mm rope lost 32 percent of its tensile strength after 25 short, factor 0.6 falls, and the impact force climbed 25 percent. After 125 drops, the rope lost 63 percent of its tensile strength.

Rappelling and frequent lowering can be rough on ropes too. A test by the German Alpine Club showed that, after 200 rappels, half ropes' strength was reduced by 70 percent. Although UV does have a harmful effect on ropes, it is relatively insignificant compared to normal wear and tear. Still, it can't hurt to minimize exposure to sunlight.

ROPE SHOPPING

So now that you know what the numbers mean, and which are more important, it's time to narrow down the rope choices. First, decide on what you will use it for.

Beginners, big wall addicts, and guides should consider an 11 mm rope for its durability. The extra longevity can easily make up for the higher

FALL FACTORS

Not all 40-ft. (12-m) falls are created equal. The severity of any fall depends upon how much rope is available to absorb the energy. The "fall factor" is the length of the fall divided by the length of rope between the climber and the belayer. As simple as this concept is, it manages to elude many climbers.

If you are 100 ft. (30 m) out from the belay and 20 ft. (6 m) above your last piece when you come off (therefore falling 40 ft.), you will take a 0.4 factor fall—scary but not too severe. However, if you fall while only 30 ft. (9 m) away from your belayer and 20 ft. above the last piece, it becomes a 1.3 factor fall that will put a major load on the entire system.

The UIAA/CEN drop test simulates an extremely hard climbing fall—a hard drop on a short piece of rope with a static anchor. In a real climbing situation, some factors that help mitigate the force include friction in the system, slippage through the belay device, and the belayer being pulled upward.

Friction in the system works in favor of the belayer and, to a certain degree, the protection as well. The force on the topmost piece of protection is equal to the two downward forces combined. So in a fairly hard fall, if the climber feels 5 kN (1124 lbf), the belayer must hold 3.3 kN (908 lbf) while the top anchor and carabiners

must hold 8.3 kN (1868 lbf). If there were no friction, the top piece would have to hold 10 kN.

But there is a catch. Friction from running through carabiners and against the rock has the effect of reducing the effective length of rope that absorbs the shock. The result is that the actual fall factor decreases more slowly than the theoretical fall factor. For example, if you are 100 ft. out and fall 20 ft., the frictionless fall factor would be 0.2, while the actual fall factor might be 0.6 or higher. Therefore, if you feel a lot of "rope drag" while leading, your topmost gear will be subjected to greater forces during a fall than you might think.

As mentioned elsewhere, an 80-kg (176-lb.) weight is used to determine forces in the UIAA/CEN single-rope test drop. This was chosen as the weight of the "average" climber. But what about everyone else?

All other things being equal, for a factor 0.5 fall on 20 m of rope, a 60-kg (132-lb.) climber will feel about 3.4 kN (765 lbf), an 80-kg (176-lb.) climber will feel 4 kN (900 lbf), and a 100-kg (220-lb.) climber will feel 4.5 kN (1012 lbf). On the same length of rope, if the climber takes a screamer with a fall factor of 1.5, the 60-kg leader will feel 5.4 kN (1215 lbf), the 80-kg leader will feel 6.2 kN (1400 lbf), and the big boy packs a wallop of 7 kN (1575 lbf).

price, but you will have to tolerate the weight and stiffer handling.

The 10.2 to 10.5 mm ropes are the best choice if you want a rope for all-around climbing and are willing to accept some trade-offs in durability or weight. These are also a good choice for working sport routes, since lighter ropes just don't hold up. Cut-resistant ropes are nice if you have the cash.

At the light end of the scale are the sub-10 mm ropes. These are great for sending that 13b you've worked and for alpine climbs. Just remember, they cut more easily and don't last nearly as long, especially for heavy climbers.

Because of the abuse they receive, "gym" ropes have a higher sheath-to-core ratio. This yields a rope with low maximum impact forces that is more abrasion-resistant and has less sheath slippage. The trade-off is that they often have high elongation and relatively poor handling. While they are great for gym owners and frequent top-rope climbers, you wouldn't want one for leading in the real world.

Other factors to consider when comparing rope systems are the weight of the rope you are dragging behind you, and how much rope you have to lift to make a desperate clip. As Chart A shows, when you're 100 ft. out, you will be trailing 4 lbs. 10 oz. (2.1 kg) of rope with a 10.5 mm and nearly 2 lbs. (1 kg) extra when using half ropes.

Chart A: Rope Systems

diameter (mm)	mass (g/m)	weight/30m (kg/ lbs.)	cut resistance	abrasion resistance	ease of use
11	75	2.3 / 5.1	3	1	3
10.5	70	2.1 / 4.7	4	2	2
10	65	2.0 / 4.4	5	5	1
9 (half pair)	100	3.0 / 6.7	1	3	5
8 (twin pair)	85	2.6 / 5.7	2	4	4

When buying half and twin ropes, it is a good idea to select matched pairs. Mismatched ropes often have different handling and stretch charac-teristics that can create problems while belaying and rappelling.

COLOR

While rope color is a matter of personal preference, there are a few considerations to bear in mind. When selecting half and twin ropes, the two should be visually very distinct from one another. I have climbed with some rope pairs in which the difference was not very obvious, creating confusion for the belayer.

Avoid colors that will cause verbal problems as well; for example, "black" sounds like "slack." For snow and ice climbing, brighter ropes, such as red and yellow, are easier to spot when conditions are less than ideal.

No matter the type of rope, white sheaths tend to hide damage while darker sheaths make it easy to spot the white core poking through. Light-colored sheaths tend to look pretty grungy after a while too.

ROPE LENGTH

For much of the twentieth century, the standard length of climbing ropes in the United States was 120 ft. From the 1960s through the 1970s most people used 45 m (150 ft.) ropes. Climbs put up in that era often have bolted belays spaced accordingly, and longer ropes can be a hassle that slows the team down.

Now the most common length is 50 m (165 ft.), and many modern routes with artificial anchors require the extra 15 ft. For most general cragging, this is still the optimal length.

Recently, 60 m (200 ft.) ropes, or longer, have become popular. For a 1000 m big wall, the extra length can eliminate four or five belays. Since the ends of the rope usually get trashed first when sport climbing, you can trim several meters off each end of a 60 m rope and still have a serviceable rope. Some newer routes require the extra length, so be sure to check the topos before heading out with a shorter rope.

The big drawbacks to 60 m ropes are a larger rack (for longer pitches), increased rope drag, and poor communication. They are also heavier, bulkier, and harder to coil than shorter ropes.

Another option for climbers doing primarily snow climbs is a 100 m (330 ft.) half rope used as a single. This allows very long pitches on moderate terrain where a fall is unlikely. The rope can be doubled for occasional crux sections. For all-around use, however, a 100 m rope is an incredible nuisance.

Many climbers are surprised to find that rope lengths are just approximations and that they vary—sometimes considerably—from the stated length. Since the rope is braided under tension, it will shrink after coming off the machine. The manufacturer needs to let it rest before cutting and then allow for continued shrinkage after that.

Your 50 m rope may actually be 52 m when you purchase it. But after you have climbed on the rope for a season, it may end up measuring 48 m or less. Since you can expect 2 to 7 percent shrinkage with use, it's a good idea to measure your ropes occasionally to avoid unpleasant surprises.

DECENT DESCENT LINES

If it's getting dark and you have a long descent or if a lightning storm is threatening to zap you, it is highly advantageous to make each rappel as long as possible. When climbing with single ropes on long routes, it is common to carry a second rope in the pack (or trailing) as a haul line and to facilitate the descent.

Some climbers use 7 mm accessory cord, but this is so light that the wind blows it all over the place. Though slightly bulkier, 8 mm is less snag-prone, more durable, and easier to grasp when hand-hauling a pack.

When rigging a rappel with a haul line, it should pass through the rappel rings. Once everyone is down, you will pull on the fatter lead rope for retrieval. Should the rope get stuck, it's better to have a fat dynamic line in your hands to solve the problem.

For snow and ice routes where rope drag is minimal, it is possible to use 3 mm cord for retrieving a rappel rope. Run your climbing rope through the anchor and tie a figure eight on a bight, then clip this back to the rope with a carabiner [Photo 1.7]. Attach the cord to the carabiner and do a single-rope rappel on the thicker rope.

Photo 1.7 Rigging a single-rope rappel with a retrieval line

CONNECTING KNOTS

The double fisherman (a.k.a. grapevine) knot [Photo 1.8] has long been trusted by climbers to connect two ropes for a rappel. However, the knot is prone to snagging due to its bulk, and it can be an incredible pain to loosen after it has been weighted. Other permutations, such as the retraced figure eight or a square knot backed up by a double fisherman, are slightly easier to untie and super-strong, yet are magnets for snags high on a cliff.

The best knot for rappelling is certainly the scariest looking—especially the first time you see someone tie a double overhand [Photo 1.9]. "You want me to rap off *that*?!" Yep, this simple, elegant knot (technically a "bend" since it connects two ropes) has the tremendous advantage of being one-sided, so it is less likely to get caught.

The double overhand is strong enough for this application (but I wouldn't use it for anything else). Of several different knots loaded to over 500 lbs. (2.2 kN), the double overhand was the only one that I could untie without the aid of a marlinspike or 10 minutes of cursing. This is now my knot of choice for most rappel situations, though I do leave long tails (at least 8 in.) and set the knot firmly.

Be especially cautious when using the double overhand with dissimilar-diameter ropes. Some sources don't recommend this at all, but I've tested several combinations to significant loads.

Since some people are leery of such a simple knot, they have surmised that a double figure eight would be safer. When I tested this knot, it had an alarming tendency to continuously turn itself inside out at about 300 lbf (1.3 kN) . . . it literally creeps along closer and closer to the end—scary.

Photo 1.8   The double fisherman knot is commonly used to join rappel ropes, but it's prone to snagging and difficult to undo after being loaded. It's the knot of choice for slinging chocks.

Photo 1.9   The double overhand bend may look scary, but it's ideal for connecting rappel ropes. Always dress it properly, leave long tails, and snug it tight!

FINAL CONSIDERATIONS

When looking at ropes in the store, run the rope through your hands; the sheath and core should feel smooth without any bumps or ridges. Flex the rope to see how stiff it is; be wary of those that are very soft or stiff. A good rope will be moderately stiff and firm; that is, it shouldn't flatten easily when compressed.

Wring a short section of the rope in your hands; a sheath with pronounced ridges is more prone to abrasion. Look carefully at the sheath; yarns that aren't a consistent color are a sign of poor quality control.

Building an inexpensive rope requires compromises: They can start with cheaper raw materials as well as increase production efficiency by cutting corners. The manufacturer can use a lower twist rate so the machines run faster. This means you often get a rope that meets the minimum specs but will lose elasticity quickly (resulting in higher impact forces) and be less durable. While cheap dynamic ropes are safe to climb on, they are not a good value.

Chart B: Descent Rope Pairs (50 m)

diameter (mm)	weight (kg/ lbs.)		diameter (mm)	weight (kg/ lbs.)		total (kg/ lbs.)
10.5	3.5 / 7.7	+	8.8	2.5 / 5.5	=	6.0 / 13.2
10.5	3.5 / 7.7	+	8.0	2.1 / 4.6	=	5.6 / 12.3
10	3.3 / 7.2	+	7.0	1.9 / 4.1	=	5.2 / 11.3
8.8	2.5 / 5.5	+	8.8	2.5 / 5.5	=	5.0 / 11.0
8.0	2.1 / 4.7	+	8.0	2.1 / 4.7	=	4.2 / 9.4
8.8	2.5 / 5.5	+	3.0	0.4 / 0.8	=	2.9 / 6.3

ROPE CARE

Nothing destroys a rope faster than sharp edges! Use runners judiciously when leading to keep the rope away from edges, and rope pads when top-roping to guard against abrasion.

Even a rounded edge can do considerable damage if the rope runs over it while weighted. I know of one case in which a rope ran around an outside edge of rough granite that many climbers would not suspect as being dangerous. When the leader fell, the 11 mm rope was shredded down to just a few core strands!

Always use at least two locking carabiners for the anchor on a top-rope—for safety and to minimize wear and tear. Make sure the carabiners are hanging below the top edge of the cliff for rappels and top-ropes.

You're better off using a fat, heavy rope for working the crux on sport climbs; save the ultralight rope for the redpoint. Occasionally alternate ends of the work-rope to give the nylon a chance to recover.

DE-KINKING

Few things are more aggravating than a rope that twists up into dozens of kinks. Often the problem isn't the rope. A good rope is neutral when it comes off the braider; in other words, the rope does not have kinks built into it. Many of the things climbers do can introduce those annoying twists.

When you buy a brand-new rope, don't simply unwind the fancy wraps and then lift the coils off the hank. This simple act puts forty to fifty twists in your rope. If you unwind it end over end, as if unspooling it, the rope will stay neutral [Illustration 1.3].

Your rappelling and belaying methods also affect how the rope handles. Many people like figure eight devices for rapping. But an incorrect hand position with the figure eight puts one twist in the rope every 10 ft (3 m). The correct position is straight down, not off to the side, with the rope running between your legs. The Munter hitch is even worse for rappelling because it can put two twists in the rope every 10 ft.

The old method of coiling a rope into big loops that can be worn over a shoulder tends to introduce twists into the rope. With practice, you can overcome

Illustration 1.3   Unwinding a new climbing rope

this, but it is still a slow technique. Butterfly coiling the rope [Illustration 1.4] does not add twists and is much faster if you start with both ends in hand and work toward the middle. The drawback here is that you need to stack the rope before leading out. If you start the butterfly from one end, it will be ready to use immediately after uncoiling it.

The best method for single-pitch climbs is to use a rope bag with a tarp—the rope will be kink free and ready to go each time you move to a new climb. The rope bag also protects the cord from dirt and mud, and it can make a convenient, dry place to set out your shoes and other gear at the base of a climb.

MARKING

It's a good practice to mark the middle (and even quarters) of your rope to simplify rigging rappels and make it easier for the belayer to estimate how much rope is left.

Some climbers elect to use tape, but this is temporary at best and has a tendency to migrate away from where it is supposed to be (dangerous when rigging a rappel). Whipping the ends and middle of ropes with nylon yarn is an old nautical trick, but it tends to abrade away rather quickly and can stick in a belay device.

For lighter-colored ropes, I prefer to use a black marking pen. Since phenol-based marking pens can weaken nylon, some climbers are concerned about harming their ropes. However, Carter's Marks-A-Lot, Sanford's Sharpie, and Binney & Smith's Majic Marker did not affect nylon in one test. If you are still concerned, BlueWater offers a marking pen that is safe for all nylon.

WASHING ROPES

A clean rope is a happy rope. Dirt particles can work their way in between fibers of the sheath and core, acting like internal sandpaper and decreasing suppleness. Using a tarp at the base of climbs and not stepping on your rope can really help.

Hand washing in a tub is the safest method of cleaning a rope. If you insist on machine washing, use a front loader on gentle cycle with cold water.

If you use a top-loading home washing machine with a central agitator, put the rope in a large mesh bag, pillowcase, or sleeping bag storage sack. To avoid making a rope salad, you can chain braid it first [Photo 1.10].

Plain cold water is often fine, but commercial rope cleansers are effective and will not remove the rope's dry coatings or lubricants. Do not use detergents or anything containing bleach (or bleach sub-

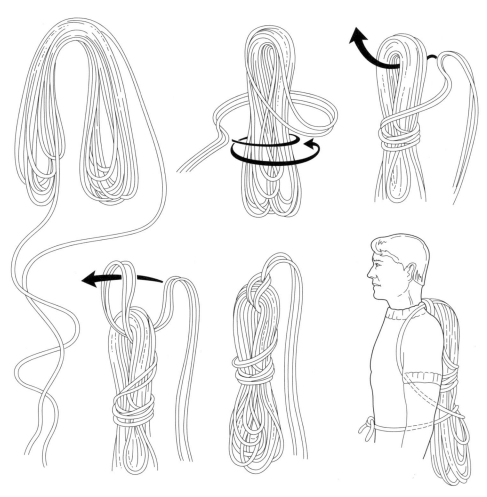

Illustration 1.4   The butterfly coil

Photo 1.10   Chain braiding a rope for washing

petroleum products will not harm nylon, that cannot necessarily be said of all the additives in those products.

The scariest contaminant is battery acid—the fumes alone can destroy a rope core, with no visible effect to the rope. At least one rope is known to have failed from contact with battery acid, with fatal results.

Fortunately for sea cliff climbers, salt water has no effect on nylon, but you should be sure to give the ropes a thorough freshwater rinse after the climb. Also, one lab test showed that DEET, the active ingredient in many insect repellents, did not appreciably harm nylon (though it sure eats a hole in some plastics).

RETIREMENT PLANNING

Sooner or later, we all have to ask, "Should I retire my rope?" If you're out there on the sharp end . . . pushing your limits . . . hands sweating . . . legs shaking . . . looking at big air below you, confidence in your lifeline is essential. If you don't feel comfortable climbing on a rope, it's definitely time to put it away.

Regardless of your rope's age, constantly inspect it while you belay and rappel. Feel for bumps, thin spots, or changes in stiffness as the rope runs through your hands; these indicate it may have been severely stressed. Look for signs of heavy fuzzing (50 percent of fibers are cut) and puffs or bulges of white core material showing through the sheath. Any of these means the rope should be retired.

With daily hard use, a rope may be ready to retire in 3 to 6 months—or sooner. The active climber who is getting out most weekends can perhaps get one to two years from a rope. The occasional climber, who gets out up to ten times a year, should be able to lead on a rope for two to four years.

Even if a rope never comes out of the plastic

stitutes). Be sure to rinse thoroughly. While you are at it, you can reapply the dry treatment to your rope with a wash-in treatment available from climbing shops. Air-dry in the shade by looping the rope loosely over a clothesline or equivalent.

STORAGE

Store ropes in a cool, dry place—ideally in a rope bag. The most deadly of sins is to store your rope near chemicals. Especially harmful are acids, alkalis, oxidizing agents, and bleaching compounds. While it is true that pure gasoline and bag, it is wise to not lead multipitch climbs on it after five years. Old ropes in good condition shouldn't break in low-factor falls, but the impact forces on your gear and body will be much higher than with a fresh rope.

We tested an 11 mm rope that was virtually un-used and had been properly stored for about twenty years. To look at it, anyone would think that it was in great shape and probably wouldn't hesitate to climb on it. The rope held one UIAA/CEN drop.

Once you decide to retire a rope from lead duty, unless it is really thrashed, it should be fine for top-roping and rappelling since impact forces are fairly minimal. Just keep a close eye on the condition of the sheath.

When it is really dead, cut up the rope so that you, or someone who does not know better, will not be tempted to use it anymore. With patience, you can weave many different patterns of floor mats from old ropes (consult a good knot book).

CHAPTER 2

CARABINERS

CARABINERS ARE AN INTEGRAL PART OF the climber's safety system, and selecting them is just as vital as choosing more glamorous equipment such as ropes and protection.

Otto Herzog is commonly credited with adapting the pear-shaped snap-links of Munich firefighters for climbing in the early 1900s. These steel *karabiners,* and new iron pitons with an eye (much like modern Lost Arrows), allowed climbers to protect faces that lacked natural protection. With this equipment and the development of felt-soled shoes, a new era was born. Between 1910 and 1914, the great limestone faces of the eastern Alps were conquered and rock climbing as we now know it began.

Until 1941, all carabiners (or "krabs" as the Brits call them) were made of steel. However, owing to steel shortages during the war, Bill House, a climber on the U.S. Army's equipment development team, worked with ALCOA to produce the first aluminum alloy (S-T 24) carabiner. These proved to be one-third lighter yet the same strength as the existing steel "'biners."

Today, most carabiners are made of 7075 aluminum alloy (sometimes called zicral), which is composed of about 88 percent aluminum, 6 percent zinc, 2.5 percent magnesium, 2 percent copper, and a smidgen of chromium, silicon, iron, manganese, and titanium.

CONSTRUCTION

Manufacturers receive the aluminum alloy in rod form and then either cold-work or hot-forge the stock. Cold working, sometimes called cold forging, simply means the rod is bent and squeezed into shape by monstrous machines at room temperature.

This is how the vast majority of carabiners are produced [Photo 2.1].

Hot forging requires heating the alloy to around 800°F (427°C) before it's pressed into a die. This latter method allows intricate shapes; the engineer can more easily put the metal where it is needed, providing strength and a broad rope-bearing surface in some places and saving weight in others. The resulting carabiners, although not necessarily stronger, are generally lighter, easier to operate, and more expensive. However, with a big-enough press, brute force cold working can achieve nearly the same strength and shapes as hot forging.

No matter the method, once the carabiner has been shaped, the body and gate must be thermally treated to achieve strength several times that of the untreated alloy. The first step is solution heat treatment at 900°F (482°C) for 2 hours, which dissolves the precipitates made up of the alloying elements. The 'biners are then quenched in water to create a "supersaturated solid solution." This prevents the formation of large precipitates that weaken the metal.

The next step is to "artificially age" the alloy at about 250°F (121°C) for 24 hours, followed by air-cooling. This allows the controlled formation of microscopic, evenly distributed precipitates, the presence of which are crucial to final strength. The result of all this heating and cooling, if properly performed, is called a T6 temper . . . and a darn strong 'biner. Everyone does it.

The treated parts are then tossed into large tumblers filled with stones that knock off sharp edges. The high luster of many carabiners is achieved by tumbling them with much finer ball bearings to polish the metal.

The next step for many 'biners is anodization, which many believe is merely a cosmetic treatment.

Photo 2.1   A massive machine forces carabiner bodies into shape.

Actually, this complex, five-step electrochemical process changes the outer surface of the aluminum to aluminum oxide, a material nearly as hard as diamond. While aluminum will oxidize slowly on its own (this is what can make your hands black when you climb), anodization can result in a much thicker, more durable surface.

Depending on the concentration of acid and the temperature of the solution, the porosity and hardness of the coating can be varied. To achieve the different colors we are familiar with, the anodized parts are dipped into tanks of dyes. The final step is to seal the outer surface by placing the carabiner in boiling deionized water for a "clear" coat, or, if it has been dyed, in a bath of nickel-acetate solution, which seals the anodized surface.

Depending on the quality and thickness of the anodization process, the surface layer will minimize corrosion (important if you live or climb near salt water). Since the interiors of gate mechanisms can hold moisture, they are most susceptible to corrosion and benefit most from anodization.

Steel is often used for gym and rescue carabiners because of the material's very high strength and abrasion resistance. However, the weight of these 'biners precludes them from normal climbing applications. Titanium carabiners have yet to become price- and weight-competitive with aluminum models.

BODY DESIGN

The shape of the body determines how the carabiner performs. All carabiners for climbing can be grouped into four categories: oval, D, offset D, and the pear-shaped HMS [Photo 2.2].

Oval-shaped carabiners have long been the standard for climbers and have been surpassed in popularity only in recent years. The design is ideal for aid climbing, rigging carabiner-brake rappels, and racking gear because of its symmetrical shape. However, when loaded, half of the force is placed on the weakest link, the gate. As a result, oval carabiners have significantly lower major-axis and gate-open strengths than other designs of equal weight—and tend to be relatively heavy. Versatility and low price help make up for these disadvantages.

Next in the evolutionary chain came the D-shaped 'biners; these are designed to bear most of the load along the spine and tend to be the strongest of the nonlocking carabiners. Their symmetrical shape is rather inefficient, but their large size makes for a good handhold. Ds generally offer the best value-to-performance ratio.

Offset Ds, by reducing the curvature of the carabiner's hinge end, save significant weight without diminishing strength or performance. Though the design dates back to at least the mid-1950s, offset Ds have gained prevalence only in the past decade.

At first, many offset Ds had a round cross-section that was relatively narrow. This thin rod stock causes ropes to wear out much faster under repeated falls. Thin-stock 'biners can also reduce the strength of wired-nut cables and wear out fairly quickly when clipped to bolts or pitons.

Newer carabiners from several companies move the metal around for better performance. The resulting tear-shaped (thin on the outside, wide on the inside) or I-beam cross-section reduces weight, yet is still friendly to the rope (pro-

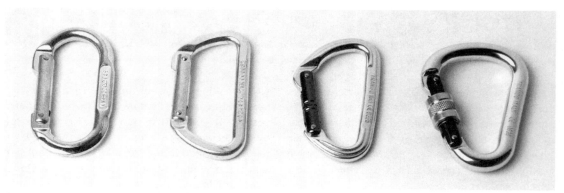

Photo 2.2   The basic carabiner shapes (left to right): oval, D, offset D, and pear

viding a broad rope-bearing surface, 10 to 12 mm thick). These designs often have significantly higher gate-open strengths than 'biners made with a round cross-section.

While offset Ds typically have a straight back, a recent trend has been to add a bend or bump for better ergonomics. These can make the 'biners a bit easier to hold and increase gate clearance. Some models have an eye for an attached quickdraw; this ensures the 'biner is ready for a fast clip and prevents cross-loading. However, to replace the sling you may have to send it to the manufacturer.

Pear-shaped locking 'biners, officially called HMS belay (*halbmastwurf sicherung*; German for half-clove hitch), are the oldest carabiner design. They are ideal for belaying and rappelling with a belay device or a Munter hitch because of the large, rounded internal profile. While primarily intended for attaching to the harness, these are also useful for top-roping and at belay stations where several carabiners are clipped into one anchor.

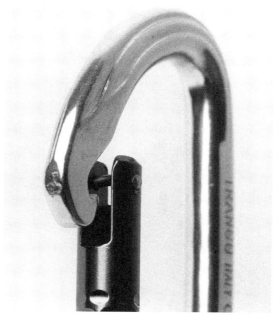

Photo 2.3 Pin-and-notch carabiner latch

LATCH DESIGN

All carabiners use one of two methods for latching the gate closed: a pin-and-notch [Photo 2.3] or a dovetail [Photo 2.4].

The pins of most carabiners' gates are stainless-steel rods that are slid into position and then flattened (peened) on both ends for security. Another option is to mill out a catch on the gate, rather than using a pin, although the body still must have a notch, which snags on slings, bolt hangers, etc.

Dovetail latches have been around almost since carabiners' beginnings. The so-called key-locks are one of the latest permutations. The newer styles have several advantages over conventional pin-and-notch carabiners, including the lack of a notch to snag on things when clipping and unclipping. About the only downside to notchless carabiners is that they are more prone to unclipping from gear slings/loops and spilling gear.

No matter the body or latch design, the profile of the nose (where the closed gate meets the 'biner body) dictates how easily the carabiner clips into mangled pins and rat's nests of webbing. The early 'biners had noses that were flush with the body, giving them a smooth profile. Most 'biners today now have a "blind gate," which means there is a bump on the nose that makes the action end much easier to locate by feel and easier to catch the rope to clip. Some models have ridges in front of the notch (on both sides) to help guard against accidental gate opening when the carabiner is pulled against or across the rock when under load [Photo 2.5].

GATE DESIGN

The gate of most carabiners is made from a straight rod of aluminum milled out at both ends [Photo 2.6]; sometimes grooves or notches are added for better

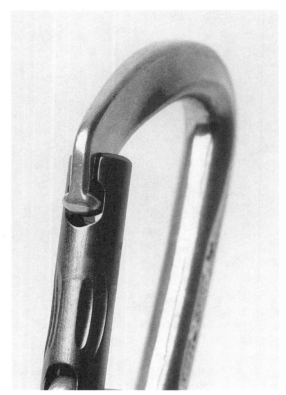

Photo 2.4　Dovetail carabiner latch

slams against the rock or is jerked hard in a fall. You can demonstrate the difference in stiffness by slapping the spine of the 'biner into the palm of your hand and listening for the click. High-speed photography has revealed that the rope running rapidly through the carabiner during a fall causes vibrations that open and close the gate briefly (gate flutter)—creating the chance that an impact at the wrong instant could result in gate-open loading and carabiner failure.

Run your finger around the inside perimeter of a bunch of carabiners, and you will feel that some models have sharp edges at the ends of the gate [Photo 2.7]. If one of these 'biners gets cross-loaded during a fall, it can shred the sheath of your rope in the blink of an eye. Better carabiners, no matter the style of the latch, have shielded (a.k.a. "shrouded") gates to protect your expensive climbing rope [Photo 2.8]. Some companies put a hole in the back of the shielded gate to help prevent snow and ice from building up.

Recently, wire gates (bent stainless-steel "paper clips") have appeared in the climbing world after decades of use in other industries. Wire-gate 'biners are significantly lighter, yet just as strong as other offset Ds. Because of the reduced gate mass, gate flutter is nearly eliminated and they are very easy to clip. Wire-gate 'biners are also less

grip. These straight rods are the most versatile style of gates and are found on the vast majority of all 'biners on climbers' racks. There really isn't anything for which straight gates cannot be used.

Carabiners with bent or dogleg gates are used on the rope end of a quickdraw (and sometimes on camming units) to assist in making the clip. The angle of the bend in some models is very pronounced, giving a good scoop for the rope, while in others it's subtler. Just remember that the easier a 'biner is to clip, the easier the rope can become unclipped accidentally.

The tension of the gate spring also affects how easily a carabiner clips and unclips. Light tension would seem to be a good choice but will result in the gate opening too easily when the carabiner

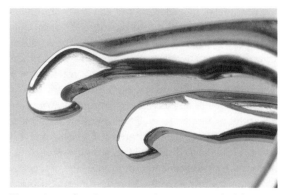

Photo 2.5　Carabiner nose designs: guarded, low-profile

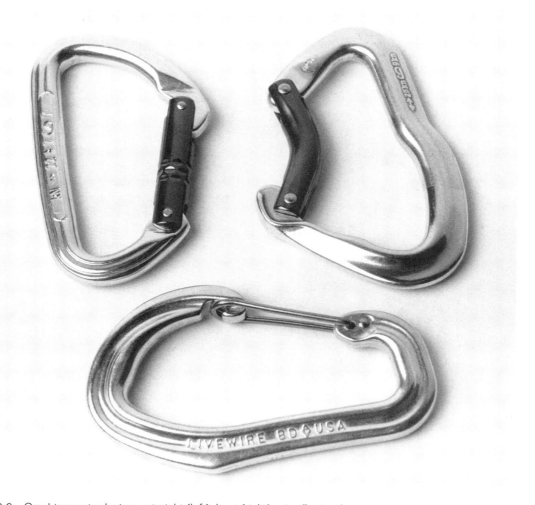

Photo 2.6   Carabiner gate designs: straight (left), bent (right), wire (bottom)

susceptible to freezing up on ice climbs.

However, if the 'biner is cross-loaded, the small radius of the wire can be very damaging to a rope. Wire gates are also prone to tangling with your wired nuts on the rack. And some companies merely throw a wire gate on an existing body with an unguarded latch for a regular gate; these gates are more likely to get pushed open by the rock.

LOCKING MECHANISMS

Since an open gate reduces strength by roughly two-thirds, keeping the gate closed is the key to safety with carabiners. The only way to assure this is with a locking mechanism on the gate [Photo 2.9]. Every climber should have several "lockers"

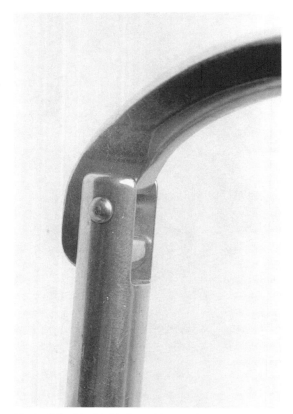

Photo 2.7   Unshielded carabiner gate

for use in clipping critical bolts and gear, rigging anchors, hauling, and rappelling.

In the past, locking carabiners were typically large and heavy. However, there is now a good assortment of lockers available that aren't much heavier than standard carabiners. These are ideal for use on quickdraws, or even clipped directly to a bolt, when the consequences of an accidental unclip could be particularly severe.

The screw-gate mechanism, in which a collar is manually twisted around the gate to prevent accidental opening, is the simplest and arguably the most reliable. Screw gates are less prone to icing or jamming with grit than self-locking models. All of the current screw gates have hidden threads, and most have a low number of threads per inch,

so it takes fewer revolutions to close them. It is important that you always twist the screw gate until it is snug; do *not* back it off a half-turn or the lock could loosen unexpectedly.

There are two styles of screw gates: body-blocking and gate-blocking [Photo 2.10]. The older body-blocking collar screws up until it wedges against the nose of the body of the 'biner. This works adequately under normal use. However, if the carabiner is loaded while the collar is screwed tightly, it will be extremely difficult to unscrew once the load is removed. Screw collars that are blocked by a stop on the gate do not suffer this problem. You can identify problem lockers by snugging the collar closed and squeezing the gate; there should be very slight play.

Photo 2.8   Shielded carabiner gate

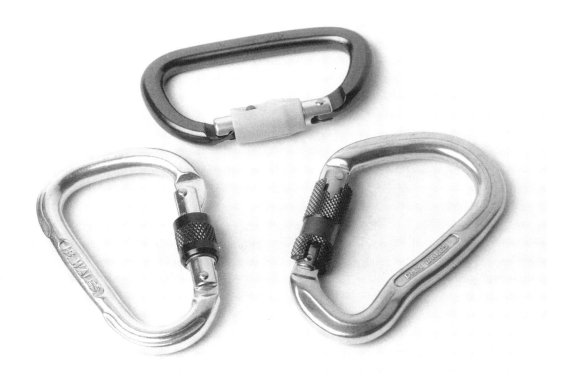

Photo 2.9 Locking mechanisms: screw-gate (left), semi-autolock (top), autolock (right)

The nicest screw gates close with an easy spin—as long as they're clean—which is helpful for locking quickly with one hand. Collars should be knurled for a good grip. One model has an additional plastic bridge that you swing into place after locking the 'biner to prevent cross-loading [see Photo 3.3 in the next chapter].

The obvious disadvantage to screw gates is you must remember to lock them each time, and they can sometimes unscrew themselves when you aren't looking (rock gremlins). Automatically locking gates reduce—but don't necessarily eliminate—these hazards. Most "autolockers" work by employing a large, spring-loaded collar that takes a quarter turn to release. Be aware that with this system, a slim possibility exists that the rock or the rope running over the gate could still twist the collar and cause the gate to open.

Some autolocks have a second security feature that you must pull or push before the lock can be unlocked, sometimes requiring two hands. Other models can be prevented from unlocking by lifting the locked collar over a hump, easily done with one hand.

A few years ago, it was discovered that when some models of locking carabiners were weighted with twice body weight, as could happen at a hanging belay, the "locked" gate could open. This can happen if the lock does not extend far enough over the nose to anticipate flexing of the 'biner when loaded. While not a major concern, it's another reason to stay aware and organized at belay stations.

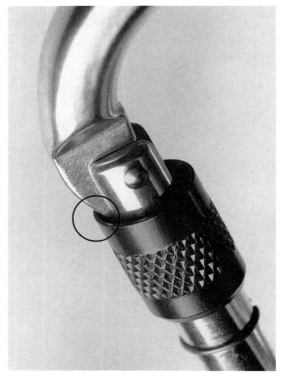

Photo 2.10   Gate-blocked screw-gate collar. Note the slight gap between the collar and nose of the carabiner.

TESTING AND RATINGS

The CEN standard specifies that with the gate closed, all general-purpose carabiners must hold at least 20 kN (4496 lbf) along their major axis. This figure is based on the 12-kN (2698-lbf) limit placed on climbing ropes; due to the "pulley effect," the top anchor is subjected to 66 percent more force than the climber feels. Oval carabiners are considered "low-load connectors" and have to hold only 16 kN (3597 lbf) with the gate closed. For each test, the load is applied at a controlled rate with two greased 12 mm steel pins until something gives—often explosively.

You may have heard the statement "modern climbing ropes do not break, but they do get cut." A similar thing can be said about carabiners: if properly clipped and not loaded over an edge, they won't break when the gate is closed.

Carabiners fail when the gate is open at the wrong moment. This can happen for a variety of reasons, including pressure on the gate by the rock or anchor; whiplash or the 'biner banging against the rock; failure of a piece of gear when the same carabiner is clipped in to two or more pieces; ripping of a shock absorber; and gate flutter from vibrations created by the rope during a fall.

The CEN minimum requirement for gate open strength is 7 kN (1574 lbf), but some of the new designs are rated to 10 kN (2248 lbf)—much better. The open-gate test is waived if the carabiner has an automatic locking gate. Oval and HMS carabiners must have gate-open strengths greater than 5 kN (1124 lbf).

Carabiners are also loaded along the minor axis to test cross-loading strength, which must be 7 kN. Unfortunately, this particular test is a bit contrived and the results can be misleading. The load is applied with two 10 mm steel pins to the center of the carabiner, no matter its shape. Since many carabiners, such as bent-gate models, would not naturally stay in this position, grooves 0.5 mm deep are filed into the body and gate to keep the pins in position.

Though this minor-axis test does strain the whole carabiner, it does not effectively simulate a cross load as it will happen in the field. This is particularly true with models that have bent gates, which tend to capture the rope at either the hinge or the latch. The standard also does not address the rope-shredding ability of cross-loaded carabiners that have uncovered sharp features along their inner perimeters. (While it's very rare, it can happen.)

Any carabiner light enough for climbing will flex a bit under body weight, but it should still open. All carabiners that pass CEN are required to open with a load of 0.8 kN (180 lbf) applied, and the beefier ones will hold more and still function properly. However, I found about 30 percent of the straight-gate offset Ds would not open with 250 lbs. (113 kg) hanging on them and had sticky gates with just 180 lbs. (82 kg)—two would not even open under body weight.

CHOOSING CARABINERS

When choosing carabiners for your rack, first decide on the body style and gate design most appropriate to the climbing you intend to do. Those who are just starting to build their trad racks should consider ovals at first because of their versatility. Later on, you can supplement with more specialized offset Ds and bent-gate 'biners.

If you look at only one number when selecting your carabiners, make it the open-gate strength. This is the figure that is most important to your safety. The other numbers (closed-gate, minor-axis strength, weight, clearance) make good trivia but are not as significant. (For most climbers, price will be the next number to consider.)

How important is weight? Let's consider using a "standard" 'biner that weighs 62 g (2.2 oz.) and a "light" 'biner that weighs 48 g (1.7 oz.) on sport and traditional racks. For a typical bolt-protected route, the climber will need about ten quickdraws; the light 'biners save 280 g (10 oz.). For an all-around rack, the total is roughly thirty to forty 'biners, and a weight savings of about ½ kg (17 oz.) can be achieved.

By using the lightest carabiners on the market (34 g, 1.2 oz.), the sport climber could save an additional 10 oz. . . . and spend over twice as much on his or her rack versus one with standard 'biners (which will also last longer). The big wall climber with a hundred 'biners could save herself well over 3 lbs. (1.5 kg) by using light 'biners. If she carries many ovals (the lightest of which is 60 g), as is likely, the weight savings will be less.

My advice? Don't be overly concerned about carabiner weight, and compare other features first. Your climbing will improve far more by removing 5 lbs. (2.3 kg) off your gut than by counting grams on your rack.

Ideally, you should narrow the list of candidates to a few models and then compare them side by side. A lot of it boils down to personal preference: how the 'biner fits your hand, gate action, size, shape, and color. Assuming you don't lose them, the decision on which models to buy is one you will live with for a long time.

Though I would climb on most modern carabiners, there are some that I would not buy because I am picky about performance, feel, and rope friendliness. Do not trust carabiners made before about 1980—even budget modern 'biners are stronger and better designed.

Ideally, look for 'biners that have a wide rope-bearing surface and a gate that lacks sharp edges along the inside perimeter. Check to make sure the gate opens smoothly, has plenty of clearance, and closes with a good snap. Examine the flattened ends of the hinge and gate pins; some stick out and have rough edges that are prone to snagging webbing.

If it's a locker, be sure the collar is easy to operate; they rarely get better in the field. You should be able to operate the locking mechanism with frozen hands while wearing mittens, in pitch-darkness.

DESCENDING RINGS

Nobody likes leaving carabiners behind on rappel anchors—that practice can get expensive in a hurry. If you are in a remote part of the world where it's highly unlikely anyone will be following your descent, then it's acceptable to rap directly off nylon runners. But if others are likely to use the anchor, it's discourteous at best to pull your rope over the runners; the friction will melt them and weaken the material.

Many climbers carry a few descending rings

[Photo 2.11] that are usually made of rolled, seamless aluminum. These are light, strong (over 2000 lbf, 9 kN), and fairly inexpensive. However, they wear out pretty fast at rap stations that are frequently used (two rings are far better).

An even more affordable alternative for high-traffic rappel anchors is an 8 mm Quick-link. This is a steel oval, which closes with a screw gate, that is far stronger than two descending rings. Do not use narrower Quick-links (hard on ropes) or Lap-links (not strong enough) for rappel anchors.

Never thread rappel rings or Quick-links for top-roping! It's much better to replace your worn-out 'biners than to wear out an anchor and leave it for someone else.

CARE

Unlike nylon products, carabiners do not lose strength with age—they will pretty much last indefinitely. The primary reasons you will need to retire a carabiner are grooves worn by abrasive

Photo 2.11   Descending rings: welded stainless steel, Quick-link, seamless aluminum

ropes, gouges caused by steel pitons and bolt hangers, and corrosion caused by salt water or even the sweat from your hands. Inspect your 'biners carefully for these signs, as well as any evidence of tiny cracks—particularly around gate pins and hinge pins.

If a carabiner gate is sticky because it's bent rather than oxidized or gritty, you should retire the 'biner. If you use your 'biners near salt water, be sure to rinse them thoroughly in fresh water, allow them to dry in a warm place, and then lubricate them before storage. Remember, it's the water inside the 'biner, where you can't see it, that is of greatest concern.

WD-40 is a good water dispersant and an okay penetrating lubricant. However, such a petroleum

USING CARABINERS

When used properly, carabiners are trustworthy connectors. Poor orientation is probably the biggest cause of carabiner failure—and it's usually the climber's fault. Be sure that the rock cannot press the gate open when the 'biner is loaded. When a carabiner is levered over an edge (the result of a poorly placed bolt or an extension sling that is the wrong length), it can break with as little as 2 to 3 kN (450 to 674 lbf) of force. Bear in mind that a factor 1 fall of only a few feet, as could easily happen right off the belay of a multipitch climb, generates about 10 kN (2248 lbf) at the anchor. For all 'biners, especially those with bent gates, make certain that the rope will not cross back over the gate when you are leading. Otherwise, a fall at this point could form a loop that will pull through the gate with nary a pause [Illustration 2.1].

Reduce the risk of a carabiner unclipping itself from a bolt or piton by always using a sling or flexible quickdraw. It is important that the rope pass from the back (rock side) toward the front of the bottom carabiner. Otherwise, the draw can twist itself around so that the top 'biner unclips either the bolt or the sling.

For maximum safety, use a locking carabiner on rigid anchors (bolts or pitons), where even a small chance of unclipping is unacceptable (such as the first bolt of a sport route). It is best to use two lockers (gates opposite and opposed) when setting up a top-rope, since this is less harmful for the rope (wider bend), and it eliminates the possibility of the rope mysteriously getting unclipped.

Clipping too many things into a carabiner at a belay anchor places much more stress on the gate, reducing strength significantly. No more than two 'biners should be clipped in to the wide end unless it's a pear 'biner. On the small end of offset Ds, only one is recommended; even the use of webbing wider than $1\frac{1}{16}$ in. is best avoided.

Although open-gate strength is an important measure, it does not tell you how a carabiner will perform when the gate notch is accidentally hooked on a bolt hanger or wire cable. While this is an obvious form of misuse, it can happen when stick-clipping or making a dicey reach. If the climber proceeds anyway and falls even a short distance before freeing the notch so the gate will close, the consequences can be disastrous. Most carabiners will hold only between 1.8 and 3.1 kN (400 and 700 lbf) when levered from the gate notch. Even with a dynamic rope and soft belay, a climber falling just a few feet can easily exceed this breaking point. You can also break a carabiner with the notch hooked just by doing a bounce test while aid climbing. If you can't clip a fixed piton without properly aligning the 'biner to load the major axis, stuff a sling through the piton's eye and clip that.

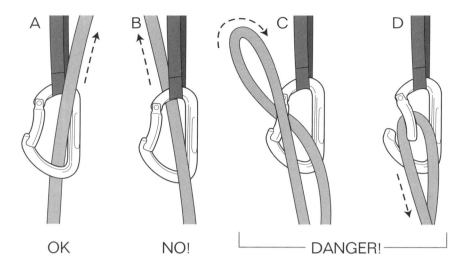

Illustration 2.1   Clipping a carabiner. A: The rope should always run from back (next to rock) to front (away from rock). B–D: If clipped front to back, the rope can unclip itself during a fall.

product can attract grit, possibly causing worse problems than what you tried to solve. A better solution for sticking gates is a dry lubricant used for bike chains.

DROPPED GEAR

Conventional wisdom says that a carabiner that has been dropped must be retired, even when there are no signs of damage. Perhaps not.

In a test conducted by REI, thirty carabiner bodies (half ovals, half Ds) were each dropped six times onto a concrete floor from a height of 33 ft. (10 m). Following the drops, their open-gate strength was measured and compared to thirty control samples from the same production batch that had not been dropped. The statistical result was no loss of strength.

According to Chris Harmston, the quality assurance manager at Black Diamond, "I have test-broken hundreds of used, abused, and dropped 'biners (even some that fell 3000 ft. (1000 m) from the top of the Salathé Wall on El Capitan). Never have I noticed any problem with these unless there is obvious visual damage to the 'biner."

While somewhat reassuring, this does not give you carte blanche to use carabiners that have been dropped a significant distance. Immediately retire any carabiner that is crooked, has deep indentations, or has a gate that doesn't operate smoothly.

CHAPTER 3

BELAY AND RAPPEL DEVICES

WHILE CLIMBERS MAY SPEND HOURS fretting about which rope to choose or protection to buy, they often give little thought to the simple gizmos that affect how ropes and protection work. But choosing a belay device is a decision that can have profound consequences.

No single belay or rappel method or device is ideal for all situations, so most well-rounded climbers end up owning several devices and choose among them depending on the style for each day's climbing. This chapter explores the options.

BELAY FORCES

Selecting the right belay/rappel device for a given day of climbing depends on a number of factors, including the style of roping up (single, double, or twin ropes); the diameter and stiffness of the ropes to be used; the quality of the protection; and the strength and weight of the climbers in the party.

In the vast majority of falls, all belay methods put the same amount of force on the protection—in other words, all belays are "static" until the rope begins to slip. It's only with high-impact falls that some belay methods are significantly more dynamic (and thus less stressful on the pro, leader, and belayer) than others.

Sport and gym climbers who usually belay from the ground often become complacent because they have never had to catch a hard fall—fall factors greater than 0.8 can happen only if the leader plummets below the belayer. (Up to factor 1 is theoretically possible, but rope stretch means the climber hits the ground.) When you enter the "real world" of multipitch climbing, however, the potential exists for very serious forces that exceed the capability of many belay methods. The age-old waist belay, for example, offers only about 180 lbf (0.8 kN) of holding capacity—without gloves, you *will* burn your hands and probably let go of the rope.

Ideally, you should be able to vary the holding power of the belay to suit the situation. However, this is far beyond the capability of most climbers, and even belay devices designed to vary holding power with their orientation essentially offer the same braking force throughout their range.

Particularly worrisome to traditional and aid climbers is the force placed on the top piece of protection in a hard fall. In one series of tests by REI, most belay devices in a factor 1 fall kept the load on the top piece to about 1000 lbf (4.5 kN), while a Petzl GriGri averaged over 2200 lbf (9.8 kN).

Another test series in Germany showed that a 0.375 factor fall with a 154-lb. (70-kg) climber subjects the top piece to about 1190 lbf (5.3 kN) with a GriGri on the belayer's harness, while a Munter yielded 854 lbf (3.8 kN) and a figure eight kept it to 787 lbf (3.5 kN). If you divide these numbers by 1.6, you'll get an idea of the force inflicted upon the leader's body.

Attaching the belay device to your harness, rather than an anchor, lessens the impact on the climber and anchors. One test showed that forces are reduced from 15 to 30 percent due to the belayer being pulled forward or lifted into the air.

If the belayer jumps in the direction of the rope while catching a fall with a GriGri, the peak force on the top piece drops to about 764 lbf (3.4 kN). That's great for sport climbers belaying on the ground. But this technique is next to impossible at a small stance or hanging belay, and the forces allowed by a GriGri should cause serious concern for the many aid climbers now using these convenient devices to belay on walls.

BELAY AND RAPPEL STYLES

Given all the variables in climbing, it's useful to be familiar with different styles of belaying and rappelling. There is no one answer for everything.

MUNTER HITCH

At a 1973 meeting of the UIAA in Italy, some Italian climbers advocated a belay hitch that had been used by Phoenician sailors for controlling ships. Though it was named for Swiss guide Werner Munter, the credit for it should more likely go to German climber Franz Ruso. After extensive testing, the *halbmastwurf sicherung* (HMS), or half-clove hitch, gained widespread popularity.

It's surprising how many climbers are unfamiliar with the Munter (a.k.a. Italian) hitch [Photo 3.1], considering its effectiveness, simplicity, and price (free). Even though you may hardly ever use the Munter, it's very useful when a belay device gets dropped or left at home.

One advantage of the Munter is a relative independence from hand position. With the Munter, you have sufficient braking power no matter the location of your brake hand. (With all of the other

EVOLUTION OF THE BELAY

In the nineteenth century, climbers used ropes for safety on glaciers but considered them dubious at best on rock, because they had not worked out the techniques of belaying. For much of the early history of climbing, if one roped climber fell, everyone fell—unless the rope broke.

Famed British climber Geoffrey Winthrop Young began advocating a controlled "springing" of the rope with the belayer's body way back in 1920. However, it would be another two decades before a satisfactory procedure was worked out. Indeed, several authors during the 1930s advocated sacrificing the falling leader to preserve the rest of the climbing party. This was accomplished by a static "rock belay" (performed by wrapping the rope around a nearby horn or over a boulder) that would practically ensure the rope would snap.

The standard technique for belaying during the first half of this century was to pass the rope around the hips, over the shoulder, and even over the knee. However, experiments by the Sierra Club confirmed what many had suspected—only a well-braced hip belay was sufficient to hold even minor falls.

Research by Richard Leonard and Arnold Wexler into the forces of falling led to the development of the "dynamic belay," codified by the Sierra Club in 1946. The belayer was taught to deliberately allow the rope to run a few feet to reduce forces. (Considering that manila climbing ropes stretched only about 12 to 18 percent before breaking, the need for some give in the system was critical.) This dynamic hip belay required practice and inevitably led to rope burns for the belayer (to which I can personally attest) unless gloves and heavy clothing were worn.

When more elastic nylon ropes (37 to 55 percent stretch) took over, clamping down tight on the rope for more static hip belays was once again advocated. In practice, however, when the fall was severe enough the rope would still be ripped through the belayer's hands.

In the late 1960s, Fritz Sticht developed an aluminum plate with a slot through which a bight of rope could be threaded and clipped to a carabiner. The resulting friction from the sharp bend in the rope allowed the belayer to comfortably hold relatively severe falls with minimal effort. Though it took a while to catch on, the Sticht plate still retains a loyal following and is the forerunner of modern belay devices.

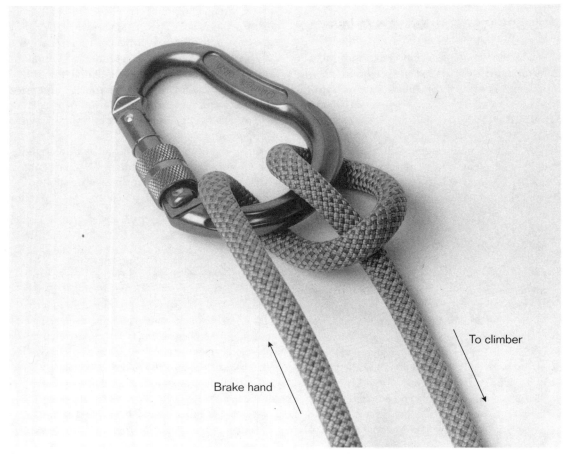

To climber

Brake hand

Photo 3.1   The closed Munter hitch gives maximum braking power.

devices, the belay hand must quickly be moved to the proper position to stop the fall. Thus if the belayer is unprepared, or the belay hand is blocked at an awkward stance, there's a good possibility of dropping the falling climber.)

A "closed Munter," with the rope on both sides of the 'biner running next to each other, has greater holding capacity—about 2.5 kN (562 lbf)—than most other belay methods. This is one of the best methods for belaying the second directly off the anchors.

However, the "open Munter," with the rope entering and exiting the 'biner in opposite directions, is more dynamic than many other devices—about 1.4 kN (315 lbf). Consequently, if there is a good chance of a severe fall, the best lock-off hand position with the Munter is opposite that used with a belay device.

The Munter can be used effectively for belaying either single or twin ropes—it does not twist the rope too badly. But it's a major hassle for double ropes, since you often need to take in on one rope while letting out on the other.

The drawback of the Munter is its unfriendliness toward ropes. The hitch does more sheath damage (melting of fibers) than any other belay method when catching hard falls (hopefully an infrequent occurrence). And you'll end up with a tangled nightmare if you try to rappel with a Munter. Use this only as a last resort when you've dropped the rack and don't have enough 'biners to rig a carabiner brake.

CARABINER BRAKE

After you get over the disappointment of watching your dropped rappel device bouncing down the cliff into oblivion, it's time to rig a carabiner brake [Photo 3.2]. This can be done with as few as three carabiners (one locking), but the standard configuration uses five (or six if you don't have a locker on the harness).

Ideally, you should rig the brake setup with two oval carabiners forming the frame, and their gates should be opposite and opposed. However, few climbers use ovals anymore (except for aid climbs), so it's likely you will have to use D-shaped 'biners. In this case, it's best to rig the 'biners with the gates

opposed but on the same side for symmetry.

For most steep rappels, you will want two carabiners clipped across as the "brake bar" to provide adequate friction. Should you have to rap with a heavy load or on a single line, it's best to use six more carabiners to double the carabiner brake.

If you are descending low-angle slabs, one carabiner will suffice as the brake bar. You can also use a *dülfersitz* (rope between legs, across chest, and over opposite shoulder) if you have heavy clothing or a high pain tolerance.

BELAY PLATES

There are now numerous permutations of the original Salewa Sticht plate, and all of them work in essentially the same way [Photo 3.3].

The standard Sticht plate (and figure eight devices using the small hole in Sticht configuration) offers fairly good stopping power—roughly 2 kN (450 lbf). However, they often jam against the carabiner at inopportune moments, such as when

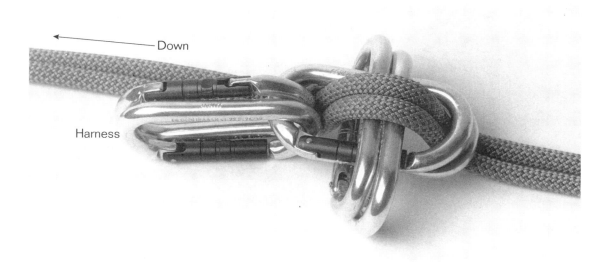

Photo 3.2   Carabiner brake

the leader suddenly needs a lot of slack to make a clip.

Some plates have a coiled spring on the carabiner side to prevent accidental locking. While effective, the spring also reduces the braking force to about 1.5 kN (338 lbf). Worse, it has an annoying habit of tangling with every piece of gear or webbing within arm's reach.

These devices tend to provide too much friction for rappelling with a doubled single rope (clipping a second carabiner between the plate and belay 'biner will allow a smoother descent). Due to the small mass, they also heat up seriously during long rappels; melting of the rope's sheath is a distinct possibility.

Because these small belay devices are easy to drop and can slide down the rope out of reach while belaying, a keeper cord is needed so the plate stays where it belongs.

For all of these reasons, there is little point in using any of the standard Sticht plates for rappelling, with or without the spring.

However, a new generation of belay plates has been engineered to overcome the problems of their predecessors. These offer smoother rappels, faster payouts, and built-in keeper wires. With the modifications, these new belay plates work about as well as many belay tubes.

BELAY TUBES

The Latok Tuber was the first in a long genealogy of belay tubes, by far the most popular all-around devices today. While similar to belay plates, their greater depth makes them less prone to locking up unintentionally.

The amount of friction generated by tube devices is determined by several factors, including the length and depth of the slot. Shorter, shallower

Photo 3.3   Belay devices: Sticht with spring and an ATC (plastic bridge prevents cross-loading the carabiner)

slots create more friction than longer, deeper ones.

A tube's effective depth is also determined by the shape of the locking carabiner selected. Large HMS 'biners have a very rounded end that will not fit up into a tube and thus give less friction and a smoother rappel. By flipping the carabiner over, the small end fits deeper into the tube for more braking power. D-shaped lockers also tend to fit deeper inside the tubes.

The thickness of the carabiner also makes a significant difference in the handling of most belay/rappel systems. Thicker 'biners offer a smoother belay. When rappelling on new, small-diameter ropes—or when rapping with a haul bag—clip a second carabiner through the bight of rope, or you may find yourself going too fast.

Rule out any belay device with a nylon keeper cord—it is guaranteed to get sucked into and jam the device as you rappel. My favorite keeper is a plastic-coated wire cable because it flexes and is quiet. (A rigid aluminum rod is noisy jangling from a 'biner.) But the cable must be fairly stiff to stay out of the way.

All other things being equal, thinner walls would wear out faster than thicker walls. However, some companies use 6000-series aluminum (or softer) and others use harder 7000-series, so the durability of different devices cannot be easily determined by looking at them. (In this case, anodizing, which creates those pretty colors, does not affect longevity.)

Mass of the device is the main factor in how hot it gets by the end of a rappel. Cooling fins and holes on belay tubes are mostly for marketing purposes, although the ribs on some devices make them easier to hold onto with wet gloves.

Belay tubes wear out faster than other belay devices—good thing they're fairly cheap. After a lot of hard use, particularly with wet, gritty ropes, the rope-bearing radius of the tubes can get alarmingly thin. Although the worn tubes still function and won't catastrophically fail, they are much harder on your expensive climbing rope.

The original round Tuber design was squared off to feed better, and it still lives on in several popular devices. These are normally used with the wide end next to the carabiner for smoothest operation. Tests by REI showed that flipping the tube around does not appreciably affect the holding power of the devices, contrary to popular belief. However, rope handling may be improved with the small end nearer the carabiner when using frozen, fat, or very stiff ropes.

Black Diamond's Air Traffic Controller (ATC) is certainly the most widely imitated belay tube and with good reason—it's a solid all-around performer. I've used an ATC for many years and don't have any major complaints.

The V-shaped notches of the Trango Jaws make a versatile belay device. With the notches on the side where the leader's rope exits, it performs much like any other tube device. (*Note:* Trango does not recommend this.) But when it's rigged so the notches are on the side of the brake hand, you get over twice the braking power because of wedging in the grooves. Jaws is ideal for using a pair of slick double or twin ropes, rappelling with a haul bag, or belaying a heavy climber. With a single rope, however, the rope tends to cross awkwardly into the wrong notch—still effective, but I prefer the simplicity of an ATC.

FIGURE EIGHT

Although I rarely use a figure eight device [Photo 3.4] anymore, they still have their adherents and a few distinct advantages. In general, these devices provide the smoothest rappels of all the standard options. Because of their larger mass, figure eights are also less prone to heating up than other rappel devices.

Although many people accuse the figure eight device of kinking their ropes during a rappel, this has more to do with pilot error. When your brake hand is positioned off to the side, with the rope running outside your leg, the rope will snarl terribly by the time you reach the bottom. Keeping the

Down →

Photo 3.4   Figure eight device in standard rappel configuration

brake hand directly below the figure eight with the rope between your legs greatly reduces tangles. Running the rope between the legs is also safer because you can use both hands for braking if necessary (friction decreases near the bottom) and it's easier to recover the rope if you lose control.

One nice feature of figure eight devices is that they are hard to drop accidentally if you follow a simple procedure. When you're climbing, keep the large hole clipped to the locking carabiner that you attach to your harness's belay loop. To rig the rappel, pass a bight of rope through the large hole and around the stem. Now you can unclip the 'biner and reclip it to the small hole without risk of losing the device. Reverse the procedure at the bottom of the rappel.

Be careful that your figure eight does not slip out of place on the carabiner. With certain combinations, the figure eight can lever against the locking

mechanism and break the gate—this has happened on several occasions, and at least one person is dead as a result! Standing on ledges part-way down sets up the potential nightmare as you unweight the figure eight and then weight it again.

Though typically thought of as a rappel device, the figure eight also serves well as a belay device for single ropes [Photo 3.5]. Using the small hole in Sticht-mode gives about 2.0 kN (450 lbf) of braking force (varies depending on the size of the hole). Rigged as if for rappels, the figure eight has a bit less holding force than other devices, about 1.2 kN (270 lbf).

The so-called "sport mode," where the bight is clipped through the 'biner instead of running around the neck, has only around 0.8 kN (180 lbf) of stopping power and has resulted in many dropped climbers.

A standard figure eight makes the most sense

for alpine climbs, when a soft catch can keep snow anchors from ripping out and the consequences of a long fall are less severe.

The Trango Belay 8 is an unusual device that works well for sport climbing because it pays out rope incredibly fast. A V-shaped slot increases holding power so a small climber can hold a big person with ease.

AUTO-BRAKING DEVICES

Belay devices that brake automatically when a climber falls have significant pros and cons. For interminable belay sessions while the leader is working a sport route, an auto-braking device allows the belayer to hold the resting climber with minimal strain.

When the leader is sketching on desperate aid, an auto-braking device can enhance safety—even the best belayer's attention will wander after a while. However, as mentioned previously, these devices put maximum force on the gear and may be inappropriate for hard aid. It's a Catch-22.

The catch, or rather the lack thereof, is that many climbers use these belay devices improperly, and people have decked as a result. Compared with belay tubes, all of these auto-braking devices are more prone to jamming when the leader needs a big swipe of rope for a clip at the edge of his or her reach.

The Petzl GriGri remains the hands-down choice among auto-braking devices, despite its considerable bulk and weight (the equivalent of four belay tubes) [Photo 3.6]. The GriGri also makes a nice backup to your ascenders for climbing a fixed rope.

The GriGri works only with ropes between 9.7 and 11 mm and should never be used on icy ropes. Because its operation is a bit unusual, and it can accidentally be rigged backward, quite a few belayers have messed up and dropped the falling climber.

Photo 3.5 Figure eight device rigged for belaying

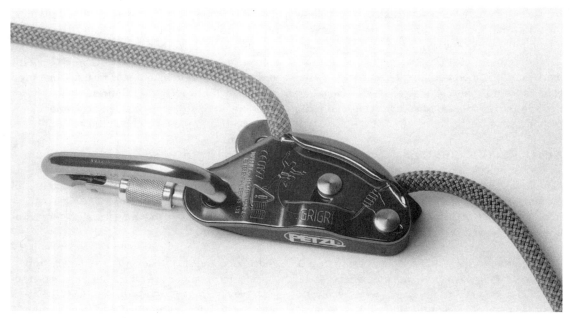

Photo 3.6   The Petzl GriGri auto-braking belay device

Photo 3.7   The Silent Partner self-belay device

Other auto-braking belay devices are available that do the job, but not nearly as nicely. Having tried them, I'd rather use a belay tube or a GriGri.

For solo lead climbing, there are several systems that "work," but only one is recommended. The Wren Industries Silent Partner is the best option if going alone is your thing [Photo 3.7].

The Kong Gi-Gi is a handy little tool commonly used on multipitch sport climbs in Europe for bringing up either one or two second climbers on ropes from 8 to 12 mm [Photo 3.8]. The leader carries it while a second belays him with a standard belay device. The Gi-Gi also works well for rappelling, but cannot be used to belay a lead climber—if you're swinging leads, you must swap devices at each belay station.

The Gi-Gi is auto-braking and needs only one hand to operate for belaying one climber, freeing the leader's other hand. With two seconds, one person can keep climbing if the other falls, so a party of three can move much faster. However, if the second is hanging free of the rock, you will not be able to lower him easily. One answer is to girth-hitch a sling through the bottom hole of the device and run it up through the anchor and down to your harness; this allows you to lift the bottom of the Gi-Gi and lower the climber.

BOTTOM LINE

The gear fetishists can argue endlessly about which belay device is minutely superior to another in some

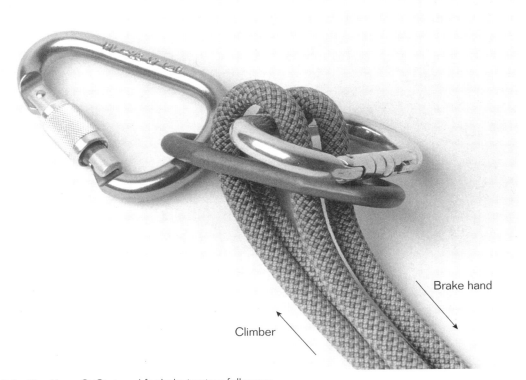

Photo 3.8   The Kong Gi-Gi rigged for belaying two followers

minor aspect. Personally, I'd rather go climbing.

For a day of cragging with single ropes, I'm most likely going to use an ATC-style belay tube for its simplicity and good all-around performance.

For belaying a sport climber at his or her limit, the Trango Belay 8 is hard to beat for speed of paying out rope, but a GriGri is deluxe for holding hangdoggers.

On a wall, I'll take both a GriGri and an ATC-style tube, the former for long belay sessions, the latter for raps, for belaying very dicey leads, and as a backup for dropsies.

When using double ropes or twins, or for climbs where I suspect I'll want a lot of holding power (a partner the size of a house, for example), the Trango Jaws is definitely my favorite. Perhaps on a snow climb, I'd take a figure eight.

When all else fails, I can resort to a Munter for belays and a carabiner brake for rappels. Even the old hip belay and *dülfersitz* come in handy at times.

No matter the device, when rappelling into the unknown or in dicey circumstances, it's a good idea to use a backup system that stops the descent when you release your hand. Commercial models are available but are heavy and bulky. Climbers are better served by an autoblock knot set up *below* the rappel device—see *Self-Rescue* by David Fasulo (Chockstone Press, 1996) for details. Do not use a prusik above the rappel device because it is difficult to loosen.

CHAPTER 4

RUNNERS AND CORDS

WEBBING AND ACCESSORY CORD ARE the ties that bind our climbing equipment. We use them for protection, as anchors, and for countless other tasks, both important and mundane.

RUNNERS

A runner, or sling, is simply a loop of webbing made by tying or sewing two ends together [Photo 4.1]. These loops are most commonly used for extending protection on trad climbs (to reduce rope drag) and for rigging belay anchors.

Though you can make runners from accessory cord, they will be thicker, bulkier, and far more costly than webbing runners of the same strength.

The thinness of webbing (about 3 mm) is also invaluable when threading tight spaces. On the other hand, one test showed that 9 mm cord was almost four times more abrasion-resistant than 1 in. tubular webbing. You can spend much more for 5.5 mm Spectra cord, but it's only a bit better than the webbing for abrasion resistance.

Even though it doesn't have great durability, webbing is cheap enough to replace regularly.

MATERIAL

Tubular webbing used to be made on shuttle looms that would spiral "weft" filaments around the lengthwise "warp" filaments. While adequate when intact, the webbing could completely unravel once damaged. Now, most webbing is made with needle looms and is identified by a seam on

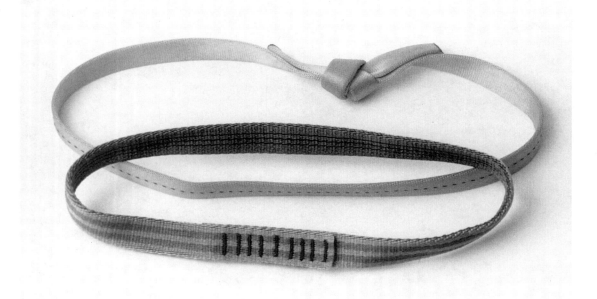

Photo 4.1   Tied (water knot) and sewn (bar-tacked) runners

one edge. Webbing produced in Europe has one contrasting-colored thread for every 5 kN (1125 lbf) of breaking strength.

Until a decade or so ago, 1 in. (25 mm) tubular nylon webbing was the material of choice for most climbing applications because it is strong—around 4000 lbf (18 kN)—and relatively inexpensive. The 1 in. webbing also comes in earth colors—a good choice if you must leave slings at rappel anchors.

Although 1 in. is still around and widely used, $^{11}/_{16}$ in. (18 mm) nylon supertape webbing, a thicker and denser weave, has gained popularity because it's about the same strength yet a lot less bulky. The narrower webbing also reduces outward strain on a carabiner's gate.

By combining an ultra-high-molecular-weight polyethylene fiber (called Spectra or Dyneema) with nylon, webbing can be made slightly narrower yet much stronger and more resistant to abrasion and cutting. Spectra runners also absorb less water and are more UV-resistant than nylon-only slings. These runners cost more and are completely static, but I think they're worth it.

Spectra webbing has two major drawbacks: low heat tolerance and slipperiness. While nylon softens at 446°F (230°C) and melts at 500°F (260°C), Spectra softens at 212°F (100°C) and melts at only 297°F (147°C). Because of the slippery nature of the material, knots loosen easily and slip under load. Although one brand of Spectra webbing can be knotted, most cannot and it isn't easy to tell them apart—none are sold off the spool, only as sewn products.

Someday you may be forced to cut and knot a Spectra runner, perhaps for rigging a rappel anchor. In this situation, slice through the middle of the stitching so there is a stub on each end. These will act as stoppers and prevent the knot from completely slipping apart.

Thin ½ in. and $^9/_{16}$ in. tubular nylon webbing is still used for slinging aid protection and tying off dicey piton placements. Neither is particularly strong—between 1000 and 1500 lbf (4.5 and 6.7 kN)—or abrasion-resistant, so don't use these unless you need them.

CONSTRUCTION

In an ideal world, a loop of webbing would be twice as strong as a single strand. However, bends create variable strain (more on the outside, less on the inside) that weakens the webbing. This is most dramatic with knotted slings, which often break at only slightly more than the strength of one strand. Sewn runners are much stronger.

The water knot, also called the ring bend, has been around at least since Isaak Walton wrote *The Compleat Angler* in 1653 and is still the preferred method of connecting webbing. It is both easy to tie and untie—the latter point being its chief advantage and disadvantage.

It's always a good idea to carry a few tied runners on a long trad climb because you may need to untie one for threading an old piton or wrapping around a boulder or tree. The water knot can be loosened by hand more easily than other knots.

Because it's as slippery as water, this knot also has a tendency to come undone on its own. Always tighten water knots by fully weighting the sling with your body and recheck them often—it's really scary when you discover a loose one! Some climbers tape the ends down to ensure no mishaps. Although the double fisherman knot is more secure, you can't loosen it once it's tight, which defeats the whole purpose of knotted slings.

Not only are sewn runners far stronger but they are also less bulky, which simplifies rigging chores. Bar tacks are among the strongest of all the stitch patterns, but this depends greatly on the sewing machine, needle, and thread combination. Most companies use computerized machines that are very precise (some can do patterns), and they test samples frequently. Do *not* try to sew your own runners!

LENGTH

Runners come in many different lengths, and which you choose is largely a matter of personal preference or the necessities of a climb.

Sewn 12 in. (30 cm) runners are versatile because they can be doubled up for racking and extended when necessary. It's handy to have a few of these on the rack, in addition to regular quickdraws, for their extra length.

The most popular size runners are 24 in. (60 cm) long. These can be worn bandolier-style across your chest for fast access. Ice climbers often hang them straight down from the neck so they can be reached with either hand while the other is locked onto a tool. On alpine climbs you may want as many as eight to ten such runners since routes tend to wander.

Shoulder-length runners can also be tripled-up and racked as quickdraws. The trick method for this is to clip a carabiner into the runner, then pass a bight of the runner through the 'biner and clip all three resulting loops with another 'biner [Photo 4.2]. When you need to extend the runner, simply unclip either 'biner from two of the loops and tug. Voilà: both 'biners are miraculously inside the loop and you're ready for action.

It's often a good idea to carry a couple of 48 in. (1.2 m) runners. These double up nicely for carry-

Photo 4.2   Tripling up a runner. The final step is to clip the webbing at the bottom into the inserted carabiner (on right).

ing over the shoulder and come in handy at belays.

Bill Forrest developed an option to standard loops called a rabbit runner, a simple 4 ft. strand of webbing with loops sewn on each end. With both loops clipped into a carabiner, you get a standard shoulder-length sling that can be extended when needed. These are convenient when wearing a lot of clothing because you can just unclip one loop and tug off the sling.

Many times one runner isn't enough and you need to extend it. Girth-hitching runners together is a common practice, though it decreases strength by about 30 percent, from roughly 6100 to 4200 lbf (27 to 18 kN) for sewn Spectra loops. If maximum strength is a concern, use locking carabiners for connecting runners.

Never girth-hitch webbing around wire cable! This reduces strength to about 1500 to 2000 lbf (6.7 to 9 kN), a force that is easily achievable in a hard fall. If you're out of 'biners, drape the sling through the wire and clip both ends.

LONGEVITY

If you've ever run across old rappel anchors with sun-faded webbing that was stiff to the touch and made creaking sounds when it was moved, you must have wondered if the webbing was safe. The short answer is: possibly, but back it up or replace it anyway.

One test showed that UV-exposed webbing and cord lost about a third of its strength in one year. Tests of old sling removed from climbs showed a very wide range of holding power. The scary part is that strength could not be judged from appearance alone—some webbing that looked fine broke under low loads, while some so faded it was hard to tell the original color was remarkably strong.

Anchor webbing without rappel rings should be inspected very carefully for rope burns that can severely weaken the material. Don't forget to check the knots too!

Inspect your climbing gear occasionally for abrasion of the webbing or stitching. Age alone isn't a major factor in the longevity of runners, unlike climbing ropes, which lose some dynamic properties with time. However, fuzzy or faded slings should be replaced—the stuff is too cheap, and important, to skimp on it.

QUICKDRAWS

Whether for clipping bolts on sport routes or extending protection on trad climbs, quickdraws are standard on the racks of most climbers. Although a quickdraw can be any runner short enough for racking with two carabiners, most of them are sewn through the middle so there is a loop on either end [Photo 4.3].

To ensure the bottom carabiner is in position for a fast clip, the lower loop is either sewn snug enough that a bent-gate carabiner must be pushed into position, or a rubber band holds the biner captive. The top loop must be large enough to allow flipping the straight-gate carabiner that connects to the anchor so it will be less likely to unclip.

Tests have shown that the top carabiner is more likely to unclip itself if the 'biner is captive in the quickdraw or when the gate is facing the bolt head. This can happen on a slightly traversing line if rope drag or your body raises the rope end higher than the bolt. It's best to rotate the top carabiner so that its gate is facing down and out from the anchor.

When clipping an anchor, be sure that the gate on the lower carabiner is facing away from the direction you will travel. Also be sure the lower 'biner will not be loaded over an edge or bulge (this can be off to the side too)—you may need to use a different-length quickdraw.

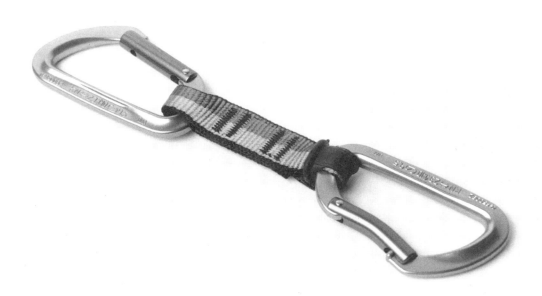

Photo 4.3   Quickdraw with a floppy end on the straight-gate carabiner and a captive end on the bent-gate carabiner (keeps the 'biner oriented properly)

LOAD-LIMITERS

Two devices are used by climbers in special circumstances to reduce forces during a fall. Quickdraw load-limiters absorb energy placed on weak aid or ice protection that might otherwise not stop a fall. Via ferrata lanyards keep you tethered to the steel cables common in Europe.

LIMITING DRAWS

The best known, and most heavily tested, load-limiters are the Yates Screamers, which use controlled ripping of precisely designed stitching to reduce impact force [Photo 4.4]. The standard Screamers activate at 550 lbf (2.5 kN), while the version made for dubious aid protection activates at 300 lbf (1.3 kN). Fully extended after a major fall, they test about as strong as a regular quickdraw.

Although both of these devices only absorb 500 lbf (2.2kN) (accompanied by a loud ripping sound), they also prolong the duration of a fall. This gives the dynamic climbing rope time to absorb an additional 300 to 400 lbf (1.3 to 1.8 kN). Thus a piece of protection that might have felt 2000 lbf (8.9 kN) in a fall receives only about 1200 lbf (5.3 kN). An additional Screamer in series could reduce the force even further, although you reach a point of diminishing return.

For difficult alpine ice climbs, where belay anchors are often poor and the protection can be

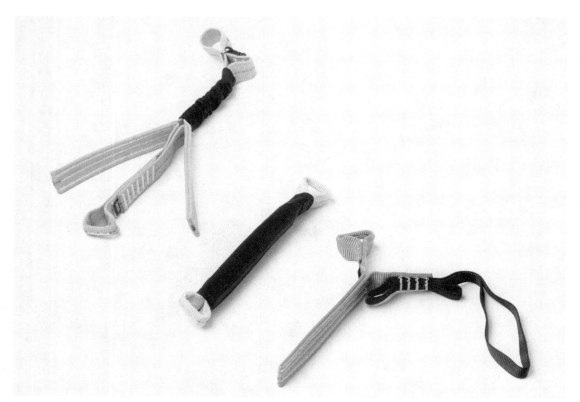

Photo 4.4 Load limiter for an ice screw (with cover pulled back to expose stitching), for standard protection (cover in place), and for very dicey aid placements

even worse, it may be a good idea to carry several load-limiting quickdraws.

VIA FERRATA LANYARDS

Particularly in the Eastern Alps, the *via ferrata* (iron highways) are widely used for reaching peaks and passes. Mostly built during the world wars for moving troops around, this amazing network of steel ladders is precariously attached to cliffs. Next to the ladders, a steel cable serves as protection for climbers who clip in to it with lanyards.

The danger with these ladders exists in the long distance between anchor points on the safety cables. Should you slip (don't laugh, the rungs can be very slick), it is quite easy for even a short fall to explode carabiners.

Several European climbing companies make a Y-shaped lanyard that attaches to your harness and has a locking carabiner on each long end. The operation of each is different (read the instructions), but they all limit the forces of a fall to tolerable levels.

You probably won't find these shock-absorbing lanyards in North America (there's really no need for them), but many climbing shops in Europe have them.

CORDELETTES

In the past decade, many climbers have taken to carrying 20 ft. (6 m) loops of accessory cord for use at belay anchors. Called a cordelette, such a loop allows a fully redundant anchor that is very fast to rig. For the best efficiency, both the leader and the second carry one with them.

Typically, a cordelette is made from 7 mm accessory cord because it is strong and affordable. Some climbers skimp and use 6 mm cord because it's cheaper and slightly less bulky, but this is cutting the margin of safety rather thin for minimal gains.

Other climbers go all out and use the expensive 5 mm cords that have a nylon sheath and a Spectra core. These work fine but can be stiff, and the

cost tends to inhibit cutting up the cordelette for backing up rappel anchors when necessary.

A nice alternative to the standard 20-ft. loop of cord is a 12 ft. (3.7 m) rabbit runner of Spectra webbing. Called a webolette, this is lighter, less bulky, and slightly easier to rig while still providing plenty of strength [Photo 4.5].

No matter whether you are using a cordelette or webolette, the rigging is essentially the same. Three anchor points are arranged so that they are all within arm's reach (you may need to extend natural pro to achieve this). A bight is clipped to each anchor and the resulting loops are all gathered and equalized in the direction of anticipated loading. These loops are tied off with a simple overhand knot.

The resulting master anchor point is redundant but will not equalize loading on the anchors if the

Photo 4.5   Webolette anchor

load shifts direction. If one piece fails, the other two will not be shock-loaded and disaster will hopefully be prevented.

The big difference between a cordelette and webolette is that the latter must always be tied off with the anchor knot. Without the overhand, if one piece fails, the entire belay fails. A cordelette without the anchor knot can shift to equalize the load. If one piece fails, the other two will be shock-loaded, but you have a chance the system will hold.

TOP-ROPE ANCHORS

There is no reason anyone should ever get hurt while top-roping! But it happens all the time. Anchor failure for what should be the safest form of climbing is inexcusable.

Top-roping anchor points (in many cases, trees) are often set far back from the rim, so extension is needed to get the two locking carabiners over the edge. Although girth-hitched slings are plenty strong for this application, a length of 11 mm static caving rope is more convenient, durable, and cut-resistant if you top-rope frequently.

Make your anchor rope long enough to reach two solid points; 30 to 50 ft. (9 to 15 m) may be needed. Slip two or three 3-ft. (1-m) sections of 1 in. tubular webbing around the anchor rope to add abrasion protection, or use other padding.

Always tie a figure eight loop for the two locking carabiners so that one anchor's failing won't mean catastrophe. It's foolish to leave this knot out just for the sake of convenience in relocating to a different climb.

CHAPTER 5

HARNESSES

CLIMBING HAS COME A LONG WAY SINCE I first tied into the end of a Goldline rope with a bowline on a coil. In those days, the pain from the loops of rope around my waist was good incentive not to fall. When that wasn't possible, three parallel red marks were often visible on the sides of my rib cage for several days.

Today, virtually all climbers wear sit harnesses, and all but the cheapest harnesses have padded waist belts and leg loops, a belay loop, and gear racks. The comfort and safety of falling, hanging, and rappelling have improved dramatically.

Most of us start out buying just one harness, and that's the rig we use for most of our climbing. We want a harness that works for climbing in the gym, all-day rock routes, and perhaps the occasional big wall or ice climb. Specialized sport, wall, and alpine harnesses are available; however, a good all-around harness will cover most of your needs.

DESIGN

The purpose of a climbing harness is not just to hold the climber in a fall but also to spread out the impact of that fall. Research by the German Alpine Club concluded that the use of a swami waist belt alone (once a common practice) can result in severe damage to the internal organs if the climber is subjected to loads greater than 840 lbf (3.7 kN)— easily attained in a moderate fall. And hanging from a waist belt can lead to unconsciousness or death after just a few minutes. A well-designed harness spreads the impact force of falls and allows you to hang in relative comfort for a long time without losing consciousness.

Harnesses come in two basic designs: the sit harness and the full-body harness (or a sit harness and chest harness combination). The full-body harness [Illustration 5.1] holds climbers upright and distributes loads better than a sit harness, but it can also subject falling climbers to whiplash or even a broken neck. Young children, expectant mothers, and climbers of girth (bellies larger than hips), who can slip out of a normal sit harness in an upside-down fall, should wear a full-body harness or a sit harness combined with a chest harness, as should those crossing glaciers while wearing a heavy pack. Nearly everyone else is better off in a sit harness, because of its comfort, ease of use, and overall effectiveness.

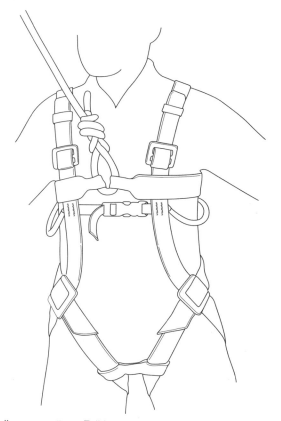

Ilustration 5.1   Full-body harness

Sit harnesses come in two forms: the diaper and the swami with leg loops. Diaper harnesses [Illustration 5.2] consist of a waist belt and a loop of webbing that pulls up through the crotch to support the legs. With a few exceptions, these have faded from the market—they are usually less comfortable for hanging, drape poorly, and lack a belay loop. Many diaper harnesses don't have a direct tie-in point, so it is possible to end up hanging sideways in them after a fall. The oft-repeated claim that the leg straps can be dropped from a diaper harness while you're still tied in to the waist belt is false. With all diaper harnesses, you must untie first in order to drop your pants or change layers. Do not use a carabiner to connect the leg loop to the waist belt because you won't hang properly.

The swami belt/leg loop style is by far the most popular harness design. Trailwise developed the first such combination in 1967, followed by Forrest a year later, and all of the current models on the market are simply variations on this theme.

What distinguishes the deluxe waist belts is the degree of factory-formed shape they have been given and the amount of lumbar support they offer. The cumulative effect of hundreds of jolting falls can be rough on your back.

The better swamis [Illustration 5.3] are wide at the back—between 3 and 4¼ in. (8 and 11 cm)—for

support and taper to about 1½ to 2 in. (4 to 5 cm) in the front, for maximum comfort when you're hanging and freedom of movement while you're climbing. It's important that the back portion is stiffened for extra support. In fact, a well-built swami that is only 3 in. wide can be more supportive than a poorly designed one that is nearly 5 in. (13 cm) wide.

LEG-LOOP CHOICES

Leg loops come in closed, semi-adjustable, or fully adjustable styles. All are attached to the waist belt with elastic webbing risers in the back.

Closed loops are traditionally sewn in the shape of double Os, and they often come in 2 in. (5 cm) size increments. These leg loops may be sold separately from the waist belt to allow a customized fit. With their light weight and clean design, these are popular for sport climbing, since your clothes and thigh size aren't likely to change often. For all-around use, however, many prefer more adjustability.

More and more harnesses are coming with teardrop-shaped (double-Y) leg loops, which have about 3 in. of built-in adjustment. These usually have a bit of elastic webbing to hold them snugly in place. Though slightly harder to pull on, these semi-adjustable leg loops are comfortable and trim, stay in place, allow easy movement, and fit most people without hassle.

The fully adjustable leg loops are usually double-Os with a buckle that allows 6 in. or more of adjustment, so you can wear them year-round with any combination of clothes. The better ones are only slightly heavier and bulkier than teardrop leg loops and are just as comfortable to wear.

No matter the style, wide leg loops (2½ to 3 in.) are the most comfortable to hang in, especially for heavier climbers. Narrow leg loops (2 in. or less), such as those found on sport harnesses, will feel like wire cables after an hour at a hanging belay. Leg loops should taper in the front to an inch or less

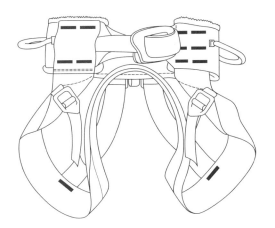

Illustration 5.2   Diaper harness

for maximum freedom of movement. Loops that stay open on their own make donning a harness significantly easier—a worthwhile luxury, especially on small rope-up ledges.

Except for climbs at your limit, the weight of the harness is mostly noticed in your hand, not when you are wearing it. In a men's large, the difference among harnesses averages around 3 oz. (85 g)—11 oz. (310 g) at the most. That may be important for hard redpoints or shaving weight on an ambitious alpine climb. However, other design aspects play more important roles in both performance and comfort.

MATERIALS AND CONSTRUCTION

Most harness makers use webbing that is about 1⅛ in. (3 cm) wide for the load-bearing structure.

Wider webbing is an inexpensive way to distribute the load, but this can result in undesirable bulk up front. Some companies use webbing that is wide in back and tapers at the front. Other ways to spread the load include stiffeners and extra pieces of webbing across the back.

The first generation of padded harnesses had either pile fabric sewn to the inside of flat webbing or foam stuffed into tubular webbing. Although both construction techniques are still used, these designs are limited to rather basic shapes.

The current standard in harness technology is shaped foam. This entails laminating foam on both sides with fabric, cutting the resulting sandwich with a die, and assembling the pieces with computer-controlled sewing machines. This production method allows more contours. Some companies vary the thickness of the foam in places or thermo-mold the foam to create air channels for better ventilation.

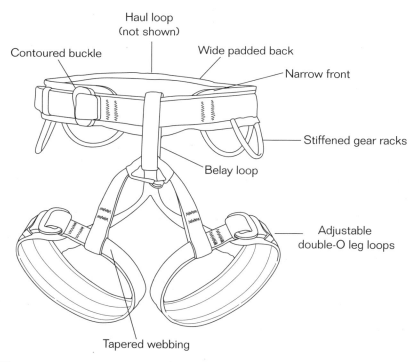

Illustration 5.3   Swami harness

HARNESSING YOUR YOUTH

Once your rugrat graduates to rock monkey, it's time to get a children's full-body harnesses.

Until about age 10 to 12 (85 lbs., 57 in. tall), kids tend to be top-heavy and have narrow hips. This makes them more prone than adults to flipping upside-down and even slipping out of a sit harness in a fall. The high tie-in point of a full-body harness keeps children upright during falls and distributes the load evenly.

Since munchkins grow like weeds but don't weigh much, their harnesses need a lot of adjustability but only minimal padding. Look for designs that keep fidgety little kids from undoing the buckles when you aren't watching.

With most laminated-foam harnesses, the firmness of the foam greatly affects comfort, durability, and price. Squeeze a harness by its edges—the mushy ones won't distribute a load as evenly and tend to break down faster. The better harnesses use foams that are stiffer and more resistant to compression. The stiff foam on my four-year-old harness has retained its feel and shape despite lots of wear and repeated crushing in a pack.

The area of a harness that receives the most wear is the rope path—the loops you tie into. These points are usually reinforced with extra material, and the better harnesses use robust fabric, such as ballistics cloth, or a double layer of webbing.

The outside of a harness, particularly the bottoms of the leg loops, also receives a lot of abrasion, and using Cordura or ballistics cloth for the shell instead of pack cloth will increase longevity. A smooth texture will be less abrasive on bare legs or backs—run your fingers firmly along the inside surface and edges of the harness to check for rough spots. Most laminated harnesses are finished with binding tape along the edges, which can be rather uncomfortable. The nicest (read: most expensive)

models have internal seams, leaving a smooth surface against your skin.

The lining should be soft and comfy, even when drenched with sweat. (Remember, closed-cell foams and coated fabrics don't breathe. I expect to see dense yet breathable foams used in harnesses soon.) Although pile linings are luxurious at first, the material is prone to pilling and dries slowly or freezes when wet. At least one harness covers up most of its plush lining with warning labels made from nasty-feeling plastic. Maybe the lawyers aim to make it so uncomfortable that people won't go climbing and expose themselves to risk.

TYING IN

The majority of harnesses on the market today close with load-bearing buckles that must be double-passed (rethreaded). The only buckle that does not require this extra step for secure closure is the Petzl DoubleBack, a brilliant design that stays doubled even when you remove the harness.

Whether the buckle is aluminum or steel is irrelevant, as long as the harness passes CEN standards and it isn't worn in a Hollywood movie. Even a 220 lb. (100 kg) climber taking a 65 ft. (20 m), factor 1.5 fall—we're talking a real screamer here—impacts with only about 1575 lbf (7 kN), and the CEN harness standard is 2248 lbf (10 kN).

Look for a buckle with a thumb tab to make threading easier; simple rectangles are harder to manipulate. Two-piece buckles that must be pried apart for rethreading are a nuisance best avoided. The tip of the webbing should be tapered, with rounded edges, and, preferably, stiffened with epoxy. If it is difficult to thread a buckle when the harness is new, it will only get worse as the webbing softens with use.

To make donning a harness easier, many companies use a pre-buckle system (Velcro and/or elastic) to hold the swami in place. Although I like this amenity, I don't care for the heart-thumping ripping sound that occurs when the Velcro parts as I lean into a rappel. Plus, once separated, the end of the belt often rides up out of place. I prefer harnesses with an elastic loop that can be threaded to hold the swami end in place.

I am amazed when I hear of climbers who refuse to use, or even cut off, their belay loop, because they "don't trust it." This is actually one of the strongest pieces of gear you own, and it's there for a reason—to make belaying and rappelling easier and safer.

Belaying from a carabiner in a loop provides much less chance of cross-loading, which reduces the carabiner's strength by more than two-thirds. The belay device will be in a better position for control, and clothes are much less likely to be sucked in on rappel. Don't be too concerned about wear and tear reducing the strength of the belay loop—the rest of the harness will need replacement before that's a problem, assuming normal wear.

FEATURES

A sturdy rear loop, large enough to hold a carabiner or two, is essential for attaching haul ropes, approach shoes, and the like. Many of these are "runner strength," though the value of this is questionable. The CEN does not test haul loops, and a harness is not designed to hold a fall or other large force from behind. No standard climbing harness is designed for the so-called Australian rappel, an absurd face-first military technique.

Any all-around harness should have a minimum of four gear loops. The industry standard is stiff 8 mm plastic tubing over cord that is sewn to the swami. Loops that point up are generally easier to clip than downward-pointing loops, but the latter are more comfortable under a pack's hipbelt (an issue for alpinists).

Make sure the rear gear loops are not too far back to reach without major contortions. Similarly, the front loops should hold gear at your side, not in your crotch. There is no standard for strength, so make sure the gear loops seem securely attached—you *really* don't want your gear clattering to the ground from midpitch.

All of the swami and leg-loop harnesses have elastic-webbing risers to hold the leg loops in place. Quick-release buckles on these make changing pants and answering the call of nature much easier. A surprising number of otherwise good harnesses lack this basic feature.

SIZING

The importance of proper sizing cannot be overstated—it directly affects harness comfort, performance, and safety.

Start with the swami belt. Make sure it fits snugly just above the hipbones. There should be enough range of adjustment to go from shirtless to a heavy sweatshirt—or perhaps to allow climbing after big holiday eating binges. The sizing among various brands ranges tremendously, so one company's medium may fit the same as another company's large.

With most harnesses, the gear loops are positioned for optimal use in the middle of the size range. If you are at one size extreme or the other, the gear loops or tie-in point may be misaligned. Harnesses with two buckles, one on either side of the tie-in, give a wider adjustment range.

Now try on the leg loops. You should be able to slip a hand between the loop and your leg. If the leg loops are too snug, you won't be able to move freely; if they're too loose, the leg loops wander around and are prone to pinching men's vital parts.

Harnesses shaped specifically for women have been around since 1980 (Forrest). With most brands, when you lay a women's harness on top of a men's, it's hard to see any width differences in the waist belts or leg loops. The real distinction is in the amount of rise, the distance between the swami and leg loops. Women generally need 1½ to 3 in. (4 to 8 cm) more rise than men. When it comes to your own butt hanging on the line, however, I recommend not getting trapped by a gender label.

CHECKING THE FIT

The best way to determine whether a harness fits is to wear it while climbing. Failing that, shop only at stores that have a rope to hang from. Hang freely in midair, and make sure the harness holds you naturally in a sitting position [Illustration 5.4].

Give each harness at least several minutes of hang time. While most of the harnesses feel fine initially, significant differences show up after a while.

With the right amount of rise, the weight will be evenly distributed between the swami and leg loops. If there is too much rise, the swami takes more of the load and rides up into your rib cage. With too little rise, more weight is on the leg loops (reducing blood flow) and the tie-in point is too low, making you more likely to flip upside-down.

To separate the contenders that pass the vertical hang test, move on to the leaning hang. Tie in short to an anchor on a wall and press your feet against the wall, as if you were at a hanging belay.

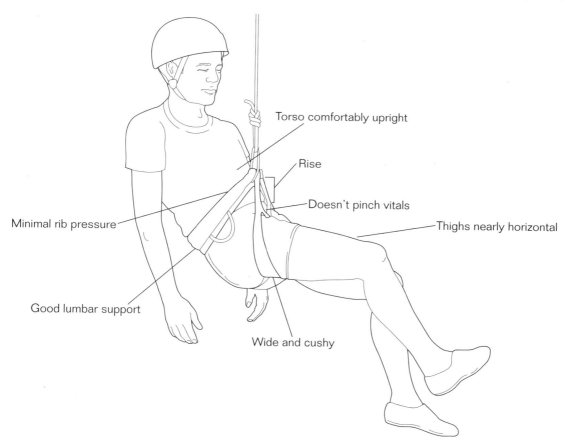

Torso comfortably upright

Rise

Doesn't pinch vitals

Thighs nearly horizontal

Minimal rib pressure

Good lumbar support

Wide and cushy

Illustration 5.4   Proper fit while hanging

This puts much more pressure on the swami than a straight hang. A poorly designed harness will soon have you begging for mercy.

PRESERVING YOUR HARNESS

I've seen climbers wearing old harnesses that were incredibly tattered and faded. Dumb move. Although age itself has little effect on the strength of nylon, wear and tear can seriously weaken it. The industry recommends that a harness be retired after two to three years of moderate use, or five years of minimal use. The date of manufacture is now placed on a label sewn to the lining.

All of the manufacturers recommend that a harness be retired after a serious fall because hidden damage can occur. Other causes for retirement include severe abrasion, torn stitching, a damaged buckle, or fading of the webbing.

Is a six- or seven-year-old harness that's in good shape safe to climb in? Probably. Is it worth finding out? I don't think so. Limiting use to minimal-load applications, such as top-roping, may be an acceptable alternative to trashing the harness. But the newer harnesses really are nicer than what was available back then.

The big killer for a harness, and possibly its valuable contents, is acid. Even the fumes can seriously weaken the nylon, without any visible damage. Keep your climbing equipment far away from car batteries and solvents at all times.

Most accidents involving harnesses happen when the climber fails to buckle properly. Double-back the waist belt through the buckle, of course, and make sure at least 3 in. (10 cm) of extra webbing extends beyond the buckle as a backup.

The single most important way to prevent fatal mistakes is to *stop talking* when you put on your harness and tie in to the rope. When you're done, double-check everything—buckle, rope path, knot—and get in the habit of buddy checks with your partners.

CHAPTER 6

ROCK PROTECTION

IN THE BEGINNING, THERE WERE NATURAL chockstones. When a climber found a rock securely wedged in a crack, he put a sling around it and clipped the rope in to it for protection. Next, British climbers began to pick up stones and hexagonal, threaded railroad nuts on approaches to climbs, and they placed these in cracks. Then machine nuts of all sizes, with their threads filed out to prevent abrasion, were prefitted with slings. And from these roots sprang a multitude.

Although there are countless variations of climbing protection, they can be divided into four basic categories: passive, active, poundable, and bolts. Passive protection has no moving parts and is most dependent upon the skill of the leader. Active protection, primarily spring-loaded camming devices (SLCDs), uses mechanical leverage. Poundable pro requires a hammer to place, while bolts require a drill.

PASSIVE PROTECTION

Over the past thirty years, innumerable designs of artificial chocks have been offered to the climbing world. Viewed with skepticism at first, this form of protection did not gain wide acceptance until the 1970s. In the interim, pitons were the protection of choice.

Until the late 1970s, most pitons from Europe were made of soft steel, which conformed to cracks, were difficult to remove, and were generally left in place. In North America in the 1960s, hard steel pitons grew in popularity because they were stronger and could be reused, thus smaller numbers were required on long routes. The second climber would remove the pin by beating it back and forth, which enlarged the crack even in granite. As routes were repeated by more and more parties, the dam-

age to the rock became very apparent. Yosemite's Serenity Crack is a classic example of this abuse—and it's easier to free-climb because of it.

Among the first climbers in the United States to recognize the potential of chocks were Royal Robbins, who imported the first models from Europe, and Tom Frost and Yvon Chouinard, who improved upon the early designs. Not only were these "nuts" less damaging to the rock than pitons but they were also easier to place, allowing much faster and more difficult ascents. For many, the decisive argument in favor of "clean" climbing, as the new style of hammerless ascents was known, was an article by Doug Robinson that appeared in the 1973 Chouinard catalog.

With all the pieces in place, the stage was set for the rapid development of metal (and even wood and plastic) chunks that could be hand-wedged into cracks, slots, and pockets. Nearly every imaginable shape was tried, touted, and abandoned. There were Ps, Ts, Vs, and Zs; hexagonals and hexentrics; cams and cogs; and every possible permutation of upside-down, truncated pyramids. What remains, for the most part, are designs that have withstood both the test of time and market pressures.

Today's chocks fall into three categories: wedges or tapers, micronuts, and passive camming nuts [Photo 6.1]. Wedges remain the most useful and reliable. Micronuts are also indispensable, but because of their small size, they are not as strong, either in construction or in placement, as larger wedges. Passive camming nuts can also be wedged, so they offer many placement possibilities. These have been replaced on many climbers' racks by SLCDs, yet passive cams can still be the best choice for many placements and should not be discounted.

The difference between many brands of chocks is minimal; the choice often comes down to personal

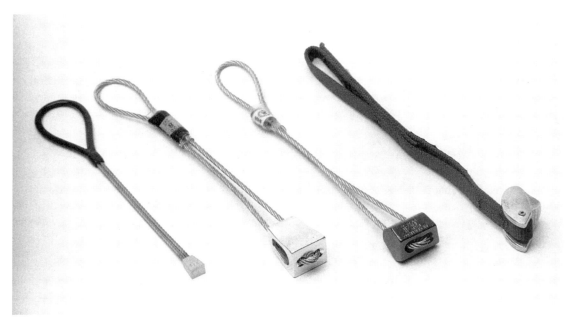

Photo 6.1   Micronut, standard wedge, and two passive cams

preference and economics. Almost any chock will work just fine in a crack with sufficient constrictions, though some may be slightly harder to remove than others. What really separates the various models is how easy they are to place and how well they hold in less-than-ideal situations, such as pin scars, parallel-sided cracks, and outward flares.

ATTACHMENT

Most chocks used to be slung with nylon accessory cord or webbing, which tended to be either bulky or relatively weak. Now ultrastrength materials allow thinner and stronger slings.

The vast majority of wedges, and all micronuts, now have wire cables. Compared to chocks on nylon slings, wired nuts are easier to rack (you can fit more on a 'biner), easier to place (you get several more inches of reach), and easier to remove (the stiff cable lets you push upward somewhat). For all but the largest hexes, which flop around too much, I now prefer cable over sling.

You usually need to use a quickdraw with a wired nut to keep the rope from lifting it out of place. On longer crack climbs that devour nuts, like those at Devils Tower, this means lots of quickdraws and more time at each placement. Some nuts have longer cables that can often be used without quickdraws—nice, but climbers who rack gear on their harnesses will find them too long.

Slings

With few exceptions, all larger nuts that can be slung are designed for use with 5.5 mm Spectra (or Technora) cord. Although expensive, this is much stronger than 8 mm nylon accessory cord, and the reduced bulk is a significant advantage (put the knot inside larger hexes) [Photo 6.2].

In fact, nuts slung with Spectra cord can be stronger than their counterparts on cable. Spectra is slippery, so tighten a triple fisherman knot under your full body weight and leave at least 2 in. (5 cm) tails.

Some companies offer pre-slung nuts with the knots already tied and the tails secured with heatshrink. You can tape the ends of your own knots to reduce snagging. You can also put a few inches of tape around both cords near the nut to stiffen them. This gives you the flexibility of a sling with the added reach and control of a cable.

Cables

Most of the larger wired nuts use galvanized steel cable. The ends of the cable are swaged together with a machine that applies even, exact pressure. (Swaging your own wires is not recommended unless you *really* know what you are doing and have testing equipment.)

Sometimes the cable will slide through the nut when you're trying to remove it; this makes it tougher to get the piece out. Applying a few drops of epoxy at the holes in the nut will prevent the cable from sliding when pushed.

Because of their small size, micronuts use stainless steel cable, which is stronger but more expensive than galvanized steel. The ends of the cable are inserted into a precisely drilled hole in the nut and either soldered into place or molded directly into the nut. The result is a connection that can be stronger than the cable. (Swaged cables usually break at the bend in the nut.) The drawback is that repeated or forcible flexing of the wire at the nut (as during removal of the nut from a placement) results in frayed cables. Inspect your micros often; if you see even a single broken strand, retire the nut—it's likely there are more that you cannot see.

WEDGES

For almost twenty years following the introduction of the first commercial wedge-shaped nut (the MOAC), almost all wedges had straight sides that tapered downward. The different models varied in angle and depth, often depending on the area where they were developed. For example, Steven Stones, made by the Gendarme, were ideal for West Virginia's Seneca Rocks.

In 1979, Wild Country introduced the first curved wedges [Photo 6.3]. These offered more placement options ("left" or "right") and greater

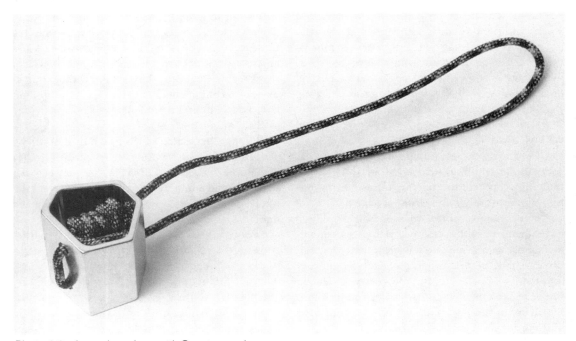

Photo 6.2 Large hex slung with Spectra cord

Photo 6.3   Wedges: straight, curved, and molded

security—they jam more tightly when set. Today, the majority of wedges have curved sides on their primary faces. Those with too much curvature or without a slight flattening of the top and bottom edges of the concave side are prone to sticking.

Another relatively recent trend is the use of nonparallel faces (a transverse taper) on wedges to improve performance in flaring cracks [Photo 6.4]. Most companies offer this feature on the end faces, rather than on the primary faces, of their curved wedges. These trapezoidal-cross-section nuts are a mixed blessing: They may work in situations in which rectangular wedges cannot, yet they can get spit out of a crack faster than you can blink. A solid piece is dependent upon perfect contact with the rock.

Rather than cut them from bar stock, many com-panies now mold their wedges (a concept pio-neered in Campbell nuts). This allows them to be sculpted three-dimensionally to form exotic shapes. Many have scoops or cutouts, which let the nut straddle a nubbin for a more secure (and difficult-to-remove) placement.

Medium to large wedges are among your most useful and versatile pieces of protection. Most are designed with a thickness-to-width ratio such that the endwise width is the same as the primary width of the next size up. In other words, a #7 placed sideways fits the same crack as a #8 placed normally. Although an endwise placement pro-vides less contact with the rock, it can often be ex-cellent with thicker nuts.

As wedges decrease in width below ½ in., they begin to lose this ratio—and thus their versatility.

Photo 6.4   A transverse taper allows placements in flaring cracks but doesn't work well in parallel placements.

They become much wider than they are thick to give maximum surface area in tiny cracks and to make room for the relatively thick cable. The result is that endwise placements for small standard wedges are very unstable and insecure.

Barring abuse or loss, wedges should last you through many years of climbing. Occasionally inspect the cables for kinks and broken strands, and replace Spectra slings every few years—they deteriorate from abrasion, UV, and age.

If you have a serviceable set of older wedges, I wouldn't run out and replace them. As you lose a few, you might want to try some of the newer designs.

MICRONUTS

In the late 1970s, Australian climber Roland Pauligk developed the RP, the first micronut

[Photo 6.5]. Ever since, these small squarish wedges have earned a place on most climbers' racks because they work where nothing else will. They require thoughtful placements—after all, we're talking about a tiny blob of metal wedged in a crack. Nevertheless, if the rock is sound, the placement is good, and the fall factor low, a micronut *should* hold—I've taken big whippers onto micronuts and lived to talk about it.

In hard rock, even with a perfect placement, the softer brass or bronze micronuts can deform and rip out. In soft rock, though, these micros tend to have a better bite than harder nuts, which can shear through the rock. Trade-offs, always trade-offs. The smallest two or three sizes are best reserved for body-weight aid placements (and a liberal dose of prayer).

Because of their design, all micronuts are more susceptible to damage from removal than are standard wedges. Don't jerk them out of the crack—this will cause the wires to break at the head. Always try to wiggle them out, or use a nut tool to prod them carefully—without digging into the wire. Inspect your micros often for telltale stray wires or unusual kinks.

PASSIVE CAMMING NUTS

Passive camming nuts are not a dead issue now that spring-loaded camming devices (SLCDs) are here [Illustration 6.1]. In fact, I will go out on a limb and say that beginners should use passive-camming nuts before they blow a wad of cash on the latest SLCD gizmos. In the long run, learning to use passive-camming nuts will make you a safer climber.

Many climbers underestimate the complexity of using SLCDs; there is a lot more to it than just injecting one into a crack and clipping in. By learning the basics first, you will acquire a better understanding of cams with moving parts.

There are practical advantages of passive cams as well: Hexentrics and Tricams are light, strong, and relatively inexpensive. For alpine climbs with long approaches, the weight advantage of a rack

Photo 6.5 Micronuts have stainless-steel cable silver-soldered to the heads.

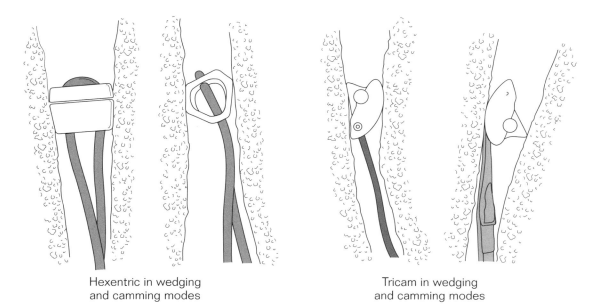

Hexentric in wedging
and camming modes

Tricam in wedging
and camming modes

Illustration 6.1 Passive camming nuts

of hexes over a rack of SLCDs can easily be several pounds. A well-placed passive cam can be far stronger and more secure than an SLCD; it can work better in horizontals and pockets, and it doesn't walk deeper into cracks that widen inward. Without passive cams on your rack, you frequently need to "waste" an SLCD or two on a belay.

Let's not forget that many of today's classic hard routes were put up BF (before Friends). Eldorado's Naked Edge, Canyonland's SuperCrack, Yosemite's Outer Limits, and numerous others were first climbed with good old passive pro.

PASSIVE PLACEMENTS

Placing passive protection is both an art and a science. To safely evaluate each placement takes a great deal of practice; reading books and articles is an important start, but certainly no substitute for experience. Ideally, you should take lessons from a certified instructor.

It is a huge step from the indoor gym and/or sport climbing to the "real world" of traditional lead climbing—there is a *lot* more to deal with than "clip and go." Start off several grades lower than you can flash on bolt routes; trust me, you'll be glad you did. I've seen 5.11 sport climbers reduced to quivering blobs on 5.7 trad routes.

When placing a chock, you should look, listen, feel, and think. Look carefully at the placement to make sure that you have maximum contact area and there are no pivot points. Tap the rock and listen to be certain there is no hollow sound indicative of fragile rock. Feel that the nut is set securely enough that it will not be dislodged as you climb past, yet is not so tight that it requires a major struggle to remove. Think about all the possible directions of loading (including an outward pull by the rope) and the consequences if the piece should pop.

There are other considerations. Endwise placements tend to be less stable. You may need to choose between using a finger or hand jam and filling that jam with a piece of pro. You may need to place a second directional piece to keep your primary pro in place. Sometimes you need to equalize two marginal nuts to get one strong placement. Often you will need to add a sling to a piece of pro to increase its security (so the rope won't pull it out) or to reduce rope drag and keep the rope running straight (which reduces the outward pull on lower pieces). Keep in mind that the quality of the rock significantly affects the strength of the placement.

When following a climb, examine each placement and try to figure out why the leader slotted that particular piece there. If the leader is experienced, you will learn something. If he or she is inexperienced, you can teach that person something. Either way, it helps to look at the piece prior to cleaning—if you pull it out the way it went in, there's less chance it will get stuck.

One way to learn chock craft is to practice "sewing up" cracks while climbing with a loose top-rope backing up the lead rope; have an experienced traditional climber evaluate your placements. You can learn a lot from aid climbing, too. Once you have the hang of placing pro, you're ready for the sharp end on easy free climbs.

NUT TOOLS

Gotta have 'em. These tools [Photo 6.6] will quickly pay for themselves many times over because they help you free stuck chocks. They are also useful for threading placements, untying knots, and spreading cheese on crackers. You can get by with a screwdriver or a shelf bracket but why? Nut tools are fairly cheap and work a lot better.

The nicer ones have a small-profile tip with a hook for snagging nuts and pulling on trigger cables. I especially like nut tools with a smooth, fat surface on the pounding end since you are often hitting it with the palm of your hand.

Attach a keeper cord to your nut tool so that it won't disappear if you drop it. It's a good idea to make this out of 6 mm accessory cord; you don't need the strength, but it could serve as an emergency prusik.

Photo 6.6   The shape of the tip on a nut tool affects how useful it will be; some are too large for tight cracks.

ACTIVE PROTECTION

Although the first SLCDs were produced by Greg Lowe in 1973, they were rather primitive and awkward to use. When Ray Jardine came out with Friends in 1978, crack climbing was revolutionized almost overnight. Parallel-sided cracks that previously were a nightmare suddenly became easily protectable. Now it's almost unthinkable for most climbers to start a trad pitch without a good assortment of active cams.

While designs vary, all SLCDs work on the basic principle of opposing cams pushing outward and creating friction on the crack walls. Because of the angle of the cams, the outward force is almost twice the downward force.

We want cams to place easily, stay where they are put, and come out without a struggle at the appropriate time. Then, of course, they should be light, compact, and durable—yet affordable.

During the early years of SLCDs, there was definitely a lot of funk being sold. Some Rube Goldberg contraptions were quite amusing to look at but scary to use. Now, most of the weird stuff has disappeared and it's hard to go wrong—most of the gear works fine, although there are important differences.

THREE VERSUS FOUR CAMS

Four cams almost always offer greater holding power in any kind of rock [Photo 6.7]. Because they generally are wider and have greater spring tension, four-cam units (FCUs) are fairly stable (the stem stays pointed in the direction you place it). However, they also have a greater tendency to walk deeper into cracks. This trait may have your second cursing if the pro is out of reach, but if the crack flares upward, the cam can open up.

The biggest advantage of three-cam units (TCUs) is that their narrower head widths allow placements in shallower cracks—a TCU with all its cams engaged has greater holding power than an FCU with only three of its cams contacting the rock. The central cam, which is fatter because it takes twice the load of the other side, acts as a pivot point, making TCUs rather unstable, but at least they can't walk.

CAM DETAILS

The majority of SLCDs have cams machined from 6061 aluminum, the same material used in passive chocks. It is strong yet soft enough to give a good bite in the rock. However, thinner cams can mushroom after a couple of falls (or one big one).

The alternative is 7075 aluminum, an even stronger alloy that is also a bit harder. This allows thinner, lighter cams, which work well in hard rock but are more prone to "tracking" (slipping) out of soft sandstone under moderate loads [Photo 6.8].

Contrary to popular belief, teeth on cams don't have a huge impact on holding power in rock. Their main advantage is to enhance stability of the unit by grabbing on crystals so the unit is less likely to rotate.

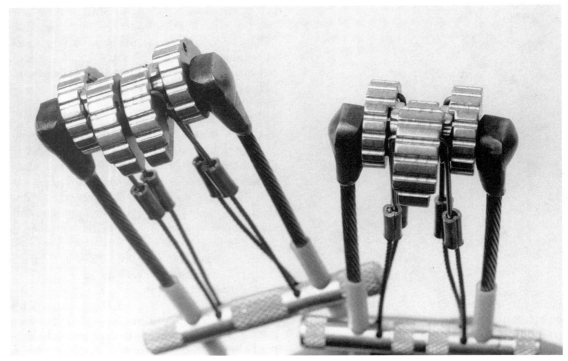

Photo 6.7 Four- and three-cam, dual-stem SLCDs—it's a choice between greater stability and fitting shallower cracks.

Most SLCDs now have cam stops milled into them that prevent the cams from collapsing if they are loaded on their tips [Photo 6.9]. This might save your neck if the unit walks upward until it's fully open. You can also place these in an open "umbrella" placement if you have to.

As the width of the camming unit relative to its range decreases, so does stability. This is particularly noticeable in SLCDs made for cracks wider than 4 in. (10 cm). For long offwidths, it's probably better to "crack jumar" with the big units (push them up as you go) and place expanding tube chocks when you need to leave something [Photo 6.10].

CAMMING RANGE

It's probably best to start off with a full set of one brand of SLCDs if you're building your first rack so that you become very familiar with them. However, eventually you may find yourself filling in gaps in expansion range with different models.

If you look at the charts in catalogs, they always list the minimum (full contraction) and maximum (full expansion) range. However, the "usable" range is actually 5 percent less on the minimum end, so you have a little wiggle room to remove it, to 60 percent less on the maximum end for a reasonable degree of stability (80 percent expansion is pushing your luck) [Illustration 6.2].

Taking this usable range into consideration, you may then see gaps in coverage on your rack.

Also be aware that the usable range severely limits the smallest SLCDs. These little guys don't have as much holding power to start with and have a working range of only 3 to 4 mm (0.12 to 0.16 in.)—

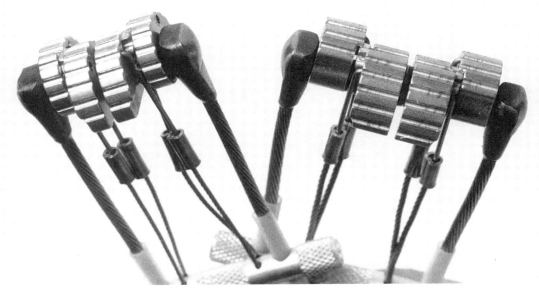

Photo 6.8   Narrower 7075 aluminum cams for hard rock and wider 6061 aluminum cams for soft rock

Photo 6.9   Milled cam stops prevent the cams from collapsing.

Photo 6.10   For protecting wide cracks, expanding tube chocks are lighter and more compact, but somewhat harder to place, than equivalent-size cams.

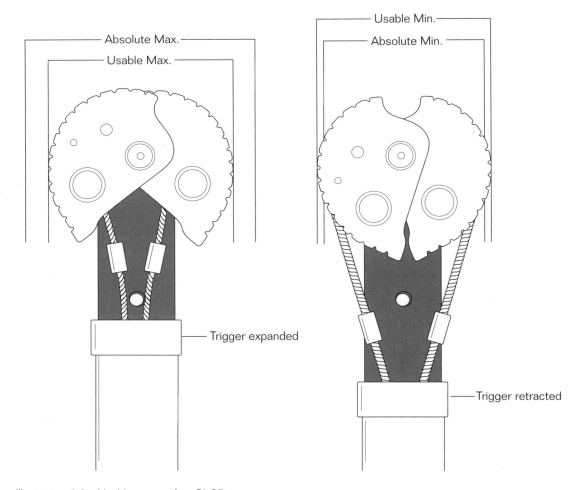

Illustration 6.2   Usable range of an SLCD

it's a fine line between what will hold and what pops.

A fairly recent innovation is SLCDs with offset cams, meaning the two on the left are a half-size larger than the two on the right. This dramatically improves their performance in cracks that flare outward, which is the majority of cracks at granite areas such as Joshua Tree, the South Platte, and Vedauwoo. Consider starting off with a set of offset cams instead of normal SLCDs if flaring cracks are common at your local areas; they also work adequately in parallel cracks.

STEMS

The original Friends had a rigid bar of aluminum for the stem, a design that is still available [Photo 6.11]. The advantages are predictable loading of the cams and superior durability. However, if the stem is levered over an edge in a horizontal placement, it can bend or break with relative ease. The workaround to this is called the "Gunks tie-off," which is made by attaching a loop of cord to a hole near the head; the loop is clipped instead of the sewn sling on the stem.

The majority of SLCDs now have flexible stems made of stiff cable that will bend over an edge instead of snapping. There are two styles: a single, central stem or a dual, U-shaped stem. Both work well once you get used to them, but there are some subtle differences. The single stem attaches mid-axle, which spreads the cams farther apart and increases stability, and it sometimes works better in shallow placements.

Although the stems are flexible, avoid falling on them when they are set in a horizontal or diagonal crack; you can permanently tweak the cable, particularly in models that are less stiff. Such bending may affect the trigger action, but probably not the strength of the cables.

TRIGGERS

Single-stem SLCDs have a trigger that you operate much like a syringe. This allows the cams on one side to be operated independently of the cams

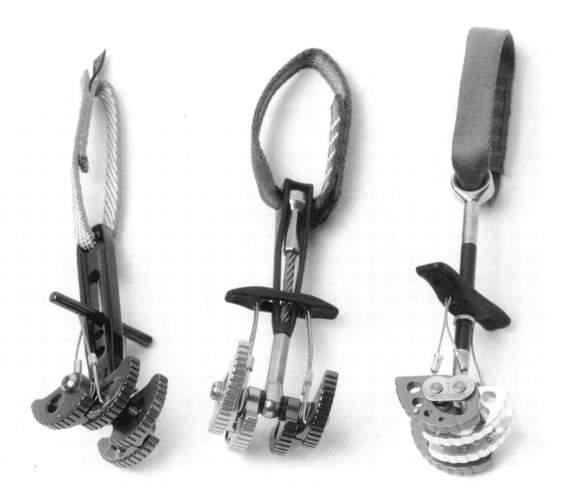

Photo 6.11   Rigid stem, flexible stem with offset cams, and flexible stem with dual axles

on the other side so that you can finagle a stuck device from a crack. However, some triggers have an annoying tendency to rotate around the shaft; this can make aligning the cams to the crack a bit tougher when you're struggling for a placement.

Dual-stem camming units generally offer more room for fingers, which can be a blessing when you are pumped and fumbling to get a piece in. These can be harder to operate while wearing heavy gloves, but often you can pinch the trigger bar between thumb and forefinger while resting the end of the stem on your palm. Since the cams cannot be operated separately, retrieval can be more problematic.

The number-one complaint climbers have with SLCDs is broken trigger wires. Some styles, and even sizes within a style, are more prone to problems than others. Often the damage is done when the cams are tossed into and pulled out of the pack, so a little extra care here can save hassles. Ideally, the trigger wires should be easily field-repairable, but often you have to send them in to the manufacturer—prior to a long trip, inspect all your cams carefully.

WEIGHT

Most of the smaller SLCDs are close enough in weight that you won't notice the difference unless you're carrying a massive rack. As they get large, however, it is worth considering this figure when purchasing. If fist cracks and offwidths are your thing, the difference in weight between some models can be very significant.

STRENGTH

All the SLCDs sold today meet the CEN standard so they can be sold in Europe. This just means the units were tested in a steel crack (with low- and high-friction surfaces) and did not pull out or break at the rated minimum strength.

Don't use strength ratings as a criterion for choosing SLCDs. In the real world, you will find that the rock is often the limiting factor in holding power. In soft rock, such as desert sandstone, many camming units are prone to tracking—they literally pull right out of the rock at frighteningly low loads, starting around 1600 lbf (7 kN). One company offers SLCDs with very wide cams that have greater holding power in soft rock.

SLINGS

All SLCDs worth your cash come with color-coded sewn slings. A good reason to start with a set of one brand is that the consistent coding helps you get dialed in—"finger locks mean red, thin hands mean blue, etc." When you're hanging by one hand, the pump meter is ticking and seconds count.

Some older cams had a sewn sling with a bottom loop just big enough for a single carabiner. To extend with a quickdraw, you must first remove the 'biner—a needless hassle. Most SLCDs now have a bottom loop that easily fits two carabiners. The nicest slings are doubled so they can be clipped short or long as needed, often eliminating the need for a quickdraw.

Most of the time, you will rack each unit with its own carabiner for rapid-fire placements. For aid routes when you have a massive rack, it may be a good idea to put two or three cams on a 'biner to reduce bulk.

SPRING-LOADED WEDGES

Since the smallest SLCDs won't even fit in many shallow cracks, you may have to resort to spring-loaded wedges for parallel RP-sized cracks [Photo 6.12]. Their holding power comes from one wedge sliding against another to create outward force . . . assuming that everything goes according to plan. Most reliable in the smaller half of their size range, they should not be considered nearly as strong as a well-placed nut but are invaluable on a clean aid rack.

ACTIVE PLACEMENTS

If you mindlessly slam SLCDs into a crack, you're in for a rude and violent awakening someday. Cams can, and do, fail to hold when placements are not analyzed for pitfalls.

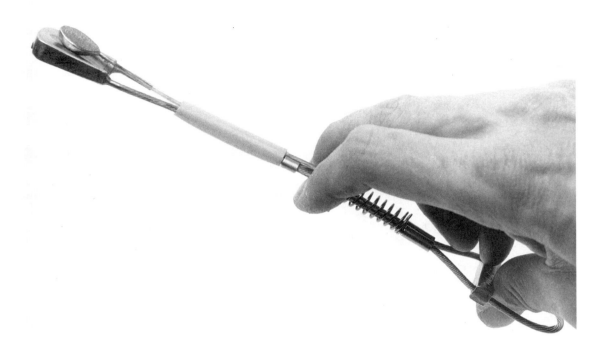

Photo 6.12   Spring-loaded wedges can work where nothing else will on hammerless ascents.

Since the rock is often the limiting factor in holding power, inspect it to avoid expanding flakes and polished, wet, or icy spots. SLCDs work best in parallel or *slightly* constricting cracks, but a bit of inward or outward flare is okay if it's well within the range of usable expansion.

Place the camming unit with the stem pointed in the direction of anticipated loading, taking into consideration what will happen if the direction changes. It's best to set the cam back from the edge of the crack so that the rock is less likely to fracture. However, don't bury it so deep that the second can't reach the trigger [Illustration 6.3].

Ideally, you want the camming unit to be mostly to halfway contracted (10 to 50 percent) so that it gives maximum stability and strength. If you cram it in at full retraction or barely close it so the cams get tipped, you may have just blown $50—the second shouldn't pay for your screw up. Use a long sling if there is any possibility of the unit walking.

Be sure that all the cams are evenly engaged with the rock, particularly with smaller SLCDs that don't have much room for error. When two cams on one side are extended (offset) more than the others, unpleasant surprises can result. This can happen in horizontal placements because the stem will rest on the bottom of the crack.

CAM CARE

For smooth, reliable operation, keep your SLCDs clean and lubricated. Particularly after a desert trip, it's a good idea to remove grit by swishing the units around in warm, soapy water, and then allow them to air-dry.

Although many people advocate using WD-40 or Tri-flow for lubrication, these petroleum-based

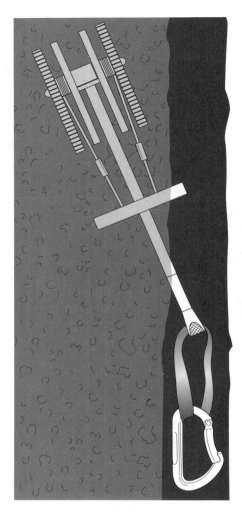

Illustration 6.3   Correct SLCD placement in a vertical crack: cams fully engaged and well inside crack with the stem pointed in the direction of loading and the trigger accessible

products don't last long and attract gunk and grime. High-quality, dry bike-chain lubricants will prevent your cams from gumming up.

For camming units smaller than 1 in. (2.5 cm), many climbers like to sling the triggers with cord to facilitate removal from cracks too small for fingers. If the piece is being stubborn, clip a sling to

the cord and give a good tug—with luck, it will pop right out. You may need to use a nut tool (or two) to retract the trigger or manipulate the individual cams.

GEAR SLINGS

Although many climbers, particularly those with a sport-climbing background, prefer racking the gear on their harness, this is very inefficient on multipitch climbs when you are swinging leads with your partner. You will save a lot of time by using an over-the-shoulder gear sling, which can be handed off at the belay station [Illustration 6.4].

Because a modern climbing rack is pretty darn heavy, you will want padding for comfort. Some climbers prefer gear slings with multiple, small loops for maximum organization, but I like the ability to be able to slide the rack out of the way. Plastic tubing over the sling makes clipping and unclipping easier at awkward moments.

Adjustable gear slings are handy if the climbing team consists of both a tall and short person. I've been very thankful for a full-strength gear sling when I reach a belay after running out of runners while on lead. (My chalk bag belt has come in handy on occasion, too.)

AID PROTECTION

Moving from the world of free climbing into the nebulous realm of aid opens up a plethora of possibilities for gear placements—and greatly increases the size of your rack. Using the term "protection," however, is a bit misleading since many aid placements can barely hold body weight, let alone a fall.

A number of specialty items are available that permit passage without destroying the rock. Small hooks for nubbins, large hooks for flakes, and camming levers for thin cracks allow progress in

PROTECTION TIPS

- Never trust your life to any one piece, no matter how good it appears. Especially, never blindly trust fixed anchors and old slings.
- Always try to have at least two solid pieces if you are facing a bad fall, as well as a directional piece for your belayer.
- No climbing gear lasts forever, not even hardware. Inspect your gear frequently—and especially after a major fall.
- If you haven't used a certain type of protection before, practice extensively at ground level before trusting it on a climb.
- Throw in a piece occasionally even when you are on "easy" ground. It won't slow you down that much and could save your butt—don't get cocky.
- As you move past, be careful not to dislodge or re-orient the cam or nut with your body, rack, or rope.
- Sling your nuts on different-colored cord to help identify individual pieces. This can save valuable time when your arms are burning.
- Mark all your gear with tape, paint, or heat-shrink if you want to hang on to it (and renew the markings from time to time). Otherwise, your rack will keep getting lighter and your various partners' will somehow grow.
- Make sure your slings for nuts are long enough, about 10 to 12 in. (25 to 30 cm) after tying. A triple fisherman (recommended for Spectra) eats up a lot of rope. Varying the length reduces the "sleigh bell" effect of nuts banging into each other.
- Rack your micro wedges on one 'biner, your medium wireds on another, and your large wedges on yet another. Some overlap between sets helps too, especially in smaller sizes.
- Rack from smallest pro in the front to largest in the back. It makes finding the right piece much easier.
- Use key-lock 'biners for racking wired nuts; they make removing a piece one-handed easier. Be aware that it's also easier to accidentally drop them too.
- Triple up runners and rack them like quickdraws; it is much easier to retrieve them from the rack than pull them over your head and shoulder.
- Warn your partner if you arrive at a fixed nut so that he or she won't waste a lot of time trying to retrieve it.
- Don't set your pieces too hard, or your second will hate you. Rarely do you need to tug hard on them repeatedly, as many beginners tend to do.
- The corollary is, don't set your pieces too loosely, or you will hate yourself when you look down to see them fall out. Learn how to use an opposition nut to hold a critical piece in place.
- Seconds who are vertically impaired (i.e., short) get really peeved at tall leaders who place pro just out of reach.
- It is a good idea for both climbers to carry a nut tool. If you don't, the leader invariably gets three-quarters up the pitch before realizing that she forgot to give the only tool to the second. Also, she who has a nut tool gets the booty!
- Take advantage of natural pro when possible: tied-off knobs, threaded slots, and slung chockstones. These can be very strong and are somehow more rewarding.
- Avoid using small trees and bushes for protection or holds; this eventually kills them. Protect our resources or we will lose them!
- Learn how to properly equalize anchors. Use load-limiters on particularly dicey placements.
- Don't get dependent on your own rack. A good trad climber should be able to pick up just about any assortment of gear and do the route.
- Don't get dependent on having the rack on your right side (or your left). Learn to be ambidextrous. Sometimes the climb dictates how you wear the rack.
- If you can't place gear you trust while leading, don't fall! Know when a climb is out of your league, and don't be afraid to back off or resort to aid.

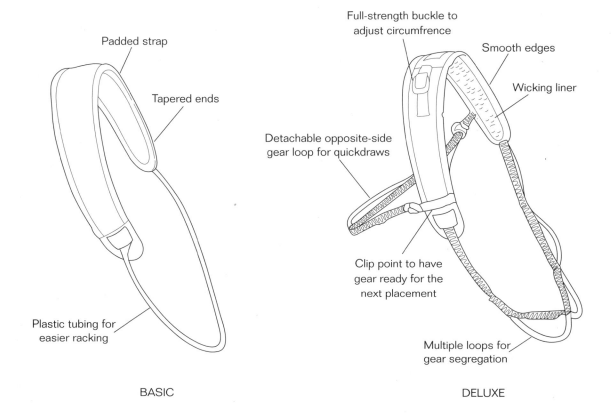

Padded strap

Tapered ends

Plastic tubing for easier racking

Full-strength buckle to adjust circumfrence

Smooth edges

Wicking liner

Detachable opposite-side gear loop for quickdraws

Clip point to have gear ready for the next placement

Multiple loops for gear segregation

BASIC

DELUXE

Illustration 6.4   Gear slings

the most unlikely of places. These should always be the first lines of attack before resorting to more destructive methods that require a hammer.

Smaller hooks, often referred to as "sky hooks," come in a multitude of shapes and sizes—and on some walls, you'll want them all [Photo 6.13]. You may even want to file down the wide tip of some hooks to a point for very slight depressions.

The wider the base on the hook, the more stable it will be as you move around on your aiders. However, sometimes a very wide base gets in the way. Make your webbing slings as short as possible to allow for maximum reach.

For flakes up to 3 in. (7.6 cm) wide, large hooks allow speedy progress [Photo 6.14]. Once made by

bending old ring angle pitons, the commercial ones work better and are more trustworthy. By wedging it in place with an angle piton, you can even leave a Fish hook as protection that won't lever out on the flake.

Cam hooks are amazing little crack ascenders that work by levering against roughly parallel walls [Photo 6.15]. A pair of these allows very rapid movement up a thin crack, but be sure to leave solid pro every now and then.

Words of caution about testing marginal aid placements . . . stand clear! The best bet is to step in the bottom rung of your aiders so that the piece is above your head and the distance of the fall is shorter should it pop. If you must be up at eye level,

cup your hand over the placement as you weight it to keep your teeth intact.

PITONS

Given modern clean-climbing equipment, indiscriminately pounding pitons into rock is inexcusable. That said, there is a time and a place for a well-driven "pin." Just think before you bash.

Assuming he doesn't drop them first, the neophyte tends to overdrive his pins, damaging the pitons, sometimes weakening the placements,

Photo 6.13   Aid hooks are threaded with ½-inch webbing. The shape and reach of the point and the width of the base determine where and how well each works.

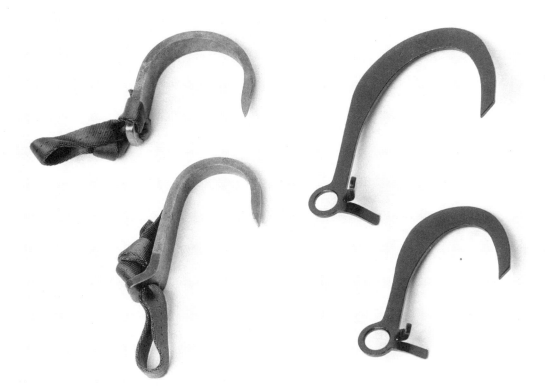

Photo 6.14   Large hooks are useful on horizontal flakes.

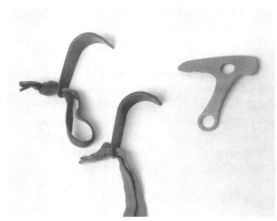

Photo 6.15 Cam hooks allow fast ascents of narrow, vertical cracks.

making removal harder, and causing more rock damage. Place pitons with a mind toward minimizing damage during the back-and-forth pounding needed for removal. Or make an offering to the mountain gods rather than destroying their temple—leave the piton there.

The majority of pitons available are made from 4130 steel (commonly called chrome-moly), heat-treated for durability and strength. Chrome-moly pitons withstand amazing punishment. However, those heat-treated to higher tempers are more brittle; heads of some pitons have been known to snap off.

By contrast, European soft-iron pitons are generally "leavers"—you often can't get them out. They're cheap, so some climbers carry a few for fixing gear. Titanium pitons weigh roughly half that of comparable steel models and, depending on the alloy, are fairly durable. Though prices have come down, these are best reserved for alpinists requiring light racks.

Pitons (and bolt hangers) with CEN approval must have a minimum eye diameter of 15 mm and a thickness of 3 mm; eye edges must also be beveled. Pins designed for protection must have blades at least 3½ in. (9 cm) long with eyes that hold 5620 lbf (25 kN) in the normal direction (perpendicular to the crack) and 3372 lbf (15 kN) in sideways pull (parallel to the crack). "Progression" (aid only) pitons can be any length, and their eye-strength requirements are halved. U.S.-made pitons don't have to meet these standards, though many would; some may not pass the 'biner-eye requirement.

Most piton design function is obvious; selection is dictated by the route, but a few shapes are particularly useful [Photo 6.16]. Narrower, pointed blades are designed for irregular limestone cracks,

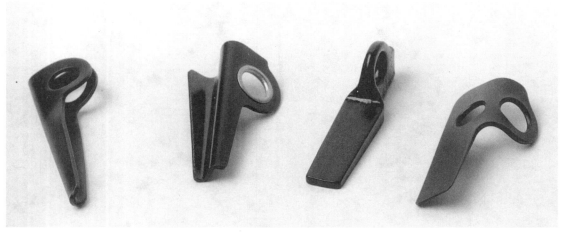

Photo 6.16 Pitons: angle, Z, Lost Arrow, and knife-blade

but wider, straight-sided blades hold better in even, parallel-sided granite and sandstone cracks. Bongs for wide cracks were once common before SLCDs but are rarely needed now [Photo 6.17].

Z-pitons hold better than angles (four versus three contact points) and, when it really gets exciting, work well for nesting pins. Stubbies (short, fat angles) work for nailing old pin scars, instead of tying off longer pins that bottom out. Saw your own from angles or buy them.

When faced with an incipient crack, you will need to resort to micropitons such as beaks and RURPs [Photo 6.18]. Beaks resemble hooks that are pounded into the thinnest of vertical cracks. RURPs (Realized Ultimate Reality Pitons) are more like the tip of a knife-blade piton and work better in horizontals. Neither is meant to hold more than body weight.

Metal shards in the eye are a painful experience. It's important to wear glasses with plastic lenses while nailing. Racking pins in alternating directions takes up less space on the 'biner.

MASHABLES

When even tied-off or stacked pins won't hold, a bashie, a blob of metal on the end of a cable, can be pounded into the most unlikely shallow cavities, depressions, or crackless jams and corners [Photo 6.19]. Corrupted from Bill Forrest's Copperheads (intended to be regular nuts), "heads" are now standard equipment on more serious aid routes.

Anyone with a swaging tool and common sense can make bashies. However, if you lack either, don't attempt it; mistakes could be fatal. Be wary of guys in parking lots selling heads. Commercially made heads are readily available and inexpensive.

The smaller heads have copper swages; larger ones have aluminum swages—less durable but they stick better. Some have two swages in a row

Photo 6.17   Bongs, named for their resonating sound when struck, aren't used much anymore now that large cams are common.

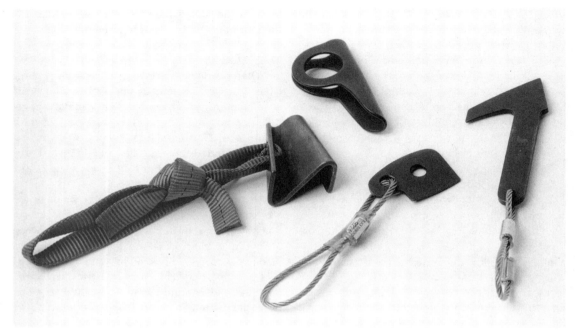

Photo 6.18   Aid protection: Z-nailer for stacking pins, stubbie piton, RURP, and a beak

for pasting a larger surface area of a seam. For horizontal seams, a bashie on a circular loop is best.

HAMMERS

After you've tried a geologist's or framing hammer for aid climbing, you'll want the real thing. A hammer designed for climbing has a large, flat pounding surface and good mass to give the most punch to your blows [Photo 6.20].

Various materials are used, but many prefer wood handles for shock-absorbency and feel. Wood dries out (and heads loosen) and may need replacement. Fiberglass handles are more durable and absorb shock well, but a rubber grip is essential. Wood and especially fiberglass will splinter from mis-hits if not protected by tape (wrap first with fiberglass strapping tape, then cloth tape). A shoulder sling and leash (so the tool can dangle below your feet) are important and shouldn't interfere with holstering.

While many hammers taper to a blunt point on one end, it may still be too awkward for pasting a mashable into a corner. If you expect to do a lot of heading, bring a blunt chisel.

I had to drill a carabiner hole in my first hammer for removing pro, but now they all have them. To remove pitons, a cleaning cable—steel cable about 30 in. (75 cm) long with loops at either end—is clipped between the hammer and the pin. A good outward flick of the hammer can pop that sucker right out of there . . . and into your teeth if you aren't careful! This is faster and less injurious to the rock than hammering the pin back and forth until it's loose.

BOLT GEAR

Although I enjoy clipping nice, solid 3/8 in. (10 mm) and 1/2 in. (13 mm) bolts and encourage the upgrade of old 1/4 in. (6 mm) time bombs, I'm not a fan of the

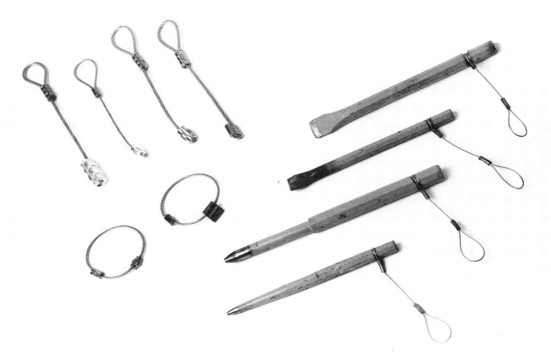

Photo 6.19   Aluminum heads, Copperheads, circle heads, and an assortment of punches are used for pasting the most unlikely of aid placements.

overpropagation of bolts and will not discuss power drills. However, hand drills do have their place and should be carried on most big walls. And you should know something about the bolts you clip.

DRILLS

It's worth the extra weight and bulk to get a hand drill with a rubber grip, preferably one with a stiff flange to protect your hand from mis-hits. A clip-in loop of some sort is essential.

Two styles of drill bits are available: the old Rawl taper bits and the new Rawl slotted drive shaft (SDS) bits [Photo 6.21]. And they cannot be used interchangeably. Carbide-tipped SDS bits, which also fit many power drills, are readily available at hardware stores but need sharpening prior to use.

Carry at least two drill bits, and all the necessary tools for replacing them. A plastic blow tube is useful for clearing holes, and safety glasses are a good idea. Bring a diamond sharpening stone if there's a chance you'll run out of bits.

The standard wrenches for bolts are ⅝ in. and 13 mm—something that's a good idea to carry on climbs even if you don't have a bolt kit. Most cheap adjustable wrenches will round off the corners of bolt heads; either get a good one or use box wrenches. Put a leash on it, too.

A good bolt placement requires a clean hole that is not wallowed out; practice on obscure local boulders beforehand. If the drill bit has twists, always turn it clockwise while pounding. Be sure to make the holes deeper than the bolt you intend to place. Never hang on a drill as it is sure to snap off, plugging the hole.

Never place a bolt that you are not positive is trustworthy! Leaving a ticking bomb for someone

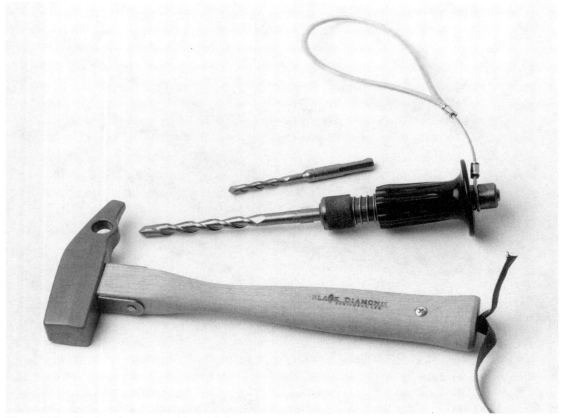

Photo 6.20   Climbing hammer and hand drill

else is irresponsible and reprehensible. Adding bolts to an established route should be done only with considerable forethought—it's usually frowned upon. But replacing ancient bolts or beefing up belay stations is a civic service.

BOLTS

When you encounter a ¼ in. bolt on a twenty-year-old route, it's reasonable to assume the thing is junk—sometimes they come out in your hand. Anything with a nonstandard bolt hanger (such as sawed-off angle iron) or thin sheet-metal hangers (ancient Leepers) is also guaranteed to be garbage.

For hard rock on moderately trafficked routes, a 3-in.-long, ⅜ in. five-piece Rawl Power-Bolt [Photo 6.22] is probably the best choice because it is strong and cheap, and can be easily replaced. For softer rock or top anchors, it's a good idea to use somewhat longer ½ in. bolts. And if you're drilling in very soft rock, use long 6 in. bolts.

Bolts on cliffs sprayed by salt water are subject to an insidious demon called stress corrosion cracking (SCC). Even stainless-steel bolts can weaken to negligible strength in as little as 18 months with *no* visible indication! Beware if you go to Thailand or other popular destinations on the ocean.

At present, the best option for sea cliffs are glue-in stainless-steel bolts because they are not subjected to tension as a bolt is tightened. However, titanium bolts currently being developed are

Photo 6.21   Taper bits (left) and SDS bits (right) are not interchangeable. Bits with carbide tips should be sharpened for best performance.

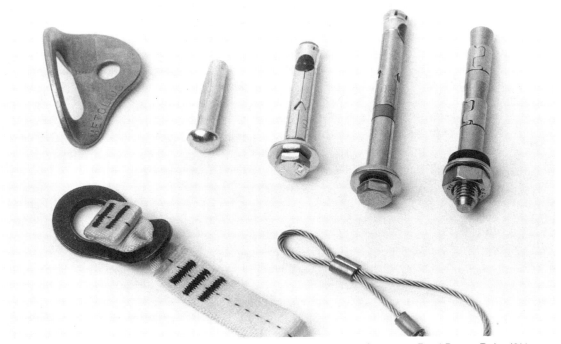

Photo 6.22   (Top) bolt hanger, 5/16-in. button head contraction bolt, 3/8-in. five-piece Rawl Power-Bolts (2 1/4-in. and 3 1/2-in.), 10 mm stainless-steel stud bolt, (bottom) cable rivet hanger, and washer rivet hanger

likely to become the standard in the future for corrosive environments.

Long sections of blank rock often allow no way up except by rivet ladder. Drill a 5/16-in.-wide hole and pound a 1-in.-long, 3/8 in. machine bolt halfway into it. Then slip on a keyhole bolt hanger and drive the rivet home until it's snug. If the route is likely to see much traffic, use 1/4- by 1 1/2-in. buttonhead compression bolts instead because they can

be upgraded (most rivets shear off and require a new hole to be drilled).

Recently, removable bolts have been introduced that allow a hole to be drilled and left empty [Photo 6.23]. These are essentially spring-loaded wedges made to fit round holes. However, the holes must be drilled at an angle (instead of straight in as for regular bolts) to prevent bending the cable. And getting them out after a fall can be a hassle.

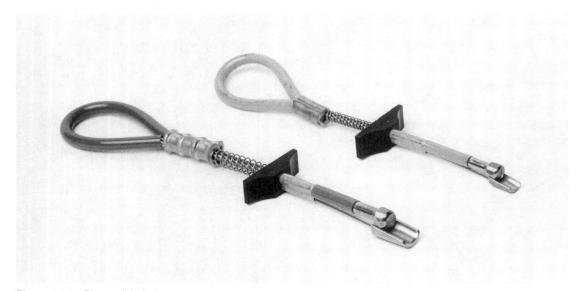

Photo 6.23   Removable bolts

CHAPTER 7

BIG WALL GEAR

IT'S QUITE IMPOSSIBLE FOR CLIMBERS, no matter their level of experience, to look at a Yosemite wall or a Karakoram tower without dreaming of vertical adventure. Scoping out lines is a reflex as natural as breathing. The big stone beckons. But if you're not prepared, it can smack you hard.

Although you can spend a small fortune on the latest equipment, it is possible to get up big walls on a budget. Indeed, there is a long tradition of climbers pooling racks from a half-dozen friends, scrounging food from awestruck tourists, and making their own gear. Be forewarned, however, that the park service takes a dim view of ill-equipped climbers who require rescue; the rescue costs and fines can be as steep as the Leaning Tower.

Don't get too caught up in the gadgetry either. As the almost-honorable Warren "Batso" Harding puts it in his 1975 classic book *Downward Bound* (obligatory reading for any big wall aspirant), "The new advancements and endless varieties of equipment can lead to an obsession with the tools of the trade, rather than the trade itself, an attitude that the equipment does the climbing, not the man or woman. When it boils right down to it, no amount or variety of equipment will make up for insufficient skill or will."

HAUL BAGS

Getting your mountain of gear from Camp 4 to the base of the climb, up the wall, and back to the valley floor requires more than the average crag sack.

Back when climbers were still using Goldline rope and swami belts, the standard haul bag was an army duffel bag with a few straps attached. Climbers quickly discovered these were nowhere near durable enough for the thrashing dished out on a wall climb. Haul bags made from heavy canvas, Cordura, or ballistics-cloth fabrics rarely lasted more than a few walls.

Until recently, the material of choice has been 28 oz. vinyl-coated nylon (VCN), most often seen in white but now available in several colors. Avoid dark colors unless you enjoy preheated drinking water on hot days. This fabric can withstand a tremendous amount of abuse, is absolutely waterproof (till you put a hole in it), and is relatively slick so it drags easily over rock.

Now 33 oz. urethane-coated nylon (UCN) has proven to be even more durable, and costly. The extra stiffness helps hold the bags open for easier rummaging.

The closure system for haul bags runs from simple draw cords to elaborate flaps that provide better weather seals. All haul bags should have a drain hole in the bottom; 10 gals. (38 l) of water weighs 80 lbs. (36 kg). Keep critical items, such as sleeping bags and clothing, in waterproof stuff sacks.

SUSPENSIONS

All of the large haul bags on the market use a four-point suspension, though some smaller haul packs just use three straps to support the load [Illustration 7.1]. Whether three- or four-point, it is helpful for the straps on one side to be a few inches shorter than on the other. This offset makes it noticeably easier to unclip one side while the bag is hanging, for access to its contents.

The backpacking suspension may seem like an afterthought on many designs. This is to keep it streamlined and, thus, out of the way in the vertical world. Nonetheless, if you anticipate long approaches and descents, the extra money for a more comfortable suspension is well spent—or strap the haul bag to an external frame.

Any haul bag should have a sleek, uncluttered,

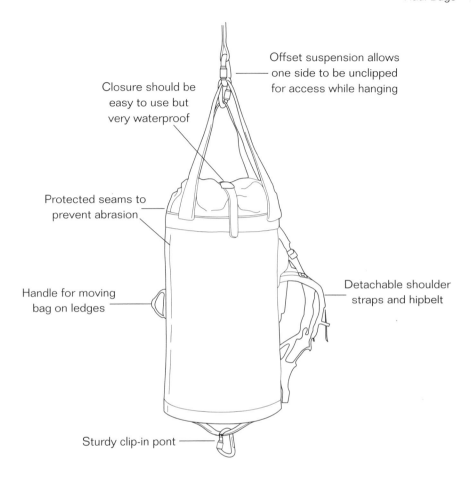

Offset suspension allows one side to be unclipped for access while hanging

Closure should be easy to use but very waterproof

Protected seams to prevent abrasion

Handle for moving bag on ledges

Detachable shoulder straps and hipbelt

Sturdy clip-in pont

Illustration 7.1   Haul bag

tapered profile to minimize snagging. Buckles and other fittings that don't tuck away, as well as critical seams, need to be covered by flaps for protection. The shoulder straps and waist belt that you use to hump the haul bag to the start of the route must be removed and stowed securely inside (you're hosed if you lose them!) or tucked away in special compartments before you fill the bag.

Because bags are often connected like boxcars when hauling, the clip-in loops underneath need to be strong enough to hold serious loads. (No matter how strong the bag, *never* jug on a rope

fixed to it!) It is also helpful to have an external handle(s) to aid in lifting the haul bag off anchors and manhandling the thing across ledges.

CAPACITIES

There are two major schools of thought on capacity: Hauling one "grade VI" mega bag, 9000 to 10,000 cu. in. (150 to 165 l), versus hauling two small "grade V" bags, 4000 to 5000 cu. in. (65 to 80 l). One heavy bag is less expensive but may be extremely tiring to carry or haul, especially on less-than-vertical slabs, whereas each of the two lighter bags is much less backbreaking to move and less apt to incur damage to its contents. It's also easier to find things in a smaller bag.

Smaller haul packs—2000 to 3000 cu. in. (33 to 50 l)—work best on long day routes where a normal climbing pack would get thrashed and a haul bag is just too big. These are also useful on multi-day climbs for sending extra gear up a zip line, for handling overflow, or for day use. Fanny or bullet packs are very useful on aid routes to carry assorted essentials.

HAUL BAG TIPS

Most haul bags are quite Spartan on the inside. Though not necessities, features such as zippered pockets and internal gear loops or daisy chains do make organization on the wall a bit easier.

You can wear a hole through any haul bag in a nanosecond if you do not carefully pack the "pig" so that hard objects (such as a can of stew) are not pressing against the outside. Line the inside of the bag with cardboard or your sleeping pads before packing.

Before you go up on any wall, patch holes, tears, and abraded stitching; an eviscerated haul bag could spell disaster. You can extend the life of your bag dramatically by covering external stitching with Seam Grip or with plastic-dip tool-handle coating.

PORTALEDGES

The original wall beds were portable hammocks designed to be tied between two trees. The hassle in rigging these, owing to a lack of properly spaced anchors, led to the development of single-point hammocks. These hammocks consisted of a sheet of fabric supported along the edges by six webbing straps that met at a single anchor point. Although much better than their predecessors, these still left a lot to be desired in comfort and convenience.

In search of a better night's sleep, climbers began to jury-rig portable ledges from objects such as lawn chairs, sheets of plywood, and gates from wire fences. These creative contraptions were obviously lacking when it came to durability and portability, so collapsible frames with fabric beds started to appear. Early models suffered from numerous problems: hourglassing, overflexing, severe rain-fly leakage, poor adjustability, and minimal durability.

Modern portaledges [Illustration 7.2] have undergone numerous refinements in the past decade—to the point where they could more accurately be termed vertical tents. Given the prices, this appellation is more appropriate; you can buy an expedition tent for less. The materials used, particularly in the frames and joints, are more robust, and assembly is even easier than before. Most important, the storm-worthiness of modern ledges is significantly better than the old ones'.

Portaledges are available with either 6061-T6 aluminum or 4130 chrome-moly steel; titanium is currently not offered. Though the manufacturers tout the virtues of one material over the other, the reality is that any of them can make a good frame; design and construction are more important.

Each manufacturer has a slightly different system for rigging the portaledge frame, using four to nine suspension straps leading to a central anchor point. Although you should adjust these straps before crawling onboard, it's helpful if they can be fine-tuned easily while you are in bed. The design and location of the buckles, not to mention their strength and durability, are very important factors. Despite conflicting claims about ease of setup, most of the ledges are comparable, with practice, if you count total time for pitching and striking.

Wherever nylon fabric runs taut over metal, it's a candidate for severe abrasion. Though all the ledges are reinforced on the wall side, most could use more protection on the other edges, where they often get banged during pitching and striking. The actual bed material needs to have high tear strength. To prevent the dreaded bathtub effect, the floor also

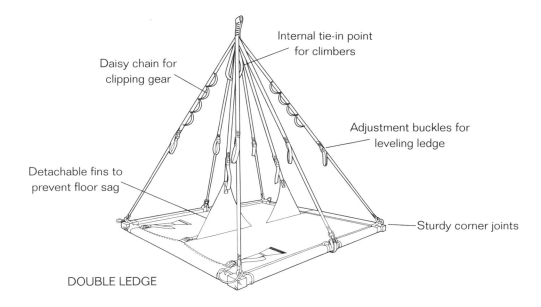

Internal tie-in point
for climbers

Daisy chain for
clipping gear

Adjustment buckles for
leveling ledge

Detachable fins to
prevent floor sag

Sturdy corner joints

DOUBLE LEDGE

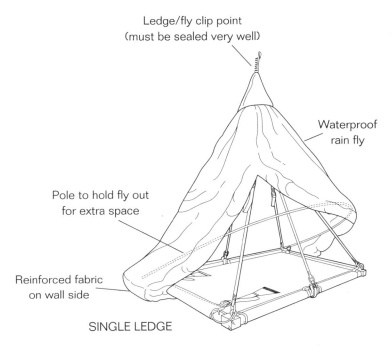

Ledge/fly clip point
(must be sealed very well)

Waterproof
rain fly

Pole to hold fly out
for extra space

Reinforced fabric
on wall side

SINGLE LEDGE

Illustration 7.2   Portaledge: single and double

needs a drain hole at the lowest point.

Another decision you must make is whether to choose a single or double portaledge. Singles have been the traditional favorite and certainly offer more privacy. Obviously, doubles give the most versatility since they also make a luxurious one-person shelter, and a hammock can be strung underneath for a person (assuming he or she is accustomed to sleeping in a ship's berth). A double saves a team roughly 10 lbs. (4.5 kg) and $500 when compared with a pair of single ledges.

RAIN FLYS

Imagine all of the water running off two vertical football fields draining directly on top of your tent, and you will begin to understand the importance of a good waterproof rain fly. Simultaneously, the wind is rushing up from below, trying to rip your pitiful campsite to shreds.

Although you should always seek out a location that won't be a natural funnel during a storm, even the best sites cannot escape nature's full fury. Because of abrasion and rockfall, lightweight fly fabrics tend to get shredded quickly. Nylon pack cloth is the current fabric of choice because of its durability and ruggedness; higher deniers are more abrasion-resistant but heavier. The best fabrics have multiple urethane coatings.

Seams can leak an amazing amount of water, so the fewer there are, the better. Thoroughly sealing the seams, both inside and out, with Seam Grip is very important. Even the outside of taped seams should be sealed, so you don't need to pay extra for this feature. Set the ledge up in your backyard, take your time to do the job right the first time, and you'll probably never need to do it again.

Water running down the anchor attachments can wick copiously through the webbing suspension straps. A waterproof squirrel guard (fabric cone) around the anchor webbing helps, but the webbing coming through it still needs special attention with the seam glue. Do not underestimate the ability of water to seek you out in a storm.

Because pack cloth does not breathe, and there is no inner canopy (as on a conventional double-wall tent), condensation is a significant problem in all portaledges. This is best combated with ventilation and the use of a good Gore-Tex bivy sack to keep your sleeping bag dry. Waterproof/breathable flys are available but work best in cold, dry conditions and cost several hundred dollars extra.

Rain flys should be designed for rapid deployment. This means that (while still in the stuff sack) the fly is clipped to the anchor and the ledge is then clipped to the fly support webbing. When the weather rolls in, you can unfurl the fly, with some hassle, when you are in bed. Especially with two people sharing a ledge, it's a good idea to set the fly up ahead of time if there is any threat of storms.

Perhaps the single biggest improvement in portaledges in the past few years is the addition of a pole for the fly. The increase in comfort during a storm is huge. The difference is directly analogous to old, cramped A-frame tents versus modern, spacious dome tents. The pole can also serve double-duty for use as a cheater-stick on long clips.

To prevent updrafts from making your fly look like Marilyn Monroe's skirt in *Seven Year Itch*, it needs to attach securely underneath the frame. A simple draw cord works most of the time but is inadequate for serious conditions. Additional lash points are important, but they need to be operable from inside your haven. You might also consider adding a clear window for checking out the weather and a cooking vent if the fly lacks one.

ASCENDERS

Next to your rope and protection, ascenders are the most valuable tools on a wall. Make do with prusiks only if you're a glutton for punishment. Most of the small handleless ascenders aren't suited to the big wall task either but are ideal for crevasse rescue [Photo 7.1]. Ascenders are made for going up a fixed rope, but they are also called upon for many other tasks, such as hauling loads.

Photo 7.1 Mini-ascenders. These are useful for glacier travel and emergencies but are not suitable for a big wall.

Ascender handles are made from cast, pressed, or extruded aluminum. Although cast aluminum is less durable, and a potential for strength-robbing air bubbles exists, all models currently available are very strong.

To pass the CEN tests, each ascender must hold a 900 lbf (4 kN) load ten times (five on the thickest and five on the thinnest recommended ropes) without damaging the ascender or sheath. (The ascender is moved down the rope after each pull.)

Unfortunately, some ascenders are poorly designed ergonomically. Models with vertical hand-grips are hard on the hands and wrists. Though some have angled, molded-plastic grips, there is still room for improvement [Photo 7.2]. If necessary, make the grips more comfortable by using foam and tape. For expedition use, be sure the handle will accept a mitten-covered hand.

Cam design largely determines how well the ascenders grip an icy or muddy rope. More aggressive teeth hold better but tend to abrade and snag the rope, particularly when down-jugging [Photo 7.3]. Some ascenders use a lever arm to amplify the clamping force on icy and muddy ropes. Though all manufacturers use steel cams plated or treated for extra durability, the teeth eventually wear down and may not grip sufficiently. Inspect them regularly.

One-handed ascender operation is key. When cleaning an aid pitch, the second often removes the top ascender from the rope and replaces it above the next piece to be cleaned; likewise, when clearing a bulge, the top ascender is removed and reattached in a higher position—over and over. Though all ascenders require manual dexterity to operate, some are noticeably easier to use than others. Small hands exacerbate the differences; try before you buy.

Most ascenders should not be used for self-belay because pebbles can prevent the cam from closing. Never use any ascender where it could be shock-loaded; rope sheath failure is quite possible.

If you will be doing very long jugs or carrying a heavy pack, consult a good spelunking manual,

Photo 7.2 Handled ascenders with comfortable grips and openings large enough for a gloved hand

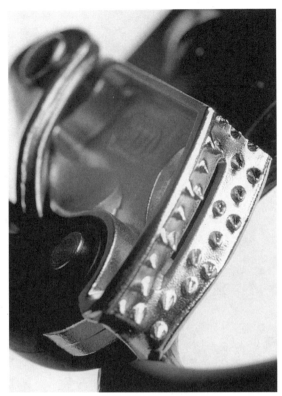

Photo 7.3 Aggressive cam teeth with a slot for clearing ice

such as *On Rope* (Padgett & Smith, 1997), for more efficient ascent techniques worked out by cavers. Chest pulley and other systems are somewhat more complicated but can save you a tremendous amount of energy.

Always tie in short as a backup when ascending. Attach a daisy chain from your harness to each ascender as an additional backup. Remember that bouncing while jugging has a sawing effect on a rope running over an edge—bad for the rope and worse for you. On traverses, clip a 'biner from the bottom of the ascender to the rope to help prevent it from popping off.

PULLEYS

You need a pulley to haul a heavy load; its quality affects how hard you work [Photo 7.4]. With a basic, no-frills pulley that has a self-lubricating, bronze bushing, about 140 lbf (0.6 kN) is necessary to lift a 100 lb. (45 kg) haul bag. With a more expensive pulley with a polished axle and quality ball bearings, only 110 lbf (0.5 kN) is necessary—which

Photo 7.4   Clockwise from top: The large pulley is most efficient; small pulley is compact; carabiner pulley is okay in a pinch; Wall Hauler is the old standard; ratcheting pulley works as a backup ascender.

will save you tons (literally) of work. Because their ball bearings are sealed to keep out grit, more expensive pulleys continue to roll easily long after cheaper, unsealed pulleys have gummed up.

Greater sheave (wheel) diameter also eases hoisting due to less rope friction. A 4:1 tread diameter/rope diameter ratio is desirable for heavy loads. Be aware: Companies typically list the outside sheave diameter rather than the more-important tread diameter.

Light-duty pulleys have nylon sheaves—fine for occasional wall use and crevasse rescue. Aluminum sheaves last much longer but are somewhat heavier and more expensive.

Given the forces that big wall climbers apply, all of the pulleys for climbing are sufficiently strong. Rescue pulleys must accommodate much bigger loads more efficiently, but they are heavier, bulkier, and more expensive.

Several pulleys have built-in rope cams, which greatly simplifies hauling. The smallest of these work well for crevasse rescue but are harsh on ropes when used on a wall. The Wall Hauler has long been the standard for big walls, but it has a maximum load rating of 90 kg (200 lbs.). Some newer self-camming pulleys will hold over 400 kg (900 lbs.), which makes them strong enough for "live" loads, and they can serve as backup ascenders.

Care: Clean grit from pulleys for maximum efficiency; use a dry lube on unsealed bearings. When hauling, attach the pulley to a sling where it can pivot (rather than to a fixed anchor) to minimize rope wear and torque on the axle.

WALL HARNESSES

Your normal harness may seem adequate for a big wall. But when your legs are numb after hours of hanging, you begin to wish for a lot more cush. The heavier you are, the greater the need for serious support.

Compared to a regular harness, big wall harnesses have wider swami belts and leg loops, and more padding. For freedom of movement, these components usually taper toward the front—this is especially important for short-waisted people. Women tend to need more taper in the swami and more rise in the front of the leg loops. A few harnesses have reinforcement across the back of the swami to provide greater lumbar support.

Most have adjustable leg loops to accommodate extra clothing. Better leg loops open completely, making them easier to remove for changing layers or sleeping, while remaining tied into the swami. The rear straps that hold the leg loops must be easy to unfasten for heeding the call of nature. Elastic straps may stay out of the way better, but webbing straps, once properly adjusted, provide more support for your haunches when you're hanging.

All wall harnesses need a belay/rappel loop on the front—this is stronger and more reliable than any carabiner you carry. A haul loop on the back of the harness for attaching a trailing line is also a must. Although this is generally full-strength, it should never be used for clipping into an anchor.

At least four strong racking loops are needed; some harnesses are set up for attaching more. I find the easiest loops to use are cord stiffened with plastic; folded webbing is inferior. Some gear loops are sized to double as hammer holsters, though a soft hammer holster is better.

Because comfort is paramount, spend at least 15 minutes hanging from any big wall harness you are considering. Any store worth shopping at will have an anchored rope for this purpose.

WALL RACKS

Major aid fests require a lot of gear. With 20 lbs. (9 kg) of metal hanging from it, a standard free-climbing gear sling feels like piano wire, and a pair of them can choke you like a boa constrictor. The solution? A well-designed wall rack with four gear loops that let the gear hang at your sides [Illustration 7.3].

Good slings feature wide shoulder straps, padded with foam and/or pile, that distribute the load evenly. A sternum strap is helpful to keep the shoulder straps in place and prevent losing the rack in the event of a fall (serious bummer). Better racks have strong extra loops on the shoulders for clipping off the rack to an anchor for sorting.

Some wall racks work as chest harnesses—important for roped soloing and radically overhanging aid routes. Because a full rack makes you top-heavy, clipping the rope into a chest harness can keep you upright after a fall.

AIDERS

You need at least one pair of aiders to go beyond free climbing [Illustration 7.4]. Standard aiders have steps that alternate sides; some have ladder-like steps. For serious aid routes, the old practice of using an aider/sub-aider combination has given way to using two pairs of 1 in. webbing aiders for greater efficiency.

Everyone with a sewing machine seems to make aiders, and there isn't much to distinguish them.

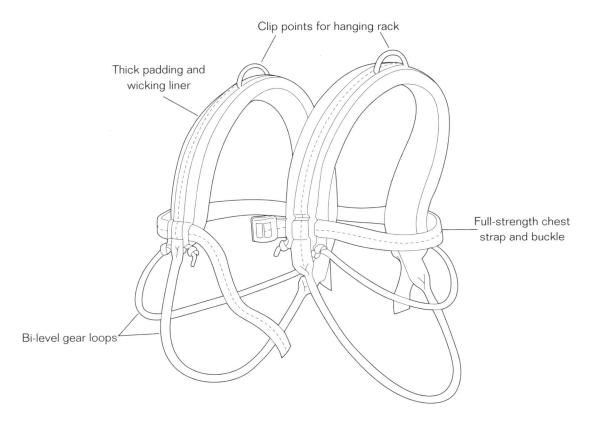

Clip points for hanging rack

Thick padding and
wicking liner

Full-strength chest
strap and buckle

Bi-level gear loops

Illustration 7.3 Wall rack

Although you can easily tie your own, I don't recommend it; the steps don't stay open and the knots hurt your feet. Commercial aiders are much nicer and relatively inexpensive.

All decent aiders feature a rugged stiffening material to hold the steps open. Those that use only additional reinforcing webbing soften with use; plastic reinforcement is desirable. A sub-step in the second rung is very useful, though one in the top rung is rarely used. Better aiders have a full-strength grab loop at the reinforced carabiner loop. A few are designed with a 'biner loop at the bottom, allowing a second aider to be clipped in or ballast to be attached (to keep the aider from flying in the wind) without collapsing the bottom step.

The typical combination is a four-step and a five-step aider made with two colors of webbing. Aiders made of ¾ in. webbing are used for alpine climbs where weight and bulk are issues and rigid boots are worn. It is best to buy aiders in pairs because the steps of different brands often don't line up—annoying at times.

Hearkening back to the days of wooden-runged *étriers*, you can also choose ladder-style aiders. These have the big advantage of being less tangle-prone in the wind. My favorites have a rigid spreader rod at the top. The second and third steps also have a piece of elastic that you flip over your toe to hold it in place while jugging.

A "new" option in the United States has been

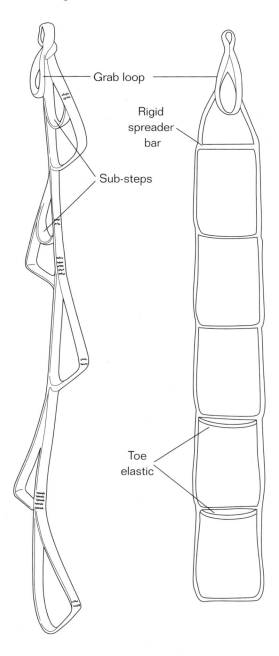

Grab loop

Rigid
spreader
bar

Sub-steps

Toe
elastic

Illustration 7.4 Standard and ladder aiders

used by Soviet climbers for decades. Called the Russian Aider System, it consists of stirrups worn on the calves that have hooks to go in rings on the "aider." For moving fast, particularly on steep and mixed terrain, it's worth considering.

DAISY CHAINS

In addition to tying the rope into their harness, big wall climbers also girth-hitch two daisy chains through the rope path (or to the belay loop) [Photo 7.5]. These indispensable multilooped slings are used for keeping your placement and attached aiders from falling the distance, and for jugging and anchoring yourself. They should be at least long enough to allow a clip at full reach—roughly 45 to 55 in. (115 to 140 cm), depending on your ape index—when girth-hitched to your harness.

Numerous suppliers make nearly identical products. Most companies use $^{11}/_{16}$ in. (18 mm) supertape nylon webbing for daisy chains because it's supple, durable, and affordable. Daisies made from Spectra webbing are stronger, less bulky, and absorb less water but cost more. The first loop for attaching to the harness should be 8 to 12 in. (20 to 30 cm) long; the better ones have a half twist for a more compact girth hitch.

The stitching on each pocket of a daisy chain is rated at around 400 to 800 lbf (1.8 to 3.6 kN), although the entire sling approaches 4000 lbf (18 kN). Never use daisy chains as the sole anchor when loads exceed body weight. When belaying, the main rope must always be your anchor! Also, you must never cross-clip two pockets; a failure of the stitching would allow the carabiner to escape the daisy.

Traditional daisies have six to eight pockets, which give a decent range of adjustment. However, some savvy wall climbers rave about using one of the infinitely adjustable daisies. Using high-grade 1 in. (25 mm) flat webbing and an aluminum cam-lock buckle that tests to over 2000 lbf (9 kN), this versatile tether makes your vertical life easier. A descending ring on the tugging end provides a good handle and ensures there is no chance of the end pulling through.

CLOTHING

For the most part, the clothing you wear and carry on a big wall should be the same as what you would use in a high mountain environment to cope with extremes of heat, cold, and rain. This includes synthetic underwear, fleece, and good rain gear (that can survive a thrash up a squeeze chimney), as well as warm gloves and a hat.

Although showing up at Camp 4 in a pair of expensive big wall pants may label you a yuppie climber, they really do have their advantages. The better ones are made of a woven stretch material that is designed to wick moisture, dry quickly, shed wind and rain, and provide great abrasion and snag resistance. They have tapered legs so you can see your feet, ankle zips for ventilation, double seat and knees, and zippered pockets. Men's versions should have a long fly that zips up (not down) to open—an advantage when wearing a harness.

KNEE PADS
No matter what pants you wear, you also may want knee pads to protect your legs from abrasion and bruising, although they don't have to be anything fancy. I prefer those that attach with elasticized Velcro straps because the pull-on variety tend to cut uncomfortably into the back of the knees. Some people like the hard-shell telemark knee pads, although they are bulkier.

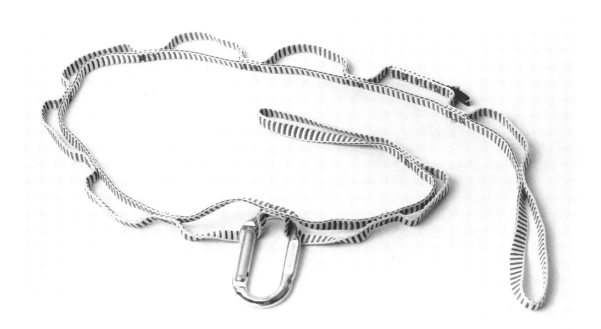

Photo 7.5　Never cross-clip a daisy chain! Just a couple of bar tacks keep that carabiner in place.

BIG WALL LUXURIES

Climbing a big wall is like going backpacking—only you get vertical. Besides your tent (portaledge) and pack (haul bags), each climber also needs a closed-cell foam pad, a bivy sack, and a synthetic-insulated sleeping bag. Everything that goes up on a wall should have a clip loop to prevent loss! Depending on the route and your dependency on coffee, you may also need a hanging stove and a portable espresso maker. There are a few other items that, although not essential, take some of the harshness out of the climb.

- Butt bags. Butt bags can have either two or three points of suspension; I find the former more comfortable and less of a hassle to use.
- Bosun's chair. Although better than hanging in a harness, butt bags don't offer the comfort of a bosun's chair [Illustration 7.5]. This is a foam-padded sheet of plywood rigged with suspension straps and a back rest for a decadent belay.
- Wall bags. The more organized you are on the wall, the smoother the climb goes. Wall bags are rugged stuff sacks with secure hang loops attached that make life much easier.
- Rope bucket. Another useful item for keeping the snafus to a minimum is a rope bucket used for stacking the rope at belays [Illustration 7.6]. These are essentially long, skinny stuff sacks that unzip lengthwise to form a flaring receptacle.
- Johns. Though required only in Yosemite at present, it's a good idea for all climbers on

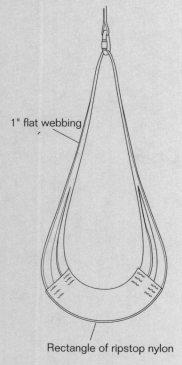

1" flat webbing

Rectangle of ripstop nylon

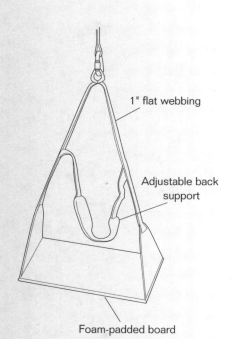

1" flat webbing

Adjustable back support

Foam-padded board

Illustration 7.5   Butt bag and bosun's chair

Illustration 7.6   Rope bucket

multiday routes to carry a portable john [Illustration 7.7]. The standard wall john is made from 4 in. (10 cm) diameter PVC pipe that has a plug on the bottom and a screw-on lid. A webbing haul loop is securely attached and the john is clipped underneath a haul bag. Do your deed into a paper lunch sack and put this and toilet paper into a plastic bag. Shove the burrito into the tube. Tossing the paper bags off is illegal and extremely bad form!

- Drinking water. Although many climbers use duct-taped, 2-liter soda bottles to carry water (most gallon jugs aren't rugged enough), modern water bags offer collapsibility and surprising durability. No matter what you use, divide your water into several containers and store those below clothing and sleeping bags.
- Sun protection. On the vertical desert, you will need sunscreen, good sunglasses, and a hat with a brim to keep from frying.

- Duct tape. Exhaustive scientific research has proven that life on a big wall is impossible without duct tape. Carry a roll, along with a sewing awl, lubricant (for camming units and ledge frames), and a first-aid kit. Be sure that everything you take up on the wall (pads, jackets, gloves, etc.) has a convenient clip-in loop.
- Tunes. I prefer a Walkman over a boom box because of its compactness, durability, and low power consumption. FM radios can pick up an NPR station on many walls in Yosemite for news and weather. Use battery-powered remote speakers if nobody else is around and you need to crank it. And don't forget extra batteries!
- Candle lanterns. A candle lantern is nice for your evening's repast and saves headlamp batteries.

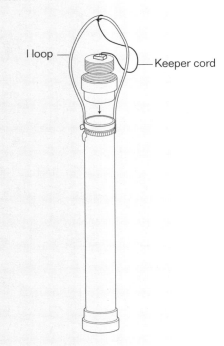

Illustration 7.7   Big wall john

GLOVES

Another item for protecting your body from the abuses of a wall climb is gloves. Some of the best include snug-fitting calfskin work gloves from the hardware store, with the fingertips cut off (glue the seams first to prevent unraveling). Bike gloves are adequate, but most lack sufficient durability and some are too thickly padded to make holding a hammer comfortable.

SHOES

Standing in aiders for hours on end places unusual demands on a pair of shoes. Primarily, they must be comfortable; have good arch support, stiff midsoles, and reinforced toes—dragging toes while jumaring wears through rands (the rubber strips set in the toe and heel) alarmingly fast—and climb well enough for moderate free moves (sticky rubber helps). High-top models give ankle protection on the climb and approach.

Though standard approach shoes may be adequate for occasional use, they are no match for real wall boots. Here is the crucial test: Grab the shoe by heel and toe and try to bend the shoe in half so the treads are touching. The easier it is to bend, the more painful they will be when you're standing for hours in aiders; the use of a stiffened foot bed may help shoes that are too flexible. The sole should be wider than your foot so your foot won't be squeezed by the webbing.

CHAPTER 8

APPROACH AND ROCK SHOES

ONCE YOU GET BEYOND HIKING ON trails and scrambling up peaks, your choice of footwear makes all the difference. Specialized shoes to get you to the cliff, and then up it, are essential if you are serious about vertical advancement.

APPROACH SHOES

The term "approach shoe" means different things to different climbers. For many, these are the lightweight shoes you wear on the short hike into Eldorado Canyon or up to Seneca Rocks—or around town [Photo 8.1]. For others, approach shoes are heavier models designed for the long hump and easy climbing leading to the Diamond or the base of Half Dome. Still others want boots

adequate for approaching (maybe even climbing) the big walls up the Baltoro.

Despite some advertising claims, no single pair of shoes will do all of these things well—let alone trail running or mountain biking. Although virtually any hiking shoe will get you to the end of the trail, climbers must be concerned with how the shoe performs on muddy or icy slopes, slippery talus, and moderate rock climbing.

With the best of the sticky-rubber approach shoes, I can climb fairly well at about three number grades below my trad limit. Approach shoes that tend more toward hiking comfort force me to drop another two grades, while normal hiking or trail-running shoes (which lack sticky rubber and neither edge nor smear well) barely allow fifth-class scrambling.

For approach shoes, not all "sticky rubbers" are

Photo 8.1   Approach shoes with lacing to the toe and carabiner loops on the heel

Photo 8.2   Lug pattern of a good approach shoe offers edging performance and traction.

created equal; some don't grip at all. But sole friction is not the only determinant of a shoe's climbing performance. Indeed, rubbers that are too sticky wear out quickly and tend to hold sand particles that act like ball bearings.

The sole's lug pattern is equally important, especially on mud and snow [Photo 8.2]. If the cleats are too small, they tend to wear quickly and lose traction. Yet, lugs that are too deep or closely spaced don't shed mud, so you may end up carrying around several pounds of gunk. Downhill traction is severely lacking on many approach shoes, a problem that will occasionally leave you flat on your butt.

CLIMBING PERFORMANCE

To a large degree, climbing performance of approach shoes is determined by how they fit. Snug, narrow shoes will climb the best but are the least comfortable for long hikes. Looser-fitting, wide shoes will keep your feet happy but may force an earlier change to rock shoes. Lacing systems that extend to the big toe (instead of the ball of the foot) offer greater adjustability but can only do so much.

The shoes that edge best are designed with a solid strip of rubber around the sole's perimeter, extending from the inside ball of the foot to the little toe. Lugs in this edging zone leave gaps that decrease performance. Forefoot plates or stiffened midsoles also increase edging performance, though sensitivity is sacrificed.

High rands of sticky rubber around the toe and heel areas significantly improve crack-climbing performance, but only a few models have this feature. Good rands also help protect against abrasion, and the better ones guard against stubbed toes.

Approach shoes are very popular for aid climbing, even though many actually perform rather poorly on big walls. If you're spending hours at a time in aiders, a soft, collapsing arch will leave you in agony. The thin toe rands on most shoes will not survive a single ascent's jugging without major reinforcement. Good wall boots are very stiff through the instep (you can't fold them in half), and they have thick toe bumpers. (You also can ask resolers to glue an inexpensive, sticky-rubber rand reinforcement to most shoes.)

SHOE DESIGN

Approach shoes come in both low-cut and mid-ankle heights. Below-the-ankle shoes are lighter and more compact, and allow greater flexibility.

Over-the-ankle shoes are far better at keeping out scree and provide much-appreciated padding when jamming in wide cracks, although the additional ankle support is marginal at best. Many shoes are available in both styles, featuring the same outer and midsoles.

Durability of approach shoes has, in some cases, been a sad joke. Scree slopes are murder on stitching, so the fewer seams, the better. Although it may be a fashion faux pas, protecting the seams with Seam Grip can greatly extend the life of approach shoes.

All-leather uppers tend to be the most durable and water repellent (though this also depends on leather quality). On the other hand, fabric-and-leather uppers are noticeably cooler on hot summer days and dry out faster when soaked.

Be sure your shoes have a strong clip-in loop on the heel. If you lose a shoe during a multipitch climb because a loop broke, it will be a long, painful walk out. For long approaches, you might consider using low gaiters to keep out sand and pebbles.

ROCK SHOES

Rock shoes *do* make a difference. True, almost anyone can climb at 85 percent of his or her capability in the best of the "beginner" shoes, usually for less than $100. However, for $25 to $50 more, you gain another 10 percent of performance and usually more comfort and durability.

You also get more all-around performance for your buck with top-drawer shoes. Well-designed shoes, if properly fitted, tend to be more versatile than the price-point models. Few climbers really need more than two or three pairs of good shoes. When you are trying to eke out that last 5 percent of your ultimate performance—whether that's 5.9 or 5.14—it doesn't really matter whether the additional benefit is real or imagined. If it works, you're happy. Funny thing, though. When we succeed on a climb, we credit our skill and training; when we fail, the shoes often take the blame.

SHOPPING FOR YOUR FIRST ROCK SHOES

I've heard far too many woeful tales of a bad purchase that could have been prevented if the beginner knew what to look for. The two biggest mistakes the newbie can make when buying rock shoes are relying on shoe reviews and bringing your significant other to the store. Do not blindly trust reviews—we can only tell you what we think, not what will work for you. And often it's best to ignore the advice of friends who are teaching you to climb—they mean well but seldom are knowledgeable enough to really help.

The first step toward a successful purchase is finding a store that is qualified to sell rock shoes. Unless you live near a climbing mecca, each store will carry a limited selection, so you may have to shop around. Ideally, the shop will carry several models from at least two of the major brands and possibly one of the lesser-known brands. The store also should have a climbing wall or, at the very least, a panel of holds that allows you to try the shoes in a variety of foot positions.

Consider mail order for rock shoes only if you can't get to a shop or your local store doesn't carry the shoe your brother insists you have to try. To get the most for your money, there is simply no substitute for trying on a lot of models and sizes.

Just as important as finding a good, service-oriented store is picking the right employee. This may sound silly, but it can mean the difference between good performance/happy feet and wasted money/foot agony. A part-timer who has been working at the shop for only a few months doesn't know beans about selling and fitting rock shoes, even if he does climb 5.13. It generally takes two to three years of shop work before a salesperson has enough training and experience to give trustworthy advice.

You're off to a good start if the salesperson asks intelligent questions about the type of climbing you do, the shoes you already own or have tried, and what you think you need now. On the other hand, run away if he starts telling you which shoes he owns, gives you the rundown on every model in stock, or bores you with the crux sequence of his latest redpoint.

After listening to your answers, the salesperson should tell you about three or four specific models that might be suitable. Then it's time to start trying on shoes. Allow at least an hour to find the best-fitting shoes. Hint: Visit the shop in midafternoon, when your feet are swollen and it's least crowded, so you'll get full attention. Trim your toenails beforehand for the best fit, and if you plan to climb in socks, bring your own.

SHOES THAT FIT

Fitting rock shoes is an art, not a science. The seasoned salesperson will start with a few sizes of one promising model and have you in the right size on the second or third try. She will understand how a particular model should fit (toes must be scrunched in some, flat in others, for example) and how much stretch to expect, and she won't waste your time with a wide shoe if you have an AA-width foot.

After your size has been determined for one model, a knowledgeable salesperson should be able to bring out sizes of other models that are pretty close. Ignore the numbers on the Brannock device [Photo 8.3] or box for now; they only get you in the ballpark. You should tighten and tie your own shoes to get the right tension. It is very important to start with them *completely* loose and work up from the bottom—this makes a real difference in fit.

Most rock shoes are designed to work best when they are comfortably tight. Shoes with thick midsoles create an edging platform, so a looser, toes-flat fit is fine. If there is no midsole, or a very thin one, you will need a snugger, scrunched-toes

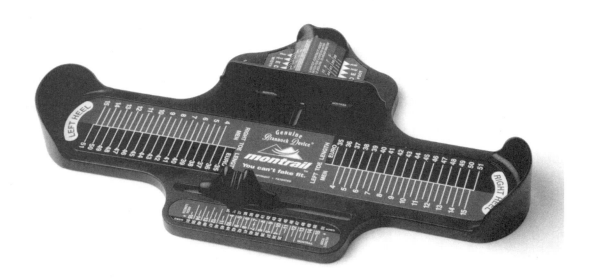

Photo 8.3 The Brannock device is just a starting point.

fit to get adequate edging performance. However, *they should not hurt.* Some climbers downsize their shoes to a point that would make a masochist cringe, yet this can actually decrease performance because flexibility and sensitivity are sacrificed.

The majority of us have one foot that is slightly longer than the other. While this isn't a problem in most shoes and boots, it can be a problem in tight-fitting rock shoes. Size to the longer foot.

Try each pair on the climbing wall. The experienced salesperson won't ask vague questions like, "How do they feel?" Instead, she will inspect the shoes laced on your feet and ask about specific aspects of fit: "Are there air spaces around your toes?" "Is your heel snug?" "Does your foot twist inside while edging?" "Is a seam creating a pressure point?" (Ideal answers: no, yes, no, no.)

When you have ruled out all but two models, you may want to try on a few different sizes of each to confirm the best pair for you. Although the consistency is much better than it used to be, rock shoes are handmade and it's possible that one pair will be sweeter than another, even within the same size and model.

After you walk out the door with your new shoes, resist the temptation to head straight to the rock gym or crags. Once you get them dirty or sweaty, shoes cannot be returned to most stores. Take the time to reconfirm your choice by wearing them at home for a while longer.

Pressure points usually don't go away (they get more painful), and most shoes don't stretch longer (only wider). Assuming that the shoes are clean, you kept the box and receipt, and they weren't on closeout, you should be able to get an exchange or refund without any hassle if you decide you got the wrong shoes.

THE LAST IS FIRST

All shoes are built around lasts, which are plastic or wooden forms that resemble a human foot [Photo 8.4]. The biggest changes in rock shoes in the past few years have come from increasing sophistication of the lasts. Shoe designers have gained a greater understanding of anatomy and are sculpting lasts to maximize performance and improve fit, especially in the arch.

The shape of the last also determines how the shoe will function [Illustration 8.1]. With some shoes, the big toes are allowed to stay pointed forward in a natural anatomical position; climbing in such shoes will be comfortable all day long. As the toes are forced to point downward, the comfort also goes down, but the shoe becomes increasingly

WOMEN

In general, women have longer toes, a narrower forefoot, higher arches, lower anklebones, and a narrower heel than men. Given the minimal amount of material in a rock shoe versus a mountaineering boot, this does not present a major problem in obtaining a good fit for most women.

The most common fitting complaint among women is pressure on their anklebones. At present, few women-specific rock shoes are on the market. But narrower-fitting unisex (read: men's) shoes are also worthy contenders for many small-footed people.

KIDS

How to shop for the wee ones is a dilemma all parents face. Spending money on rock shoes they will soon outgrow may not be appealing, but look at the bright side—your kids could be into alpine $kiing.

Starting young climbers in an old pair of sneakers with sticky rubber glued to the bottom is one option, but this will quickly lead to a performance plateau. If you really want your child to enjoy this sport, there is no substitute for the real thing. It's probably best to size the shoes with at least one pair of thick socks so there is some growing room.

powerful for edging and pulling with the toes.

Performance and comfort can be augmented by curving the sole more toward the big toe [Illustration 8.2]. This asymmetric design is a more natural position than the traditional symmetric shape, which shoves the big toe over (and probably ruined some climbers' feet with bunions and hammertoes).

How the shoe is assembled around the last also affects performance [Illustration 8.3]:

- Board lasting. When the shoe is board-lasted, the insole (usually leatherboard or a synthetic composite) is nailed to the last, and the uppers are sewn and glued to this assembly. The result is a stiff, supportive shoe that can survive numerous resolings [Photo 8.5]. These are the best choice for many crack climbs, all-day edging, and general comfort.

- Slip lasting. The majority of rock shoes today are

Photo 8.4   Rock shoes assembled around lasts

made by sewing the upper into a sock [Photo 8.6] and slipping it over the last before gluing on the rands and sole. Slip-lasted shoes, which may or may not have a midsole, will generally be more sensitive, flexible, and lighter than board-lasted shoes, though they are not appropriate for all climbs or climbers. Since they get their support from compressing the feet, the fit must be tighter for optimal performance.

MORE DETAILS

Another part of rock shoes that has seen significant improvement in recent years is the rand. On the better shoes, complex shapes and a variety of

FLEXED

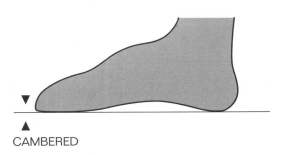

CAMBERED

Illustration 8.1   Last profiles

RESOLING

Keep a watchful eye on the outsoles and rands, particularly around the big toe, where they wear out first. Reglue any separations with Barge cement as soon as they appear.

Although it's possible to do a good job of resoling your own shoes, the odds are against it your first time. This is something which practice, and the right tools, make perfect.

Often, if the shoes aren't too far worn, the cobbler can put on a half sole instead of replacing the entire sole. If you put off the repair until you've worn a hole in the rand by your big toe, you can expect to spend considerably more and risk getting back shoes that don't fit the same as before.

Since turnaround time can be several weeks during the height of the climbing season, it's a good idea to have your shoes resoled long before your big trip.

Photo 8.5   Rock shoes: board-lasted lace-up, board-lasted Velcro, slip-lasted lace-up, slip-lasted slipper

  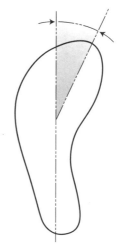

Symmetric   Asymmetric   Radically asymmetric

Illustration 8.2   Last symmetry

materials are used to minimize empty space inside the shoe and to cajole—rather than cram—your foot into the proper position.

Most rock shoes have uppers made of split-grain leather, although the quality varies. The addition of a lining helps increase support and minimize stretch—and keeps your feet from turning bizarre colors—but decreases flexibility somewhat. Some shoes have partial linings to give the best of both worlds while others use webbing strips to control stretch.

Compared to basic design and fit, the other details about rock shoes are of minor importance. The materials used in the uppers affect weight and breathability but quality of construction has more to do with durability.

Don't sweat too much over rubber. After Boreal introduced sticky rubber in 1983, there was a lot of competition to improve performance. All the brands are fairly competitive nowadays, and you can always resole your shoes with the flavor du jour if you want.

If you are new to climbing, it will pay to choose a pair of shoes with thicker rands; poor technique

Board-lasted

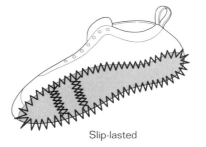

Slip-lasted

Illustration 8.3   Board and slip lasting

Photo 8.6   Sewing the uppers of a slip-lasted rock shoe

wears these out fast. If you are hooked and intend to stick with the sport, you will save money in the long run by springing for a better-quality pair of shoes to start with. It's cheaper to grow into something ability-wise than to quickly outgrow it and need to upgrade. You are also likely to get more resoles out of a higher-grade shoe.

Two pairs of shoes are desirable for the active climber. You don't want to be sidelined because your only pair has to be resoled in the middle of the season, and you get more versatility with two. Three pairs can be useful to cover the range of climbing, but you really don't need five or six pairs of rock shoes unless you have a fetish or get pro deals.

SHOE AND FOOT CARE

I've heard lots of elaborate methods for breaking in shoes before you climb, from soaking to stretching. After having tested dozens of models, I don't believe the tricks are needed—just wear the shoes.

When you get home from a day of climbing, be sure to air out your shoes. Sweat-soaked shoes left in your pack will cultivate critters that could be used for biological warfare. Not only does this result in horrendous odors but it also hastens the demise of the uppers.

If your shoes' odor brings tears to your eyes when you pull them from a pack, it may be time for drastic actions. Among the folk remedies I've heard are tossing in cedar chips or car fresheners, throwing the shoes in a washing machine or storing them in the freezer. Commercial foot powders work great at controlling smells. For hard cases, wash the uppers with soap and water and air-dry the shoes in the shade. If all else fails, try sizing your next pair so you can wear socks in them.

Sticky rubber is prone to picking up dirt, which reduces its friction. Before a redpoint or comp, wash the soles with water (never use solvents) and a rag, then allow them to air-dry, followed by lengthwise rubbing with a stiff brass-bristle brush.

The rubber on shoes that have been stored for a while will harden from oxidization (ozone is the main culprit), so it may take more aggressive brushing to remove the outer layer and restore their stickiness. Some climbers carry their rock shoes in storage sacks to help keep contaminants at bay.

Most important: Never leave your shoes in a car on a hot day. The heat will delaminate them.

Climbers have lots of theories on why rock shoes cost so much (conspiracies, price gouging, and marketing are some), but it really boils down to two words: skilled labor. Open up one of the newer shoes and look inside, all the way up to the toe, at the elaborate, smooth seams. Study how the rands are applied to produce variable tension, and notice the little details that increase comfort.

Desirable Features

- Two heel loops, or a really big one, make it easier to pull the shoes onto your feet.
- More ventilation is usually a good thing.
- Unless you're trying to climb 5.14, padding in the tongue should be copious.
- Flat laces are more comfortable and stay tied better than round ones.
- Seams in the toe and heel region should be smooth.
- The top edge of a shoe shouldn't bite your ankle.
- On hot, sunny days, light is right. Black or dark-colored shoes are mini-ovens.
- Quality leather or a lining keeps your feet from turning weird colors.

CHALK AND CHALK BAGS

What sticky rubber is to our feet, chalk is to our hands. Made from magnesium carbonate, chalk absorbs sweat and enhances friction. The great boulderer John Gill is credited with bringing chalk to the climbing world from gymnastics in the early 1960s . . . and white splotches have marred the rock ever since.

Although chalk is unsightly, most climbers rely on it to climb near their limits. Chalk is sold as loose powder, as compressed blocks that you crush, or in mesh balls that slow usage and prevent spills. Some deluxe brands have additional drying agents, although it isn't clear that they really help.

Typically, chalk is carried in a small bag worn

on a belt. A good chalk bag has a wide mouth that stays open when needed yet closes securely to keep chalk from getting everywhere. Better chalk bags are also hinged in the middle to help prevent spills and have a pile lining to hold loose chalk and make chalking easier.

For bouldering, larger chalk buckets are set on the ground nearby. These are handy for groups of climbers and keep a cloud of chalk from exploding when you land on your back, as often happens when wearing a chalk bag.

Colored chalk, intended to match the rock, has been tried by several companies but has never achieved performance equal to the white stuff. Likewise, chalk alternatives created for other sports have proved unsuitable for climbing.

Although it's harmless to the rock, chalk is one of the main issues that threaten access. Everyone must do their part to minimize visual impact that disturbs nonclimbers. Along with periodic chalk cleanups at popular areas, climbers can keep crags clean by avoiding "psychological dips," brushing off chalky holds after an ascent, and always erasing "tick marks."

At the famous sandstone boulders of Fontainebleau, near Paris, France, climbers have long used powdered resin to enhance their grip. Called "pof" and carried in a handkerchief tied into a ball, the resin mixes with your sweat to create a tacky compound. However, resin also clogs the rock and never washes off (as chalk does), so it should not be used anywhere else in the world.

CHAPTER 9

HELMETS

I HAVE A VERY TANGIBLE FEEL FOR HOW much force it takes to break bones. If my head, instead of my knee, had hit that tree while skiing, I almost certainly would not be writing these words. That doesn't mean I'm a born-again, proselytizing helmet zealot. But my skiing accident made me look closer at why I don't always wear a helmet for climbing.

Like most of you, I never think twice about protecting my head for alpine or ice climbing, where falling projectiles are the rule, not the exception. Wearing a helmet while mountain biking is also a no-brainer; I won't even ride with someone who doesn't have one.

Yet, like most of you, I have stubbornly resisted wearing a helmet when rock climbing, despite knowing about many deaths that might have been prevented had the climber been using a brain bucket.

KNOW THE RISKS

When you're standing around the base of El Cap or any other tall cliff, cogitate on this: A carabiner dropped from 650 ft. (200 m) up will approach the ground at 140 mph (225 kph) and hit with roughly the same force as an 11 lb. (5 kg) rock falling 6 ft. (2 m). You never climb big walls? Well, say you're pulling a tenuous move and pop off for a 20 ft. (6 m) fall that flips you upside-down. Depending on your weight and the nature of the fall, your head can impact the rock with thirty to fifty times the force of that 'biner or block.

Would a helmet save you from a granite missile or the impact of a fall? There's a lot of anecdotal evidence from the climbing world of smashed helmets and relatively uninjured climbers, but there's little real data. However, a look at the bike market gives a good indication.

In 1991, only 18 percent of the estimated 66.9 million bike riders in the United States wore helmets regularly—and 836 cyclists died. By 1997, the number of bike riders was up to 80.6 million, but with routine helmet use increasing to 50 percent, the number of cycling deaths actually decreased, to 808.

Just as important as a helmet's ability to ward off violent death may be its potential to prevent traumatic brain injury (TBI).

If you get off lucky and don't require rehab, a moderate brain injury will cost only about $18,000. The average medical and nonmedical cost (e.g., home modifications, vocational rehabilitation, health insurance) for a severe TBI runs nearly $196,000—and can reach $4 million. If you need it, acute rehab will typically keep you hospitalized for 55 days with the meter ticking at $1000 per day. Even death isn't a cheap way out since brain injury fatalities average $455,000. This all adds up to $48.3 billion dollars spent annually in the United States for care of brain injury victims.

Obviously, the majority of the 1.9 million annual TBIs occur in highway accidents, yet sports and physical activities make up 20 percent of that total. TBIs account for 34 percent of all injury deaths in the United States.

About 80 percent of TBIs are mild and generally considered inconsequential—you often hear something like, "He was back climbing a week later." However, follow-up neurological studies are rarely performed on such patients, and the impairments that are not at first apparent can be significant and long-lasting—even devastating. Violence and antisocial behavior are often associated with mild TBI. (There's a significant incidence among the homeless and death-row inmates.)

Other cognitive and emotional functions may be affected by accidents that don't even send people to the hospital. A good knock on the ol' noggin can result in motor, perceptual, speech, and language deficiencies, as well as regulatory disturbances and personality changes.

Mild TBIs are particularly insidious because there are usually no obvious mental or physical impairments. However, they often result in dramatic life-altering changes that friends and relatives don't really understand. It's even worse for survivors of severe TBIs, who typically experience depression, anxiety, and alienation.

Unlike other tissues, damaged neurons are incapable of repairing themselves; all brain injuries, except for swelling, are permanent. Fortunately, it is possible to compensate by retraining other parts of the brain, though it is a slow process and can only go so far. Even ten years after an accident, patients will still be making progress in their recovery.

The good news is that helmets can greatly reduce the chances of such injuries. And the even better news is that modern climbing helmets are so light and unobtrusive that I have run out of excuses for not wearing them.

DESIGN AND CONSTRUCTION

Climbing helmets can be divided into three basic types: fiberglass shell, plastic shell, and "microshell" [Photo 9.1].

Without question, fiberglass shells are the most durable—and the heaviest. The best are made with epoxy resin and woven cloth of glass, Kevlar, and/or carbon that is vacuum-molded. Substituting polyester resin, chopped fibers, and conventional molding substantially reduces cost and durability, but can still give decent protection.

Stiff, plastic-shelled helmets have gained popularity in recent years and now comprise the bulk of the market. These are generally lighter than fiberglass helmets, but also more susceptible to degradation from ultraviolet light, chemicals, and general wear and tear. Despite their shorter life spans, helmets with stiff plastic shells offer both good protection and value.

Nearly all hard-shell helmets rely upon a suspension system to absorb the energy of an impact. In theory, these can survive multiple impacts better than foam-core helmets, which permanently deform or break after a single blow. However, all helmet makers warn you to retire a helmet after a severe impact because of the potential for hidden damage.

The newest generation of climbing helmets uses thin plastic over expanded polystyrene (EPS) foam. The thin microshell does not spread or absorb impacts, as rigid shells do, but merely protects the foam inside.

These new-wave helmets are designed to give much better protection against front, rear, and side impacts than most traditional styles. They are also

Photo 9.1   Helmets: microshell, plastic, and fiberglass

light, comfortable, and better looking than other helmets. The drawbacks: they are relatively bulky, have a limited life span, and at present, are rather pricey.

STANDARDS

All climbing helmets are made to pass the CEN standard, which is derived from outdated UIAA helmet tests. These tests are in some cases tougher and in other cases weaker than those for bike and ski helmets. It's fair to say they have not kept up with current climbing technology or trends and could be greatly improved.

Also, it's important to realize that all of the helmet standards are pass/fail—they tell you nothing about the level of protection offered by various models. While some helmets are undoubtedly better than others, we are left guessing by the industry.

Helmet tests were conceived in the days when climbers rarely fell, and thus the emphasis was placed on protection from rockfall instead of protecting the head from impact against the rock. Very demanding tests for falling objects were devised, using a heavy blunt object weighing 5 kg (11 lbs), dropped from 2 m (6.5 ft.). Another test drops a 1.5-kg (3.3-lb.), pointed cone four times from the same height onto slightly different spots on the helmet. These standards make climbing helmets far superior to bike or kayaking helmets for protection from falling objects.

But climbers fall far more frequently these days, and the UIAA standard included only a minor frontal-impact test. As an afterthought, the CEN standard added the same test for side and rear impacts (a 5 kg flat plate dropped half a meter). According to Ed Becker, executive director of the Snell Memorial Foundation, which sets helmet standards, climbing helmets receive only about a quarter of the testing for such impacts as bike helmets get. For protection during tumbling or swinging falls, most climbing helmets leave a lot to be desired.

So can you just use a bike, ski, kayaking, or hockey helmet for climbing? Nope, because they offer very limited protection from falling objects. The ideal climbing helmet—lightweight, full protection from falling objects and front, side, and rear impacts, plus real durability—has yet to be designed. Nevertheless, one fact remains clear: Almost any helmet is better than no helmet in a head-threatening accident.

DETAILS

Besides the obvious features of shell type and suspension system, there are other details to consider when shopping for a helmet. Among the most important is ease of adjustment, particularly for alpine climbing, where you often need to add or remove a hat. Many helmets use a fidgety buckle behind your head that is awkward to adjust; others use Velcro that isn't much better. The best helmets adjust sizing with the turn of a dial.

The buckles on many helmets are a nuisance to open and close, especially with gloves on. Others are too long, making them uncomfortable. Try out the buckles before buying.

All climbing helmets have a provision for attaching a headlamp, though some of these systems are a bit of a jury-rig. It is helpful to have keeper cords both in front and back to hold the light in place [Photo 9.2]; otherwise the headband tends to creep up the smooth helmet shell. For the newer microshell helmets, you need to buy an accessory kit to hold a headlamp.

Examine the inside of the helmet for protruding rivets and sharp edges, which are especially common on cheaper models. In theory, the suspension should hold your head away from these lacerators, but you're better off if they aren't there. Absorbent headbands are nice in theory but tend to get rather skanky after a while, and they still don't keep sweat out of your eyes if you're working hard.

Photo 9.2   A good helmet holds a headlamp in place fore and aft. This one has detachable plugs for the ventilation holes to increase warmth and dryness.

LIFE SPAN

No matter what the construction or materials, your helmet has a limited life span. If it receives a major impact—as in, "I'd be history without it"—then you got your money's worth and you need to retire it.

Hopefully, you will use your helmet for years without ever really "needing" it. But all of those little knocks and bangs, hours of ultraviolet light exposure, and the steady evaporation of plasticizers have a cumulative effect. The standard recommendation is to retire all helmets after five years of use. In practice, this is far too conservative for the better fiberglass helmets, which can last ten or more years, and very optimistic for the lighter, microshell helmets, for which two years is probably more realistic with frequent use.

Research by the British Mountaineering Council in the early 1990s showed that plastic helmets aged at an alarming rate, especially when used in a school environment. They found that many four-year-old helmets would not pass the CEN impact test. The deterioration was strongly correlated with mileage; plastic helmets were pretty much trashed after two years of heavy use.

Ultimately, retiring a helmet is like retiring a rope—do it when your gut instinct outweighs the pain to your wallet. Write the date you started wearing the helmet on a piece of tape inside in a protected spot.

The question of durability is particularly important on an expedition or big wall, where you will not have the option of replacing a broken helmet. The lightest helmets can break even if sat upon or dropped while inside a pack. For remote climbs, you're better off with a sturdier brain bucket that can withstand some abuse.

By the way, if you simply must decorate your

helmet with stickers, it's safer to choose a fiberglass or microshell helmet. The adhesive used in some stickers can significantly weaken thermoplastics, though I have not heard of a helmet's failure actually being traced to this cause. Applying paint to plastic helmets is an absolute no-no.

THE RIGHT FIT

Probably two-thirds of the helmets worn by climbers are not adjusted properly, and the level of protection can be severely compromised by the level of flip-flop on your head. To make matters worse, the instruction manuals included with most climbing helmets have terrible fitting instructions.

Finding the right size and shape is the first step; be prepared to accept that the helmet you want may not be the helmet that fits. Climbers with particularly small or large heads may have a particularly hard time with fitting.

Unfortunately, there are no extra-large climbing helmets on the market. Indeed, the only option for size 8 (24½ in. or 62 cm in circumference) and larger may be the Bell Kinghead, a bike helmet that fits up to size 8¼ (26 in. or 66 cm).

Parents may also opt for bike helmets for their children because there are more models to choose from at reasonable prices. Remember, however, that bike helmets offer very limited protection from falling objects.

The bike world figured out long ago that a lot of people have ponytails that need to be accommodated in helmet designs. If you have long hair, your choice of climbing helmets that fit properly may be limited. Try them out first.

Making the basic adjustments (circumference and chin strap) is pretty easy on most helmets.

They should be snug but not uncomfortably tight; if you can get two fingers under the chin strap, it's too loose. For winter climbs, be sure the helmet can be adjusted to accommodate a hat. By the way, helmet liners may look dorky, but they are great in the cold and are more comfortable than standard stocking caps or balaclavas (which often raise the helmet too high, decreasing protection).

The hard part of helmet fitting is getting the Y-junctions on the straps in the correct spot (just below the ears) and properly tensioned. Most climbers' helmets fail what I call the Homer Test. Smack the heel of your hand upward against your helmeted forehead while saying "Doh!" Odds are, you now have a large expanse of exposed skull asking to be beaned. This means that either the Y-junction is too far to the rear or the front straps are too loose. The result? You will not be protected in a tumbling fall.

When the straps are properly adjusted, the helmet brim should be three finger-widths above the bridge of your nose. The bottom of the helmet should not lift more than an inch, no matter how the helmet is tugged. It may take 20 minutes to get the perfect fit, or to discover that a helmet is simply incompatible with your skull. However, this is time well spent. Ignore at your own peril.

CHAPTER 10

ICE TOOLS

SNOW AND ICE ARE AT THE VERY HEART of mountaineering. Indeed, the ice ax is a universal symbol of the noble sport. According to French alpinist extraordinaire Gaston Rébuffat, the ice ax "is at once the mountaineer's tool and his closest companion" (*On Ice and Snow and Rock,* 1970).

Only two decades ago, the standard practice was to use a 70 cm (28 in.) ice ax for everything from snow climbs to vertical water ice. Now the difference between alpine climbing gear and that for waterfall ice is as great as that between mountain and road bikes. While they share some attributes, it is better to discuss them separately.

MOUNTAINEERING AXES

From the mid-1800s—when the Grivel family began modifying pickaxes—until the mid-1970s, ice-ax heads were hand-forged and fitted to a wooden shaft. At first the shafts were about 1.5 m (60 in.) long and designed for assistance in walking on glaciers, chopping steps in ice, and self-arresting falls on steep snow; picks were straight and long, and had no teeth.

The advent of crampons with front points in the 1930s opened up steeper terrain, and ice axes gradually shrank. Today, mountaineers usually carry an ice ax of about 70 cm [Photo 10.1]. While curved picks date back at least to 1938, they did not gain popularity until about 1966 when Pit Schubert and Yvon Chouinard redeveloped the concept for *piolet traction* (pulling up on the shaft of a tool with the pick planted in ice). The final major step in the evolution of modern mountaineering axes came in the 1970s, when metal shafts were developed.

LENGTH

The length of your ice ax is primarily determined by the steepness of the terrain you intend to climb, but your height and personal preference enter into the decision too. For most alpine climbers, 70 cm is the ideal length. When the ice ax is held like a cane, *piolet canne*, the tip of the spike should just reach the anklebone.

Longer shafts provide stronger anchors when sunk to the hilt in snow and are comfortable for relatively flat glacier walking. However, they are unwieldy on moderate slopes and are heavier;

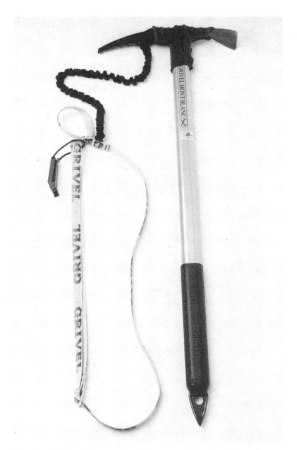

Photo 10.1   Mountaineering ax with a body leash and a rubber grip on the head for warmth

trekking poles may be a better choice. A shorter shaft, such as 55 cm to 60 cm, is often preferred on steep alpine climbs, but will be more difficult to use for self-arrest.

HEADS

Ice-ax heads are no longer forged by hand from steel. Instead, they're either cut or stamped from sheet metal—like cookies—with the adze welded on (the majority) or machine forged [Photo 10.2]. Either method yields a very strong, relatively inexpensive product.

Because you frequently use your ax like a walking stick, its comfort in your hand is an important consideration. Many of the "cookie-cutter" heads can be made more comfortable by rounding the edges with a file (this also reduces wear and tear on your gloves). With few exceptions, today's machine-forged heads are more comfortable right off the shelf.

Aluminum is used for the heads of the very lightest ice axes, often used for ski mountaineering and adventure racing. However, unless weight is absolutely critical, a steel head is a better choice because it is stronger and more durable, especially when you need to pound the ax into the snow for a belay anchor. Aluminum heads also tend to bounce off when swung into ice or even hard snow because they have so little mass.

While omnipresent for waterfall-ice tools, modular heads are not necessary for mountaineering. It is unlikely you will ever wear out a pick unless you are gonzo abusive. Ice axes with interchangeable parts tend to be much heavier, less comfortable, and more expensive than conventional axes.

For extended periods of snow climbing, particularly in very cold weather, you may want to pad the center of the head with foam insulation. Commercial versions are less bulky and easier to remove than pads that are duct-taped into place.

Photo 10.2   Forged heads (left) with smooth, contoured edges can be more comfortable in your hand, and kinder to gloves, than welded heads (right).

PICKS

The old debate continues between positive versus negative pick clearance [Illustration 10.1]. Pick clearance makes no difference on soft snow; for ice, a positive-clearance pick is superior—it penetrates deeper when it is weighted and doesn't bounce out when swung into the ice. The potential disadvantage of a positive-clearance pick is a greater likelihood of having the tool ripped from your hands during a self-arrest on hard snow; a pick with negative clearance is more likely to bring you to a gradual stop. In reality, however, no pick works on hard snow or ice once you're a few seconds into the slide and going fast. It is very easy to hand-file a negative clearance back to positive, but not the other way around (without shortening the pick).

Chopping steps is very nearly a lost art, so no one makes ice axes with straight (perpendicular to the shaft) picks anymore. General-purpose ice axes have curved picks with angles of 70° to 75° to the shaft. Tools with steeper pick angles (60° to 65°) are better for steep climbing, but not quite as good for chopping. Radically steep picks (less than 60°) work well only on vertical ice. Bear in mind that chopping steps is still an important technique for

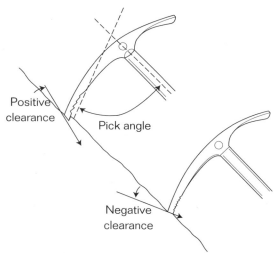

Illustration 10.1   Positive- and negative-clearance picks

the mountaineer. For short sections of ice, it can be easier and safer than stopping to put on crampons; for load carries on expeditions it can save you lots of energy; and it could even save you if you ever lose or break a crampon.

Teeth on a pick increase its holding power in hard snow or ice, but make it harder to withdraw the pick. For this reason the pick on the typical general-purpose ice ax is moderately angled with teeth along the lower edge of only its distal half (near the tip). Sharp teeth near the shaft perhaps add more security but can tear up gloves.

ADZES

After years of experimentation with adze design (droops, curves, scalloped edges, etc.), most companies have gone back to what works best for all-around use—minimal droop (75° to 80°), relatively flat, with a straight edge. If finished well, this is more comfortable in the hand and is efficient at chopping steps, bollards, and ledges. The only advantage a steeply drooped (70° or less), curved adze has is in rotten snow and ice, where it is used like a pick.

SPIKES

The spike should be made of steel and have a symmetric, pointed shape. Avoid ice axes with spikes that are aluminum (dulls easily), asymmetric (works well in only one direction), or tubular (plugs with snow). Other than that, don't fret about the spike.

SHAFTS

Almost all ice-ax shafts are now made of oval-cross-section aluminum-alloy tubing, which is light, strong, and affordable. Although not as aesthetically pleasing as wood, and heat-robbing when noncoated, aluminum shafts are far more durable and are strong enough to pass the CEN test for shaft strength of "technical" ice tools: 4 kN (900 lbf), marked by a T inside a circle. A few ultralight axes meet the lesser standard for "basic" ice tools—2.5 kN (562 lbf), marked by B inside a circle—though even this is still stronger than most wood shafts.

About one-third of today's ice axes have a thick rubber coating on their lower half for improved grip, insulation, and vibration damping. Such shafts may not penetrate snow as easily, but they also resist pulling out better. More than half have smooth, painted shafts that are easier to plunge into firm snow. (The epoxy coating also provides a bit of insulation.) Several axes have a smooth, thin rubber coating on the lower shaft that combines the best of both worlds.

A frequently overlooked consideration is how much vibration is transmitted to your hand when using the ice ax as a walking stick, particularly on rock and ice. This is a subtle quality that is not readily quantifiable, but I can tell you that some axes ring like a tuning fork when the spike is rapped against a hard surface while others are very dampened. Dampening also helps reduce shattering of ice when setting the pick.

LEASHES

Leashes keep your ax with you should you fall or just suffer an episode of the dropsies. But not everyone likes them: Gaston Rébuffat claimed a leash "is an evasion, an easy way out and is in fact inadvisable: it can cause an accident and, in the case of a fall, injuries" (*On Ice and Snow and Rock,* 1970).

A wrist leash can be cumbersome when zigzagging up a slope—you may have to change hands every time you change direction. But when venturing into crevassed areas or mixed climbs, and when learning to climb, some sort of leash is a good idea. There are several nice commercial leashes available, or you can make one from nylon webbing [Illustration 10.2].

Many climbers prefer a long wrist leash (the length of the ice ax), particularly in steep terrain, because it reduces strain when hanging from the ax and when chopping steps. A long leash adds control to your blows, and you can clip into it at a belay. On the downside, if you lose control of the tool during a fall, it may be difficult to grasp as

you're falling—and it could impale or slash you.

Another option is a short wrist loop on a ring that slides along the shaft, keeping the ax nearby in a fall and when doing mixed climbing. Many axes come with a stop screw on the shaft to keep the loop from sliding off. If there isn't a stop screw, you can drill and tap a small hole for a screw. (A tight hose clamp will work, but that's as tasteless as wearing shorts over long underwear.) If you remove the screw, be sure to plug the hole with epoxy to keep water out of the shaft.

Some climbers prefer a body leash to avoid the hassle of zigzagging and to ensure that there is no chance of accidentally losing the tool. This usually consists of webbing that is long enough to reach from the ax head to the climber's harness or a shoulder sling. To prevent dragging or tripping, elastic cord is often strung inside the webbing so the extra length is there only when needed.

WATER-ICE TOOLS

Climbing ice is easy. Modern ice gear works so well that once-desperate routes that instilled terror in the hearts of aspirants are now considered moderate, suitable for teaching beginners. The result has been a surge in ice-climbing popularity, and standards at the top end today are pushed more on icy rock than on frozen waterfalls.

Climbing ice is also dangerous. Modern gear has not changed this other truth of the sport. Just because you can do the moves doesn't mean it is safe to do so. Even if ice protection were as reliable as rock pro, the consequences of a fall with all those sharp points attached to you are potentially much more severe.

Modern ice tools are so superior to those available a decade ago that it is hard to go wrong with your choice. However, tools vary widely in suitability for different styles of climbing, "feel," and price. If possible, borrow tools or participate in an ice demo before purchasing.

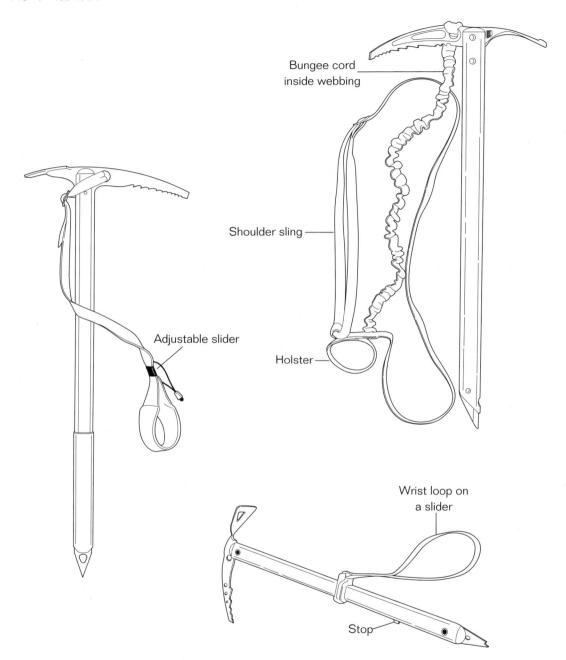

Illustration 10.2 Leashes: long wrist loop (left), short wrist loop on a slider (lower right), body leash (upper right)

SHAFT DESIGN

Your first consideration should be shaft design: straight, lower bend, upper bend, or compound bend [Photo 10.3].

Straight shafts are the traditional favorite for alpine climbs because they are easiest to plunge into snow. They also swing most naturally when reversed for hammering pitons. Simple webbing leashes on straight-shafted tools will be very supportive because of the angle of your wrist (a small "shelf" is formed).

Shafts with a lower bend have gained wide popularity for steep water ice. These offer a more natural swing for placements than do straight shafts, and you gain a bit of knuckle clearance (but will still bash them with bad technique). Lower-bend shafts also relax the angle on your wrist, so they require a much more supportive leash. Though I don't find bent shafts significantly harder to plunge into firm snow—assuming there is no funky spike—they may not resist pulling out as well as straight shafts. And most bent shafts are less effective for hammering; choking up often helps.

The newest innovation in shaft design is a bend near the top of the shaft. These tools provide extra clearance around bulges, making them superb for steep ice. However, they are somewhat less stable for dry tooling because the center of gravity is moved farther from the axis of rotation (a line between the tip of the pick and the spike). The upper bend can also interfere with hammering, particularly in tight places, because the shaft can hit the surface before the head does.

Compound bent shafts may appear bowed (a combination of a lower and upper bend) or S-shaped. While some of these are highly effective water ice tools, others leave a lot to be desired.

Bottom line: If you want one set of tools for water ice and mixed climbing, choose shafts with gradual bends—either low or high—that feel best for your swing.

SHAFT CONSTRUCTION

Most tools currently available feature 7000-series aluminum alloy shafts, though fiberglass, carbon fiber, and titanium alloys are also used. There can be significant differences in specifications of the aluminum alloy, temper, and extrusion. As with bicycle frames, this can affect the feel of the tool as well as its durability.

While the shafts and head attachments are generally quite durable, beware any shaft that has many holes (especially large ones) drilled in it, because they create stress points that may lead to failure.

One of the CEN tests for technical ice tools

Photo 10.3   Shafts: upper bend, lower bend, and straight

resembles a boot-ax belay with a 900 lbf (4 kN) force applied to the head for 1 minute. Another test simulates a "stein-puller" move, in which the head is fixed with the pick pointed upward and a 200 lbf (0.9 kN) downward load is applied to the shaft 50 cm from the head.

Strength is not the only consideration—some ice tools vibrate more than others during placements or hammering. You can get a feel for this by holding the tool at the grip, giving the tool a quick tap with a knuckle in several places, and noticing how much vibration reaches your hand. More dampened tools are better because they don't tend to shatter the ice. However, testing a tool on real ice will give you a much better feel for shaft vibration.

Shafts with thinner diameter grips will be more comfortable for those with small hands. But even those with large hands find that thinner shafts are less tiring to hold and easier to swing accurately. As Jeff Lowe puts it, "Try doing pull-ups on a 1 in. (2.5 cm) bar and then a 3 in. (7.6 cm) bar—the former is much easier."

The rubber on the grip provides insulation and a tacky surface to hold; it should be durable enough to not be destroyed when rapped against a crampon for clearing balled-up snow. Rubber on the upper shaft serves little function, adds weight, and makes holstering more difficult; some climbers even trim it off.

BALANCE

The overall weight of a tool is worth considering—particularly if you don't have arms like Arnold Schwarzenegger. The weight range among tools of the same length is more than 7 oz. (200 g). This may not seem like much until you try swinging them overhead for an hour. On the other hand, the lighter tool is more likely to bounce out and may take more strikes to get a solid plant.

Ideally, most of the tool's mass should be in the head, giving more momentum to your strikes. This weight distribution is one of the most notable distinctions between price-point tools and high-end models.

Many tools accept removable weights, which allow you to customize them with a heavier head for waterfalls or a lighter, less bulky design for mixed climbs. You can also make your own head weights with nuts and bolts from the hardware store.

LENGTH

For technical ice and mixed climbing, most people prefer a tool about 50 cm long (the only size available for many tools). Tools 45 cm in length are appreciated by some, but less than that is only useful for a third (spare) tool. Longer ice axes are unwieldy and impractical in the vertical realm.

HEADS

Modular heads have become the de facto standard [Photo 10.4]. Although hammers and adzes are seldom swapped, replacing picks is essential. In twenty years of climbing ice, I have never broken a pick, but I know other climbers who snap à couple every season. More often, picks just wear out from heavy use and lots of resharpening.

If you climb with a set of matched tools (often a good idea since it means fewer tools and spare parts), you will probably want a hammer head for your dominant hand to pound pitons. The weaker hand may appreciate an adze, which is typically 1 to 2 oz. (28 to 56 g) lighter. Climbing with two hammers is fine unless you have to cope with rotten ice or loose snow (common when topping out) or need to chop a belay step.

A larger surface area on the hammer allows more room for error when placing pins. Watch out for hammerheads with thin, unsupported necks; they have been known to snap off when hammering a piton or torquing in a dry placement. A smaller, angled adze works rather like a fat pick but is less effective than a broader, flatter adze for hacking out ledges.

Many of the newer hammers and adzes are designed for hooking on rock edges and camming in cracks. These still work well for pounding and chopping, and they certainly increase your options when the ice runs out. But staring at a sharp pick pointed

Photo 10.4   Modular head with a good hammering surface that can be wedged into cracks

at your eye while hooking can be unnerving.

Some tools come with aluminum head assemblies. Make sure these have a steel hammering surface or an anvil on the pick for pounding the tool into ice or snow. Steel heads are more robust—something you may appreciate if you have an adze and must start a screw or picket with the side of the tool head.

Many heads have holes large enough to accept a carabiner. However, if you clip these directly as part of your anchor, it tends to lever out the pick. It may be better to clip the leash (if full strength) or the spike for a more secure, multidirectional backup to your anchor.

Considering the price of ice tools, don't settle for sloppy workmanship such as metal filings trapped inside a shaft where they rattle around for eternity. Parts should disassemble easily, or field changes will be almost impossible. Bolt heads designed to be turned with the pick of another tool should be deep, or they may strip easily. Be leery of aluminum bolts or any that project too far; tool heads receive frightful abuse.

TOP PICKS

The style and angle of the pick, as well as the shape of its tip, greatly affect the tool's performance [Photo 10.5]. All of the current tools come with reverse-curve picks, though other styles may be available. These steeply angled picks, if properly designed, allow a good arm swing with a snap of the wrist at the end, which uses the mass of the head to set the pick.

Lesser angles, such as on drooped and classic

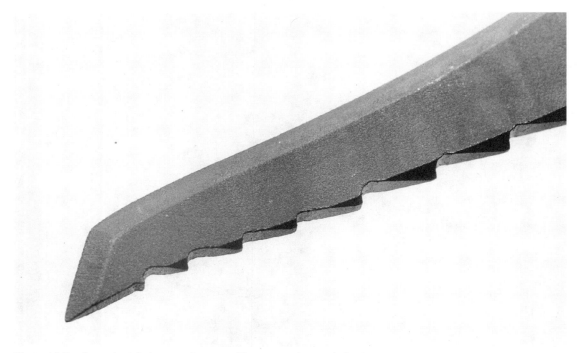

Photo 10.5 A stock pick that needs no modification and just a little sharpening

picks, allow a more natural arm swing but are much less effective at hooking chandeliered ice or dry tooling. If the pick angle is too steep, it requires a less efficient downward jab at the end of the swing.

A few companies offer half-tube picks for use in very brittle or soft ice. However, tubes are nearly worthless for dry tooling, mediocre for hooking, and notorious for breaking; dull easily; and are a hassle to sharpen. Leave them alone unless you have a specific need.

Thinner blades (3 mm or less at the tip) penetrate brittle ice with less fracturing than the standard thickness (4 mm). However, thin blades tend to be weaker, so be careful.

Any blade can bend, or even snap, if you wedge the pick in a crack and torque hard enough on the tool. The CEN test for pick strength is performed by clamping the first 2.5 cm (1 in.) in a vise and torquing on the shaft. The pick must not break nor permanently bend beyond a minimum range. The picks for technical tools are also fatigue-tested by clamping as before and torquing back and forth with a light load of 18 lbf (80 kN) at least 50,000 times (12,000 for tube-style picks).

Many picks require a fair amount of modification to the tip to bring them up to a suitable level of performance. Make sure the top edge is sharp (for easy removal), the bottom teeth are detuned (some are too grabby), the first tooth is steeply angled (for thin ice and dry tooling), and the point is angled back (so it won't bounce) and sharp [Illustration 10.3].

Picks will get a lot of filing as a result of the abuse they receive. It is best to do this by hand with a flat file; using a bench grinder can overheat the metal and ruin the temper. If the first notch is close to the end, you will file into it fairly quickly and need to replace the pick sooner than you may wish.

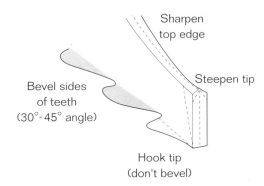

Sharpen top edge

Steepen tip

Bevel sides of teeth (30°-45° angle)

Hook tip (don't bevel)

Illustration 10.3 Tuning a pick: For maximum pick performance, sharpen the top edge and bevel the teeth inward (for easy removal); hook the first tooth (for thin ice and dry tooling; and angle the point back (so it won't bounce). Keep the tip razor-sharp.

Buy spare picks when you purchase a new tool, if there is anything left in your wallet. If you wait too long, the parts may no longer be available, and you could end up with an expensive dust collector.

SPIKES

The spikes almost seem an afterthought on technical ice tools, but they can affect performance [Photo 10.6]. Bulky spikes make the shaft harder to plunge into snow and to remove from a holster. Forward-raked spikes allow climbers on low-angle ice to grasp the shaft a few inches below the head and punch the pick and spike into the ice for a quick hold—call it *piolet* doorhandle—unless the rubber grip gets in the way. Many spikes must be sharpened or they will skate on hard ice.

Most spikes have a clip-in hole, used when the pick is driven to back up an anchor. Few companies rate these for strength, however, and there is no CEN standard for the strength of the spike's attachment to the shaft.

LEASHES

A well-designed leash is very helpful for climbing on steep terrain to prevent a severe forearm pump. Most tools come with wrist leashes, but some of them are pathetic—both uncomfortable and hard to use.

If the leash attaches at the head, the tool dangles out of the way when placing a screw or making mixed moves but makes one-handed retrieval harder [Illustration 10.4]. A leash attached at midshaft is much easier to flip back into your grasp but the tool hangs horizontally and can get in the way. Knots for attaching a leash are bulky, while large metal rings can make an annoying clank with each plant (tape over them).

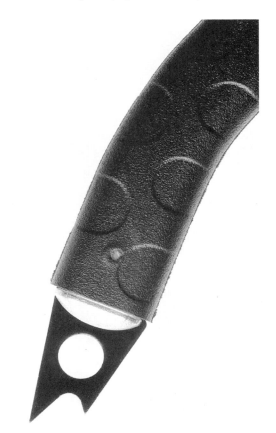

Photo 10.6 A good spike allows the shaft to be plunged into hard snow and contacts the ice when the pick is set.

While a couple of twists in the leash webbing keeps some climbers secure, most prefer a more solid lock around the wrists. Look for a system that can be operated with your teeth. However, the nicest ones can be opened and closed with just a hand movement. Avoid models that use Velcro because it is prone to freezing up.

Several removable leashes are now available that allow you to set a tool, unclip the leash, perform a task such as placing pro or wiping snow from your glasses, and then reclip the leash [Photo 10.7]. The early versions left much to be desired, but improvements continue, and remov-

Photo 10.7   A removable padded leash

able leashes could become the norm.

The stiffener on the wrist loop is important for mobility, comfort, and keeping the loop open. If the pad is too wide and stiff, it interferes with wrist flexibility and digs in. With the overhanging nature of some modern routes, a lot of time is spent hanging from the leash and comfort is important.

The majority of leashes are not runner-strength (there is no standard), and you should never expect a placed tool to hold a serious load as an anchor.

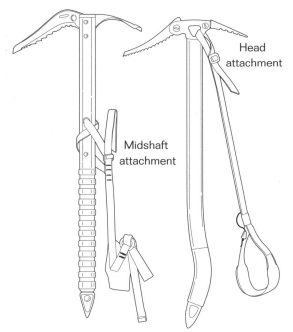

Head attachment

Midshaft attachment

Illustration 10.4   Head and midshaft leash attachment

CHAPTER 11

CRAMPONS

CRAMPONS HAVE COME A LONG WAY since Oscar Eckenstein redesigned them for climbing around 1910. (Basic crampons date to at least 500 B.C.) These were superior to nailed boots for steep snow and ice and reduced the need for chopping steps—a slow, laborious process.

The relatively soft snow conditions in the French Alps, where the Eckenstein crampons were developed, is conducive to a flat-footed style of climbing. "French technique" still has many advantages on low- to moderate-angle slopes, not the least of which is a reduction in calf strain.

In 1932, Laurent Grivel invented twelve-point crampons with two forward-slanting points that allowed ferociously steep snow and ice to be easily climbed. The Germans and Austrians first realized the potential of this method on the harder snow and ice common to their region. This "German technique" of front-pointing is particularly efficient on steep terrain when stiff-soled boots are used.

CRAMPON TYPES

In the past twenty years, crampons have undergone a surge in development leading to greater performance and specialization. There are now several types of crampons from which to choose.

INSTEP AND APPROACH

The lightest option for occasional stretches of snow is an instep crampon consisting of four spikes on a small plate. Attached with straps under the center of your foot, they are better than nothing but rather insecure.

An approach crampon is a full-length flexible plate with eight to ten spikes. These strap onto nearly any shoe or boot and give reasonable secu-

rity on moderate-angle slopes. Approach crampons are ideal for getting to the base of alpine rock climbs but not something you'd want for climbing a long, steep couloir.

ALPINE

For extensive walking and climbing on level and moderately angled snow and ice, a flexible crampon with a moderately stiff boot is the best choice [Photo 11.1]. This combination allows a more comfortable rolling action with each step—and helps keep the snow from balling up under the crampon.

There are two styles of flexible crampons: those with a hinge under the arch and those with a metal plate that bends with the boot. I can't tell much difference in performance, but the ones with big metal plates feel slippery on rock.

The front points on alpine crampons are oriented horizontally for greater surface area. These points work best on snow and soft ice and still do a commendable job on hard ice and rock.

For all-around versatility, especially walking and rock climbing, downward, or slightly forward-raked, "mixed" secondary points (the pair behind the front points), are the way to go. Crampons with sharply forward-raked secondary points, sometimes called ice points, are great with stiff-soled boots for alpine gullies where you are on your calves the whole way. When used with soft-soled boots, these raked secondary points give no support and poor mixed performance.

TECHNICAL

A rigid-framed crampon on a rigid-soled boot is the ultimate combination for climbing vertical ice—it reduces vibration and offers superior support. However, these are often clunky on level ground, prone to balling (a dangerous buildup of snow), and heavy.

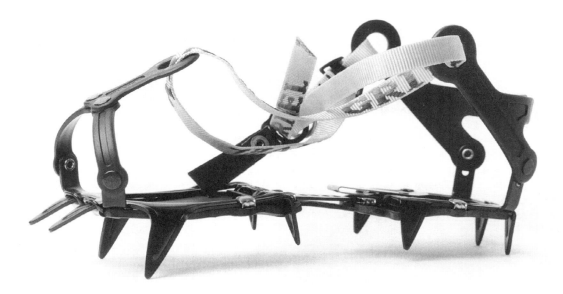

Photo 11.1 A ten-point alpine crampon with horizontal front points and a strap-on binding. A tooth is added on each side under the ball of the foot for twelve-point crampons.

For steep ice, crampons with vertically oriented front points rule because they slice into water ice with minimal fracturing. Vertical points are also superior on rock because they can be cammed in cracks or placed on minute dimples.

Dual front points are the traditional choice that offer the most support with the least calf fatigue [Photo 11.2]. If you want one pair of crampons for the widest range of conditions, these are probably the best bet.

However, mono points (a single front point on each crampon) are superior for nearly all steep ice and mixed conditions [Photo 11.3]. The mono allows your foot to pivot on small holds for dropknees and backsteps; you can take advantage of small divots and thin cracks in rock or ice; and you

Photo 11.2 The vertical dual points of a technical crampon resemble ice ax picks.

Photo 11.3 Vertical mono point and forward rake of the secondary points provide tripod stability.

can toe-in to pick holes for greater efficiency and ice preservation (something your second appreciates on thin routes). Alex Lowe claimed, "Monos are much more precise—and more fun."

HYBRID SYSTEMS

In between the extremes of rigid boot/rigid crampon and flexible boot/flexible crampon is the nebulous area of hybrid packages. Flexible crampons used with rigid boots essentially become rigid but tend to have more vibration than with rigid crampons. Rigid crampons on flexible boots have a greater potential for popping off, as well as stress-fracturing the crampon, but some combinations work quite well. In both cases, you usually end up with equipment that is better on steep terrain but not quite as good on either the flats or vertical ice.

Another potential setup frequently attempted is using crampons with telemark ski boots. Technically, it works, if you can get a good fit with a crampon that has a toe bail (sometimes tough). The problem is that telemark boots make lousy mountaineering boots. Because of the square toe, flexible forefoot, and stiff ankle, they are poor when kicking steps up a snow slope, and they are lousy on rock. Nevertheless, crampons do allow you to climb up what you are about to ski down.

ATTACHMENT METHODS

To strap or to clip? Attaching crampons with straps is traditional, and it still has advantages: many hiking and older mountaineering boots have insufficient welts to safely accommodate clip-on crampons, and overboots often require straps to hold the crampons. Nowadays straps are made of neoprene (best) or nylon webbing and use fast and easy lacing systems—you should be able to lace your crampons wearing mittens.

Clip-on crampons are more convenient, and if you're wearing leather boots, they won't impede your circulation the way crampon straps can (not a problem with plastic boots) [Photo 11.4]. Some models of clip-ons are available with toe straps instead of bails—they're just as easy to use as bails

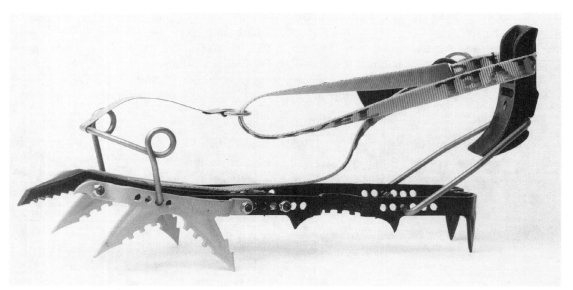

Photo 11.4 Technical ice crampon with clip-on binding system

and may work with overboots. Although you can easily clip a crampon wearing mittens, the safety straps on some models might require barehanded dexterity. Quick-release plastic buckles are used on some safety straps, but I've seen so many break that I don't trust them for this vital job.

I am leery of heel clamps that use cables rather than solid metal rods—although cables offer greater adjustability, they're more susceptible to breaking. Cables wouldn't stop me from buying a pair of crampons that fit well, but I'd carry spare cables on an expedition—with nuts and bolts—just in case.

Because few clip-on models have side posts (most strap-ons do), a tight fit is especially important to prevent lateral movement of the midsection. This can be a problem with soft-heeled leather boots because the heel lever can put painful pressure on your foot.

FIT

Achieving a good crampon-to-boot fit is so important that this should be the determining factor in selecting a pair of crampons. If there is any movement at all, you won't be secure when you need security most: on a section of steep ice, with no pro, looking at the slide of a lifetime.

The crampon's front points should extend past the front of the boot by 3 to 4 cm (about an inch)—based on personal preference and the conditions you typically encounter. If there are side and rear posts, they should fit snugly to the boot, so that if you pick the boot up and shake it, the crampon stays in place. (Do not try to bend them; this can stress the tempered metal and greatly increase the chance of breakage.) Heel points should lie beneath, without extending past, the rear edge of the boot.

Crampons with toe bails and heel levers typically do not fit all boots—and not just those lacking deep welts. There are so many variables (toe width and shape, heel width, sole thickness, etc.) that it's just not possible to fit everything.

Some toe bails fit better than others, and it is difficult to bend the hardened steel (install boot and apply hammer). Some heel wires are too narrow for some boots, which makes them unnecessarily hard to close. The heel lever should closely contour to your boot, especially if you climb in leather, or a painful pressure point can result.

The best advice is to try several models of crampons to find the best fit; don't just take the pair a friend recommends or the clerk hands you. If you will be using supergaiters or overboots, be sure to take them with your boots to the fitting. Crampons are difficult to mail-order—it's unlikely you'll get the right fit unless the catalog company also sells the boots you own.

Learn how to fit and repair your own crampons (carry spare parts and tools), and test them before going on a major climb. Practice putting them on at home before you have to do it in the dark with frozen hands.

Ease of adjustability of crampon length is a non-issue as long as you just use your own single and double boots; the length difference is easily accommodated by adjusting the heel lever.

CARE

Crampons rarely break these days as long as they are properly adjusted and maintained. The CEN requires that downward spikes withstand 270 lbf (1.2 kN), dual front points 337 lbf (1.5 kN), and mono points 450 lbf (2 kN).

To avoid problems with rust, dry your crampons and spray them with WD-40 after each trip. Periodically inspect the straps and check the tightness of all bolts and rivets. If any of the points are badly bent or you find stress fractures, it is time to replace parts or retire the crampons. Keep all of your points fairly sharp with a hand file, but don't get zealous about it unless you anticipate hard ice.

ACCESSORIES

Wet snow clumping under your crampons can be a serious, potentially life-threatening, problem. Most companies now offer very durable anti-balling plates as an accessory—I consider them a necessity, even for technical crampons [Photo 11.5].

You can make your own by cutting thick plastic bleach bottles to shape and taping or wiring the outlines in place—these work but get ripped up quickly and feel slick on rock.

For transporting crampons, I prefer using a crampon bag (especially when traveling) or just strapping them unguarded to the top of my pack. Many people use the rubber point protectors that resemble spiders, but I find they are both a nuisance and don't last long.

Photo 11.5   Anti-balling plates to prevent snow from clumping between the points are a necessity.

CHAPTER 12

SNOW AND ICE PROTECTION

THE TERM "SNOW AND ICE PROTECTION" is almost an oxymoron since, given the highly variable nature of the medium, it is always questionable whether the gear will really protect you if you fall. While popping off a rock route is usually no big deal, it is a most unwise practice when climbing on snow or ice. Even when the gear does hold, you run a high risk of puncture wounds from sharp points or a broken ankle from crampon teeth stopping cold.

SNOW ANCHORS

The first rule of using snow anchors: Try to get a good rock anchor. Because you often don't have this luxury, the second rule of using snow anchors is: Recheck them constantly. Which brings up the third rule of using snow anchors: Don't trust them.

It is true that in good, firm snow, properly set flukes and pickets can be remarkably strong (though nobody makes any holding-power claims).

It is equally true that in the real world, ideal conditions rarely exist, at least for long.

FLUKES

A snow fluke (or deadman) is like an aluminum shovel blade with a cable attached to its center [Photo 12.1]. If properly placed, the fluke dives into the snow when loaded, providing a dynamic belay. I witnessed a test in which a fluke pulled by six people traveled almost 10 m under the snow before stopping. To be effective, the angle of placement—45° to the direction of loading—is vital; otherwise, the fluke can fly out [Illustration 12.1]. The better models have cable stops that maintain this angle. It is also important to dig a slot for the cable—or *flukus ejectus*.

PICKETS

A snow picket is basically a giant stake that is pounded into the snow at a 60° angle to the direction of loading. These tend to work best in snow or ice too hard for flukes but not hard enough for ice screws.

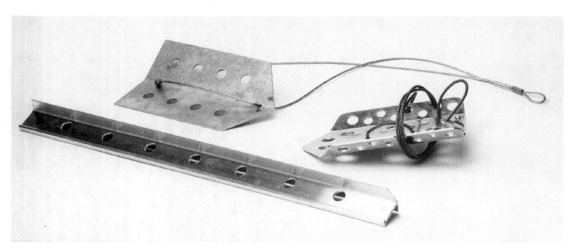

Photo 12.1   Snow flukes are more compact but pickets rack better and are faster to place.

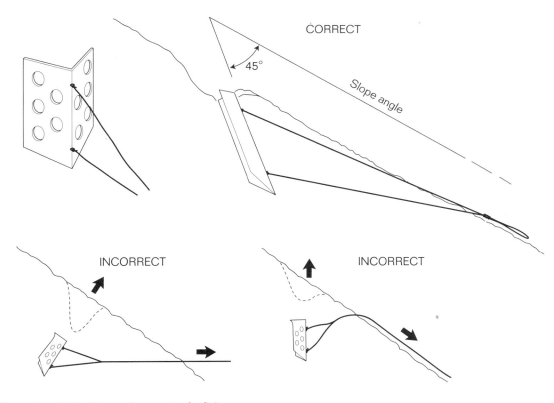

Illustration 12.1 Proper placement of a fluke

All things being equal, holding power is dependent upon both surface area and rigidity (the stiffer the better) of the picket. If you are using pickets, you will find it handy to have an ice hammer with you, although you can use the side of your ice ax's head to pound in the picket. A picket (as well as many ice axes) may be buried horizontally and tied off at its midpoint for use as an effective deadman in softer snow conditions.

Shorter (2 ft. or 60 cm) pickets are probably the easiest snow anchors to carry on a rack, an important consideration when leading on a 100 m (300 ft.) rope. Although it may be tempting to drill lots of holes to lighten your snow pickets, this can seriously compromise their strength and is strongly discouraged. Pickets usually have carabiner holes for racking and clipping runners, but the best have

pre-attached steel cable and reinforced hammering surface.

ICE PROTECTION

First rule of ice climbing: Don't fall. Yeah, yeah, I know. Ice screws can hold a huge force—when the ice is solid, the placement is perfect, the planets are favorably aligned, and your karma is good. However, it's impossible to predict how strong ice pro is in the real world because the variables are nearly infinite.

SCREW DESIGN

The biggest recent improvement in ice screws is the quality of machining, which greatly affects how easily they place [Photo 12.2]. Sharp, beveled teeth, a smooth finish (inside and outside), and a slightly larger tip diameter all help reduce the amount of force needed to screw into hard ice. Give your screws a tune-up with a file as needed, and don't clear the ice core by knocking the threads against your crampon.

Steel screws with a shaft diameter of about 17 mm have become the standard because of their strength, durability, and ease of use. Titanium and aluminum screws are 1 to 2 oz. (28 to 56 g) lighter. However, these screws usually have a larger diameter, which increases their holding power in softer ice but also makes them harder to place.

Look for hangers roughly 3 in. (8 cm) long with a right-angle bend so that the clip-in hole is perpendicular to the ice, orienting the carabiner properly. The nicer hangers have a smooth, rounded top edge, so you don't shred the palms of your gloves during placement, and the edges of the eye are beveled to minimize carabiner damage.

A "coffee-grinder" spinning knob attached to the hanger makes screws unbelievably fast to place and remove. Once you've tried these, it's hard to go back to conventional hangers.

Beware the cheap, no-name titanium screws coming from Russia and Eastern Europe. They often do not pass standards but make okay lightweight "leavers" for rappels. If you expect a titanium screw to hold a fall, stick with tested screws from trusted names.

SCREW STRENGTH

In lab tests performed by Black Diamond—more realistic than the lame CEN standard—the company's 17 cm screw rated at 2248 lbf (10 kN) had an average strength of 4853 lbf (21.6 kN), but ranged from a high of 8333 lbf (37 kN) to a low of 1979

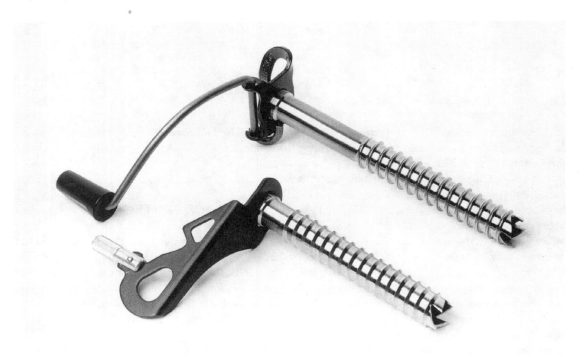

Photo 12.2   Two styles of ice screws with coffee-grinder handles that flip out of the way

SCREW PLACEMENT

It's much faster and easier to place screws at hip level rather than overhead, since you have more leverage. Because your hand is lower than your heart, it also has a chance to warm up.

Look for placements that are in a depression or on a large expanse of flat ice; avoid the lips of bulges and columns of ice, which are more prone to fracturing. Clear away rotten surface ice and create a small depression to start the screw in; as you place the screw, feel for any decrease in resistance, which may indicate an air pocket.

You can improve placements in waterfall ice by doing something counterintuitive. Instead of angling screws downward from perpendicular to the ice, as many of us were taught, place them angled 15° upward into ice in the anticipated direction of the load [Illustration 12.2]. During a leader fall, this reduces the fracturing of ice that occurs at the lip and can thereby double the strength of the placement.

Very important: This upward placement applies only to screws with a good concentration of high-protruding threads, and the ice must be very solid and cold. In unavoidable rotten or very sunny ice, place the screw straight into the ice or angled downward. Obviously, placing secure screws depends on judging ice conditions accurately.

Always sink your screws to the hilt for maximum holding power. Carry some short screws if you suspect thin ice. If you bottom out a longer screw, and if no more than 2 in. (5 cm) is sticking out, it's best to clip the hanger. That's because, if you fall onto a tied-off screw, the tie-off sling often slips to the end as the screw bends under load, putting even more leverage onto the screw and frequently cutting the sling. In this case, you would be better off clipped directly to the hanger.

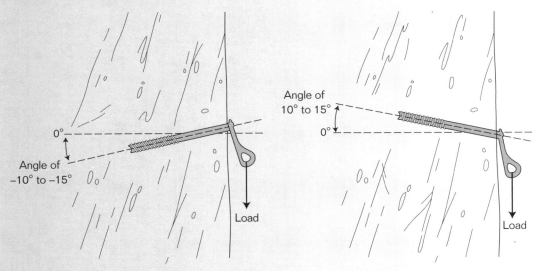

Illustration 12.2   A downward angle (left) is strongest in questionable ice (and for screws with small threads). An upward angle (right) is strongest in cold, solid ice.

lbf (8.8 kN). Sounds good—at first.

According to Chris Harmston, Black Diamond quality-assurance manager, "If we applied our 3-Sigma [statistical analysis] system to the 17 cm screws placed in ice, we would have a rating of 554 lbf (2.5 kN)—meaning 13 out of 10,000 could be expected to fail below 554 lbf." It is noteworthy that Black Diamond's 3-Sigma rating on its 22 cm screw would be 1109 lbf (4.9 kN) and on the stubby 12 cm screws the rating would be only 454 lbf (2 kN). In other words, longer is better.

The upshot: Place screws in the best and deepest ice you can find, place them at full length, place screws often, and use rock protection when available.

ALTERNATIVES FOR ICE

When the ice doesn't allow good protection, it's time to whip out the ice hooks [Photo 12.3]. Larry Penberthy, of Mountain Safety Research fame, developed the first "Ice Hawks" in the 1970s. When placed as a piton in an ice-filled crack, these can hold significant loads. Hooks in thin, brittle, or rot-

Photo 12.3   Use an ice hook only when you can't get a good screw or piton placement. They can be surprisingly strong in chandeliered ice and frozen cracks where nothing else will work.

V-THREADS

Nobody likes leaving expensive equipment behind when they rappel an ice route. Famed Russian mountaineer Vitali Abalakov developed the V-thread, in which two intersecting ice-screw holes are threaded with a webbing runner [Illustration 12.3]. In good ice, these have been tested to over 2000 lbf (8.9 kN).

To thread the V, you will need a tool to pull the webbing through—it can be as simple as a bent coat hanger. Another option is a commercial model made of sheet metal that can also be used to clear the cores from ice screws. Yet another version is a flexible cable with a hook on one end and a 'biner loop on the other that is less prone to getting in the way.

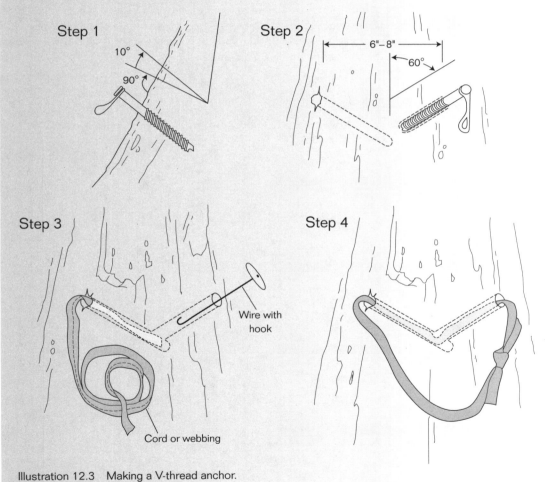

Step 1

10°

90°

Step 2

6"–8"

60°

Step 3

Wire with hook

Cord or webbing

Step 4

Illustration 12.3   Making a V-thread anchor.

ten ice should be considered desperation measures rather than reliable protection. Load limiters are a good idea.

Pound-in ice tubes (and especially ice pitons) are essentially obsolete because the current generation of ice screws require so much less energy and time to place and remove. I've often heard the statement, "Screw the second, he's on a top-rope," but I see little point in flaming out your partner if she has to lead the next pitch—and she may decide to get even. Still, some climbers carry a pound-in or two for emergency measures. Some of the newer pound-ins have longer hangers than the old Snargs, which aids in their removal, as long as the leader remembers not to place them in a corner.

ACCESSORIES

Several options are available for racking your ice screws that will speed up access—futzing around getting the pro you need while hanging by one arm is gripping at best. The nicest racking systems orient notchless carabiners so the gates are held facing outward.

Instead of attaching holsters to your harness (if even possible), consider using a separate belt with a quick-release buckle. This allows you to easily slide your holstered tools out of the way when scrambling.

CHAPTER 13

CLOTHING SYSTEMS

WHEN THE TEMPERATURE IS WELL BELOW freezing, the wind is howling, and snow is piling up fast, you will either be loving life—or hating it. Your reaction will be determined partly by your attitude and largely by the performance of your clothing.

As alpine climbers, we alternate between periods of intense activity, such as skiing uphill on an approach or leading a strenuous ice pitch, and inactivity on interminable belays. No other sport places such demands on clothing for insulation, ventilation, and protection from the elements.

The virtues of a clothing system consisting of base, insulating, and shell layers are well known. All too often, however, consumers purchase these components separately, and incompatible garments can lead to poor performance, excess weight, and wasted money.

Lest we get carried away with high-tech euphoria, bear in mind the remarkable achievements of our predecessors. Most of the classic routes in the Alps were done prior to 1940 by climbers wearing wool clothing. Furthermore, all fourteen of the 8000 meter peaks were climbed before synthetic fleece and waterproof/breathable fabrics were invented. That said, climbers are accomplishing more—and doing so with greater comfort—with modern clothing.

SYSTEM CONCEPTS

For an integrated clothing system to work well, you need to start with the base layer and work outward [Illustration 13.1]. Many people underestimate the

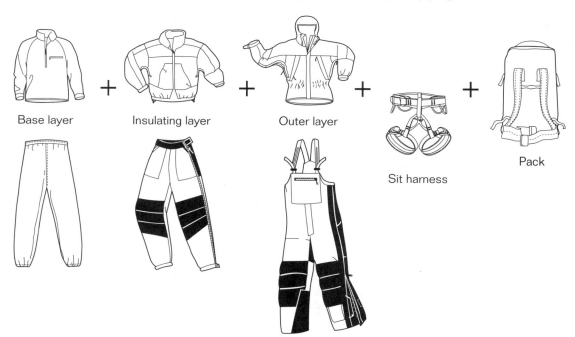

Base layer + Insulating layer + Outer layer + Sit harness + Pack

Illustration 13.1   The complete layering system, including gloves and gaiters, must work together.

importance of this first layer for transporting moisture away from your skin—it can make or break the system. The next layer(s)—the insulating layer—should trap warm air and aid the outward flow of moisture. Finally, your shell must allow body moisture to escape, prevent outside moisture from entering, and stop convective heat loss. For extreme cold, the shell is replaced with an outer insulating parka.

Stopping to layer is anathema to alpinists. Removing a pack and/or harness, finding or stashing a jacket, then putting the pack and/or harness back on several times a day wastes precious time. Thus you need clothing that can handle a wide range of conditions and is easily adjustable on the move; a lot of backpacking designs fail miserably here.

All of the components also need to work together to prevent the dreaded "gaposis"—a serious disease common in poorly designed systems. The symptoms include sleeves that expose the wrists when you're climbing, bottom hems that ride up to the belly button when your arms are raised, pants that expose your butt when you crouch, and legs that ride up to calf level when you high-step while wearing a harness.

Some climbers think they need battle armor for maximum durability, and there are plenty of companies willing to supply it. However, for peak performance, light is right. The difference between a heavy-duty suit, for example, and one made of lighter, carefully reinforced fabric, is more than a pound and a half. Although more abrasion-resistant than lighter cloth, the rougher fabric is also more likely to hold water on its surface; this reduces the garment's breathability and increases weight, and the shell can freeze solid.

Even if you have gone to extraordinary efforts to save weight in your clothing system, you will be wasting a lot of energy if you can't move easily because of a restrictive cut or layers that bind. Climbing is hard enough that you don't need to be fighting your clothing as well as gravity. Beware of combining too many stretch garments; the overall effect can actually be confining.

When shopping, try on everything you will wear and go through all the motions of climbing to make sure there is no binding while high-stepping or making a long reach. Once home, evaluate the clothing indoors while wearing your harness and helmet, a loaded pack, and mountaineering boots. This is when you discover that a lot of so-called clothing designed for climbers is adequate only for backpackers or city dwellers—find out while you can still return it.

FIT FOR A WOMAN

Women don't need to be told that they are shaped differently from men—or that relatively few companies recognize this. The present situation is far better than a decade ago, when a "women's" label meant a men's shell in pretty colors. However, women still don't have the complete selection of performance outerwear designed for climbing.

Women are usually offered second-tier garments instead of the same companies' top-of-the-line styles available in men's sizing. And a women's medium is **not** the same thing as a men's small.

A parka made specifically for women has a smaller neck opening, narrower shoulders, wider hips, and shorter torso and sleeves than the same parka for men. Pants have a higher rise in the back, narrower waist, wider hips and thighs, and a shorter inseam.

NATURE'S CALL

Most clothing designers have obviously never used their products, especially while wearing a climbing harness. If they had, going to the bathroom would be much easier. The most complicated designs are rainbow seats, which can be difficult to use, add weight, and trap snow under the flap. Drop seats are a better alternative but still require a lot of futzing (even more if you wear bibs). Furthermore, most crotch zippers are too short; male genitalia get rather small in the cold and a harness often bunches up one's pants.

For men and women, the most convenient system is a through-the-crotch zipper that extends up the back [Illustration 13.2]. Earlier designs had many flaps that made them stiff and wide, leading to chafing, but newer systems are trim and convenient. Obviously, this design makes an integrated clothing system with corresponding zippers or flaps important. Your underwear must have a very large vertical opening or the system can backfire on you in a most rude manner.

STYLE

Color is a personal choice, but be considerate of others. Countless otherwise stellar photos have been ruined by thoughtless models wearing dull clothing—a little splash can make a big difference. Bright colors also offer a safety factor, particularly in a whiteout; yellow is the most visible day or night, but reds and oranges have the most "pop" on film. However, friends don't let friends wear neon. Even pastels or lighter colors are better than black or earth tones.

There's nothing wrong with being a little self-aware of how you appear even in a wilderness setting—show a little panache. While you may not

Illustration 13.2   Through-the-crotch zipper

mind looking like a bum, your partners and other climbers have to look at you.

BASE LAYER

Clothing has changed a lot since the days when everyone wore wool underwear. Many of us went through the polypropylene stage; early versions were scratchy, retained odors, and melted in a dryer. Polyester was the next material to make a major inroad, and it is still the standard against which others are compared. However, new generations of polypro (a.k.a. olefin) and wool have overcome many of the old problems and are now making a comeback.

Transferring moisture away from your skin is the primary roll of base layers, and their effectiveness at this task has been greatly enhanced by new fabrics. Indeed, sometimes they work too well—when you stop, the moisture can be moved away so quickly that you feel a sudden chill (called flash-off).

Many new garments are made from bicomponent fabrics, in which different-diameter yarns are knitted together so the side next to your skin wicks perspiration away, and the exterior surface helps it evaporate. First used in performance athletic wear, this fabric technology works best in snug-fitting clothing that maintains contact with your skin.

Moisture transfer also may be enhanced by chemical treatments to improve wicking. Some of these use a hydrophilic (water-loving) finish that bonds to fibers and helps spread moisture; eventually, however, these treatments can wash out. Others work by an electrostatic principle that ionizes the fibers to move moisture; fabric softeners can temporarily weaken the performance of these. Although not as effective as bicomponent underwear in my experience, these chemical processes do not rely on body contact, so loose-fitting clothing is still effective at moving moisture.

Most of the base-layer garments are offered in

different weights. The thinnest are great for running or cross-country skiing but offer little insulation value. By far the most versatile are the midweights, which provide a good combination of warmth and moisture control. If you'll be standing around in severe cold, the expedition weights are nice, but they do not wick moisture nearly as well as lighter fabrics.

Most of the new synthetics are quite a bit better than what was available ten years ago. However, claims of superior odor prevention for one brand over another are marketing hype; there is no standard for comparison. All fabrics I've tried still show signs of pilling after a while. Some manufacturers say pilling of underwear and pile garments can be reduced by washing the clothing inside out with a fabric softener. Salt buildup from sweat will diminish wicking performance; occasionally rinsing the underwear in fresh water helps a lot on extended trips (your tentmate will appreciate it too).

DESIGN

Some people like the feel of loose-fitting base layers, which aid ventilation. However, underwear that hugs your body is warmer, because of reduced airflow, and fits better under stretch insulating layers [Illustration 13.3].

Fabrics with smooth exterior surfaces enhance freedom of movement by allowing subsequent layers to slide over them easily. A brushed or patterned interior surface reduces contact points with the skin, trapping more air without holding water. While not as attractive as regular seams, flat-stitched seams are more comfortable and stronger—and all too rare. White or light-colored fabrics are more versatile than dark-colored ones because you won't roast on a warm day (crucial on a glacier).

I prefer zip turtlenecks for temperature regulation, but only if the neck fits snugly (many don't) without choking. Henley's (three-buttons) or crew necks are popular alternatives. A long tail prevents gaposis.

Bottom layers with a high waist will help reduce the bulk from overlapping waistbands, and they stay up better under a pack. Also, wide elastic bands are less prone to rolling under a hipbelt. The intimate layer, bras and briefs, should also be made of synthetic, wicking fabrics. Briefs with a wind panel on the front can be critical for men!

INSULATING LAYER

Insulations work by trapping warm air near your body—the more air that is trapped, the warmer the insulation. Wind resistance is desirable but is often at odds with another important attribute: managing moisture generated by high-intensity activities.

NATURAL INSULATIONS

Wool is the traditional favorite because of its ability to also keep you relatively warm when wet. Because it is absorbent, wool pulls moisture from your body and slowly releases it to the environment so you don't get the flash-off chill of some synthetics. Although newer processing techniques have made some wool garments much more comfortable to wear, they still carry significant penalties of weight, bulk, and drying slowly.

I have a closet full of wool sweaters and jackets that I use for day trips because they look nice; my wool knickers and pants are only keepsakes. But for serious climbs and extended trips, nearly all the wool stays behind.

Once common because of their light weight and compressibility, down vests and sweaters have also fallen out of favor for insulating layers. These can get saturated from sweat when wearing a pack, lose most of their insulating quality when wet, and a small tear can make a big mess.

FLEECE

Ever since the late 1970s, when Yvon Chouinard began marketing synthetic fleece similar to that used by Norwegian fishermen, it has become the insulating material of choice for climbers. Far

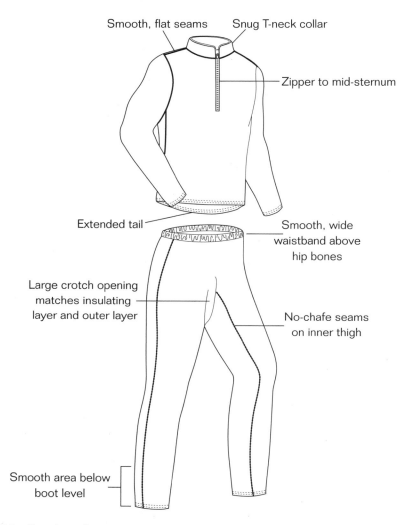

Smooth, flat seams

Snug T-neck collar

Zipper to mid-sternum

Extended tail

Smooth, wide
waistband above
hip bones

Large crotch opening
matches insulating
layer and outer layer

No-chafe seams
on inner thigh

Smooth area below
boot level

Illustration 13.3   Base layer features

lighter and faster-drying than wool, fleece now comes in hundreds of fabrics of widely varying performance characteristics and quality.

The most common, and widely imitated, fleece is Polartec 200, a midweight (8 oz. per sq. yd.), double-face (fuzzy on both sides) material. This is a good all-around product well suited to stop-and-start activities, although it's a bit warm for aerobic sports.

The lighter Series 100 (6 oz.) is more suitable for multiple layers; this can be either double- or single-faced (fuzzy on one side, smooth on the other). The heavier Series 300 (11 oz.) is too warm for all but really cold conditions, and more efficient options are available.

The standard polyester fleece fabrics stretch a little and breathe well—and the wind cuts right through them. Better-quality fleeces have a water-repellent finish that helps them shed water and dry faster. Some fleeces come from recycled materials; they cost a bit more but otherwise have similar characteristics. An average jacket will keep twenty-five 2-liter soda bottles out of landfills, while saving more than a quart of oil and reducing toxic emissions.

Often referred to as synthetic chamois fabric, microdenier fleeces are made from a fiber so fine that a thread 27 miles (43 km) long weighs less than a teaspoon of water. Although luxuriously soft and fairly wind-resistant, the material does not breathe well and tends to pill.

For clothing that requires greater freedom of movement, stretch fleeces add about 7 percent spandex (a synthetic rubber made of polyurethane; Lycra is one brand). Garments with too much spandex (more than 10 percent) tend to be heavy and slow-drying. One minor nit with stretch fleeces is that they are harder to remove than regular pile—rather like a Chinese finger puzzle.

Even greater performance can be attained by combining materials. For example, PowerStretch fleece has brushed polyester inside (60 percent) to pull moisture away, a smooth nylon face (30 percent) with greater abrasion and wind resistance, Lycra (10 percent) for stretch, and a chemical wicking finish.

A normal fleece has equal "loft" on both sides. Higher-performance fleeces have a loose, high pile on the inside and a denser, low pile on the outside. The result is 10 to 15 percent more warmth, improved wind resistance, better water and snow repellency, and reduced pilling, without additional weight. Waffle-like grid patterns help reduce weight and bulk without sacrificing warmth.

WINDPROOF FLEECE

Well-designed windproof fleece clothing can be a good choice for alpine activities. Garments made with these materials are sufficient for a wide range of cool weather conditions and still work well under a shell when the weather turns nasty.

Early versions of windproof fleeces sandwiched a membrane between two layers of standard fleece, but this was too warm for many conditions. Now, lighter fleece is used on both sides of the film, or fleece is put on the outside and mesh inside.

Because breathability is decreased, non-windproof side panels or pit zips are needed for ventilation. Windproof fleece vests often have a highly breathable back—these are among my favorite cool-weather garments.

Another extremely functional clothing option is a lightweight, woven bicomponent fabric sewn inside a wind shell (e.g., the Marmot DriClime Windshirt). The lining is very efficient at transporting moisture and offers a bit of insulation, while the outer fabric cuts the wind and allows moisture to pass at a rate that prevents flash-off. The shell also makes a smooth sliding surface under fleece, so freedom of movement is enhanced.

Some companies offer a heavier fleece covered by a rugged windproof shell that is highly breathable. These work well in near-freezing, damp conditions (think Scotland) but are less versatile in other climates.

SYNTHETIC INSULATIONS

For a warmer layer than midweight fleece, I prefer clothing insulated with the same synthetics found in sleeping bags (see Chapter 14, Sleeping Systems). Synthetic-insulated sweaters and pants are excellent items for severe cold. Compared to heavyweight fleeces, these are lighter, more compact, more wind-resistant, and more water-repellent. Because of their slick nylon inner and outer shells, they also offer better freedom of movement within a layering system. Unlike down-insulated clothing, you don't have to worry about saturation with water, or tears spilling the contents.

PHASE CHANGE MATERIALS

The newest category of insulation works to maintain comfort by storing and releasing heat. This emerging technology uses micron-sized, spherical particles of paraffin encased in a durable shell wall (microencapsulated Phase Change Material, or PCM). These "beads" are imbedded into foam, into a fabric coating, or within fibers; the more PCM, the greater the storage capacity.

The paraffin is made to melt at specific temperatures, a process that absorbs heat. As the temperature drops below this melting point, the paraffin solidifies and releases heat. The overall effect is an active buffering of temperature fluctuations.

This PCM technology appears best suited to activities where occasional "recharging" is possible, such as going into the lodge when alpine skiing. Climbers waking from a cold bivy will need to generate a lot of heat before the PCM can do its thing . . . and that could take hours. In the meantime, you could actually feel colder than with conventional clothing while the PCM pulls heat from your body.

It's still too early to pass final judgment on clothing with PCM, as the technology is certain to be improved. However, just because a product contains a phase-change material doesn't mean it is up to the job.

VAPOR BARRIER

Yet another concept for staying warm in cold conditions is to prevent any moisture from moving outward. Vapor barrier (VB) clothing does indeed work (see Chapter 14, Sleeping Systems, for a more thorough discussion), but it is best suited to constant-intensity, extreme-cold activities. Many find it too difficult to regulate a VB clothing system effectively when output and temperature vary widely. And moisture buildup within synthetic clothing insulation is rarely the problem it can be with sleeping bags.

In theory, VB clothing will actually decrease sweating and thus your rate of dehydration so you will need less water. If you intend to cut it this close to the edge, you had better experiment first and have the entire system wired!

DESIGN

Once you have chosen materials for your insulating layers, it's time to compare fit, features, and price [Illustration 13.4]. Zip up the jacket and make

sure the collar seals out drafts without choking you. Unfortunately, collars that are too wide are the rule rather than the exception. Some designs add a drawstring so you can snug up the neck, though these aren't quite as comfortable as a snug fit.

For medium- and heavyweight tops, I like underarm zippers (pit zips) that extend into the body of the garment. Abrasion patches on the shoulders and elbows, while often more fashionable than functional, can extend the life of your top but decrease breathability, add weight, and slow drying. Do not buy any fleece top that has knit cuffs or waistbands; these retain water and dry slowly. Built-in hoods are nice in ugly conditions, but they get in the way when not in use; I prefer a hat and neck gaiter.

Whether you choose a jacket or pullover is a matter of personal preference. A jacket is obviously easier to put on and take off and has better ventilation; however, some people don't like the bulk of the zipper and its storm flap. If you choose a pullover or anorak, look for a model with a long neck zip (reaches below your sternum) that allows effective cooling; a side zipper also makes pullovers *much* easier to put on.

Typically, stretch-fleece bottoms are worn all day. Sort of like fuzzy tights, these are comfortable, allow easy movement, and have few bells and whistles. Although ankle zippers make donning such pants easier, the zipper pull can become a pressure point inside tall mountaineering or ski boots. Ankle stirrups are both uncomfortable and unnecessary.

Because they can often be too warm, heavier-weight fleece or synthetic-filled pants need to be easily removed and ventilated; full-length side zippers are highly recommended. Often worn as outerwear, many of these have hand-warmer pockets, a crotch zipper, and abrasion patches on the seat and knees. Since these bottoms are worn outside your boots, a somewhat shorter pant leg, with no elastic in the hem, is advantageous.

If you know it is going to be consistently cold, a stretch-fleece sleeveless suit is a great choice. Not

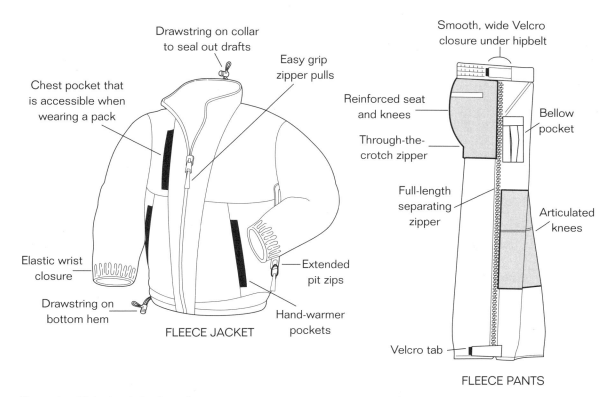

Illustration 13.4   Insulating layer features

OUTER LAYER

The outer shell is your primary line of defense when the elements turn against you. If your shell's not up to the task, life is not good. No matter how great the rest of your clothing system, you'll fight to stay comfortable in harsh mountain environments.

WIND SHELLS

Unless it is precipitating or water is dripping on you, there is little reason to wear a waterproof shell. Even the most breathable of the waterproof/breathables is easily out-sweated by highly aerobic activities. You can save a lot of weight, bulk, and expense by choosing a water-resistant wind shell. For running, cycling, and high-altitude mountaineering, these may be a better choice than fully waterproof parkas.

Microfibers

Microfiber shells are extremely breathable, highly wind-resistant, and somewhat water-repellent because of the very tight weave of the fabric. The lightweight fabric has a soft hand, is quiet (a hidden blessing), and very compressible. Water repellency is often increased by a coating, although these tend to decrease in effectiveness with time.

Because they are not particularly abrasion- or

only does this add insulation to your core area but it is also more comfortable, with no waistband, shoulder straps, or gaposis.

tear-resistant, microfiber shells are better suited to "low-impact" activities; you'll likely thrash them with hard use. For extended trips in polar conditions, microfiber shells are the best choice because condensation will not build up inside your clothing.

Enhanced Fabrics

Although microfiber fabrics do a pretty good job at keeping you dry in light precipitation, greater wind- and water-resistance can be achieved by laminating fabrics with a membrane (Gore Windstopper) or encapsulating fibers in a polymer film (Nextec). These enhanced fabrics are completely windproof yet still highly breathable (water vapor can pass easily). Because they don't rely on a tight weave for windproofness, the fabric can be lighter and more compressible.

You will get wet wearing an enhanced fabric if it's really raining (the seams aren't sealed) but less so than in a microfiber. Thus these enhanced-fabric shells are ideal for aerobic sports in damp, windy conditions. They are not particularly durable for high-abrasion activities, and you may pay a hefty premium for a moderate performance increase.

Rugged Stretch

A relatively new category of wind shells is made from high-performance stretch fabrics. These are densely woven with a rugged outer nylon surface that is quite abrasion-resistant and sheds snow. High breathability and remarkable freedom of movement make these fabrics ideal for climbing and skiing.

Perhaps the best application of these fabrics (Schoeller and Malden are currently the leading manufacturers) is in pants—these are unbeatable for the alpine environment. The material also works incredibly well for jackets, although fewer companies offer these because of the high cost.

RAIN SHELLS

Don't rule out an old-fashioned, waterproof rain shell for some activities. A well-designed polyure-thane-coated nylon shell, with good ventilation, will likely give performance equal to that of the cheaper waterproof/breathables at a fraction of the weight and cost.

During the summer, I often leave an inexpensive rain shell in the bottom of my climbing pack for unexpected afternoon showers. If you are going to a tropical region, the high humidity and warm temperatures reduce the driving effect of moisture to almost nil, so there is little advantage in wearing a waterproof/breathable rain shell.

WATERPROOF/BREATHABLE SHELLS

Back in the days when we wore waterproof *cagoules* and breathable 60/40 parkas, we dreamed of having one shell that would keep us dry in the rain and stop the wind yet allow moisture to pass. Since then, tremendous advances have been made through much trial and error.

However, there are no miracle fabrics, and you need to understand the limitations or face disappointment and discomfort. Considering the price of some modern parkas, you'd expect them to offer perfect protection for everything from steamy jungles to Himalayan summits. Reality check: Don't expect any of these jackets to work well in all possible conditions.

Although people often refer to a "waterproof-breathable (WP/B) fabric," this is a confusing misnomer. We're actually talking about a woven outer fabric to which a WP/B material is laminated or coated [Illustration 13.5].

Discussions of performance, durability, and weight largely revolve around the outer fabric, not what's inside it. Frequently, the mills that weave the fabric are unrelated to the company that laminates the membrane. W. L. Gore, for example, does not actually make fabrics; it just applies its technologies to other companies' products.

Outer Fabrics

A lot of companies would like you to believe that all similar fabrics, such as taffetas or taslans, are the same, yet this is far from the truth. Two fabrics that look the same to the untrained eye can vary greatly in performance and price.

Most high-end shell fabrics are made with filaments of nylon because it has a high strength-to-weight ratio for both tearing and abrasion. For very light fabrics, the nylon may be tensilized (molecularly aligned by heating) to increase tear strength further. Polyester is less expensive and has a nice hand, but it is significantly less durable.

The filaments are twisted into yarns (threads) of different weights, as measured in denier (d). A denier of 30d is very light, while the thicker 70d is relatively strong, and Cordura can be 1000d. If the number of filaments (f) per thread exceeds the denier, the result is a microfiber fabric. Two or more yarns can also be twisted together to increase strength further.

To increase abrasion resistance, the yarn may be texturized by mechanical processes. Taslan fabrics are created by abrading the threads with air jets prior to weaving; this yields a soft, cottony feel, but the rough surface does not hold chemical treatments well and is prone to "wetting out" (becoming saturated). False-twist fibers are made by twisting a thread, heat-setting the molecules, and then untwisting the thread; this results in smoother, silkier fabrics that are more abrasion-resistant (because the threads are undamaged) and naturally water-repellent.

The yarns are then woven into a fabric—those that run the length of the roll are called warp, and those that run across the roll are called fill. The number of warp and fill yarns in a square inch is the thread count; generally, higher thread counts provide greater durability and have a softer "hand"(the softness and feel of the fabric). The weight of a given fabric is for one square yard, without any laminates or coating. For example, the full specs on Supplex 330 (one of the best taslans) reads: 70d/66f x 70d/66f/two-ply, 160 warp x 68 fill, 3.3 oz.

After weaving, the fabric is dyed by one of three processes. Beam dyeing is the most efficient and is generally used on taffetas and ripstops; jig

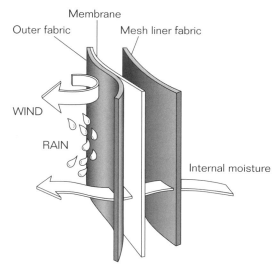

TWO-PLY FABRIC

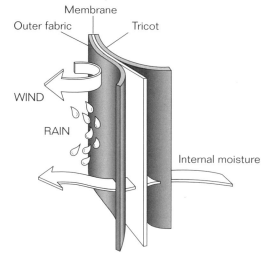

THREE-PLY FABRIC

Illustration 13.5   Fabric laminates: two-ply and three-ply

dyeing gives a somewhat better hand and is common on heavier taslans; and jet dyeing gives the best hand. Few fabrics are jet dyed because it is a pricey process.

Membranes: Waterproof and Breathable?

After a mill has made the fabric, it is often shipped off to be laminated or coated. For lamination, the fabric is calendered (smoothed with pressure and heat) on one side before the membrane is glued on.

Gore-Tex is a bicomponent membrane of expanded Teflon protected by an oleophobic (oil-hating) coating. The pores in the membrane (9 billion per sq. in.) are 20,000 times smaller than a drop of liquid water and 700 times larger than a molecule of water vapor. Unless it is punctured, it is physically impossible for the membrane to leak. Problems with clogging pores and delamination were solved many years ago. Now over twenty years old, Gore-Tex's newest generations still set the standard against which other WP/Bs are judged.

Another laminate (Sympatex) uses a hydrophilic, monolithic film (no pores) of polyester that is windproof, relatively waterproof, and somewhat breathable. It moves water through the film by breaking down the liquid molecules and releasing the vapor on the other side.

Several microporous, polyurethane coatings on the market (such as Entrant, H2No, Helly Tech, and Triple Point Ceramic) also claim to be waterproof and breathable. The effectiveness of these coatings is dependent upon their porosity and thickness. The latter can vary greatly, even on the same roll of fabric. Most coatings are applied as a single layer, a process that is cheap but imprecise. Better coatings use two or more layers to ensure even application.

Early versions of these coatings were downright terrible—they tended to be waterproof yet barely breathable, or they breathed okay but let you get wet from the outside. However, the technology keeps improving and a few of the contenders are now nipping at Gore's heels. Indeed, with good design and quality outer fabrics, some outperform midrange Gore-Tex shells. A new, more breathable Gore-Tex, called XCR, ups the ante once again, so expect the competitors to keep working at it.

There are many different lab tests to measure waterproofness, water repellency, breathability, and durability, but there's little agreement on which ones to use or how well they correlate to real life. Without reading the entire test procedure, it's difficult to draw meaningful conclusions from data.

Marketing departments use the confusion to their advantage and produce technical-looking documents that mean very little. For example, different standardized tests for moisture vapor transmission rate (MVTR), a measure of breathability, give a wide range of results, so you can't just compare numbers provided by the companies. Even independent lab results should be greeted with caution; read the fine print.

It's important to realize that all WP/Bs perform their best when it's dry and cold outside. This environment provides the maximum "driving effect" for the warm, moist air near your body. As the temperature and humidity outside the shell increase, the resistance of the fabric to vapor transport becomes more of a factor. Thus more breathable fabrics (higher MVTR) work significantly better in suboptimal conditions than moderately breathable fabrics.

On cold, rainy days, wearing thick insulation prevents most of your body heat from reaching the shell. This means the WP/B material is near ambient temperature and there is very little driving effect, making condensation likely. Removing a layer of insulation will warm the shell and allow your clothing system to work effectively.

Linings

The membrane or coating generally needs to be protected on the inside from abrasion to prevent leakage. There are two ways to do this: suspend a lining inside the two-ply shell, or laminate an inner layer (making it a three-ply).

Although once quite popular, shells with linings

are no longer worth considering for technical users. In general, two-ply shells are heavier, bulkier, and less durable than comparable three-ply models. The linings tend to become saturated and cling to you or freeze stiff.

The innermost layer of three-ply materials is an ultralight knit mesh that helps spread moisture over a wider surface area for quicker drying. Either nylon or polyester tricot can be used, but the latter is more hydrophobic, so it helps moisture transport. New generations of three-ply fabrics have a soft hand and are nearly as quiet as two-plies (though cheap three-plies are still pretty stiff and crinkly).

An alternative to the tricot mesh is a layer of raised dots (Gore PacLite) for abrasion protection. This saves about 3 to 4 oz. (85 to 115 g) off a typical jacket and decreases bulk when stuffed by about 15 percent. Even though the dots themselves are nonbreathable, the overall breathability of the fabric is claimed to be 25 percent better than with three-ply because more surface area is exposed (gluing on the mesh blocks pores). One drawback to PacLite shells, similar to coated shells with no lining, is that they tend to cling to wet skin or clothing, making them rather difficult to slip on and off.

Water Repellency

The last step in making the WP/B fabric is the application of a durable water-repellent (DWR) treatment, the quality of which makes a huge impact on performance. When people complain about their shell leaking, most of the time the culprit is a failure of the DWR, not the WP/B material.

For any WP/B to work its best, the water on the outside surface should bead up and roll off. If the fabric becomes saturated, the material still breathes but at a greatly diminished rate. More important, this layer of water promotes condensation inside the shell (that damp, clammy feeling), which may be interpreted as leakage. The wetted-out fabric is also much heavier and can freeze.

To enhance beading, a fluoro-polymer coating is applied to the fabric, greatly increasing surface tension. The quality of DWRs varies greatly. If a catalog talks about testing, look for 90 points (out of 100) after twenty machine washings, which means the DWR is still effective after twenty washings. Cheaper ones are rated at around 70/10—they wet out after only ten washes.

WASHING SHELLS

If you've ever waxed your car only to find water no longer beads up after a few days of driving around the city, you'll understand why DWRs stop working. Dirt, smoke, and other contaminants mask the effects of the coating. Water repellency is easily restored by washing. (Never take WP/B garments to the dry cleaner, which strips the DWR, or use liquid detergent, which has surfactants that prevent beading.) It's important to zip up the shell, avoid detergents, and toss the jacket in a warm dryer at the end (the heat reactivates the DWR).

Eventually, even the best DWRs will wear off, particularly beneath packs. Use Gore ReviveX or Nikwax TX-Direct (follow instructions carefully) to restore your garment to working order.

CONSTRUCTION

The best materials in the world are all for naught if a shell is compromised by design flaws. Gore found this out the hard way back in the late 1970s, when its laminate was widely used without design constraints. To ensure that the garment works properly, Gore now requires products using its technology to meet certain design criteria. For Gore's highest standard (Black Label), the shell must not leak during 1 hour in a storm chamber that simulates a deluge of 22 in. of water per hour. However, the mannequin is set up for hiking instead of climbing, so I don't consider the test to be "extreme."

Despite grumbling, the net effect of Gore's policy has been an overall improvement of outerwear—even on non-Gore products. Today we take for granted that critical seams are factory-taped and that zippers shouldn't leak.

However, although even the most basic shells now meet minimum design requirements, there are still huge differences in the details—especially when it comes to fit and ease of use.

Zippers

It's safe to say that all of us have struggled with zippers. Either they don't start, are hard to operate, or snag on fabric—usually when the weather has just turned for the worse. I've seen climbers screaming and cursing at shells with uncooperative zippers.

The front zipper receives the most abuse, particularly at the starting tangs. Large-toothed (#5 or #8) zippers hold up much better than coil zippers in this high-wear area. Look closely at the reinforcement area around the tangs—this is often the first place to fail. A snap at the bottom will hold the jacket closed when the zipper is partly undone for the rope to reach your harness or for ventilation.

The newest innovation to appear is water-resistant coil zippers (similar to those on a dry suit). These are likely to become more popular as an alternative to the befuddling flaps and Velcro found on most shells with conventional zippers.

DESIGN

For year-round versatility, a hip-length parka and pants are probably the best combination [Illustration 13.6]. If you are going to have only one shell system, this is a good starting point.

Some climbers prefer waist-length jackets because they don't get in the way of gear on the harness. However, to ensure adequate overlap, you need to compensate for the shorter length with either bibs or high-waisted pants. Bibs give more protection and warmth than pants, but they can be way too warm unless highly breathable material is used from the waist up.

For winter mountaineering, you can't beat the protection of a one-piece suit, although these can be too warm at times. Because one-piece suits eliminate the midriff overlap of two-piece systems, they are lighter, more comfortable, and warmer.

Fit is of paramount importance for shell gear. Pay particular attention to your freedom of movement when trying on garments, and be sure to wear the heaviest layers you anticipate using underneath. Bend, reach, high-step, crouch, stem, and stretch to make sure you are not hindered. Look for articulated (pre-bent) elbows and knees, as well as gusseted armpits and crotch. You should be able to swing your arms overhead without creating a gap at the wrist.

The parka should be large enough to fit comfortably over a heavy pile jacket, but it should not be so huge that you are swimming in it with a tee shirt underneath. If a shell is baggy enough, range of motion is not a problem. However, these are real flappers on windy days, and they are also snag-prone and heavier. A well-tailored shell does not interfere when you're climbing nor feel like you're wearing a kite.

Ventilation

No matter how well a fabric is supposed to breathe, ventilation is a key consideration. Even a simple wind shell can be too warm when you're carrying a heavy pack up a steep hill.

Underarm zippers (pit zips) are the most common vents, and these work well if they are at least 14 in. (35 cm) long, stay open, and extend into the chest (instead of stopping where the sleeve ends), and your insulating layer has corresponding zippers. Unfortunately, many shells have a complex system of Velcro weather flaps that make the pit zips difficult to operate.

Chest vents are viable alternatives or adjuncts to pit zips that help cool your torso directly. Chest vents are easier to operate because of their location, act like air scoops when opened, and let you reach into a pocket of your pile jacket. However, some designs don't stay open very well, and you

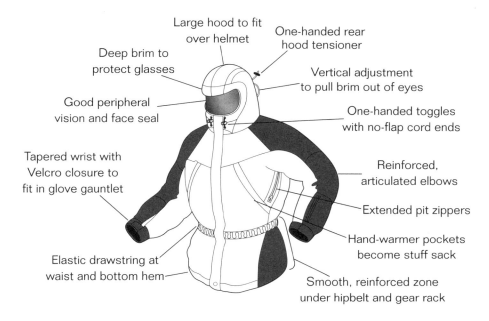

Large hood to fit over helmet

One-handed rear hood tensioner

Deep brim to protect glasses

Vertical adjustment to pull brim out of eyes

Good peripheral vision and face seal

One-handed toggles with no-flap cord ends

Tapered wrist with Velcro closure to fit in glove gauntlet

Reinforced, articulated elbows

Extended pit zippers

Hand-warmer pockets become stuff sack

Elastic drawstring at waist and bottom hem

Smooth, reinforced zone under hipbelt and gear rack

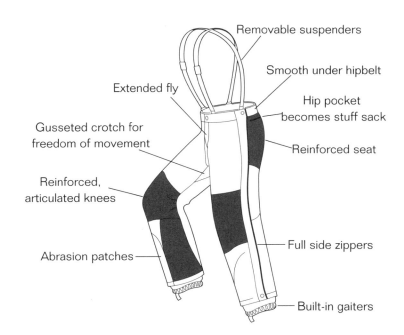

Removable suspenders

Smooth under hipbelt

Extended fly

Hip pocket becomes stuff sack

Gusseted crotch for freedom of movement

Reinforced seat

Reinforced, articulated knees

Abrasion patches

Full side zippers

Built-in gaiters

Illustration 13.6   Outer shell features

need matching layers for chest vents to work well.

Some shells, particularly lightweight models, have ventilating pockets that are lined with mesh fabrics. In general, I find these less effective than pit zips or chest vents because they are often filled with other things—such as the hat and gloves you took off when you started heating up!

Hoods

Waterproof fabrics are of little value if large gaps let moisture in when the wind is blowing or you're looking up. The best hoods have elastic running through a deep fabric tunnel that encircles your face. Some hoods make it hard to turn your head because there isn't enough fabric in the neck. This gets worse if you wear a heavy hat, and you may not be able to move at all with a helmet.

When slipped off your head, the hood should lie flat against your shoulders, so it doesn't fill with snow or form an uncomfortable ball under a pack. Most hoods that stow inside a collar pocket sacrifice performance for fashion. Such hoods often don't seal around your face as well as regular hoods, and the collars feel like a fat pillow around your neck.

Although most companies have figured out how to adjust lateral vision (usually by using a drawstring on the back to pull back the hood), many of the hoods are vertically challenged. It's annoying if you can't look up at a climb or down at your rack. The good hoods have Velcro tabs on the rear to help hold the brim back for upward views; a good cut enhances downward vision.

The brim on the majority of hoods is woefully inadequate for anyone who wears glasses (which is virtually everyone in the mountains). Better hoods have a larger, projecting brim that can be easily adjusted or folded back. After it's crunched in your pack, the brim should pop out. Stiffeners that stay bent out of shape are irritating.

Better hoods have drawstrings that can be adjusted one-handed without a lot of finagling with bare fingers or unzipping. Thankfully, most companies have figured out how to keep the ends of a hood's drawstrings from whipping you in the face. However, in some cases the cords are prone to getting caught in the zipper.

Fuzzy fleece next to your chin seems like a good idea, until you experience it clogged with ice against your face or frozen to your beard. Smooth knits or plain fabric are preferable. Hoods will generate untold frustration when the zipper snags on a flap in the last few inches. If it's a nuisance in the store, it will be a nightmare in a blizzard.

Stiff fabrics crinkle loudly next to your ears, while hoods with linings impede sound. There's a lot to be said for actually hearing distant shouts from your climbing partner.

Parka Details

Many people get sticker shock when they look at state-of-the-art shells, and the natural inclination is to blame the WP/B material for the high costs. The truth is that the laminate or coating represents a tiny fraction of the overall cost.

To significantly cut the retail price, compromises that affect performance or durability must be made at every step. Less-sophisticated patterns, with fewer curves, require less-skilled sewers and are faster to assemble. Fewer stitches per inch means the sewing machines can run faster. Taping of seams can be either meticulous or expeditious.

Chest pockets should be large in volume and located high so they remain accessible when you're wearing a pack or harness. Reach-across, Napoleon-style pockets are a bit easier to operate one-handed and then locate items inside, but same-side, diagonal pockets make nice hand warmers. Interior pockets are also handy; some will hold a water bottle or water bladder.

Some shells have waterproof pockets so the snow that inevitably gets inside when you stash your hat or climbing skins won't melt and soak your clothing. However, these pockets require two or three layers of WP/B fabric, which greatly decreases breathability and stiffens the shell.

For winter conditions, storm skirts make a huge difference in warmth. However, storm skirts add weight and are largely unnecessary in warmer weather. If you choose a parka without a skirt, bibs can make up for the deficit.

A few shells come with crotch straps, and some have loops for attaching straps. These serve to hold down the bottom hem in wind or deep snow, as long as you don't mind a constant wedgie. I find them an uncomfortable nuisance and unnecessary if the jacket has a good cut.

Shoulders, elbows, and knees are obvious wear points where heavier fabric is often used. Avoid shells that have extra patches sewn on; these add weight and trap water. The waist of parkas is a wear area that is less frequently protected. The elastic drawstring, which pulls in the shell to minimize airflow, forms bunched fabric that receives a lot of abrasion from your pack. Beware jackets that have a partial waist drawstring; these place a hard cord lock between your hipbone and pack belt.

The subtle features of good design all add up to a more pleasurable wearing experience. These include cuffs that seal out water when you're climbing (a weak point on many shells), a cuff on the right sleeve whose Velcro tabs won't snag the zipper flaps (a surprisingly common foible), one-handed cord locks, pockets or keepers for dangling cord ends, and an attachment point for ski-lift tickets (zipper pulls are a poor substitute).

Avoid any shell with an extra zipper track for a zip-in liner. While okay for around town, this extra zipper adds weight and makes the jacket stiffer. And if you actually use the zip-in feature, you get a cold gap up the front of the shell where there is no overlap. Pockets on the sleeves of some shells are pretty much useless gimmickry because they are too small for more than lip balm.

Pant Details

On pants and bibs, the most useful pockets are those that bellow outward and are located on the side (not the front) of your thigh. Handwarmer and chest pockets often are covered up by clothing, a pack, or a climbing harness.

For easy dressing while you are wearing skis or crampons, shell pants and bibs should have full-length, separating side zippers. One-piece suits are generally worn all day long, so leg zippers are needed for ventilation. Suspenders or nonelastic belts are necessary on pants and suits to keep them in place when you're wearing a pack.

Built-in gaiters are convenient and save weight, but separate gaiters can provide a trimmer fit, protect your shell, and solve problems with gaposis. If the shell has gaiters, they need to fit over all of the boots you wear, stay in place when you're post-holing and high-stepping (grommets for an instep strap are important), and not pooch out to catch on crampon points.

The instep region of pant legs is often reinforced to midcalf height, which is fine for hiking and skiing. However, when you're alpine climbing with crampons, extra protection is helpful all the way to the top of the calf because the rear crampon points tend to snag material.

OUTER PARKAS

For standing around when it's really cold, it's great to have a nice, warm parka and pants to pull on over everything else. Although down-insulated parkas have been around for ages, they leave a lot to be desired when that "frozen" waterfall is dripping on you.

If you will be climbing in cold, but not arctic, conditions, synthetic insulation is the best bet. When it is worn over the top of your climbing clothes at a belay, moisture from sweat or snow will move outward through the temperature gradient. Thus you can dry your "working" clothes without fear of compromising the clothing system.

Since these belay parkas are rather bulky, you may want to share one between you and your partner unless you both need it for a bivy. You probably won't be climbing much in these, so heavy-duty shell fabrics are not needed. Instead, the outer shell should be extremely breathable and dark in color for faster drying.

The parka should be sized big enough to pull

over everything you are wearing, including a helmet. A longer cut in the back to insulate the glutes and a shorter cut in the front for a harness tie-in are desirable. As any musher will tell you, a tunnel around the hood opening adds a lot of warmth.

Down still has a place on high-altitude or polar expeditions where weight and bulk are rationed. A fully baffled, expedition down parka and pants are the way to go unless a sponsor gives you a one-piece. Because you will be wearing this down clothing while climbing, an extremely breathable yet totally windproof outer shell (such as DryLoft) is a good idea.

GLOVES

Keeping your hands warm, without sacrificing dexterity, while climbing or skiing is no easy task. Not only are you grabbing cold rock and tools, but whatever you wear inevitably gets soaked from sweat and meltwater.

Women, of course, have an even tougher time. One study showed that women's fingers average about 5° to 7°F (3° to 4°C) cooler than men's. I would have guessed even colder. Depending on your circulation, you may need mittens when the guys are content in midweight gloves.

Climbing is hard on gloves, so it's a good idea to protect all the seams on the outside with Seam Grip (this can triple the glove's life). Multiple rappels will wear through palms of many gloves rather quickly. Some climbers carry inexpensive leather gloves to prevent trashing the expensive mountaineering ones.

My experience has been that the thinnest liner gloves wear out in a nanosecond and aren't worth the bother. I generally either go without or use expedition-weight polyester liners, which are still thin enough for manipulating a camera or cooking dinner. Some people like fingerless gloves, but my tips get so numb in them that I can't feel the rock.

Perhaps the best application for windproof fleece is in lightweight gloves. My all-around favorites, these are far superior to standard wool, fleece, or neoprene gloves. Windproof fleece gloves generally have palms and fingers reinforced with a rubberized material that also aids your grip.

Next up in warmth and durability are alpine ski gloves, preferably with leather palms. These give good midweight protection yet are thin enough that you can manipulate an ice screw or binding. The better ones have an internal WP/B bladder for waterproofness. I find the warmth about equal to liner gloves with overmitts, but ski gloves are less of a hassle to use.

Mountaineering gloves are warmer yet and generally feature removable liners for faster drying, sealed seams to prevent leakage, long gauntlets to seal out snow and drafts, and padded knuckles to reduce conductive cooling and bashing. All these features contribute to the hefty price tags. Trigger-finger mittens (thumb and forefinger separate from the other three) seem like a good idea at first, but to me they are such a compromise that you get the worst of both worlds—neither great warmth nor good dexterity. It's a good idea to attach keeper cords so you can dangle the gloves from your wrist when fine movements are required.

MITTENS

Only in the most extreme cold will I bother with mittens, but others may reach for them much sooner. The obvious advantage is that keeping your fingers together is much warmer than encasing them separately. A side benefit is you can slip a chemical heat pack between the shell and liner for luxuriously toasty fingers.

Standard mittens generally have Gore-Tex or similar shells with removable fleece linings. These are about equal in warmth to good mountaineering gloves but are less expensive. Size them big enough that you can wear glove liners without impeding circulation.

Expedition mittens are sleeping bags for your hands that are insulated with down or a synthetic fill. A less compressible insulation on the palm region is a good idea to prevent conductive heat loss while holding a metal ice ax.

RAYNAUD'S PHENOMENON

While we all suffer cold fingers and toes in frigid weather, there are some who must endure serious circulation problems. Termed Raynaud's Phenomenon, the symptoms are digits that suddenly turn white, then blue, becoming cool to the touch and numb. After warming, they flush a deep red and may tingle and throb. While usually triggered by exposure to cold, emotional upset and stress can also start an episode.

It appears that about 5 to 10 percent of the general population suffers from Raynaud's Phenomenon. It mostly affects women (75 percent of cases) and usually appears between the ages of 15 and 40; men tend to experience it later. Though not a danger in itself, Raynaud's may be an indicator of underlying problems such as scleroderma, lupus, or rheumatoid arthritis.

Biofeedback has been effective for some people with Raynaud's. Another method is to condition the digits by sitting in a cold area while keeping the hands in a container of warm water. This is repeated three to six times daily, every other day, for 3 to 4 weeks. The conditioning may taper off after several months but can be repeated.

HATS

You have probably heard the old adage, "If your feet are cold, put on a hat."

Although windproof fleece would seem to be an ideal application for hats, I find that I overheat in them faster than with a standard wool or fleece hat.

And covering your ears with windproof fleece makes it hard to hear shouts.

Many otherwise nice hats are cut straight across the bottom, which can result in frozen ear lobes on nasty days. Contoured headbands can be worn with a hat to solve the problem or alone when it's cool but nippy. Though I used them for years, I've given up on wearing traditional balaclavas because of their bulk and poor fit.

Good helmet liners may not be the height of fashion, but you won't be complaining on cold, blustery days. These fleece skullcaps have flat seams and a low profile to make them more comfortable inside a helmet than typical hats.

I've never understood the popularity of the bomber-style hat. The earflaps sit up on your head collecting snow until it is time to pull them down—ugh. Earflaps that tuck inside are much nicer and don't look as goofy. A visor is helpful to keep the weather off your face.

Don't forget a hat for the sun, too; these are vital on a glacier. Baseball caps are a popular fashion statement but do nothing to protect your ears and neck. Choose a white hat with a wide, full brim and decorate it as you wish.

ACCESSORIES

When it's subzero and the wind is howling, a simple neck gaiter can provide remarkable warmth. Just a tube of fleece, it will seal out drafts and can be pulled up around your mouth.

If it's incredibly bitter out, then it's time to break out a full face mask. I've tried models made of leather and of neoprene but found them uncomfortable and prone to fogging goggles or glasses. The nicest face masks use windproof fleece and have large mouth and nose openings covered by mesh to keep out blowing snow and warm the inhaled air.

CHAPTER 14

SLEEPING SYSTEMS

YOU MAY BE EXHAUSTED FROM CARRYING a heavy pack, sore from hard climbing, and nauseated from altitude, but if you can sleep comfortably, life ain't so bad.

A sleeping bag is a significant investment, and it may even save your life in extreme circumstances. The key to buying the right bag, however, is to think in terms of an entire sleeping system, including clothing, pad, liners, and bivy sacks. They all work together to keep you warm.

HEAT LOSS

Think of a sleeping system as a big thermos bottle. It does not add warmth; it simply keeps warm things warm. Place a severely hypothermic person into a superlofty bag without additional heat, and he or she won't recover.

To minimize heat loss, we need to protect ourselves from four major and three minor robbers of heat.

MAJOR ROBBERS

- Convection. A major source of heat loss, convection occurs in several ways: when the air warmed by your body rises and is replaced by cold air; when body movement inside your bag forces warm air out and draws cold air in; when slight breezes within your tent rob heat from the bag. The more wind-resistant the shell fabric, the more convection is reduced. Draft collars and hoods with face seals also reduce convection.

- Conduction. Conduction is the heat transfer between solids. Because of heat loss into the ground and compression of insulation under your body, a good sleeping pad is vital.

- Saturation. Even in very cold weather, sleeping in tents with condensation and in snow caves can dampen the bag and its insulation. It is critical to prevent saturation of the insulation. A water-resistant/breathable outer shell or bivy sack can help to keep your bag dry.

- Evaporation. You output about 1 oz. (30 ml) of insensible perspiration per hour (about a cup of water per night). Heat loss through the process is minimal (an insignificant 96 kilocalories compared with over 2000 kilocalories of intake every day), but all that moisture getting into your bag is the problem. To combat in-bag condensation, some climbers use waterproof, vapor-barrier (VB) liners, i.e., either an inner shell made of nonbreathable material or a separate waterproof liner added to a standard bag.

MINOR ROBBERS

- Radiation. The long waves of heat radiation from your body are stopped within the first inch of the insulation. Radiant barriers added to insulation have yet to provide significant benefits.

- Distribution. Some people believe that because some parts of the body lose heat faster than others, more insulation is required in corresponding parts of the bag. However, according to Dr. Murray Hamlet at the U.S. Army Soldier Systems Command in Natick, Massachusetts, the nation's leading cold-weather research center, an even distribution of insulation in the bag and wearing down booties and mittens to bed is more effective.

- Respiration. You can minimize heat lost through breathing by covering your mouth and nose, but many people find this uncomfortable. Also, the considerable moisture contained in each exhalation accumulates inside your bag if you breathe into it. Don't.

DOWN VERSUS SYNTHETIC

The first step in choosing sleeping equipment is deciding what you will use it for. Most of us want one bag that is good for everything, from winter climbs to big wall adventures to car camping. Since nothing does everything well, we need to start making compromises based upon our needs.

Down, the soft underfeathers of waterfowl, has been the insulation of choice in bedding and clothing for centuries. To date, high-quality down is unsurpassed for its warmth-to-weight ratio, compressibility, and durability.

But as we have all been told, and a few have experienced, down is useless when wet. The feathers turn into a glom of material that takes ages to dry and regain its loft. So for those who venture into wet conditions where they can't guarantee their bags will stay dry (big walls and hard alpine climbs), synthetic insulations are a good choice.

When first introduced, the synthetics were primarily spin-offs from the huge carpet industry, so they were relatively inexpensive. Innovations such as hollow fibers were developed not for superior insulating qualities but because they did not show dirt in carpets as readily. The early generations of synthetic bags, which are still around, are significantly heavier and bulkier, though much cheaper, than average-quality down bags.

In the past decade, we have seen the introduction of new synthetics that have been designed from the ground up as insulators. The result is that the gap between down and synthetic bags has been greatly reduced. A decent down bag is now only 10 to 20 percent lighter and more compact than a high-end synthetic bag, though the latter costs nearly as much.

Given that, plus the superior wet performance of synthetics, why would you still consider down? For starters, virtually any down bag from a good manufacturer will probably outlast two to four synthetic bags. While a decent down bag now has only a slight weight and bulk advantage, those with the best grades of down are significantly lighter and more compact than the best synthetics. Also, no synthetic has yet to equal the luxurious feel or wide comfort range of good-quality down.

It is interesting to note that in an attempt to make synthetic bags appear less expensive, almost none of them come with a storage sack. A standard $15 accessory included with all better down bags, these extra-large cotton or mesh bags are one of the best ways to store any bag when not in use.

THE UPSIDE OF DOWN

The two biggest factors affecting the insulating value of a down-filled bag are quality and quantity. The quality of the down refers to the percentage and size of the down clusters. This is quantified as the "fill power," which is the number of cubic inches that an ounce of down occupies. Color of the down does not affect quality, although gray down looks rather ugly if a light shell fabric is used.

About a decade ago, the industry standard was 550-fill down, with 625-fill being touted as the best available. Now 700-fill down is widely claimed, with 800-fill being trumpeted as the crème de la crème.

Higher fill powers have become more available and less expensive with the opening of Eastern European countries, where the birds are raised to an older age than in China, the leading source. The size of the down clusters is largely determined by the size of the bird when killed (the bigger, the better) and the thoroughness with which the down is processed and cleaned.

Most of the 550-fill down comes from Chinese geese that are processed for food at about 12 weeks while they weigh about 6 to 8 lbs. (2.7 to 3.6 kg). Higher grades of 650-fill to 700-fill down generally come from European birds that are raised for food (16 to 20 weeks) or breeding (28 to 32 weeks old) and are in the 14 to 16 lb. (6.4 to 7.3 kg) range. The highest loft down comes from "guard geese" raised by Eastern European farmers for their own food supply and to protect the other livestock. These big honkin' birds are about two to three years old and can weigh 20 lbs. (9 kg) or more. While it is possible to get high-loft down from Chinese geese by careful processing, because of the immature clusters it does not tend to maintain that loft in the long run.

The fill power of down is measured by placing an ounce inside a clear plastic cylinder 9½ in. (24 cm) in diameter and 24 in. (60 cm) tall. The room is kept at 70°F (21°C) and 65 percent humidity to prevent static from giving a false reading. The down is stirred up, and a 2 oz. (57 g) lid is placed inside the cylinder and allowed to settle. This test is accurate only to plus or minus 5 percent so that 700-fill down could actually be 665, unless the company claims the fill power is a minimum.

An ounce of down contains approximately 23,000 clusters with over 2 million filaments to trap air. The U.S. Federal Trade Commission used to specify that products labeled "down" must be at least 70 percent clusters with the rest being plumules, fibers, and feathers. In practice, the high-fill-power downs are well over 90 percent clusters.

According to the International Down and Testing Laboratory, the highest fill power they have ever seen is in the low 800s. Higher grades of down may eventually be marketed; however, you reach a point of greatly diminishing return in terms of weight saved per dollar spent. Eiderdown, collected by hand-picking the clusters from the nests of the cliff-dwelling ducks, takes this principle to absurd levels . . . and prices.

Any down will lose 5 to 15 percent of its fill power once it is placed inside a bag or garment, even more if the product is compressed for overseas shipping. Down can lose that much again once it becomes dirty from body oils and grime. Even though you paid for 700-fill, it could end up as 500-fill without proper care. Hence, it is important to store your down bag in a large, breathable storage sack and to wash it occasionally.

In three-season bags with the same warmth, the weight difference between average and very good-quality fill is only about 4 oz. (115 g). However, in a winter bag, the good down can save you 10 oz. (285 g), and the exceptional down can save nearly a pound (450 g) from your load. Another way to look at it is that for the same weight, higher-fill-power down will add correspondingly more warmth to the bag.

BAFFLES

Down tends to flow downhill. To prevent this and maintain even loft over the sleeper, baffles are used to compartmentalize the down [Illustration 14.1]. Depending upon the intended final product, designers can use—in order of increasing stabilization and weight—a box, slant box, trapezoidal, or V-shaped baffle.

Almost all of the lightweight bags use either a box or slant-box construction because they provide the most thermal efficiency for the least material. The slant box is somewhat easier to build, and if sufficiently filled acts like a box baffle. The spacing of the baffles is directly related to their depth; 5 in. (13 cm) is considered optimal for lighter bags.

Most companies use either no-see-um netting

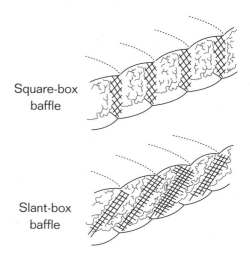

Square-box baffle

Slant-box baffle

Illustration 14.1   Baffle designs

or stretch mesh for the baffle material because they are light and the down interlocks with the fabric to minimize shifting. The advantage of the more expensive stretch mesh is greater durability after repeated unstuffings.

While companies often talk about the quantity and quality of their down, they rarely mention fill pressure. For example, a 500 cu. in. baffle chamber can be filled with 400, 500, or 600 cu. in. of down. At first, they will be roughly as warm, but as the down loses loft, the latter will maintain warmth longer. A few of the smaller companies offer optional "overfill," an extra 2 or 3 oz. (55 to 85 g) of down, which increases warmth and longevity.

A standard feature on a winter bag is a side-block baffle that separates the top of the bag from the bottom. Most lightweight bags leave this off to save weight and money, while allowing better temperature regulation. If it is really hot out, you can pick up the bag by the top edge and shake most of the down so it is underneath you. Conversely, on chilly nights, you can redistribute most of the down on top of you.

SYNTHETICS

All insulations work by trapping air; the more air that is trapped in a given space, the greater the insulative value. However, air trapped between insulation fibers is less important than the air trapped on the surface of the fibers. The reason that down, which has filaments as small as 7 microns (human hairs are 50 to 150 microns), is so effective is because of its extremely high surface-area-to-volume ratio. The goal of modern synthetic insulations is to maximize the surface area by minimizing the diameter of the fibers while retaining a good feel.

There are two basic types of synthetics: short staple, in which the individual fibers are a few inches long, and continuous filament, or long staple, in which the fibers can be up to 500 miles (800 km) long.

SHORT STAPLE

To produce a sheet of batting, short-staple fibers must be bonded together with resins and/or heat and then bonded to a paperlike scrim. Often the marketing people leave the scrim out when giving statistics on weight-to-performance ratios.

The first synthetic insulation to approach the performance of decent down was Primaloft 1. This short-staple microfiber (7.5 microns) batting still offers impressive thermal performance (both dry and wet) and durability. However, it is more expensive than other synthetics and doesn't look as warm because it requires less loft. This perceived lack of warmth has given Primaloft problems with public acceptance.

The short-staple Lite Loft (15 microns) has now been relegated to moderately priced bags or abandoned altogether by many manufacturers. Though highly compressible and thermally efficient, it does not have the best reputation for maintaining loft or retaining warmth when wet.

LONG STAPLE

Polarguard products all use continuous filaments, which are mechanically kinked to give loft. This construction makes it very strong in one direction of pull, but weak in the other, and requires no scrim. The current standard is Polarguard 3D, a thinner version of Polarguard HV (14 microns versus 23 microns) that is a hollow version of the original Polarguard. By decreasing the diameter, this continuous-fiber batting achieves a significant improvement in thermal protection, yet retains its softness and much of its legendary durability. The stuff is still bulky, but the minimal bag weights are impressive.

QUILTS AND SHINGLES

The most common methods of synthetic-bag construction are offset quilting and shingling [Illustration 14.2]. It's fallacious to say that one construction is vastly superior to the other because both have been used successfully for decades.

- Quilting. A quilted bag is made by sewing one

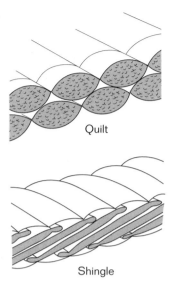

Quilt

Shingle

Illustration 14.2   Synthetic bag construction

layer of insulation to the outer shell and another to the inner shell. Because the stitching compresses the insulation, creating a cold spot, the seams are offset to minimize heat loss. Most, if not all, winter bags with this construction also have a third or fourth insulating layer sandwiched between the shells and stabilized along the edges.

- Shingling. As the name implies, shingle construction is created by overlapping batts of insulation, like shingles on a roof. One edge is sewn to the inner shell and the other edge is sewn to the outer. With a good design, there are always at least two layers of insulation between you and the cold, cold world. Because many large voids exist within the shell, the shingle technique can create a falsely inflated impression of total loft compared to a quilted bag.

OUTER SHELLS

After you choose the temperature range and insulation material that suits you, you need to consider the shell fabrics. Many companies offer more than one fabric for each model. The ideal fabric would be as light as possible, without letting the contents leak out or wind and water in. Abrasion resistance and tear strengths are minor concerns.

Fabrics tend to be either very breathable and inexpensive but minimally wind- and water-repellent, or less breathable and very expensive but highly wind- and water-repellent. The difference between nylon and polyester for sleeping bag shells is not worth discussing.

The least expensive outer-shell fabric today was the standard for performance twenty years ago—a lightweight ripstop or taffeta nylon, with a fairly high thread count (300 threads per in. or more), often calendared (melting the fibers together, creating a slick look) to keep down and microfiber insulations from escaping. You can generally assume that water-repellent treatments, if applied at all, are minimal.

The next step up in performance—and price— is microfiber fabrics. These have more filaments per thread than the denier of the yarn (more tiny fibers), resulting in a luxurious, satiny feel and much greater water repellency than standard fabrics have. If you plan to use your bag extensively inside a bivy sack, bags with microfiber shells are the best option because of their very high breathability. For most people, under "normal" conditions, microfiber shells offer the most bang for the buck.

Fabrics with the Gore DryLoft laminate give the best protection against the elements while offering good breathability—at a hefty price. A thinner version of the Gore-Tex film, DryLoft is roughly twice as breathable, to reduce condensation buildup. The barrier is completely windproof, which increases the warmth by about 5° over standard fabrics. DryLoft adds 2 to 4 oz. (55 to 110 g) and causes the bag to puff up like a balloon during compression, making the bag a bit harder to cram into a stuff sack.

DryLoft can be laminated onto a number of different fabrics. When it was first introduced, everyone used a textured polyester ripstop that had a nice feel, but was heavier and harder to stuff because of friction. Most high-end bags have now gone to lighter, smooth ripstops that don't hold snow or dirt, but are crinklier.

Tip: Though not a necessity, a bright, cheery shell color won't be quite as gloomy on day 3 of the storm. It's hard to put a rating on "psychological warmth," but I am convinced it is real.

INNER SHELLS

While not critical to performance, the bag's lining does affect your comfort. Again, high thread-count fabrics are preferable for downproofness and a luxurious feel. Attempts at decreasing radiant heat loss with special linings have so far produced meager results.

Fortunately, many manufacturers have given up on soft, fuzzy inner shells. This material makes it more difficult to move around inside the bag and adds weight and expense without increasing warmth. Several companies are hyping wicking liners that are supposed to draw moisture from the skin, but the real benefits are dubious.

A few companies use a slightly heavier fabric in the foot section to minimize wear from boots brought inside the bag—nice, but not a huge factor. Some companies use "tuck" stitching to attach baffles so that no thread is exposed. It's rather a nonissue since bags aren't subjected to much abrasion.

The inside of any sleeping bag should be dark in color, preferably black, so it absorbs more solar radiation when you are drying it in camp.

SHAPE

The less cold air that needs to be heated, the more efficient a sleeping bag [Illustration 14.3]. Ideally,

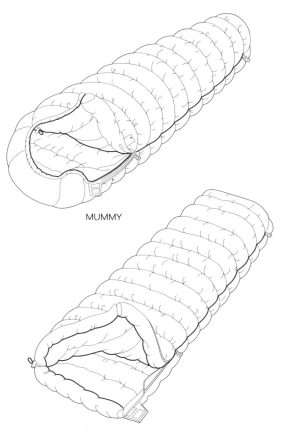

MUMMY

SEMIRECTANGULAR

Illustration 14.3   Bag shapes

the bag would hug you like a second skin, which is what a narrow mummy bag does, but many people find such a tight cut to be too confining. A slightly wider bag allows more room for tossing and turning during the night, as well as wearing additional layers inside. (Many people bring inner boots and water bottles inside to prevent freezing.) For those who are claustrophobic, be sure to compare the girths of bags, particularly in the foot section— a few bags are made with extra fabric and elastic seams so you can thrash at night.

Semirectangular and rectangular bags, while comfy, are too wide in the foot section and often lack hoods, so they are a poor choice when weight and bulk are a concern. For couples with semirectangular bags, several companies offer a doubler (bed sheet with corresponding zippers, and pockets to hold sleeping pads). This saves weight and bulk and is a lot easier to clean.

Virtually all of the good sleeping bags on the market have a differential cut; that is, the inner shell is smaller than the outer shell. This helps reduce weight, maximize loft, and minimize compression of the insulation when a knee or elbow presses against it. A trapezoidal foot section is harder to manufacture than an oval shape but allows better foot movement [Illustration 14.4].

Adding more insulation to specific parts of a bag is akin to underfilling the other sections—heat es-

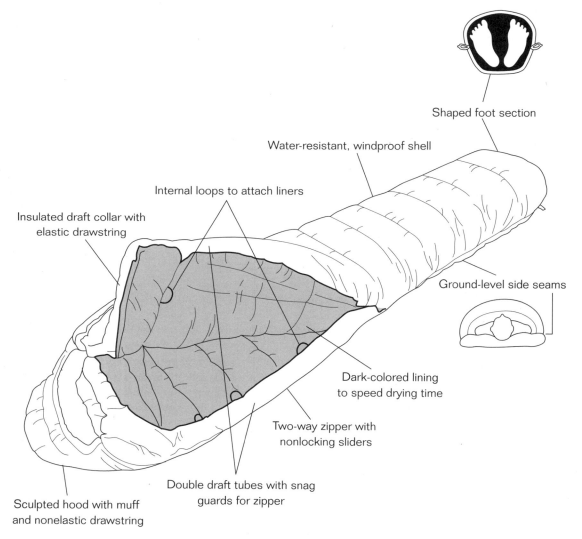

Shaped foot section

Water-resistant, windproof shell

Internal loops to attach liners

Insulated draft collar with elastic drawstring

Ground-level side seams

Dark-colored lining to speed drying time

Two-way zipper with nonlocking sliders

Double draft tubes with snag guards for zipper

Sculpted hood with muff and nonelastic drawstring

Illustration 14.4   Sleeping bag features

capes from the most vulnerable areas. Most companies put more insulation on the top of the bag than on the bottom (it's usually a 60/40 ratio) because what is underneath is compressed by body weight and insulated by the ground pad. Sometimes called differential fill, this does save weight and bulk and works well for three-season bags.

However, few people sleep on their backs all night, and the hood on a winter bag is often drawn up snugly. You can't breathe through the side of a hood, so you roll the bag up on its side, exposing the underinsulated bottom. Result: an uncomfortable night's sleep. Winter bags with a more even distribution of insulation (50/50) are preferable.

If a top with greater loft is used, it should at least wrap around the body to ground-level side seams to minimize the exposure of the underinsulated areas. This ensures uniform loft without cold spots and helps the draft tubes stay in position. A few companies use vertical sidewalls, which they claim give better protection. In a well-designed bag, either method is effective.

FEATURES

- Hoods. A well-designed hood will contour around your head and minimize the escape of warm air. A hood that lies flat on the ground is inefficient compared to one that is sculpted three-dimensionally. When closed, it should leave a small breathing hole without bunching or gaping; many designs are weak in this regard. The nicest type of hood forms a seal around your face, trapping warm air and adding comfort. Ideally, even the hood of a shell with standard fabric would be lined with DryLoft to keep moisture from your breath out of the hood's insulation.

- Drawstrings. The drawstring should be easy to operate from inside and not compress the insulation around your face. Because of the stretch, hoods with elastic, instead of cord, are much harder to close. Watch out for cold metal or plastic fittings that may press against your face.

- Draft collars. Don't even consider a winter bag that lacks an internal draft collar (these seal around your neck). Flaps that just hang from the top of the bag are insufficient in very cold weather. The better collars are several inches thick at the base, well insulated, and deep enough to close with no gaps. Unlike the hood, the collar should close with elastic, so you can reach a hand out once it is closed up. Though essential, collars can be the biggest hassle to deal with; some are fussier than others, making getting in and out of your bag more difficult. (And if you are hydrating properly, you will be waking once or twice during the night to fill the pee bottle.)

- Draft tubes. The draft tubes behind the zipper are another critical feature. If they are prone to gaposis, you suffer. Make sure that the draft tube hangs from the top no matter whether it is a left- or right-hand zip. Winter bags should have two well-filled, baffled tubes (one on top and one on the bottom) that mate closely. A good compromise is a single large top tube that nests into a cutout on the bottom; this saves weight and is less prone to snagging zippers. The down is poorly dispersed in many draft tubes; you may need to knead it into position. Turn the sleeping bag inside out and zip it up. This will reveal whether the bottom end of the zipper is adequately protected—a weak spot in cheaper bags.

- Zippers. The industry standard is the #7 YKK nylon coil zipper. These have proved extremely reliable and easy to operate over the years. As a result of this de facto standardization, virtually any left-hand zip bag can be joined to a right-hand zip for commingling of occupants.

- Anti-snag. Some type of stiffener, such as webbing, along the zipper helps to prevent snagging of the lightweight fabric. Draft flaps on the outside of zippers are not only worthless but also more likely to get caught in the zipper; avoid them.

- Sliders. I'm convinced the person who invented the locking slider for zippers is a graduate of the Marquis de Sade School of Design; they got extra credit for using a single zipper pull that flips to both sides. These insidious devices have pervaded the industry for no good reason, but fortunately they can be replaced with normal, nonlocking sliders with pulls on both sides, which worked better all along. A regular slider allows you to escape your bag in a hurry, which can be a legitimate safety issue. A Velcro closure at the top effectively prevents the zipper from opening accidentally.

- Liner loops. Some companies also offer liners to go inside their sleeping bags. Assuming there is enough room, these can significantly increase the bag's warmth. Be sure that the liner attaches via snaps or ties so you don't get tangled up inside. You can add tie loops later if your bag lacks them, but doing so is a nuisance.

- Stuff sack. All manufacturers provide you with a stuff sack, but they have a wide range of opinions on how tightly you need to pack it to get it closed. As a result, the published stuffed sizes are highly unreliable.

RATINGS AND TESTING

Any discussion of sleeping bags inevitably includes temperature ratings and their accuracy—or, more specifically, the lack thereof. A consumer survey of people who purchased bags illustrates the problem. Eight percent felt their bags were much warmer than rated, 18 percent said they were somewhat warmer, 47 percent thought the ratings were about right, 19 percent thought the bags were slightly overrated, and 8 percent considered the bags significantly colder than the ratings stated. Unfortunately, the responses were not broken down by gender.

Honest manufacturers will give a rating with at least a 10°F (6°C) range. However, even these ranges are a poor means of comparing bag warmth between brands. Therefore, the sleeping bag industry is trying to develop testing standards under the auspices of the American Society for Testing and Materials (ASTM). The standards should help level the playing field but won't be the final word—it is important to understand their limitations.

The most important standard is the heated-mannequin test. For this, an unclothed, human-shaped mannequin, with an average surface temperature of 90°F (32°C)—82°F (28°C) at the hands and feet—is placed in the sleeping bag on an uninsulated nylon cot inside an environmentally controlled chamber. A "Clo" value is determined for the sleeping bag based on the energy necessary to maintain the mannequin's temperature for 30 minutes.

The thermal resistance of clothing insulation is stated as a Clo, with one Clo being equal to the amount of clothing required to keep a sitting person comfortable in a 70°F (21°C) room with no wind. A sleeping person requires two Clo at 70°F (21°C), and every 10°F (6°C) drop in temperature requires about one extra Clo of insulation.

The independent laboratory many companies use is run by Dr. Elizabeth McCullough at Kansas State University. Widely held as the foremost researcher on insulation and sleeping bags, she chaired the task force for developing the new standard. Though admitting the test is not a perfect simulation (the bags are brand-new, and the mannequin of one arbitrary size and shape doesn't toss and turn), she argues it is a reasonable comparison of materials and designs.

CHOOSING A TEMPERATURE RANGE

Use the following guidelines to decide how warm your sleeping bag should be. Adjust these recommendations based on your own personal circumstances. A person who is an ectomorph (lean) will likely want a warmer bag than an endomorph (rotund) or especially a mesomorph (muscular).

Other variables that affect your warmth include diet (amount of fuel for the furnace), level of fatigue, clothing worn to bed, humidity, altitude, size, and type of tent (single versus double wall). It is quite possible for a person to be shivering one night and toasty the next even though the sleeping bag and outside temperature are the same.

The majority of us do most of our camping in the spring, summer, and fall with only occasional winter forays. For lower altitudes, below 6000 ft. (1800 m) or so, and latitudes, a bag rated to around 30° or 40°F (–1 to 5°C) will probably suffice. As you venture into higher elevations or travel farther north, most people will want something in the 20° to 30°F (–7 to –1°C) range as their all-around bag.

Choose a bag rated around 0° to 10°F (–18 to –12°C) if you will adventure in the early spring and late fall, as well as the summer (but you can ex-

pect to sleep a lot with it partially unzipped). Beyond this range is too hot and too bulky to be of practical use in the summer for most people.

Many climbers choose the –10° to 0°F (–23 to –18°C) range for use as a lightweight winter sleeping bag that can be augmented with clothing. This system gives a lot of versatility, but the bag must be cut wider to allow room for a warm parka.

The standard winter bag for most people is rated around –20° to –30°F (–29 to –34°C). This range works well for winter excursions in the Lower 48, as well as normal-season climbs in Alaska and the Himalayas. The weight and bulk of bags rated to –40°F will dissuade all but those heading to Denali in winter or crossing the Antarctic.

While nobody likes to be cold, the drawback of purchasing a bag that is too warm is that you will often be carrying more weight and bulk than you need. 'Tis a far, far better thing to use a layering

WARMTH BETWEEN THE SEXES

Men agree, few things on the planet are colder than the hands and feet of their significant other when she first crawls into bed. Though widely held, this generalization has led to a number of misconceptions about the thermostatic differences between the sexes.

According to Dr. Murray Hamlet of the U.S. Army Natick labs, body type, not gender, determines heat loss. The differences in metabolism and circulation in men and women are insignificant compared to differences in basic physics. In short, small things get colder faster than bigger things. Larger people have a lower surface-to-volume ratio, so they don't cool as rapidly. This is why toes—on men and women—get cold before legs. Individual body-fat percentage and metabolism rates also play important factors in our cold tolerance.

Another popular misconception is that since certain parts of the body lose heat faster than others do, bags require more insulation in

different areas. Adding more insulation to specific parts of a bag is rather the same as underfilling the other sections; heat will escape the most vulnerable area.

There is a lot of hype about women's sleeping bags these days, but it is driven more by marketing than reality. The real issue is that for far too long, most companies offered sleeping bags in only two lengths: regular and long. While these do fit the majority of the population, people at the ends of the bell curve were left wanting. A 5 ft. 2 in. (157 cm) woman will be swimming—and shivering—in a regular bag meant to fit someone who is 5 ft. 10 in. (178 cm). Some companies vary the internal width at the shoulders and hips of their bags by an inch or two; this may increase efficiency slightly for some people.

Be sure to spend time in any sleeping bag you are considering to make sure you can tolerate the cut; you will own whatever you choose for a **long** time.

system just as we do for clothing. This can include the use of one or all of the following: a thicker pad, a vapor barrier liner, an insulating liner, an insulating overbag, and a bivouac sack.

Wearing all of your insulated clothing inside a sleeping bag can be as effective as using a liner. However, going to bed wearing wet clothes will ensure a cold, miserable night; it requires a great deal of heat to evaporate water. It is also true that if your clothing is so bulky that it compresses the insulation or restricts your circulation, you are better off without the additional layers.

CARING FOR BAGS

Whether you have a down or synthetic bag, a little TLC will ensure many pleasant nights. Without it, your 10°F (–12°C) bag may be warm to only 30°F (–1°C), though no lighter or smaller.

As soon as you get home from a trip, pull your sleeping bag out of its stuff sack. Leaving the bag tightly packed when not in use is the fastest way to permanently flatten the insulation. Down bags come with a large cotton or mesh storage sack that is ideal for this purpose. I recommend purchasing one for your synthetic bag as well.

Most bags have loops on the end for hanging in your gear closet. This is fine, but I know of a case in which the local feline resident decided to use a really nice bag as scratching post—*bad* kitty. If you get a semirectangular bag that unzips around the foot section, you can use it as a comforter on your bed in the winter (sew two bed sheets together to make a case for it).

Dirt and body oils will degrade any insulation, so it is important to keep the bag clean. Start with preventive action by wearing long underwear and socks to bed; sleeping nude is not recommended. A silk bag liner is nice but adds weight and bulk. (I use one during the approach march on expeditions). When sleeping under the stars, use a ground

cloth under your pad to keep the bag out of the dirt.

Eventually you will need to clean your bag. Don't let this intimidate you. Whether it's down or synthetic, the process is the same. For down bags, it is worth using a specially formulated down soap available from most outdoor retailers. For synthetic bags, Ivory Snow is a good bet. Avoid strong detergents and anything with bleach. Most sources recommend against dry cleaning any sleeping bag; the process strips natural oils from down and can leave noxious fumes behind.

Use a large, commercial, front-loading washing machine—never a top-loader or agitator machine—on a gentle setting and run through the rinse cycle at least twice. If you hand-wash in a bathtub, fill the tub and then submerge the bag while it is in the stuff sack before pulling the bag from the sack (this keeps air out). Rinsing thoroughly is the key.

Be careful when moving the bag to the dryer so that baffles don't get torn by heavy down. If the bag has a DryLoft shell, turn it inside out. Use a low-heat setting, get a good book and a lot of quarters, and then sit back and watch. It can take from 2 to 6 hours to dry a down bag; be patient. Synthetic bags can be air dried overnight. Never store any sleeping bag while wet.

SLEEPING PADS

Without adequate insulation from the cold ground, you will be shivering inside even the world's warmest sleeping bag. Standard air mattresses are comfortable but just about worthless for insulation because air circulates within them. Spongelike, open-cell foam is also comfortable but needs to be very thick and bulky to provide adequate insulation, and it absorbs water, so a nylon case is needed for protection.

Closed-cell foam (such as EVA) provides good warmth and stays dry but leaves a lot to be desired in the comfort department. When you're sleeping

SLEEPING WARMER

Here are a few simple steps to minimize condensation problems and let you sleep warmer:

- Try to find shelter from the wind, and don't camp in the bottom of a valley.
- Increase blood flow by taking a brisk walk around camp prior to going to bed; you will sleep warmer if you start out warm.
- Make sure you are well fed and hydrated. A meal with a high-fat content takes longer to digest and generates more heat. Keep a water bottle nearby and bring some snacks to bed (unless you are in bear country).
- Prewarm your bag, especially in the foot, with a bottle filled with hot water. Be sure it won't leak!
- If possible, avoid crawling into a down bag while wearing wet or damp clothing.
- If you bring your boot liners into the bag to prevent freezing, first place them inside the sleeping bag's stuff sack, after turning it inside out, and close it.
- The U.S. Army preaches warming your bag first by getting in wearing underwear and then putting on additional insulation (such as pile clothing, down booties, mittens, a hat) during the night.
- An old wives' tale has it that sleeping nude is warmer than sleeping clothed. According to most experts, sleeping nude is not as warm because there is less total insulation around the body. In your bag, always wear at least long underwear; it prevents chills and cooling of the skin, and keeps the oils on your skin from contaminating the bag's insulation, resulting in a loss of loft.
- According to Dr. Hamlet of the Natick labs, 15 oz. (0.4 kg) of clothing equals 2 lbs. (0.9 kg) of extra down in a bag. This is because the warmth is trapped closer to your body and there are fewer voids to be heated. However, overly tight clothing, which restricts circulation, can make you colder than no clothes at all.
- Use a pee bottle for calls of nature during the night. Choose a wide-mouth bottle that is a different shape from your drinking bottle to prevent confusion in the dark.
- First thing in the morning, compress and then fluff your bag several times while it is still warm. This drives some of the moisture out of the insulation before it has a chance to freeze.
- Because everyone has a unique physiology and differing equipment, it is vital that you experiment with your sleeping system prior to going on an extended trip in extreme cold. What works for someone else may not work for you. Find out ahead of time when the consequences of a cold night out are not so severe.

on snow, many closed-cell foam pads are inadequate and need to be doubled up. An R-value of at least 3 is needed to keep from melting into the snow. Many pads have ridges or dimples for extra comfort, but these make it harder to sweep off snow or spilled soup.

Combining different materials can yield the best of both worlds, although there are some trade-offs too. Laminated open/closed-cell foam pads are a bit bulkier than closed-cell alone, though far more comfortable, but need to be covered to keep the foam dry.

Self-inflating air/open-cell foam pads are very comfortable on hard, rocky ground and can provide good insulation—these are my favorites. However, a small hole renders them useless. Extra care is required to prevent punctures, and the pad should be carried in a stuff sack when strapped to your pack.

Holes can be patched; however, you probably won't feel like it in the middle of the night, and cold makes the task trickier.

INSULATING LINERS AND OVERBAGS

Liners are usually lightweight sleeping bags that are cut narrow so they can be slipped inside other bags. To prevent you from getting all twisted up, it is very helpful for the liner to attach inside to loops on the main bag. The more sophisticated designs work well as sleeping bags in their own right; indeed, they may be all you need.

As the name implies, an overbag is simply an extra-large sleeping bag intended to house a normal bag without compressing the insulation of either. These typically add about 20°F (11°C) to the rating and can be used as very roomy 40°F (5°C) summer bags on their own. However, neither liners nor overbags are very efficient for boosting a bag's warmth. When weight and bulk are critical, include your insulated clothing in the system.

TO VB OR NOT VB

On an expedition to the North Pole in 1986, Will Steger's team used synthetic-filled bags. By the end of the trip, the bags had gained about 35 lbs. (16 kg), roughly a pound each night, in accumulated ice. Fortunately, they were using sleds to haul them.

Your skin transpires nearly a cup of water nightly, and this accumulates in your bag's insulation on longer trips. In extreme-cold conditions, it freezes and can result in a significant buildup of moisture, which fills dead-air spaces and reduces loft. High-altitude climbers have less of a problem with condensation buildup because they typically don't spend as much time in the extreme cold. On polar expeditions, a retreat to basecamp isn't possible.

To combat in-bag condensation, some use waterproof, vapor-barrier (VB) liners. Though these can make the space around you clammy, wearing long underwear mitigates this. VBs do, however, require more work on your part to prevent overheating that results in sweating; you'll need to adjust the ventilation throughout the night. Some people find this easy; others, who perhaps sweat more, find this regulation a real nuisance. Inside VB liners, you must remove most of your clothing, only to put it all back on when you wake up to relieve yourself, often getting chilled in the process. An alternative is VB clothing, worn over your underwear and under other layers. This works well in camp, but VB clothing is impractical during the day's exertions because you can't ventilate it well enough, so it must be carried. I am not aware of any ultralight VB jacket and pants currently on the market. Although the VB concept is effective for some people, most (including the U.S. Army) find it impractical.

CHAPTER 15

TENTS

THE FIRST SUMMER MOUNTAINEERING tent was designed by 22-year-old Edward Whymper in 1862. This technological marvel, which he used for his solo attempt on the Matterhorn, weighed 23 lbs. (10.4 kg) and rolled up to 6½ ft. (2 m) long. The A-frame shelter was made of the latest materials: unbleached calico walls, waterproof mackintosh floor, and four 1½ in.- (3.8-cm-) thick ash poles with iron points. According to Whymper, it was "sufficiently portable to be taken over the most difficult ground, whilst combining lightness with stability" (*Scrambles Amongst the Alps,* 1871), but required a Swiss guide to carry it.

Thirty years later, Alfred Mummery was using a two-man tent that weighed only 3½ lbs. (1.6 kg) and used two ice axes for support. As early as 1917, a London firm was selling a roomy, "waterproof" tent made of silk that weighed only 12 oz. (0.3 kg)! The tent had to be strung in a forest, however, since it had no poles.

Today's tents range from 2 lb. (0.9 kg) solo shelters to behemoths better delegated to basecamps and car camping. However, most tents are not suited for the special demands of climbers. While performance and weight are important, climbers should consider: How easy is it to set up in a howling wind? How hard is it to take down and stow after a freezing rain? How livable is it when you are stormbound for several days? How hard is it to crawl into during full conditions?

There are times when a tent assumes ultimate importance—if it blows down, you die. Quite literally, your life may depend on aluminum tubes the diameter of a pencil and fabrics thinner than your underwear. Mountaineering literature is filled with accounts of tents shredded by gale-force winds or crushed under the weight of snowfall.

TENTS FOR CLIMBERS

The right tent for you will depend on where and when you plan to use it. Standard backpacking tents are fine for camping in forests or on riverbanks during the summer. However, climbers who plan to visit the high country must think about tents that are sturdier.

THREE-SEASON ALPINE TENTS

These most versatile tents are often referred to as "extended three-season," "four-season backcountry," or "convertible" [Photo 15.1]. They are beefier than standard backpacking tents but still light enough to carry for less-demanding trips. Ideal for use during the summer months at tree line, they are also suitable for occasional winter trips in protected areas.

Since high winds are common in alpine environments, thunderstorms can be ferocious, and it is not unusual to get a foot of snow dumped on you at any time of year—the tent's performance in these conditions is critical. Also important for three-season tents is their effectiveness in heavy rainfall, as well as hot, muggy weather. On some models, the tent body can be left at home and the fly erected just using the poles and a purpose-built groundsheet—a good way to save weight if there are no bugs.

WINTER TENTS

In many respects, winter (expedition) tents are just beefier versions of their three-season siblings. The poles are of larger diameter and there are more of them. Additional guy points are added, there is generally a second door, and the fly is often a bright color to help locate home in a storm.

Photo 15.1   Three-season alpine tents come in many shapes and sizes.

Winter tents used to offer such features as snow flaps, frost liners, tunnel entrances, and cook holes. With few exceptions, these have all gone away. My experience has been that snow flaps (pieces of fabric sewn around the perimeter of the tent that you pile snow on to help anchor the tent) add weight, often freeze in place, and really aren't needed.

Full-coverage flies that extend right to the ground, and better ventilation, have eliminated the need for heavy, bulky cotton frost liners. By trapping a layer of "dead air," the inner tent is made significantly warmer and condensation is minimized.

Tunnel entrances, while nice in a storm for crawling through without bringing in the weather, are heavy and flap a lot in the wind. Zippers have improved enough that they very rarely fail if a good-quality zipper pull is used. Cook holes, of course, leak in wet conditions, and most winter tents now have open vestibules for cooking.

While many companies refer to them as "four-season" tents, this is stretching the truth. Winter tents are definitely overkill for most summer camping below 15,000 ft. (4600 m). Sure, you *can* use them, but you have to lug around a lot of unnecessary weight and bulk; they also tend to be uncomfortably hot.

TENT TARPS

An alternative to traditional tents, these have a single wall of coated fabric and set up with a minimal structure, often just a single center pole. Most do not have a floor or windows, so weight and cost are kept to a minimum.

Tent tarps may actually be better suited to winter camping than summer, when mosquitoes and black flies will eat you alive. The tarps can hold up to significant wind and snow if they are pitched well.

HIGH-ALTITUDE TENTS

These are the true portable bomb-shelters: light, easy to set up, capable of withstanding nearly anything . . . and expensive. Since you seldom have time or space to build protective snow walls, these tents need to withstand the full force of the wind.

High-altitude tents are often built with waterproof/breathable fabric, reducing the weight and bulk of an equally strong double-wall model. These materials work best in cold, dry air and perform rather poorly in a jungle environment. Single-wall tents can be as much as 20° colder than double-wall tents with full-coverage flies.

Because one wall must bear all the wear and tear, single-wall tents are not as durable as double-wall tents in the long run. When the rain fly of a conventional tent is damaged by UV rays or by shovels hitting it while you're digging out from a snowstorm, the inner tent still remains strong. It may even be possible to replace the fly. A single-wall tent can be destroyed with one errant shovel swipe.

DESIGN

For the first hundred years, most backpacking tents had A-shaped profiles. These were relatively weight-efficient but did not offer much headroom and required dozens of stakes. With the arrival of new materials in the mid-1970s, geodesic dome and parabolic hoop tents proved to be stronger and roomier. Today, the better tents are shaped to fit human activity and equipment without wasting space [Illustration 15.1].

Geodesic dome tents tend to be stronger, due to overlapping poles, and more spacious than tents that require stakes for support. However, "freestanding" is a misnomer because, even though the tents may stand on their own, many of them require stakes for vestibules. More important, these tents must be staked down in high winds. When left unattended, they roll easily in the wind—even with gear or people inside them!

In recent years, geodesic designs have been refined to make them stronger and more efficient. Rather than a hexagonal floor plan that wastes space, the floors are elongated to fit you and your

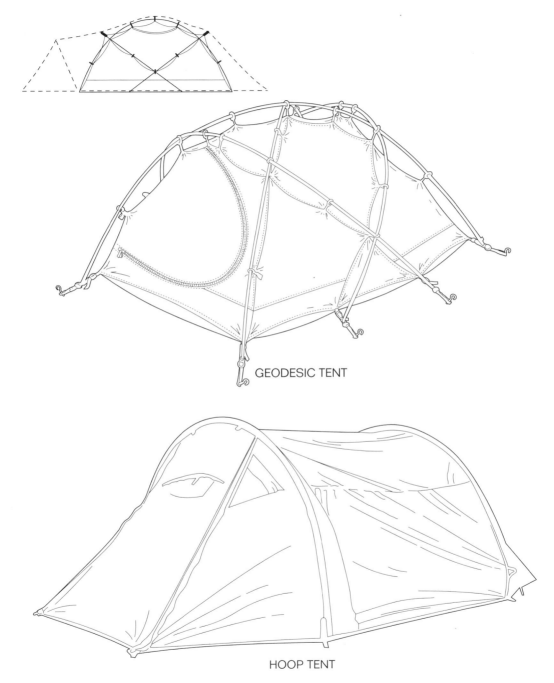

GEODESIC TENT

HOOP TENT

Illustration 15.1   Geodesic and hoop tents

EXPEDITION TENT TIPS

When setting up camp, probe the area for crevasses first, and then stamp out a good platform in the snow. Build snow walls at least as far from the tent as they are high, or you will get drifted in—make sure they are thick enough that they won't topple! Digging a small knee-deep pit in front of the door makes it easier to get in and out.

You can maximize guylines and minimize stakes by tying a long leash from a corner stake loop to a guy point above it [Illustration 15.2]. This way one stake does both jobs. Two guylines attached to a guy point at an angle provide greater stability than a single line.

If you must leave your tent in a high-wind situation, you might consider collapsing it so that it is still there when you get back. Pull out the poles and pile snow blocks on top (make sure they won't melt and soak your sleeping bag), and mark the spot with several wands.

When stuck in a tent for days on end, livability becomes a concern. Lots of side pockets are very useful, and gear lofts make a good place for drying stuff. Be careful using candle lanterns or you could easily end up with wax all over your expensive sleeping bag—permanently. Carry a 1-liter container for use as a pee bottle; practice your aim outside first. For basecamps, some people like to completely cover the tent floor with ⅛ in. closed-cell foam pads, a nice luxury.

Cooking in a tent without spilling your dinner, scalding your partner, or killing both of you is something of an art, but a few rules help. If cooking inside will be a frequent activity, get a hanging stove.

Always try to start gas and kerosene stoves outside (not necessary with cartridge stoves), but if that isn't possible, use fuel paste to minimize flare-ups. Be prepared to throw the ignited Molotov cocktail until it has settled down **completely**; keep the nearest door unzipped and within tossing range (and make sure someone else's tent isn't in the line of fire). Always keep multiple vents open when a stove is running, no matter how bad the storm—it beats dying of carbon monoxide poisoning.

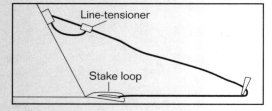

Reducing stake points

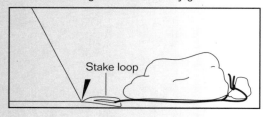

"Staking" the tent on rocky ground

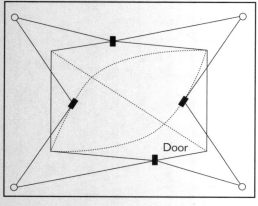

Increasing stability for high winds

■ Guy points — Guylines ○ Stakes or rocks

Illustration 15.2   Guying out a tent

gear more comfortably. The intersections of poles are also located higher off the ground to increase strength.

Hoop-style tents, which are held up by three to four stakes, tend to be lighter, more space-efficient, and faster to pitch than freestanding models. In many cases, they offer better ventilation and remarkable strength, too. About the only disadvantages are that they aren't as easy to move around or pick up to shake out dirt.

Rain flies that attach with quick-release plastic buckles are the easiest to use and allow the fly's tension to be easily adjusted as the fabric stretches. However, should the female half of the buckle break, a field repair may be difficult. Flies that use hooks or grommets and elastic to attach to the ends of poles are fussy and a nuisance to take apart when frozen to the ground.

To prevent flapping and reduce weight, the individual panels of the canopy and fly are cut with concave instead of straight edges. Termed a "cat-enary cut," this allows the tent to be pitched tauter.

There are two basic floor styles: bathtub and bias-taped [Illustration 15.3]. The bathtub floor has a minimum of seams to leak since the fabric wraps up the side of the tent. Bias-taped floors are sewn onto the sidewalls, leaving a seam all the way around the perimeter that allows a tauter pitch and provides greater strength than bathtub floors. In theory, bias-taped floors are easier and cheaper to replace should they be worn out or damaged.

Floor area and volume are merely starting points for comparisons of tent size. The amount of usable space in a tent is more important, but unfortunately there is no standard for this comparison. For mountaineering, be aware that narrow tents will fit in many places that wide ones will not.

VENTILATION

Perhaps the most frequently overlooked, yet critical, aspect of tent design is ventilation. Your comfort depends upon adequate air circulation

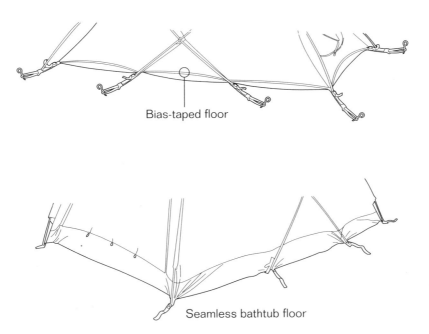

Bias-taped floor

Seamless bathtub floor

Illustration 15.3   Bathtub and bias-taped floors

when the tent is buttoned up against driving rain and blowing snow. Since cooking inside the tent is a fact of life in the mountains, good ventilation is also vital to prevent carbon monoxide poisoning, as well as steam soaking everything.

The best ventilation system allows cool, dry air to enter at the bottom and warm, moist air to exit at the top. The tent must also have good hot-weather ventilation for those sultry nights when you need protection from bloodthirsty insects.

Conventional tents have an uncoated nylon canopy, which allows moisture to pass through, and a waterproof flysheet, which keeps out the wet. Usually the fly stops several inches above the ground to allow air circulation. On winter tents, the fly extends to the ground, termed full-coverage, which makes the tent significantly warmer in cold weather but less comfortable on hot nights.

FABRICS

The more expensive tents use better grades of fabric with thinner fibers and higher thread counts. These fabrics are lighter, stronger, and more resistant to stretching than standard materials, and they hold coatings better.

A lot of unsubstantiated technobabble is thrown around concerning tent fabrics. Companies often list the weight per yard, and occasionally the denier (thread diameter), of the various fabrics, but this has little meaning unless they also provide such data as tear strength and waterproofness.

Some manufacturers use polyester instead of nylon for rain flies because the material does not stretch as much when wet and is more resistant to UV rays. In practice, high-quality nylons can out-perform cheap polyesters.

Compared to other fabrics, ripstops are lighter weight and more tear-resistant. Taffetas are generally more abrasion-resistant and have greater strength. Realize, however, that tear strengths are often given for uncoated fabrics; the strength of-

ten goes down substantially after coating because the fibers are bonded together. Many tent manufacturers build floors with a more abrasion-resistant fabric and a thicker waterproof coating.

Although fabric breathability varies, proper ventilation remains the most critical factor in reducing condensation. No fabric alone can vent the large quantities of moisture encountered in winter. Aside from the one to two pints of water vapor that each person exhales and perspires every night, there is also all the snow that gets tracked into the tent and the moisture trapped inside clothing and sleeping bags. Look for good ventilation first.

FLAME RESISTANCE

Nobody likes to condone it, but the reality of severe weather dictates that sooner or later you will end up cooking inside your tent. Unfortunately, this greatly increases the risk of a potentially disastrous fire.

Several states do not allow any tents to be sold that do not pass the Canvas Products Association International (CPAI)-84 flame resistance tests. This is a great idea for the cabin tents, dining flies, ice-fishing tents, and play tents for which the tests and laws were originally designed. However, several high-tech fabrics that are ideal for mountaineering tents are not offered in the U.S. because of this standard.

Many companies won't use fabrics that don't meet the standard simply for liability reasons. This is why you cannot buy a Gore-Tex tent in the United States anymore. The glue that holds the laminates together prevented the fabric from passing the standard, so W. L. Gore no longer allows its product to be used for tents.

Another fabric that does not pass fire-resistance tests is silicone elastomer–coated nylon. Compared to the standard polyurethane coating, the silicone makes the fabric stronger (so that lighter fabrics can be used), easier to stuff, and more UV-resistant. But since the material does not pass CPAI-84, these tents are not available everywhere.

I certainly wouldn't hesitate to buy a tent that

met my needs simply because it didn't pass the flame-retardancy tests. On a practical level, I'd still be just as careful when cooking inside a tent that *did* pass the tests—they still burn!

WATERPROOF/BREATHABLE FABRICS

Not long after Gore-Tex was introduced in 1976, the first tents made with waterproof/breathable (WP/B) fabrics appeared. Despite the criticism of naysayers, these tents (from Bibler, Early Winters, and Marmot) worked reasonably well once the designers figured out some of the bugs.

The fabrics are laminated on the inside with a fuzzy, meshlike material. This inner laminate protects the film or coating from abrasion, disperses moisture over a wide area to speed drying, and acts as a frost liner to keep the internal snowstorm to a minimum.

When discussing the breathability of tent fabrics, it is important to realize that there is much less driving effect to push moisture to the outside than in clothing systems where your body is close to the shell. It is unrealistic to expect even the most breathable WP/B fabrics to be totally condensation-free.

While venting is important, tents that have more breathable fabrics dry out noticeably faster, as do their contents. With all tents that use internal poles, you will notice significant condensation on the cold metal; they appear to sweat.

Though breathable to water vapor, none of the fabrics in these tents is air-permeable—an important distinction. Oxygen can pass through some WP/B fabrics fairly easily, but the larger carbon dioxide molecule does not fit through the membrane or coating very well. This means you can suffocate inside a single-wall tent that is tightly sealed up in a storm. Climbers have died from this.

SEAMS

Lap-felled seams are the industry standard for strength but leave two rows of stitching [Illustration 15.4]. Overlocked seams have also proved themselves in demanding conditions and are easier to seal. For either seam, look for eight to twelve stitches per inch and careful workmanship.

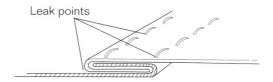

Illustration 15.4   Lap-felled seam

If you combined the thousands of needle holes in a tent into one, they would probably equal the size of a quarter. Hence it is necessary to seal these holes if you want to stay dry. If you are willing to take the time (4 to 6 hours over several days) to carefully apply Seam Grip, your tent will keep you dry for years.

Factory-taped seams are a nice feature that is becoming the industry norm. If done properly, the tent should be good to go right out of the bag. However, slipshod workmanship or cheap tape will force you to apply Seam Grip anyway.

For monsoon or tropical conditions, you still may want to seal the seams on the outside. Water can get inside a seam from the outside and move by capillary action to a weak point to the inside. Here in the Colorado Rockies and on high peaks, I don't bother, but for other areas of the country, it may be a good idea.

POLES

If the fabric is the skin of the tent, the poles are the skeleton. Many people think that the poles should make the tent completely rigid for maximum strength. However, testing and experience have shown that some give in the poles is desirable to spread forces more evenly through the structure.

Practically all high-quality tents use aluminum poles from one of two manufacturers. High-tech fiberglass tubing, made with multilayer S-glass and epoxy resin, can be incredibly strong and light, but it tends to be too flexible.

The Easton 7075-T9 poles are made by welding

sheets of metal into a tube, which is then drawn and tempered. This alloy is susceptible to corrosion (poles used near the ocean are much more prone to breakage), so the poles are anodized both for protection and color-coding. Finally, the ferrules are glued into place.

The Dongah 7001-T6 poles are extruded and drawn, so there is no seam. The ferrules are either peened into place or the tubing is butted (as on a bike frame) to eliminate the ferrule altogether. These poles are at least as strong, stiff, and durable as Easton's.

Poles come in several different diameters, the most commonly used sizes being 0.34 in. (8.5 mm), 0.36 in. (9 mm), and 0.38 in. (9.5 mm). Obviously, the larger the diameter, the stiffer and stronger the pole. But the trade-off is increased weight and bulk, so bigger isn't necessarily better.

No matter the pole material, for winter conditions good shock cord is important. Cheap shock cord wears out quickly and loses elasticity in severe cold, making pole assembly difficult at best. Quickly jerking the pole sections apart may help warm the elastic somewhat but should not be necessary.

Always carry at least one pole repair kit, those oversize tubes that can splint a broken pole. This is such a critical item, which weighs and costs nearly nothing, that it should not even be called an accessory.

POLE SYSTEMS

While virtually all modern tents use shock-corded aluminum poles, there is much disagreement among tent makers on how to attach them to the structure. The most common approach is to thread the poles through sleeves sewn into the seams. Sleeves made of nylon mesh, versus solid fabrics, allow greater air circulation that enhances ventilation and reduces condensation.

The old approach required threading a pole through several sleeve segments—a nuisance at best during a storm. Better designs use a single, continuous sleeve for each pole, which greatly simplifies setup. Tents that have color-coded poles and sleeves are rare but worth looking for; you'll appreciate the convenience when exhausted and rushing to get inside your haven.

Using plastic clips, instead of sleeves, to attach the poles has become very popular because they allow superior ventilation and reduce weight. Clip systems are often claimed to dramatically reduce setup time. However, some tents have so many clips that this is highly debatable. Although people may worry about strength and durability, clips have withstood the test of time and mountain storms.

The lightest and fastest pitching method for supporting the structure is to eliminate pole sleeves and clips entirely. Only single-walled tents can do this. The drawback is that you typically need to crawl inside the tent to position the poles and secure them in place (easier on some designs than on others).

How the pole ends attach to the tent greatly affects the speed of setup and takedown. Many manufacturers use grommets that pole tips pass through—the nicest ones have locking tips that make it much easier for one person to set up. Another popular style is a pocket that the pole slips into. This works well as long as the pocket is designed properly—many are not. My least-favorite design is the pin that slips into an open pole end, since it is harder to assemble while wearing gloves and the pole can fill with mud and snow.

REINFORCEMENTS

The strongest tents are those in which everything—tent, poles, fly (if there is one), and guylines—works together. In particular, guylines should attach directly to the pole structure, not just to the fabric panels or seams. Without this connection, the tent can wander under the fly in strong wind, making it more prone to collapse.

For double-wall tents, the underside of the fly

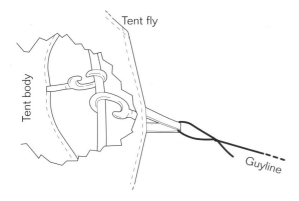

Tent fly

Tent body

Guyline

Illustration 15.5   Guyline attachment (inner and outer)

should have attachments to the body of the tent, preferably at pole intersections [Illustration 15.5]. (The external guylines should attach at a corresponding point on the outside.) These guyline attachment points need to be solid and wide so they don't pull free or concentrate stress forces. Underside fly attachments do make the tent harder to set up, but you need to use them in only the most severe conditions.

Some manufacturers also offer internal guylines that cross-brace the tent. For the most extreme conditions, these are a good idea, and you might consider adding them to a tent that lacks them.

Most companies provide guylines that are difficult to see when you are stumbling around at night—black is the worst. Red or yellow cord with reflective material is much more visible—a great retrofit. The three-holed plastic line tighteners are easiest to use on icy cords; knots and two-holed tighteners either slip or are difficult to adjust.

The strength and ultimate life of a tent is in large part determined by the reinforcements of stress areas and wear points. Critical points in seams should be backstitched or bar-tacked and the ends of webbing melted (not cut). Wear points, such as corners, should be protected with heavy material. Thoughtful manufacturers provide matching fabric swatches for minor repairs.

ESTIMATING WIND SPEEDS

2 mph / 3 kph	A barely perceptible, cooling breeze
5 mph / 8 kph	A definite breeze that's felt on your face
10 mph / 16 kph	A gentle breeze that requires staking the tent during setup
20 mph / 32 kph	A "fresh" breeze that sways small trees and turns tents to sails
30 mph / 48 kph	A "strong" breeze that starts to interfere with walking and makes pitching your tent challenging
40 mph / 60 kph	A gale that makes walking difficult and tent setup a nightmare
50 mph / 80 kph	A strong gale in which you have to brace yourself
60 mph / 96 kph	A full-blown storm that makes you wonder how strong the tent is
70 mph / 112 kph	You now understand why this is called a "violent" storm—forget walking.
80 mph / 128 kph	Welcome to the hurricane zone . . . where there are no atheists. This is when you're glad you spent the big money on a good tent.

STAKES

Of course, the guylines are only as good as their connection to the ground [Photo 15.2]. The tent skewers most companies include will bend with little provocation. Invest in good stakes that can be pounded into dirt, and they should last nearly as long as your tent.

For snow and sand, the long half-tube aluminum stakes are light and provide great holding power, but they can't take much pounding. When the ground is too rocky or frozen to use stakes, tie a 2 to 3 ft. (0.6 to 1 m) piece of cord to each stake loop. Then tie the other end of this cord to a small rock or stick and pile big rocks on top of it—much more secure than just tying the line to a rock.

When on the go in winter, ice axes, skis, and ski poles make great stakes. But when you need to take your gear and leave the tent behind, good, long snow stakes or deadmen (soft stakes or stuff sacks filled with snow) are required. Deadmen have great holding power but can freeze in place, making removal difficult.

FEATURES

It's the niceties that can make a tent great. On the other hand, minor annoyances can really detract from an otherwise commendable shelter.

- Side-zip doors. Doors that zip open to one side, instead of to the ground, hang out of the way and don't get trampled on. Better doors operate smoothly with one big arm motion; two hands should not be required.
- Vestibule. Poorly designed vestibules force you to reach all the way across your gear to use the zipper. Better ones also unzip from the top with a big opening so you can get in and out easily by stepping over the door sill.
- Door ties. Ties for holding furled doors open should be easy to operate. Large hooks and buttons work well, but if they use elastic this may eventually wear out. Reflective nylon tabs attached to zippers are easier to grab with gloves than the zipper pull alone.
- Windows. Rain flies with clear windows are a fairly recent innovation that make being stuck inside much more pleasant. These windows now have a good track record (no problems with hazing or cracking in the cold) and are becoming more common.
- Big stake loops. Long tent-stake loops, 4 in. (10 cm) or bigger, give you more working room than short ones and allow skis and ice axes to be used as stakes. If the loops have a half twist to hold them open, they are even easier to use.
- Multiple pockets. It's almost impossible to have too many pockets inside for stowing things. An abundance of loops allows hanging stoves or candle lanterns and stringing clotheslines. Many tents now have an optional gear loft

WIND FORCE

The force that a gust of wind exerts increases with the square of the wind speed. This means that as the wind speed doubles, the force it exerts on you (and your tent) quadruples. In practical terms, a 40 mph wind exerts thirty-two times as much force as a 5 mph breeze.

Your location on the globe also affects the force of wind. Because of the effects of the earth's rotation, air density decreases with increasing latitude. Since Denali sits nearer the North Pole, the air is slightly less dense at 20,000 ft. than at the same altitude in Nepal.

Another complicating factor is altitude. When you are gasping for oxygen at 20,000 ft. after minor exertion, you realize that the air is much less dense than at sea level. This decrease in density also affects the amount of force the wind exerts. The table below lists an approximation of equivalent wind forces.

A 40 mph / 64 kph wind at sea level equals:

43 mph / 69 kph wind at 5,000 feet / 1524m
46 mph / 74 kph wind at 10,000 feet / 3048m
50 mph / 80 kph wind at 15,000 feet / 4572m
54 mph / 87 kph wind at 20,000 feet / 6096m
59 mph / 95 kph wind at 25,000 feet / 7620m
64 mph / 103 kph wind at 30,000 feet / 9144m

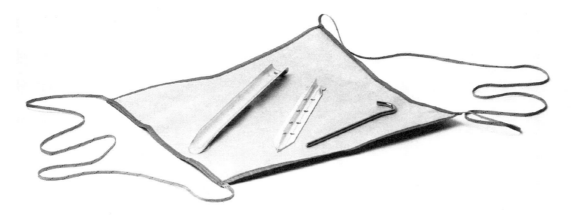

Photo 15.2   Snow/sand stake (left), aluminum T-stake (middle), tough 7001 aluminum skewer (right), soft stake (fabric underneath the other three stakes)

available that makes a convenient shelf and drying rack. These can interfere with headroom, however.

- Real stuff sack. Most tent makers provide long, skinny stuff sacks that are virtually worthless for life on the trail. An oversize sack is much easier to stuff, will hold a wet or frozen tent, and allows the tent to be smashed into odd corners of a pack.

- High visibility. The color of a tent, inside and out, is more important than many people realize. Low-impact exterior colors, such as tan and green, are nice for backpacking. But if you will be using the tent for alpine climbs, a bright color is much easier to find in a storm. Guy points with reflective webbing will light up in the dark from your headlamp hundreds of feet away.

- Pleasant ambiance. The interior of a tent preferably should be bright with a slightly warm tone. If a tent is bluish or dark inside, it will feel cold and oppressive. If the interior color is too yellow or red, it may increase tension and make it difficult to identify colors. Dark mosquito netting lets you see that incredible view outside more easily than white netting.

BIVY SACKS

A good bivouac sack is the next best alternative to a tent when the weather turns ugly. In essence, these are all-weather, no frills envelopes that are just big enough for you, a sleeping bag, and a little bit of gear. While most share the same concept, the design and performance vary significantly.

Most bivy sacks on the market have a three-ply Gore-Tex laminated fabric on the top for breathability and waterproofness. To reduce costs, many manufacturers use a polyurethane-coated fabric on the bottom of the sack. However, these do not breathe adequately when the sack is zipped up, hence condensation can be a problem. Bivy sacks that use Gore-Tex on the top and bottom give the best performance and are worth the extra money if you will use them often.

No matter the materials used, it is important that all the seams be sealed. While it is convenient to put your pad inside the sack, leaving it outside helps protect against abrasion.

The design and location of the zippers make a big difference in a bivy sack's performance. The simplest and most leak-proof design is a horizontal opening; however, these make the sacks a nuisance to get in and out of. Some companies provide a horizontal closure and one down the center of the sack. My favorite designs are those that curve across the chest and down the side of the bivy. Effective flaps to protect against leaks are important for any style of closure.

Although Gore-Tex is "breathable" to water and oxygen molecules, it does not allow carbon dioxide to pass readily. This means if you seal the bivy sack tightly, you may find yourself gasping for air as CO_2 builds up inside the enclosed space.

Rolling off the side of a cliff during the night is best avoided. Therefore, we need to stay tied in. Some sacks allow this by running the rope through the zipper (if it's in the right place) or an opening made for this purpose. Others offer a runner sewn into the sack itself, which can be sealed better against leakage.

Having spent a few sleepless nights without one, I can attest to the value of mosquito netting in a bivy sack. While certainly not necessary in all environments or year-round, the option of a removable one is well worth considering.

Many people like hooped bivy sacks that hold the fabric away from your face. These really do increase comfort; however, they add weight, bulk, and complexity. Although they're great for solo backpackers, I would consider one for climbing only if it could be used equally well without the poles.

For the most efficiency, a two-person bivy sack combines body heat and reduces weight. Their

TENT TLC

Anyone who lays down hundreds of dollars for a tent wants it to last. The number-one requested repair is replacing zippers. The main culprit is sand in the zipper track that acts as an abrasive, so keep doors out of the dirt. Try blasting them with a hose if they get really dirty.

Do not shake out shock-corded poles for assembly if you want them to last—this can cause nicks and stress fractures. Slide the pieces together. When you disassemble the poles, start from the middle and work to the ends so the elastic is not excessively stressed. Always carry a pole-repair sleeve and some duct tape.

Many companies sell custom ground cloths for each tent to help protect the floor against abrasion. However, they are rather expensive and don't work much better than a sheet of plastic trimmed slightly smaller than the tent. When weight and bulk are an issue, you certainly don't need a ground cloth, but it's a great idea for car camping and short trips.

The biggest enemy of your tent is ultraviolet (UV) light; it attacks the fabric just as it attacks your own skin. At high altitude, the problem is so severe that noticeable fading can occur after one expedition. Eventually the fabric becomes so weak that you can put a hand right through it.

The only solution to UV degradation is to minimize exposure as much as possible. Avoid setting up your tent in the middle of the day. If at basecamp for an extended period, rig a tarp over your tent. Leave the rain fly on, even if you don't need it, because that is the cheapest component to replace (if it is still available).

Another way to destroy a tent is to store it while wet. Mildew will attach to the waterproof coating, causing it to delaminate (and, no, that is not a warranty problem). Aluminum poles will corrode, which can eventually weaken them, if stored in a damp environment.

Do not wash your tent in a washing machine with an agitator—it can weaken the seams. The best cleaning method is to use a sponge and mild soap, and then air-dry it completely. Never put a tent in a clothes dryer.

main drawback is the frequent lack of bivy sites big enough for two people. Using a bivy sack will easily add 5° to 10°F (3° to 6°C) to the rating of your sleeping bag, even inside a tent.

ZDARSKY TENT

Over seventy years ago, Matthäus Zdarsky developed a simple alternative to bivouac sacks that is ideal for a team of alpine climbers. The Zdarsky tent is made from lightweight, coated fabric; has no poles; and is open on the bottom.

Since there is no floor, you can pull the tent over your head while wearing crampons or skis to get a quick respite from a blizzard. Two or three climbers cuddled together inside a single shelter are warmer than individuals in separate sacks (which are also heavier and bulkier than a Zdarsky tent but afford more wet protection).

These are seldom commercially available but are very easy to make [Illustration 15.6]. The most common versions are the width of the fabric, usually 60 in. (1.5 m), and have two tunnel vents in the middle (like stuff sacks with no ends). Refinements include quickdraws sewn into the corners, so you can anchor in, and a few snaps on the bottom hem to help keep the tent from billowing in the wind.

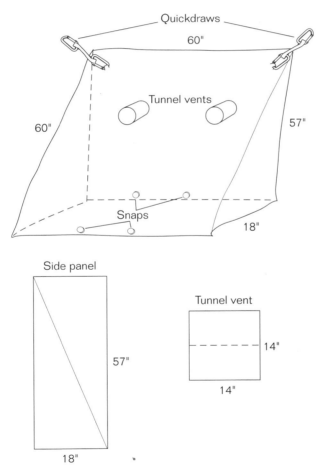

Illustration 15.6   Zdarsky tent

CHAPTER 16

PACKS

CONSIDER A 2-DAY CLIMB OF THE BLACK Ice Couloir on the Grand Teton. First, you need to carry climbing gear, bivy equipment, clothes, food, and camera up to the Lower Saddle—4800 vertical ft. (1477 m) in only 7 miles of hiking.

Unless you're incredibly Spartan, or wealthy enough to buy ultralight gear, this load can easily exceed 40 lbs. (18 kg), and your shoulders will scream in agony without a decent suspension system on your pack. The next day, however, when you're balancing on front points and running it out for hours, a huge, unwieldy pack with a thick waist belt will have you cursing.

The demands that climbers place on packs are more rigorous than those of hikers. Characteristics such as freedom of movement, stability, and durability are much more important. We also want them to be lightweight and simple, yet capable of handling heavy loads. With so many demands, you will likely end up owning several packs for your different adventures.

TYPES OF PACKS

Despite some claims, there is no single pack that will do everything the multifaceted climber may need. You may end up owning an assortment of packs from the following categories.

HIP PACKS

When traveling light and fast over a lot of terrain, a large hip pack (a.k.a. fanny pack or bum sac) is often ideal. The bigger ones are about the size of a small daypack, around 15 liters (900 cu. in.), yet are more stable when running and less obtrusive when climbing.

CRAG PACKS

Practically any midsize daypack is fine for getting your gear to the climb. Crag packs typically range from 25 to 40 liters (1500 to 2400 cu. in.) and are built with beefier fabrics. Most of the time, a frame is neither needed nor wanted. Features and style (top-loading or front-loading) are largely a matter of personal preference. Since it's hard to go wrong, crag packs aren't covered here, although you can glean some helpful hints on what to look for from the discussion of larger packs.

ALPINE PACKS

Of all the categories of packs, none requires more versatility than alpine-climbing packs [Photo 16.1]. Indeed, if you're on a limited budget and choose wisely, you could get by with an alpine pack for the majority of your climbing adventures.

Many companies claim to make an alpine pack, but a lot of those manufacturers have no clue how their packs are really used in the mountains. Sure, any pack with sufficient volume will "work," but some so-called alpine packs weigh more than 5 lbs. (2.3 kg), others interfere with your freedom of movement, and still others don't have the features required by climbers.

Packs around 50 to 60 liters (3000 to 3700 cu. in.) are about right for a long day of ice climbing or a multiday summer alpine climb. You may need a bigger pack for longer, Peruvian-type alpine climbs or winter ascents. Don't plan to use a pack's expanded capacity for anything but approach hikes—packs become very unstable when maxed out.

Most alpine packs are single-compartment, top-loading designs with extendable top pockets. These have the greatest range of volume, hence the most versatility.

Photo 16.1   Alpine pack with a beveled bottom

Many alpine packs eliminate the frame to reduce weight. But this hardman's approach has lost much appeal thanks to new technology. You would do well to choose a pack with either a simple frame or one that is removable to handle 40-lb. (18 kg) climbing loads. The weight increase of a good system is minimal compared to the energy savings and comfort.

EXTERNAL FRAME PACKS

Until the mid-1970s, the standard for mountaineering on extended trips was external frame packs such as the venerable Kelty Tioga. The rigid aluminum frame, to which the pack is attached, effectively transfers weight onto your hips while allowing good back ventilation. These remain the packs of choice for extended trail hikes.

Quality external-frame packs tend to be much less expensive than comparable-volume internal-frame packs. Probably half the people who buy internal frames would be better served by a good external. For those who do most of their hiking on trails or routinely carry very heavy loads, external frames remain the best choice.

That said, I don't recommend external for most climbers and skiers because the frame is largely inflexible and the load is far from your center of gravity—both of which make the pack relatively unstable. They usually have a wide profile too, so snagging trees is more common. External frames are also more susceptible to destruction by baggage handlers at airports.

EXPEDITION PACKS

When your excursions are longer than a few days out, you will need even greater capacity than alpine packs offer [Photo 16.2]. Lowe Alpine revolutionized the industry in 1967 with the introduction of the internal frame Expedition. Constructed using two parallel aluminum stays inside the pack, the new design offered better balance and freedom of movement when climbing or skiing.

Packs have come a long way since then—the best internal frame packs are remarkably comfortable even when carrying the heaviest loads. To achieve this, and fit everyone at the same time, suspension systems have become very complicated.

Most average-sized climbers and skiers will probably want an expedition pack in the 90 to 100 liter (5500 to 6000 cu. in.) volume range. For longer expeditions into remote areas, you may need a pack around 115 to 150 liters (7000 to 9000 cu. in.).

Because of the loads these can accommodate, and the hours you will spend carrying the pack, it really pays to shop carefully. Second only to the hiking comfort of your boots, selecting the best pack for you is of vital importance.

Photo 16.2   Expedition pack with a flat bottom

VOLUME

Because the industry standard for measuring pack volumes is still being worked out, the numbers manufacturers list are useful in making comparisons only to their other packs. Packs listed with the same capacity by different companies vary widely in true volume.

How much volume do you need? You should take into account the size or type of gear you'll be packing (for example, the size of your sleeping bag), the time of year (winter gear is bulkier), and the nature of the trip (some climbing trips require more gear than others).

Abundant capacity is alluring. But resist the temptation to buy the largest behemoth out there,

unless you absolutely need the room. The extra girth inhibits arm movement when climbing or skiing and gets in the way when bushwhacking or just passing through airport crowds. The increased depth also shifts the pack's center of gravity farther from your own.

Once you own a monster pack, you usually find a way to fill it, resulting in a perpetually heavy pack even on an overnight summer trip. If you somehow manage to keep the excess to a minimum, many of the big packs, even with their myriad straps, do not compress well when underfilled; they sag out or flop around.

On the other hand, if in doubt, err on the large side. Strapping stuff on the outside is just asking for lost or damaged gear, as well as an invitation to the evil tree spirits that grab passing packs.

The death knell for any large pack is "round-out," that bloated barreling that moves the center of gravity outward and throws you off balance [Illustration 16.1]. Tall and skinny is better than short and fat.

External compression straps alone are incapable of maintaining a pack's flat profile. The packs that have the best ride have an internal structural shelf that maintains the proper shape. The second-best alternative is a compression panel, which pulls the front of the pack into the small of your back.

SUSPENSION SYSTEMS

You can put the body of a Ferrari on the chassis of a Chevy Nova and get a great-looking, expensive car that still handles terribly. Likewise, the world's best pack bag is little more than fluff if the suspension and frame aren't up to the task. With cars and packs, most shoppers tend to get caught up with the body rather than what carries it. A pack that doesn't fit well causes sore shoulders, chafed underarms, and black-and-blue hips.

A good suspension system consists of a frame

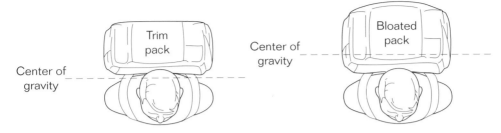

Illustration 16.1 Packs viewed from above: skinny versus fat

and harness that distribute the pack's load equally around the circumference of your hips and provide stability for the pack and the wearer. This requires careful tailoring and lots of adjustability to accommodate the range of differently shaped torsos. As is the case with footwear, fit should have the final say.

ALPINE FRAMES

Traditionally, few alpine packs had a stiff frame to transfer the weight off your shoulders and onto your hips. Though lightweight, soft packs cannot comfortably support loads over 35 lbs. (16 kg). Despite some companies' claims, plastic frame sheets and folded foam pads don't add much support.

Truly comfortable, well-balanced suspension systems used to mean backpack weights of 5 lbs. (2.3 kg) or more. But new packs using high-tech materials keep the weight under 4 lbs. (1.8 kg), yet still provide frame stays to carry heavy loads comfortably.

Just because a pack has stays, however, does not necessarily mean it will support a full load without sagging onto your shoulders. It's worth the extra money to look for stays made of 7000-series aluminum. If the company doesn't mention the alloy (the term "aircraft grade" is marketing gibberish), you can bet it is using cheap stuff that will do little more than add weight. An otherwise nice pack can often be upgraded with stiffer stays.

Stabilizer straps running from the top of the shoulders to the pack will pull the pack closer to your center of gravity and minimize shifting. However, few alpine packs have stays tall enough to actually lift the load off your shoulders. If you anticipate frequently carrying heavy loads, look for a pack with stays that rise about 3 in. (8 cm) above your shoulders when the pack is weighted. A removable sleeping pad built into the suspension system can be useful, and many alpine packs have this feature. Look for a long, rectangular pad rather than a square pad for bivy comfort. Many designs require a struggle to get the pads stuffed back in place; often it means emptying the entire contents of the pack. If this is hard to do in a showroom, imagine what it will be like after you've shivered at a bivy all night long and it's storming as you pack up.

EXPEDITION FRAMES

Most companies are loathe to admit it, but virtually any pack with a minimal frame and suspension can handle 45 lbs. (20 kg) with ease. If you plan to carry much more, however, the quality of the frame determines performance and comfort.

Originally, almost all pack makers used parallel aluminum stays, and this design is still the standard for smaller and less-expensive packs. Most companies use either 2024 or 6061 aluminum bar stock—both are easy to bend and affordable. While adequate for lighter loads, most of these frames are insufficient for supporting heavy loads. If the metal is easily bent by hand, it will sag onto your shoulders under 60 lbs. (27 kg) of gear.

A few companies use much stronger and more expensive alloys (7075 or 7001) that can be shaped to your back with difficulty. Some utilize carbon-fiber stays in their pack frames, although these are one-shape-fits-most. Other pack manufacturers beef up the standard aluminum stays with a plastic rod bent into a U-shape.

Some companies claim weight-distribution and support benefits of their plastic frame sheet. However, at most, these simply help the pack maintain shape and keep your stove from digging into your back.

Because internal frame packs ride so close to your back, they often prevent you from looking up—especially when you're wearing a helmet.

WOMEN'S PACKS

Just because a pack has a women's label doesn't necessarily mean it is going to fit a woman better. After all, the pack is fitted to your body; it doesn't know your gender. The differences between men's and women's models are rarely significant in alpine packs, as long as the pack is sized properly. With heavy loads, however, anatomically correct designs mean greater performance and comfort.

The hips of women generally have more flare than those of men. Thus, the hipbelts on women's packs are angled more. To accommodate less distance between the top of the hipbone and the bottom of the floating rib, the hipbelt is narrower.

Women tend to have shorter torsos and narrower shoulders than men. As a result, stays and shoulder straps are closer together and packs have a narrower profile.

Because the upper body of many women is curvier than that of men, shoulder straps need more contour so they don't dig in on one edge and to give even pressure distribution. Larger-chested women also appreciate low-profile straps that taper at the ends and a sternum strap with an up-and-down adjustment.

Bending the stays back from the top of the shoulders helps increase clearance.

ALPINE HARNESS

Some argue that foam is unnecessary on the hipbelts of alpine packs, since your clothing will provide plenty of padding. Bunk! A lot of summer alpine climbing is performed in light clothes, and many of us lack natural padding over the iliac crest. Hipbelts with stiffer foam (give them a Charmin squeeze) spread heavy loads more effectively, but they also get in the way more when climbing.

Since you'll often wear the hipbelt with a climbing harness, look for 1½ in. (3.8 cm) webbing versus the bulky 2 in. (5 cm) stuff that is standard on big packs. Removable hipbelts can save weight when you're traveling fast; you don't really need a hipbelt for loads of less than 20 lbs. (9 kg).

Shoulder straps should be relatively narrow, so you can move freely, yet reasonably padded for comfort. Stay away from any shoulder straps with rough inner fabric or seams since this will chafe you raw even when you're wearing a light shirt.

Radically contoured shoulder straps require the sternum strap all the time to keep them in place. For the moderate loads typically carried in an alpine pack, I find a sternum strap more hindrance than help because it inhibits breathing and makes it harder to ventilate clothing. Straighter shoulder straps give the option of using the sternum strap for climbing or skiing and leaving it open for hiking on trails.

Lots of adjustability in an alpine pack's suspension translates into more weight and things to go wrong. Better to choose a model that comes in several sizes, so you can find one that fits you without excessive adjustments. Changes in clothing layers mostly affect the shoulder straps, so make sure they're long enough for heavy insulation.

EXPEDITION HARNESS

The support that expedition hipbelts provide depends on the foam quality, method of attachment to the pack, shape, and design. Inadequate hipbelts will sag and force you to tighten the straps so much that your gut gets squished. Those that do not cup the hipbones can create pressure points and tend to slip down easily.

Low-bulk, S-shaped shoulder straps are noticeably more comfortable and offer better freedom of movement than those that are thick or straight. With packs of this volume, a sternum strap is pretty much a necessity to help distribute the load.

Hipbelts and shoulder straps are often made of open- and closed-cell foam of various densities that are laminated and then stuffed into fabric shells. This works well when high-quality foam is used. Inexpensive foams, on the other hand, break down quickly and do not distribute the weight evenly under heavy loads. Thermo-molding allows three-dimensional sculpting of foams, but other methods can be equally supportive and comfortable.

The hipbelt and shoulder straps must solidly attach to the frame; the strength of this connection greatly affects stability, fit, and durability. Stabilizer straps should be easy to reach and operate with gloves. Watch out for packs that require the bottom compartment to be properly stuffed for the stabilizers to work well.

FABRICS

The industry went through an ultralight craze in the early 1980s that produced some fabulously lightweight packs. Unfortunately, the materials available at that time did not hold up well, and few of those packs survived for long. This led the pendulum to swing in the other direction to an infatuation with heavy-duty nylon fabrics that are much more abrasion-resistant.

The raw material of choice for pack fabrics is nylon because it offers greater durability than polyester or canvas. However, by aligning the molecules, two to three times' greater tensile strength can be achieved, making a much more durable, and expensive, high-tenacity nylon.

CORDURA

The most popular material a decade ago was Cordura, a high-tenacity nylon textured by air jets. The standard 1000 denier (d) Cordura is among the most abrasion-resistant pack fabrics, but the 140 filaments per thread make it very coarse. By doubling the number of filaments, Cordura Plus gets a much better hand while only slightly reducing durability. Beware: There are now numerous cheap imitations that look similar but are made with low-tenacity nylon or polyester.

While still used in pack bottoms, 1000d Corduras have largely fallen out of favor because of weight—11 oz. per sq. yd.—and the difficulty and expense of applying a good waterproof coating. Look closely at the coating of a budget pack and you will see a thin layer with numerous pinholes. For any pack fabric, a quality polyurethane coating is important not only to keep water out but also to prevent the fabric edges from unraveling (the leading cause of blown seams).

In the past few years, 500d Corduras have become popular because they are lighter—8 oz. per sq. yd—yet still fairly rugged and reasonably affordable. The tighter weave allows a much better polyurethane coating—1½ oz. per yd. is preferable—and provides a softer hand.

The problem with all textured fabrics however, is they hold water and dirt, making it harder to brush snow off them and making them more prone to freezing stiff. A 1000d Cordura pack gains well over a pound of dead weight when wetted out (fabric saturated) in a rainstorm.

RIPSTOP

Many companies have jumped on the heavy-duty ripstop bandwagon. These fabrics can be remarkably tough, yet have a smooth finish that sheds snow. What differentiates the new materials from those of a decade ago, and the current cheap imitations, is the use of high-tenacity nylon, more intense (colorfast) dyes, and better durable water-repellent (DWR) coatings.

This is where real weight reductions are made.

The 420d pack cloth is about 7 oz. per sq. yd., compared with 210d fabrics that are only 4 oz. per sq. yd. Considering there are roughly 3 sq. yds. of fabric in an alpine pack, weight savings of a 8 oz. to 1 lb. are possible.

The trade-off for less weight, of course, is reduced abrasion resistance. It will be easier to wear a hole in the pack, but a grid of stronger yarns will prevent it from growing into a gaping rift. Using a larger-denier fiber is the least expensive method of increasing tear strength. Aramid fibers, such as Kevlar and Technora, have been used as well, but they are not particularly abrasion- or UV-resistant.

The current ripstop nylon of choice is reinforced with oriented ultrahigh-molecular-weight polyethylene (e.g., Spectra) yarns. Since this incredibly strong fiber does not hold dyes, it is white so the fabric has a distinctive look. It is also difficult to apply coatings because of its low melting point, so these high-tech fabrics tend to be less waterproof. Unfortunately, appearance alone is no guarantee of quality, because some imported fabrics have white nylon grid patterns to imitate Spectra without the cost or strength.

MESH

A lot of companies use a different fabric for the panel next to your back, ostensibly to enhance comfort. Mesh materials may be more breathable; however, they are also not very rugged (important if the pack is hauled) and they hang on to snow and pine needles. Ideally, the fabric is smooth yet fairly abrasion-resistant. Textured fabrics are rough on skin and clothes; you don't want them on the back panel, shoulder straps, or belt.

CONSTRUCTION

A climber's pack needs to be rugged enough to survive chimneys and occasional hauls up cliff bands.

FITTING

Fitting a pack properly requires practice and patience. This is where it helps to have an experienced salesperson assist you in size selection and customization. It also behooves you to learn how to adjust your pack, because there won't be a salesperson around on day 3 of your 10-day hike. Subtle changes can have a profound effect on comfort.

In matters of fit, your overall height has little to do with the size of the pack that best suits you. What counts is the length of your torso; this is measured from the top of your hipbones (iliac crest) to your seventh vertebra (C7, that big knob at the base of your neck). That same measurement will translate into different sizes, depending on the pack brand [Illustration 16.2].

Try on several packs, loaded with weight close to what you plan to carry. Spend some time with each pack—5 minutes or a light load won't do it. Don't just walk passively around the store; move like you will in the wilds. Make sure you can take a high step without the bottom of the hipbelt interfering. Swing your arms. Look for odd pressure points or undue pressure on the back of the shoulder blades.

Be sure to vocalize potential concerns; minor pain in the store can multiply into misery on the trail. The more time you spend carrying loaded packs before you make a purchase, the happier you will be afterward.

Customizing a pack's fit includes bending the stays of the pack to conform to the shape of your back. This is best achieved by removing the stays and bending them with your thumbs or over your knee so that they contour to your back.

A pack can be made out of the most exotic materials and still fall apart if it isn't assembled well.

Look carefully at the interior of any pack you are considering. Quality packs are sewn with #69 bonded nylon thread and have eight to ten stitches per inch. All straps must be bar-tacked in place or they will eventually pull out. Every joined seam (even inside pockets) should be protected by nylon binding tape, or the edges of the fabrics will fray and the seams may eventually blow out.

Be sure the rear haul loop appears indestructible and big enough to grab with a mittened hand. If the pack will be hauled frequently, make sure there are two sturdy front haul points so the pack hangs vertically.

Straps and buckles that are ¾ in. (20 mm) wide are plenty strong and can save significant weight over larger ones. However, some people find them harder to manipulate than 1 in. (25 mm) accessories, particularly when wearing gloves. For the same reason, look for the newest generation of ladder-lock sliders with big lips. Any buckle that is critical, such as those on shoulder straps and tool tubes, must be absolutely bombproof, easily replaceable, or, at the very least, designed so it can be jury-rigged with cord or wire.

For pockets, #5 YKK zippers are strong enough, but must be held by two rows of stitching and have nickel-plated sliders for durability. If the pack has a main-body zipper, it should be a size #9 or #10 coil, or you may learn the meaning of evisceration when the pack spills its guts. Reflective tabs on the

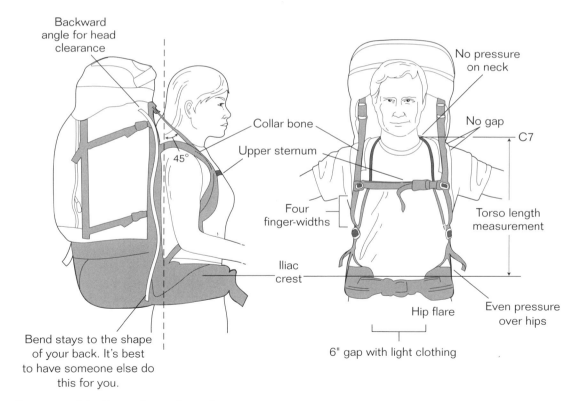

Illustration 16.2   Proper fitting of a pack

zipper pulls are nice luxuries when you're half-asleep in the predawn.

COMPRESSION/EXPANSION

An alpine pack must be compressed to a manageable size for traveling light or climbing. However, many packs use too many gewgaws to accomplish this. The result is lots of flapping straps, buckles that constantly need adjusting, and excess weight. Less is more.

Some packs use an external flap as part of the compression system. This can double as a place to carry a shovel, stash a sweater, or cram frozen ropes, but it adds weight and complexity, so think hard about whether you really need this feature.

A top compression strap running across the outside of the pack opening can be more hassle than help. It often doesn't do much except help hold a rope in place, and you must operate it every time you want in or out, otherwise it dangles. A compression strap inside the pack, however, can be left unused when headroom isn't needed.

For a time, many alpine packs had very tall—16 to 24 in. (40 to 60 cm)—extension skirts intended for use in a bivy. While possibly useful on rare occasions, these tend to get in the way the other 99 percent of the time and don't control the load as well when the pack is overstuffed. Most skirts now are around 10 in. (25 cm) tall, which still reaches up to crotch level on most bivying climbers. Grommets for drawstrings will rip out of light skirt fabrics unless they are reinforced.

A detachable top lid can save weight on climbs (though I usually leave the lid attached and flip it inside the pack, so I can still use its pockets). Many packs now have lids that convert to hip packs: okay for day hikes but too small for summit bids. If this is a feature you will use often, choose a pack that has a foam pad in the lid to give the fanny pack structure and cushioning.

While it is desirable to carry as much gear as possible inside the pack, there are times when you need to strap stuff outside. Side compression straps should be long enough to attach skis or a sleeping pad, and should have quick-release buckles. Most packs come with daisy chains for attaching additional gear; daisies with flat loops are less prone to snagging than raised loops, and they keep gear from flopping around.

Some expedition packs convert into a smaller climbing pack for versatility on backcountry trips and expeditions. These tend to be too stiff and heavy for serious climbing but adequate for easier terrain. Others take a modular approach by offering small packs that attach to the larger one, but these are still too small for alpine day climbs. Probably the best solution is an ultralight, no-frills pack that you can use as a sleeping bag stuff sack for approaches.

FEATURES

Little details count big-time in packs. They mean the difference between mediocrity, or worse, and stellar performance with many years of enjoyment.

The shape of the pack's bottom, when viewed from the side, is rarely considered. Some heavily contoured packs have a sloping bottom that gives a bit more clearance when you are descending very steep hillsides. However, these packs have an annoying tendency to flop over on the ground when you set them down. Flat-bottomed packs are more convenient most of the time—they stand up, and don't interfere all that much going downhill.

When you want to look up, head clearance becomes a problem on larger packs, especially if you're wearing a helmet. Consider packs that have an additional cutout between the stays to make room for your melon. Make sure the pack has a strap inside to maintain this space, or when you fill up the pack, the head notch may invert and exacerbate the problem.

As pack volume increases, accessibility of gear

decreases. Though some abhor them, I find vertical zippers a great convenience on huge packs. Sleeping bag compartments add expedience, but also weight and complexity. Some are far too small for winter bags.

High-stress zippers should be a #9 or #10 coil with nickel-plated sliders, not painted ones, for durability. Zippers that make tight-radius turns close with a great deal of trouble; the straighter the zipper, the better. Grab loops at the ends of zippers are useful, especially when you're wearing gloves.

Look for pocket zippers on the lid that are accessible by simply reaching overhead without removing the pack. This lets you stash or retrieve a hat or munchies without stopping.

Flapping straps that whack you in the head on windy days are incredibly annoying; plastic keepers that prevent the danglies are a solution. You can also cut off the excess webbing after you determine what you don't need. Color-coding on the straps that you use most frequently is very helpful but all too rare.

Some packs have a third rear strap in the center of the lid to help hold it in place. The result is an annoying flapping strap right behind your neck that does next to nothing.

Avoid packs made with dark fabrics. Finding something in the depths of these black holes is a real nuisance. Even worse, drab packs kill photographs. As alpinists, we go to some of the most beautiful and dramatic locations on the planet but you will find it extremely difficult to bring home great images of a climber wearing camouflage. Choose a pack that is bright red, orange, or yellow, even light pastels, though it doesn't need to be garish.

CLIMBING-SPECIFIC FEATURES

Traditional ice-ax loops still work fine for most axes, but hammers are prone to falling out if the loop is too big (adjustable loops are nice). Tool tubes with quick-release buckles at the bottom are more secure and convenient than old-style loops. Make sure the buckles are sturdy and the tube is big enough to insert a bent-shaft tool with a frozen leash.

Crampons should go inside the pack or vertically on the back, not on the top pocket, where they'll drip on you and make the pocket flop around. While straps with quick-release buckles do the job, I prefer the ease of a crampon pouch. Many packs come with slim bungee cords for attaching jackets or pads—don't use these to hold crampons or you may lose them.

Since the gear loops on your climbing harness are usually covered up by a pack, it is helpful to have gear loops on the hipbelt for carrying pro or crevasse-rescue gear. I also like a separate holster for stowing an ice tool.

Though designed for mountaineering, few packs address the fact that mountaineers rope up on glaciers. A mountaineer's pack needs to accommodate both a sit harness and a chest harness to keep a fallen climber from flipping upside down in the crevasse.

Some climbers clip a carabiner to a shoulder strap as an impromptu chest harness. If you do so, back up the shoulder strap with a sling to the haul loop—you don't want to trust the shoulder-strap buckle alone if you need to shuck your pack.

No matter which pack you choose, you will probably find several useless straps and buckles to trim off. I know one person who cut more than half a pound of dead weight from his pack!

HYDRATION

Perhaps the best innovation to come along in the past few years is the in-pack hydration system. This is a flexible bladder and a hose with a nipple, all housed in a pocket of the pack [Photo 16.3]. The bladders hold approximately 2 liters (2.12 qt.) of water when full, compress to almost nothing when empty, and are lighter than a single Nalgene bottle. Better packs are designed to hold the bladder and route the hose through a slit near the back.

Because the hose is poised for sipping at will, its convenience promotes greater fluid intake—a significant benefit to aiding both performance and

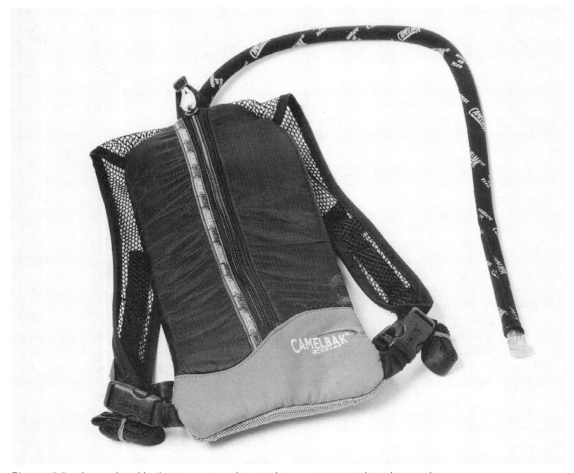

Photo 16.3 An insulated hydration system that can be worn or carried inside a pack

altitude acclimatization. Your water is less likely to freeze if insulated by the pack. (You can also blow air into the hose to keep it from freezing.) Look for a hydration system with a high-flow nipple and a sack that refills easily by simply plugging a water filter into the hose.

ACCESSORIES

No matter how good a pack's waterproof coating, in very wet conditions it will leak through all the seams and openings. If you will be hiking in a monsoon, use a pack cover to keep your gear dry.

For only about $30 and a few ounces, it makes your life much more comfortable. Mine has lasted for over a decade; trash bags will be lucky to survive a weekend.

A generic-looking travel duffel can protect your gear from abuse and prevent pilfering. The best ones are made of heavy-duty vinyl, have lockable zipper pulls, and have handles on both ends.

Pockets that ride over the top of the hipbelt are often very handy. They give you a place for assorted sundries needed while hiking, such as sunscreen, snacks, camera, hat, and crevasse rescue gear.

HIKING COMFORT

It's amazing how much clothing that is supposedly designed for hiking is actually quite poor at the task. Look for synthetic hiking shorts with a smooth waistband: belt loops, seams, drawstrings, and the bunched fabric over elastic can all create painful pressure points if they lay over the top of bone. One solution for people who get chafing on the inside of their thighs is athletic lube from running shops.

Synthetic tee shirts are far better in the heat than the cotton ones we are all used to. Check that your underwear has flat seams; many don't and can chafe.

Watch out for jackets and pants that have snaps or zipper pulls at the waist. Pants that rely on elastic waistbands to stay in place have a tendency to creep downward under a hipbelt. Bibs are much better at staying up and minimize midriff overlap, but they are just too hot for all but winter adventures. Choose a low-profile climbing harness that fits under the hipbelt comfortably.

Use trekking poles with heavy loads [Photo 16.4]. Nothing else even comes close to poles for reducing knee strain, saving energy, and increasing stability. A single pole is far less effective than two. Good trekking poles (unlike ski poles) have grips and straps that are comfortable for bare hands, shock absorbers to reduce impacts, trekking baskets that won't snag, and replaceable tips.

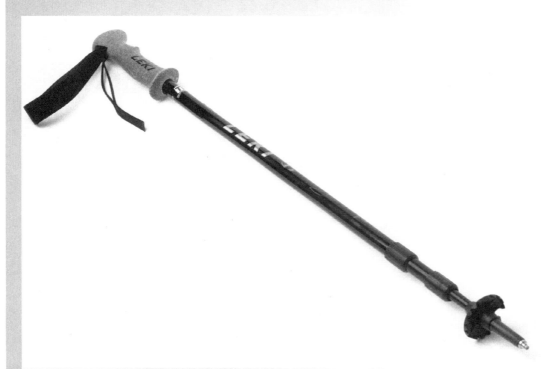

Photo 16.4   Three-section trekking pole with shock-absorbing system, cork handle, and trekking basket

CHAPTER 17

COOKING SYSTEMS

AMONG THE EFFECTS OF THE "ICEMAN," whose 5,200-year-old remains were found at about 10,000 ft. (3050 m) in the Tyrolean Alps, were a flint for starting fires and a pouch containing dried mushrooms for kindling. This ancient climber, who is now on display in Bolzano, Italy, was equipped with state-of-the-art gear for survival in the mountains. Fire is just as important for the mountaineer today, though our means of transporting and controlling it are a bit more sophisticated.

A sleeping bag or tent may be a luxury on a multinight alpine climb, but a reliable cooking system is a necessity. Without a way to melt snow and ice for water, dehydration can become a life-threatening problem. And a warm meal can make a huge difference in both comfort and performance.

When deciding upon a stove, you need to consider how and where on the planet it will be used. The gourmet may prefer a stove that simmers easily; the expedition climber needs a blast furnace to melt a few cubic feet of snow; the big wall climber wants a system she can hang from a 'biner. As with most things, there is no one stove that does it all.

Nor one pot. It's easy to get caught up in the gadgetry of stoves and fail to consider the rest of the kitchen. However, for maximum performance, cooking pots and heat reflectors play a significant role; don't overlook them.

FUEL

The major consideration when buying a stove is the type of fuel it uses. This affects not only heat output and safety but also reliability and cost of operation. For international travelers, the availability of fuel is also a significant factor.

Some stoves burn solid fuels (e.g., twigs, pine cones, charcoal); these are impractical for climbers. Likewise, stoves that use alcohol are nice for summer backpacking, but they lack the heat output for speedy meals.

LIQUID

Liquid-fuel stoves generally offer the highest heat output and are the most economical in the long run [Photo 17.1]. Since liquids do not burn, these stoves must convert the fuel to vapor prior to reaching the burner head. This is the reason for the priming (preheating) process.

Liquid fuels are classified as either "light" or "heavy," depending upon their Final Boiling Point (FBP). Light fuels (white gasoline, automobile gasoline, aviation gasoline, and Stoddard solvent) have relatively low FBPs, are more volatile, and burn cleaner. Heavy fuels (kerosene, diesel, and jet fuel) have relatively high FBPs, require more priming, and produce a lot of soot and carbon monoxide.

White Gas

In the United States, white gas is the fuel of choice because it is readily available from all camping stores as well as most hardware and grocery stores. White gas generally refers to a type of gasoline that is highly refined and somewhat less volatile than auto and aviation gas, but the term is not strictly defined. You'll hear both "white gas" and "naphtha" used for substances whose only commonality is that they are petroleum products.

The quality of white gas significantly affects your stove's performance. Because the fuel is most commonly sold in gallon cans and most of us use only a pint or two at a time, a good quantity often sits around for a year or more. The problem is that fuel degrades with exposure to air, resulting in lower heat output and stove-clogging deposits.

After you open a can of white gas, it's best to store the remainder in smaller, air-tight fuel bottles

Photo 17.1   Liquid-fuel stoves: Top-center has a ported burner head, and the other two have plate burner heads.

if it won't be used within 6 months. For trips on which performance is critical, always use fresh gas. You can safely dispose of excess white gas by pouring it into the tank of your car.

The gas you put into your car can also be used in *some* liquid-fuel stoves (choose the lowest octane available), but it should be used only as a last resort. Although inexpensive, these fuels have many additives in them that tend to clog stoves. They are also more volatile than white gas, especially if purchased in winter, when extra butanes and pentanes are added to ensure easier engine starts in cold weather. Furthermore, their fumes are highly toxic.

Kerosene

Once you venture away from North America, white gas becomes the exception rather than the rule. It may be available, but it's often known by confusing names and found in unlikely places, such as a pharmacy. The more remote you get, the greater the likelihood of having to resort to heavy fuels such as kerosene, which has even more confusing names abroad.

Because of their higher molecular weights, heavy fuels are much less volatile than gasolines—they do not evaporate at room temperature. This makes kerosenes safer to handle but harder to ignite; hence, a more volatile starter fuel is needed.

Many liquid-fuel stoves will also burn kerosene, but most require the swapping of parts to convert them. When using kerosene, your best friends are a fuel-filter funnel (to remove impurities), a tube of priming paste, a maintenance kit, and a bandanna for wiping the soot and smelly oil off your hands. Try to obtain the best-quality kerosene available (it should be clear and without perfumes), or use Jet-A1 (a commercial jet fuel, not to be confused with the extremely volatile aviation gas).

CARTRIDGE FUELS

Stoves that use fuel cartridges are far easier and cleaner to operate than liquid-fuel stoves [Photo 17.2]. Because the fuel turns to gas at atmospheric pressure, no priming is required—just turn the valve, ignite, and start cooking. Of course, anything this easy has to have its downsides, not the least of which are high fuel costs (roughly five times that of white gas), poor cold-weather performance, and the ethical conundrum of throwing spent cartridges away (puncture them first so they won't explode if incinerated).

Until recently, the only options for fuel cartridges were butane or propane, which were introduced in the 1960s. Butane works well in warmer temperatures but poorly or not at all in cold weather. At sea level, butane vaporizes at temperatures only above 31°F (–1°C). At higher elevations, reduced air pressure greatly enhances performance—at 10,000 ft. (3050 m), butane vaporizes at 12°F (–11°C), and at 20,000 ft. (7000 m), it vaporizes at –3°F (–19°C).

Propane vaporizes at –43°F (–42°C) at sea level, which gives it good cold-weather performance. However, propane must be stored at very high pressures, so heavy steel is used for the cartridges. Great for car camping and boating, propane is impractical when weight is an issue.

Two new cartridge fuels (isobutane and gas blends) are now more readily available. Very similar

Photo 17.2   Cartridge fuel stoves with ported burner heads

to butane, isobutane vaporizes at 12°F (–11°C) at sea level, which significantly improves heat output in colder conditions.

Several companies offer butane/propane blends of either 80/20 or 70/30 (the difference is insignificant) to increase heat output and cold-weather performance. When the cartridge is full, the blending makes a significant difference. However, because propane has a higher vapor pressure and is more volatile, it burns off first, leaving mostly butane at the end. A new blend of isobutane and propane may be the best answer yet, but is harder to find.

Screw-in cartridges are now the most common style, and they all use the same threading so you don't need to buy cartridges sold by the company that made your stove. The major exceptions are the Camping Gaz cartridges, which have a unique fitting that works only with their own stoves and lanterns.

Cold Weather

Though the new fuels are an improvement, few of the cartridge stoves have the heat output of a white-gas stove in cold weather. Furthermore, as the fuel in the cartridge is consumed, there is less pressure. Performance drops by about 50 percent when the cartridge is nearly empty.

The fuel in pressurized cartridges is in liquid form, which expands about 270 times in volume as it vaporizes. Because of those inescapable laws of nature, this expanding gas also cools. This principle serves us well for refrigerators and air-conditioners, yet it creates a problem for our stoves. After extended nonstop use, as when melting snow, this cooling can severely diminish stove performance. Contrary to what some people think, the cooling effect is intensified by insulating the cartridge with foam. Exposing the cartridge to the air—even air that feels frigid to us—can warm the fuel.

There are several solutions to these cold-related problems, the efficacy of which depends upon your particular stove. One option is to simply turn off the stove and swap the cold canister with one that has been warmed inside your parka or sleeping bag. For all but hanging models, you can set the car-

tridge in a pan filled with an inch or two of cool water, assuming you have a spare pot. You can also warm the canister with your bare hands, but holding a cold metal object in below freezing weather is an unpleasant experience.

The method I often use with a hanging stove is to heat the bottom of the fuel cartridge for 3 to 5 seconds every couple of minutes with a butane lighter. Just make sure the stove is running, and don't get too carried away with the lighter. An exploding cartridge could ruin your day.

Another popular option for extended winter trips is to jury-rig a heat exchanger for the stove [Illustration 17.1]. Wrap a flattened, heavy-gauge copper wire once or twice around the cartridge and run a loop up into the flame. When using a heat exchanger, an insulating foam case helps efficiency. Make the case from scraps of an old closed-cell-foam sleeping pad and duct tape, and then line it with aluminum foil to help minimize melting. Be careful not to burn yourself on the hot wire.

LIQUID-FUEL STOVES

Many liquid-fuel stoves are designed to burn white gas, unleaded gas, and kerosene. Multifuel stoves don't cost much more than white-gas-only models, and they offer the peace of mind of accepting whatever fuel is available. Unless you're sure you'll never leave the United States with your stove, I see no reason to buy a white-gas-only model.

The predominant style of liquid-fuel stove has detachable fuel-bottle tanks. Pioneered in the early 1970s by Larry Penberthy, the interesting character who started Mountain Safety Research (MSR), this design has undergone much refinement and imitation. Detachable tanks give you the flexibility to use the appropriate-size canister for the length of the trip. For longer trips, that means you're not constantly refilling a too-small tank, and for shorter ones, you're not carrying extra weight and bulk. They're also easier to check

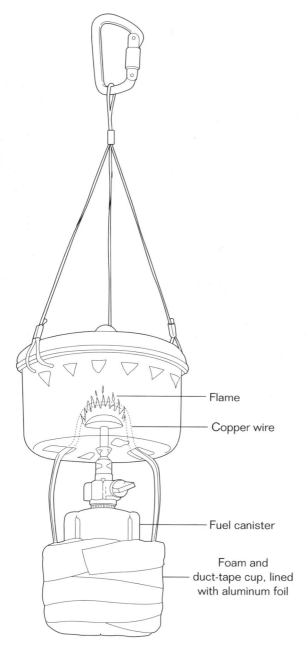

Flame

Copper wire

Fuel canister

Foam and
duct-tape cup, lined
with aluminum foil

Illustration 17.1   Heat exchanger for hanging stove

for fuel level and to refill, and they save space in your pack.

Although the MSR stoves were originally designed to use with Sigg fuel bottles, these are no longer recommended. My old Sigg bottles are all heavily dented and the bottoms on some have bulged out; I now use them only for storage. MSR's bottles are much more durable and designed to hold some internal pressure.

A liquid-fuel stove with neither a pump nor the option of adding one is not even worth considering for trips in cold weather. The point to remember is that you're not pressurizing the liquid but, rather, the air space inside the tank. If the air space is small (with a full tank), using a little fuel causes a relatively large reduction in pressure and more pumping is required. Once the tank is partially empty, very little additional pumping is needed to maintain the flame.

A common problem for any liquid-fuel stove is for the pump to fail to pressurize. This is usually caused by the pump leather drying out and is solved by oiling it and spreading the leather apart. You can use vegetable oil, margarine, or even lip balm in a pinch, but it's better to use light machine oil.

Another common complaint with some liquid-fuel stoves is that they fail to simmer properly. Often this is a result of overpumping by the complainant. Any stove will simmer better with the addition of a metal disk, such as the top of a large can, between the flame and the pot.

PRIMING

The standard method of priming a stove is simple but takes: pressurize tank; open valve; look and listen for trickle of gas; shut valve; ignite the liquid; wait for flame to almost die; reopen valve. If all has gone well, your stove will start with a steady blue flame.

The trick is knowing when enough liquid is present for priming—without overdoing it. You must also direct the flame to the generator tube (the whole point of this procedure is to get it hot) by moving the stove or blocking the wind with your

COOKING IN THE TENT

All tent and stove manufacturers warn against the use of stoves inside a tent—with good reason. Besides the obvious nasty consequences of an exploding fuel tank, flare-ups have left their share of immolated tents, and the consequences of burned skin and no shelter can be dire indeed. Sooner or later, though, you're going to be stuck in a storm so ferocious it isn't possible to cook outside. If at all possible, start liquid stoves outside and bring one in only after the flame has settled down. Treat all stoves like the barely controlled explosions they are.

A more insidious and equally deadly problem is the buildup of carbon monoxide (CO) inside the tent as a result of the combustion process; a number of climbers have died from this. This odorless, colorless gas binds with hemoglobin and prevents the uptake of oxygen, which is already in short supply at high altitude. It is critically important that a tent be well ventilated when cooking inside. Cracking a window or two isn't enough; you need a good flow of air moving through the tent.

Research has shown that lowering the pot support to decrease boil times greatly increases CO production due to incomplete combustion. Water condensing on the sides of the cooking pot and dripping into the flame also significantly increases CO output. The best way to melt snow is to heat a small quantity of water, and then add snow slowly enough that the pot stays warm.

A spilled dinner can be a disastrous event, particularly if it occurs inside the tent and near sleeping bags. Hanging stoves are clearly the best way to prevent this. Floor models with a low center of gravity are somewhat more likely to stay upright than those with a higher center of gravity. Because the ground is not often level and many pots are slick on the bottom, stoves with teeth on the pot supports are highly recommended. If yours lack these, you might want to file notches in the pot supports for extra friction.

hand. If the generator is not hot enough, when you open the valve the second time, bright orange flames will leap high into the air, terrorizing all in the immediate vicinity and drawing laughter from those a safe distance away. With practice, none of this is a big deal—the hair on the back of your hand will grow back.

Some people object to the messy soot that results from priming stoves with white gas. For them, and anyone using a heavy fuel, alcohol or priming paste are the solution. Be careful with alcohol—if it spills while lit, the flames are invisible.

CARTRIDGE STOVES

Turn the knob, press the button, and cook dinner. There certainly is something to be said for cartridge stoves, particularly those with piezo lighters (but carry a lighter too). In addition to being easy to use, they are also quiet and clean, and require virtually no maintenance. The negatives are the expense of the fuel, cold-weather hassles, and cartridge disposal.

Stoves designed so that the burner sits on top of the tank, which acts as the base, are the most compact, but they're also inherently less stable. The heat from the stove tends to reflect downward and warm the cartridge somewhat, helping cold-weather performance. If you're using a good windscreen, however, most of the heat will be reflected up toward the pot.

Stoves that have the tank connected via a hose have a bigger base and lower center of gravity; they tend to be more stable for large pots. The most spillproof systems are the hanging stoves [Photo 17.3]; however, many are poorly designed.

Photo 17.3   Hanging stove

THE WHERE AND HOW OF COOKING

There seem to be two types of people in the world—those who have a healthy, happy relationship with their stoves, and those who can never figure the darn things out. People in the former group can make fluffy omelets at high camp and field-strip any stove in a matter of minutes. Those in the latter camp can burn water and cause spontaneous combustion simply by walking past their stoves.

The difference between these groups may just be practice and familiarity. It helps to know that the principle behind all stoves is that vaporized fuel is forced through a jet and directed at a burner. Prior to a serious trip, use your stove in as many conditions as possible. Learn its idiosyncrasies, find out what can go wrong, and figure out how to fix it. When you purchase a new stove, buy any available spare parts or maintenance kits. Stores are often out of stock when you most need obscure parts.

Because boiling water is the key to many mountain meals, everyone wants to compare boil times for different stoves. The problem is that these numbers are almost worthless for comparing different companies' stoves. The lack of any standards for altitude, fuel pressure, starting water temperature, and type of pot prevent reliable comparison. There's also a lot of room for interpretation of what constitutes "boiling" (from a few bubbles to a rolling boil).

For example, for one stove model I've seen a half-dozen published boil times that range from 3½ to 5½ minutes. While some stoves are unperturbed by a light breeze, others lose significant performance—a fact not reflected by most tests. And nearly as important as boil times is the time it takes to set up a stove and get it running at full blast.

Anyone who has gasped for air at high altitude knows there is less oxygen up there—your stove knows it, too. It burns rich (too high a fuel-to-air ratio), causing a cooler, yellow flame that burns farther from the burner. To minimize wasting fuel and maximize heat output, don't overpump, and make sure your stove's windscreen is well ventilated.

Plate-style burners work better at high altitude and give off a reassuring roar when cranked, but muffle out conversations. Ported burners spread the flame more effectively, are much quieter, and tend to simmer better.

At a minimum, carry one stove for every three people in the group. An expedition would do well to carry a backup or two—you may have to retreat if a stove is lost or goes kaput. At all times, carry spare parts, the instruction manual, and a spare lighter or matches inside a zip-lock baggy in the stove's stuff sack, along with the necessary tools and another lighter.

COOKING AT ALTITUDE

Elevation in ft. (m)	Air Density (percentage)	Boiling Temp. in °F (°C)	Cooking Time (minutes)
Sea Level	100	212° (100°)	1.0
5000 (1524)	86	203° (95°)	1.9
10,000 (3048)	74	194° (90°)	3.8
15,000 (4572)	65	185° (85°)	7.2
20,000 (6096)	52	176° (80°)	13.0

COOKWARE

A pot is a pot is a pot, right? Not exactly. Your choice of cookware not only affects cooking times but also fuel efficiency and cleanup hassles.

In recent years, more and more people have been opting for shiny, stainless-steel cooksets—the lightweight, uncoated aluminum cookware that used to be so ubiquitous is fairly scarce now. Despite their weight, stainless-steel pots have gained popularity because they are much more durable and easier to clean. Stainless-steel pots also distribute heat more evenly and are less prone to hot spots that scorch food.

Heavier-gauge, coated-aluminum cookware is quite durable, heats more effectively than stainless, and is about the same weight. Teflon coatings on aluminum pots prevent the metallic taste aluminum can give some foods. The Teflon also makes the pots easier to clean than stainless steel. However, metal utensils can scratch the finish. Titanium pots are wonderfully light, if you can afford the exorbitant price.

Regardless of the metal you choose, look for pots with gently rounded corners. These are much easier to clean and allow heat to flow up the sides, which increases efficiency. Pots that are blackened on the outside will absorb heat more readily.

FLIGHT PLAN

For most of us, the "trip of a lifetime" starts at an airport. If you haven't done your homework, this great beginning can quickly turn into a "day from hell."

In today's climate of billion-dollar liability suits and terrorism, the airlines and the Federal Aviation Administration (FAA) take a dim view of people who carry explosive or flammable materials in their luggage. Indeed, the fine is a whopping $25,000. This means you will have to buy your fuel at your destination or ship it (properly packaged) weeks or months ahead of time—accompanied by lengthy forms and pricey fees.

According to the FAA, a properly purged stove and fuel container are legal to transport by air. (To purge, empty the equipment of fuel and expose it to air and sunlight for several hours.) However, the airlines are free to set stricter standards, no matter how illogical, and many now do. Numerous travelers have had their stoves confiscated at the airport, often for no good reason.

A survey by the American Hiking Society reported that some airlines allow only new, unused stoves to be transported; used stoves, even if completely purged, must be sent by airfreight. A few airlines allow purged, used stoves but not used fuel bottles or tanks (a real problem if your stove has a built-in tank).

The moral: Check with your airline, and do so well ahead of time.

You can spray-paint them with flat black stove paint, or simply use them over a campfire a few times. Generally, two nesting pots are best, one for water and the other for food. When going light, it's possible to get by with one pot.

Make sure pot lids are tight-fitting to prevent heat loss. Look for pot lids that you can grab with a gloved hand—it's sometimes too cold to cook bare-handed.

ACCESSORIES

Many people use cut-up pieces of closed-cell-foam sleeping pads to insulate the stove from the snow or tent floor. Although cheap, these have an unfortunate tendency to melt or burn when used under stoves with low-to-the-ground burners. The blade of a metal snow shovel works adequately, but this is often needed for other camp chores, and it will eventually melt into the snow. While folding stove stands are available, a good, inexpensive solution is to carry a 1 ft. (30 cm) square of ⅛ in. (3 mm) Masonite covered with heavy foil; it is light, insulates adequately, and won't burn too easily.

Wind is an evil force when it comes time to cook dinner. It robs heat by cooling the sides of the pot, pushes the flame away from the pot, or extinguishes one side of a ported burner. The majority of stoves come with windscreens inadequate for anything more than a light breeze; many cartridge models have none.

A good wraparound windscreen can increase efficiency dramatically—it both blocks the wind and channels heat up the sides of the pot. If your stove doesn't come with one, consider buying or making your own from heavy foil. The style that resembles a Japanese folding screen is not as effective as those that completely enclose the burner.

You can increase efficiency even more by using a heat exchanger or pot cozy; for longer trips, these can easily save their own weight in fuel [Photo 17.4].

CAMP LIFE

Though certainly not a necessity, miniature cartridge lanterns add a welcome touch to any campsite. They put out a lot of light (equivalent to a 75- to 100-watt light bulb), are easy to operate, and add physical and psychological warmth. If you're using a cartridge stove, these lanterns are great for finishing off canisters that are too spent to work well on your stove. Candles and candle lanterns pale by comparison.

Good coffee may be a luxury for some but it's a necessity for me and many others—don't even talk to me about freeze-dried. Drip filter systems are okay, but I prefer the heartier flavor from a French press (some are now built into insulated mugs).

Many popular backcountry climbing destinations are also prime habitat for bears. You're in for long, sleepless nights while critters maraud your supplies unless you pack along a bear-resistant food container. Many well-planned trips have been cut short with the score Animals 1: People 0. Suspending your cache from trees is simply a delaying tactic that the National Park Service no longer recommends. Bear containers are sturdy plastic drums that hold about 5 days' worth of food for one person but weigh only a couple of pounds. Besides keeping your odiferous objects (including hygiene and first-aid kits) away from grizz' and 'coons, you get peace of mind and numerous hours saved not dealing with complicated rigging that is doomed to failure.

For longer expeditions, do yourself (and your teammates) a favor by bringing a solar water shower. These are also a great source of hot water for cleaning pots and dishes after meals.

WATER TREATMENTS

Sadly, you can no longer trust the water from any stream in North America because of the hidden nasties that lurk in it. The main concerns are protozoa (*Giardia lamblia* and *cryptosporidium*) and bacteria—both pathogens can be removed by filtration. However, when traveling in Third World countries near the tropics, you must also guard

Photo 17.4   Increase fuel efficiency with a portable "oven" or a heat exchanger.

against viruses, such as hepatitis, that are too small to be blocked by filters.

The easiest method of ensuring safe water is to simply boil it, although this isn't always practical. Temperatures above 150°F (66°C) will kill everything in the water—there is no need to boil for additional time.

Iodine has long been popular for treating water; however, it has a number of drawbacks, not the least of which is the terrible taste. Since it does not kill *crypto*, requires up to 30 minutes in cold water, and the tablets have a short shelf life once opened, I no longer recommend any iodine products. Also realize that vitamin C deactivates iodine, so you cannot mix drinks until after the treatment period.

Newer chlorine dioxide–based treatments solve nearly all the problems of iodine and are superior to other chlorine-based methods. However, you still have to wait 20 to 35 minutes before imbibing. On the plus side, the two small bottles are far lighter and more compact than any filtration system.

When they work, water filters do a good job of giving you fresh, clean water that you can drink right away [Photo 17.5]. The catch is, these mechanical gadgets weigh nearly a pound and are prone to clogging, leaking, or simply refusing to cooperate. I've tried many different models and they all have idiosyncrasies—on a long trip, carrying a backup treatment method is a good idea.

The most basic water filters remove particles down to 1 micron in size (some go to only 4 microns);

Photo 17.5   Water treatment options: bottle with built-in filter, two-part chemical treatment, and pump filter.

these eliminate *giardia* and *crypto* but not bacteria, which are even smaller. For most backcountry travel, a microfilter that goes down to 0.2 micron is a better choice because it removes most bacteria that other humans spread.

To get maximum protection, you need a water purifier that adds a chemical treatment stage to a microfilter. Alternatively, you can first treat the water with iodine and then run it through a microfilter (many have charcoal that removes the taste).

CHAPTER 18

MOUNTAINEERING BOOTS

PICKING A SUMMER MOUNTAINEERING boot used to be easy. There were the Galibier Super Guides, and then there were the rest. The legendary Super Guides required hundreds of miles of walking and countless blisters before they broke in (or was it our feet that broke in?), by which time they were ready for resoling.

When I went on my first winter mountaineering trip into the Wind Rivers over twenty years ago, my feet were shod in the state-of-the-art of the day: a pair of Lowa Triplex boots. These leather triple boots were undeniably toasty, but they weighed close to 10 lbs. (4.5 kg), took years to break in, and, when wet, would freeze into icy blocks.

Then in the 1980s, plastic-shelled double boots swept the climbing world, and it seemed as if leather mountaineering boots were in danger of dying out. But recent technology gains have once again made single boots the choice of many alpinists.

No matter the material, mountaineering boots today are lighter and more comfortable, and accept step-in crampons. The new generation of boots also has more ankle flex for French technique, or flat-foot cramponing, than early plastic boots. But some boots are better suited to off-trail hiking and scrambling than for long snow and ice climbs or alpine rock.

Before shopping, pick your goals and prioritize them. The footwear you select will fit somewhere between expedition climbing, where warmth is of paramount importance, and technical alpine and ice climbing, where a precise fit is critical for performance.

BOOT STYLES

It is no longer possible to make sweeping generalizations about leather and plastic boots except they cost about the same. Some plastics are lighter than some leathers, some leathers are warmer than some plastics, some plastics flex nicely, and some leathers are superstiff.

Now it's less an issue of materials than a question of which style to choose: single, insulated single, or double boots.

No question, a good single boot is the optimum choice for summer mountaineering with moderate temperatures and lots of trail hiking and snow climbing [Photo 18.1]. These tend to be the most flexible (reducing fatigue on the trail) and relatively breathable.

For an expedition, where you must wear boots for days on end, or for extremely cold conditions, double boots are still the best bet [Photo 18.2]. The ability to remove the liners for drying, or simply wear them around camp, is a huge benefit. It is often possible to do more customizing of the fit of double boots, and you can use different liners as the conditions dictate.

Plastic boots are totally waterproof in theory, a real advantage when climbing "frozen" waterfalls or stomping through spring slush. They require no maintenance, have virtually no break-in period, and are very durable.

The gray area comes with the new insulated single boots [Photo 18.3]. At first glance, these seem to offer the best of all worlds, but there are trade-offs. For example, they can be too hot for that long hike into the Wind Rivers during August. Yet they probably are not warm enough for a climb on Denali or an 8000 m (26,240 ft.) peak.

Where the insulated singles shine is on the majority of winter ice climbs and mountain routes in the mid-latitudes (e.g., the Lower 48 and the Alps). Most are lighter, more flexible, and less bulky than plastic boots, so climbing in them is joyful by comparison. And their extra warmth over uninsulated single boots is certainly appreciated at long belays.

Photo 18.1   Single boots that accept step-in crampons

Photo 18.2   Plastic double boot

SOLE

FLEX

The stiffness of the sole is primarily what separates hiking and mountaineering boots. Boots that are softer are more comfortable for long hikes but are poor for climbing on rock and have trouble holding crampons.

Whether the shank is wood, steel, or plastic is largely immaterial. With the new integrated sole units, which combine the outsole, midsole, and rand, the flex is engineered in.

Although many people talk a lot about "rigid" boots, it's a misleading term because virtually all single, and some double, mountaineering boots flex somewhat. Even though they may feel rigid when you try to flex them by hand, the boots bend to different degrees when you're walking and climbing.

Boots that are stiffer longitudinally are better for

Photo 18.3   Insulated single boots with sticky rubber rands

toeing-in on rock edges and reduce calf strain when front-pointing. Rocker is built in so that they walk adequately, but such boots are still relatively clunky and take some getting used to.

Boots that bend more at the ball of the foot will friction better on low-angle slabs and tend to be less tiring by the end of a long day's hike. Make sure that when it flexes, the boot is not pressing down on the top of your foot.

Torsionally stiff boots give the best edging performance—soft boots require more energy to climb. Recent technology allows boots to flex longitudinally while remaining torsionally stiff.

If a fully rigid crampon is worn, any flex of the boot sole is eliminated, so all mountaineering boots work for technical ice. When used with flexible or semi-rigid crampons, the stiffer boots are ideal for alpine climbs, but softer boots may cause your calves to burn partway up a long snow slope or ice gully.

DESIGN

Along with boot stiffness, the outer sole plays a large role in hiking and climbing performance [Photo 18.4]. Both the hardness of the rubber and the pattern of the lugs are significant.

Once Vitale Bramani developed a lugged rubber outer sole in the late 1930s, the era of nailed boots was destined to end. The classic Vibram sole pattern, based on those nails, has graced mountaineering boots for decades [Photo 18.5], though recent improvements in design and molding give even better performance. For off-trail hiking and snow climbing, most boot soles with deep lugs work just fine. When it comes to rock climbing, however, outer soles with soft rubber or wide gaps between lugs under the big toe do not edge nearly as well as soles with stiff rubber that won't deform and a solid inside edge for edging.

It is possible to have boots with the modern integrated lowers resoled when the time comes. A

Photo 18.4 Mountaineering sole offering good edging and superior traction

boot-repair shop can grind off the remainder of the sole and glue on a substitute.

UPPERS

No matter what material is used, the fewer seams in the upper, the better. It's cheaper to assemble small pieces of leather or fabric than to use one large piece of quality material, but stitching inevitably leaks and wears out.

LEATHER

More than any other factor, the quality of leather used in mountaineering boots affects their performance, durability, and price. Cows may not have changed much in the past two decades, but thanks to advances in the tanning process, the leather made from cows sure has. In case you are wondering, good boots are made from the butts of adult bulls, most of which lived in southern Germany and were slaughtered for beef.

Modern leathers are processed both with vegetable (tannin) and metal (chromium) tanning agents for durability and water resistance. Anfibio leathers are further treated with silicon to make them virtually waterproof, while still allowing the leather to breathe—at least, in theory.

After tanning, because the leather is too thick for manufacturing, it is "split" with a band knife. This is not a precise process, so the leather thickness in a given boot model often varies. Thicker leather makes boots more durable, supportive, and water repellent, but also heavier and less breathable.

The only leather worth considering for a mountaineering boot is termed full-grain, because it includes the dense, topmost skin layer and a good portion of the corium (middle layer). This is the most durable and naturally water-resistant portion of the hide.

If boots are made with the smooth, outer side of the leather facing out, the boots look great, shed water, and quickly get trashed by abrasion that removes the best part of the hide. In rough talus, jam cracks, and ice climbing, these won't last as long as boots made from reversed (a.k.a. rough-out) leather. This is full-grain with the skin side facing in, so it is protected from abuse. Because of improvements in tanning, newer boots made from reversed leather also break in much faster and stay drier longer than my ancient Super Guides.

Nubuck is the term for leather that has the skin side micro-abraded and buffed for a velvety finish. Ostensibly, this allows better penetration of treatments and does not harm the leather. However, as with smooth-outside leathers, the most important part of Nubuck leather—the skin side—is exposed to abrasion.

FABRIC

Although reversed leather sets the standard for performance in boot uppers, new fabrics may start to give it a run for the money. By blending high-tenacity nylon for abrasion resistance with Kevlar for strength, companies can achieve amazingly rugged materials. These are backed with a waterproof/breathable membrane to keep the elements at bay.

Fabric boots offer very quick break-in and good support, and they seem to breathe slightly better and dry faster than leather boots. However, since these entered the market only recently, it's too early to tell how they'll perform after five years of climbing. And most of the current fabric boots are no lighter than leather models.

Photo 18.5   Molding boot soles at the Vibram factory in Italy

PLASTIC

For durability and waterproofness, plastic is still where it's at. The early shells were often too stiff in the ankles and could crack, but newer materials have allowed considerable improvement. However, plastic boots still don't offer the lateral ankle flex of single boots.

Outer plastic shells come in two styles: hinged two-piece and flexible one-piece. Hinged models have relatively stiff lower shells and an upper cuff made of a softer plastic. The hinge point near the ankle joint allows fore-and-aft flexing of the cuff. One-piece shells are engineered so the upper flexes to a certain degree; these are generally heavier.

Plastic shells are made from polyamide or polyurethane, and despite some marketing claims, the differences are minor. Less-expensive plastic boots may stiffen in very cold conditions, although supergaiters can reduce the effect. Some shells are not sealed well against leakage, so crossing glacial streams can soak the liners. Better boots keep you dry when ankle deep.

LINERS

Most of a double boot's insulation and comfort comes from its inner boot, or liner. You have two basic options for inner boots: breathable or waterproof. The breathable liners generally use either wool felt or open-cell foam (commonly polyurethane) for padding and insulation. Breathable liners are more comfortable in warmer weather, but they can become wet unless you use vapor-barrier socks.

Any inner boot made with closed-cell foam will not breathe at all, so you'll need to be especially careful about changing socks. The commonly used EVA foam (Alveolite is one brand) is very light, yet eventually gets compressed and loses some insulating value.

If your liners are worn out, uncomfortable, or just not warm enough, you can replace them with new ones. Theoretically, all manufacturers offer replacement liners, but trying to get them can take months—or eternity. There is no law that says you have to use liners made by the manufacturer who makes the outer shell—as long as they fit inside the outer without bunching or wrinkling.

Thermo-molded foam liners provide a custom fit to your mountaineering boots and are lighter and warmer than most stock liners. They are comfortable and easy to put on (no inner laces), but your feet do sweat a lot. By the time my liners reached basecamp at about 16,000 ft. (4875 m) on Gasherbrum II, the heat of the trek and the altitude caused them to loose their set and expand; remolding was a nuisance.

Lace-up liners hold your foot more securely and accommodate a wider range of foot shapes than laceless ones. Laceless inner boots are lighter and easier to slip on and have fewer seams, but they're entirely dependent upon the tightness of the outer boot for a secure fit.

Most liners have textured rubber or plastic walking soles for camp and hut use. On some, the sticky material runs partway up the side of the liner, which makes it difficult to insert the liner into the outer shell; when making an alpine start at 3 in the morning, I don't need extra hassles. Taping over the sticky part may eliminate this nuisance.

MOISTURE CONTROL

Water is your feet's enemy, no matter whether it comes from inside or outside. Wet boots are heavy, cold, and susceptible to freezing, and cause blisters the size of bagels. It's essential that boot linings and padding materials, including the foot beds, transfer this moisture away from your feet.

Calfskin leather has been the traditional favorite for lining single boots because it is soft, molds to your feet, and can be durable. But many companies use a Cambrelle (or similar synthetic) lining because it wicks moisture, dries fast, and is light. A few mountaineering boots have calfskin in the heel and Cambrelle in the toe box. Calfskin must be treated with conditioner, such as Lexol or saddle soap, or it can wear out faster than synthetics.

Adding a waterproof/breathable (WP/B) membrane layer to the lining is an obvious necessity on fabric boots. And some leather boots also have built-in WP/B linings to provide more protection, although the breathability part is questionable.

Full-length rubber rands go a long way toward keeping external water out of leather or fabric boots and significantly increase durability. Rands made with sticky rubber also help greatly for jamming in cracks. Toe caps or partial rands don't offer the same level of protection, but are far better than none at all. However, be aware that very high rands add significant weight.

The initial factory treatment on leather boots lasts a while but will eventually need rejuvenation. Wax-based products (like Sno-Seal) waterproof a leather boot but also prevent it from breathing, and some contain oils that can oversoften the leather. Carry extra waterproofing on multiweek trips.

FEATURES

Forward ankle flex on all boots is adequate for hiking. However, rear and lateral flex are other desirable characteristics that are lacking on some models [Illustration 18.1]. Without sufficient rear flex, walking downhill becomes a painful task. Lateral ankle flex allows French technique on moderate-angle slopes. You can increase ankle mobility by loosening the lacing, but this is not practical in the middle of a climb.

Pay attention to where the uppers flex at the ankle. With some boots, this point tends to dig in when the boot is flexed forward or jammed in a crack. A few boots use a nylon lacing loop here instead of a lace hook to increase comfort. Good padding in the tongue and around the top of the boot are important to prevent shin bang and other painful experiences.

If it comes down to a choice between two boots that fit similarly, take the one with a well-designed, low-friction lacing system over the model with standard D-rings. These pulley systems make it much easier to fit a boot snugly over the entire forefoot [Photo 18.6]. Be warned that they work so well, you can easily cut off circulation to your toes.

For boots without pulleys, thick, flat laces are easier to grasp than round ones, especially while wearing gloves. Lace locks can be very helpful for tightening the fore and aft of the boot separately.

Once heralded as the dawning of the new age, buckle closures on mountaineering boots have become extinct. Buckles were heavy and not easily

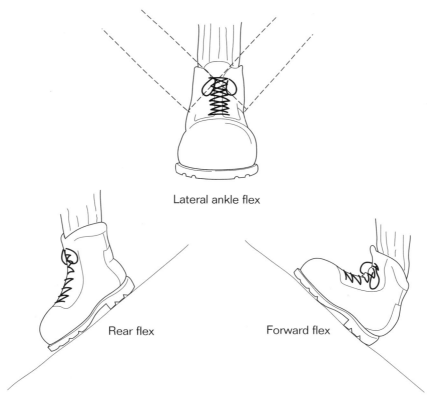

Lateral ankle flex

Rear flex

Forward flex

Illustration 18.1   Ankle flex: rear, lateral, forward

repairable in the field, and did not provide the fine adjustment possible with laces. But I won't be surprised if buckles reappear with improved technology.

Watch out for seams inside the boot, particularly in the heel area—they can cause blisters and eventually the seams may blow out.

Webbing loops on the heel and tongue can make it easier to get the boots on and provide handy clip-in points.

FIT TO BE TRIED

If you don't take the time to properly fit your boots, you'll be in for major misery. Fitting is best done in a store with a good selection and an experienced staff—the mail-order prospect is grim at best. Fitting starts with trying on several different models and choosing the right size, but it goes far beyond that. How your feet compare to the theoretical average that boots are made to fit is as important as size.

For hiking and telemark boots, the arch length (heel to first metatarsal—big toe) is the most significant measurement, because that's where the foot bends [Illustration 18.2]. For stiff mountaineer-

Photo 18.6   Pulley lacing makes life easier when your fingers are frozen.

ing boots, the overall length (heel to toe) is most important; these boots don't bend much, and the toe clearance is critical for front-pointing. Ignore the size marked on the boot; it can easily be a full size (or more) off your Brannock-device size with heavy socks.

The best way to check your size for double boots is to pull the liners from the boots and put them on over the socks you intend to use. Make sure there are 1 to 2 cm in front of your longest toe. For single boots, unlace them and kick your toes to the front until they touch. Make sure you can get one finger (and no more than two) easily behind your heel.

When trying the boots on, it's best to wear the same foot beds and socks you will use on the trail. Walking up and down a ramp can help determine whether your heel is slipping or there is too much pressure. Try the boots out on a climbing wall to see whether your foot is securely held when edging, and use a boulder to see how it frictions.

When laced, the uppers should snug across your forefoot like a big hand laid on top [Illustration 18.3]. Be sure your feet and the boots are flexing in the same place; no amount of breaking-in can overcome this problem.

In even the stiffest boots, there should be virtually no vertical lifting of your heels when toeing in. Some people say as much as a ¼ in. of heel lift is acceptable, but that's unnecessary and asking for trouble.

If you have replaced the foot beds and the length is right, you can eliminate excessive heel slip with padding. Alpine-ski shops carry special foam pads that you can attach to the outside of the inner boot. If it's properly located, your heel will feel comfortably locked in place. Spend a lot of time making sure the position is right before making the adjustment permanent. Duct tape will help keep the parts in place.

WIDTH

Almost no mountaineering boots are available in different widths these days. To check the width,

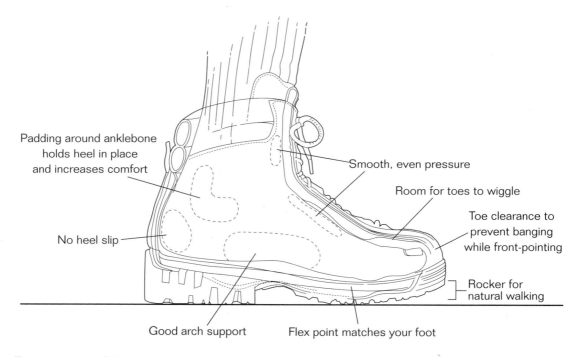

Padding around anklebone holds heel in place and increases comfort

Smooth, even pressure

Room for toes to wiggle

Toe clearance to prevent banging while front-pointing

No heel slip

Rocker for natural walking

Good arch support

Flex point matches your foot

Illustration 18.2   Fitting a mountain boot

place your sock-covered foot on the boot's foot bed insert. Observe whether there is room to spare (narrow) or you are overflowing (wide). If either case is extreme, you'll need customization.

If you have very wide feet (EE and wider), choose a plastic shell that can be punched out by an alpine-ski shop. This voids any warranty against cracking, yet it may be the only solution short of surgery. Leather boots without rubber rands can often be stretched in the forefoot to give you more volume.

People with very narrow feet (AAA) can fill some excess volume with thicker foot beds. Double boots can be padded on the outside of the inner boot with horizontal foam strips to keep your feet from swimming.

ARCH

Do you have a flat or high arch? High-arch folks will probably want a double boot with a lace-up liner; it gives you more options for customization. The largest artery in the foot *(dorsalis pedis)* runs across the instep, and pressure here can ensure cold feet. With a lace-up liner, you can change the lacing pattern and even remove eyelets to reduce pressure points. A low-volume foot with a flat arch may benefit from padding to fill in large voids.

WOMEN

The main gender difference for feet *of the same length* is that women tend to have a narrower heel and lower ankle bone. Because nearly all the good alpine boots are made to a man's last, this does create a problem. Some women's mountaineering boots are available, though rarely top-of-the-line models. If you have longer feet (women's 7 and up), you often have a much bigger selection and may be able to make a men's boot fit (possibly with the use of foot beds and fitting aids). Taller boots may be a problem, since women's calf muscles are often lower than men's, but this is more of an issue with ski boots.

TAKE-HOME EXAM

Once home with your new boots, it's important to wear them around the house or at work for at least several hours before going outside. This is your last chance to cure a potentially expensive mistake if the size or fit isn't perfect. Be sure to align the tongue every time you lace up the boots; leather has an amazing memory.

Avoid misery by trimming your toenails and pre-taping your heels if you are especially prone to blisters. Recheck the lacing and tongue position after a half-hour or so; they tend to slip. Slowly increase your mileage in the boots before making a long approach.

SOCKS

Wool—there's just no substitute. Of all the high-tech materials, none has surpassed the performance of wool for socks. In case you haven't noticed, your feet have more sweat glands per square inch (about 3300) than almost any other part of the body. Each foot produces about 1 liter of sweat per week.

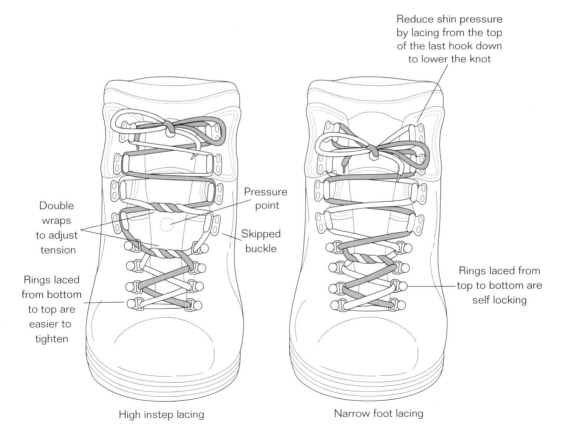

Reduce shin pressure by lacing from the top of the last hook down to lower the knot

Double wraps to adjust tension

Pressure point

Skipped buckle

Rings laced from bottom to top are easier to tighten

Rings laced from top to bottom are self locking

High instep lacing

Narrow foot lacing

Illustration 18.3   Vary the lacing technique to improve fit.

All this moisture creates one of the biggest reasons your feet become cold, because water is thirty-two times more heat-conductive than air. In addition to insulating and cushioning, wool absorbs 30 percent of its weight in moisture. This helps keep your feet dry and comfortable, something synthetic socks cannot do. The water absorbed into the sock tends to evaporate rather than go into the boot lining; this can be facilitated, of course, by a frequent change of socks. Wool socks are also much less prone to "stink foot" after numerous days than synthetics.

Traditionally, wool socks have been made by knitting them into the familiar ragg style; a blend of nylon is usually added for durability. Although these are okay, the newer terry-loop knit construction is far superior. The loops trap more air, reduce blister-causing friction, and provide additional cushioning. The best socks are now engineered with extra padding on the bottom, an elasticized arch brace that increases support, and smooth, flat-lock seams that don't create pressure points.

You may have noticed that I didn't start this discussion with liner socks. Liners are smooth, thin synthetic socks that reduce the friction of ragg wool socks. Liners are no longer needed if you purchase good, terry-loop wool socks. This may seem like blasphemy to those used to the dual-sock system, yet it is true. The loops eliminate the friction problem, and high-quality wool is so soft that it doesn't scratch the way the cheap stuff does. If the liner is a tube rather than a fitted design, you will have problems with wrinkles that can give you blisters.

COLD-WEATHER SOCKS

If you are buying footwear for extreme cold, you'll need additional insulation. You have several options. The first is to use two, or even three, pairs of heavy socks. This works well, albeit with a couple of major concerns. The combination of socks must not impede capillary circulation, so the outer sock may need to be of a larger size. Furthermore, your boots must be fitted with the double/triple-sock combo and will only work with it. If you try to cram an extra pair of thick socks into a boot sized with one pair, you can almost guarantee frostbite.

A better option is to use a vapor barrier (VB) layering system. This consists of a liner sock (for comfort), a waterproof sock, and the normal heavy sock. Your feet stay warmer because no evaporation takes place. The VB sock prevents the outer sock and boot liner from getting wet, a major bonus on extended trips. Because the liner and VB sock are each very thin, they do not significantly affect the sizing of your boots.

Although it works well, there are downsides to the VB system. It is very important that you change liner socks every night and give your feet a chance to dry out; otherwise, you could get a serious condition called trench foot. Because you are creating a warm, moist atmosphere, bacterial and fungal growth is a problem; the use of a foot powder is advised. (Some people also use antiperspirant on their feet.) If you want to try the VB-sock concept before buying commercial ones, plastic bread bags work well. Personally, I rarely bother with VBs.

The last, and least desirable, "options" for warmer feet are to use neoprene socks or battery-powered, heated socks. To get a decent fit, neoprene socks need to be sized snugly, which can impede circulation. This problem may be exacerbated by large altitude changes; the gas bubbles in the foam expand, making the socks even tighter. There are no advantages to using these in mountaineering boots, although they work great with sport sandals for stream crossings.

Even worse are heated socks, which require you to strap a battery pack to your calf or waist belt. Aside from the ridiculous amount of weight, they are expensive and prone to failure. Should they quit or the batteries die, you are left with a sweaty foot in a mediocre sock.

GAITERS

For hiking on rocky trails and corn snow in the summer, a pair of low gaiters can be a wonderful asset. The trim-fitting stretch-material gaiters breathe well in hot conditions yet keep unpleasantness out.

Knee-high gaiters are the clear choice for most alpine climbing where postholing is common [Photo 18.8]. Spend the extra money on a good pair!

Coated fabric above boot height ensures hot, sweaty calves and feet. Uncoated fabrics are very breathable but tend to flop down, so you need to always close the drawstring at the top just to hold the gaiters up. Laminated WP/B fabrics both

FOOT BEDS

Your foot contains 26 bones and 112 ligaments; these are operated by more than 200 muscles. Without even support, these muscles work overtime to correct for imbalances. This is significant even while standing and walking, and it's especially noticeable when front-pointing. Rotational movement (associated with pronation) of your foot within the boot leads to bone spurs on the heel and anklebones as well as bunions on the first and fifth metatarsal.

Throw away those 50-cent pieces of foam that come with many boots—they're garbage. Quality foot beds can increase comfort, conserve energy, improve your climbing, increase warmth, and prevent foot, joint, and lower-back problems. Your feet and lower legs will be more relaxed with proper foot beds, and many boot-fitting problems are solved.

Over-the-counter foot beds have improved greatly in recent years and are probably worth a try as an affordable alternative to custom footbeds [Photo 18.7]. However, feet are as different as faces, so there is only so much a generic fit can do.

Competitive athletes have used custom foot beds for years, and there is no reason climbers can't enjoy them as well. Good foot beds are not cheap, but they're worth every penny and will last a long time. Because you can generally use the same foot bed in your boots, they can get plenty of use.

Three routes exist for obtaining custom foot beds: an alpine ski shop, a specialty foot-bed maker, or a podiatrist who prescribes orthotics. The last choice is hyper-expensive and probably only necessary if you have serious foot problems.

Good ski shops have trained employees who spend a lot of time custom-fitting downhill boots. Most offer heat-moldable foot beds in a variety of styles.

Specialty foot bed makers offer several styles for different sports and can help with unique fit problems. Their services are worth seeking out if you want maximum performance and comfort. Some even offer mail order and will send you a kit, for taking impressions, that you return to have the foot beds made.

Photo 18.7   Aftermarket foot beds can enhance fit and performance.

breathe acceptably and are stiff enough to leave the gaiter open at the top when you aren't in deep snow.

It may not seem obvious in the store, but the gaiters should be easy to put on while you're half-asleep in predawn hours with frozen fingers. The front-opening styles win over side- or rear-opening for convenience—don't even consider simple tubes. The zipper should be easy to start; I've never had any trouble with wide Velcro strips freezing or not closing.

The gaiters should fit snugly to your boots and calf (the best come in sizes) or you *will* snag a

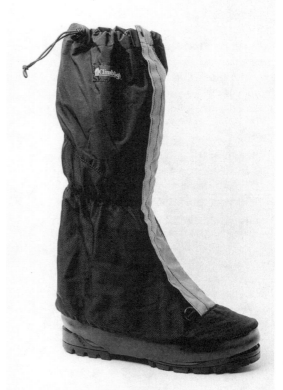

Photo 18.9   Insulated supergaiter with sticky rubber rand that does not interfere with step-in crampons

Photo 18.8   Fitted gaiter with neoprene instep strap and front Velcro closure

crampon point and trip. Without a tight seal to the boot, a gaiter will allow snow to force its way up inside, where it is trapped next to your foot. Look for abrasion patches on the inside of the leg extending to midcalf or higher; this area is often underprotected.

Parachute cord wears out on rocks far too quickly for use as an instep strap. Wire cable and nylon-reinforced urethane strap make the most durable instep strap materials, but nylon-reinforced neoprene strap is an acceptable alternative. No matter the material, the strap should be designed for easy replacement in the field.

SUPERGAITERS

Plastics and leathers have many good properties for boots, yet are fairly poor insulators. Regular gaiters work well to keep snow and other elements out, but these do not extend below the anklebone. A supergaiter takes the protection right down to the welt, leaving the sole exposed for walking and climbing [Photo 18.9].

Insulated supergaiters can easily double the warmth of your boots. For leather boots, supergaiters also offer protection against abrasion and the otherwise inevitable soaking.

Photo 18.10   Insulated overboots should be used with strap-on crampons.

Two basic styles are available: welt-cinch and rubber-rand. Those that cinch around the welt provide insulation slightly closer to the ground, but they're more difficult to hold in place, particularly with flexible boots. Attaching baling wire to strategically located grommets can solve this problem.

Supergaiters that use heavy-duty rubber rands have gained popularity in recent years. These stretch very tightly onto the boots and generally stay in place (slick, round-toed boots may require adhesive) and are quite rugged. This style leaves an uninsulated section that runs around the boot at toe level. If you're using rubber-randed supergaiters on leather boots, during storage be sure to pull the rands off or use shoe trees; otherwise, the toes of your boots may permanently curl upward.

OVERBOOTS

When supergaiters aren't enough, you'll get maximum protection from cold with overboots [Photo 18.10]. By insulating the soles of the boots, too, you can triple the boots' warmth. The obvious drawback is that overboots work only when used on crampons, skis, or snowshoes—the bottoms are too slick and not durable enough for walking or climbing.

These are the sort of thing you carry in the pack until it's time for the summit bid. They also make great mukluks when worn over inner boots or down booties, but choose a traction sole . . . slipping while going to the bathroom is embarrassing at best, fatal at worst.

Most overboots are theoretically designed to be used with step-in crampons; however, don't count on it. Be extremely careful when attaching the crampons to an overboot; if a crampon falls off, the mistake could prove deadly. Crampons with toe straps and step-in heel bails are more secure than those with toe bails. You may have to use strap-on crampons with some overboots.

TIPS FOR KEEPING WARM TOES

Take your shoes and socks off. Now look at your toes. Do you want to keep them?

The literature of mountaineering is filled with accounts of digits frozen into black blocks of ice. Denali and the Himalaya have probably claimed the greatest share, and even New Hampshire's Mount Washington has taken a large toll. Go out in severe winter conditions at any elevation and you're at risk.

It is far easier to keep your feet warm than to heat them up after they are cold. If the blood isn't warm going into your extremities, it certainly won't be warm when returning to your body's core. Dressing your legs warmly will not only help your feet but also improve performance by allowing the muscles to operate efficiently. The old adage "If your feet are cold, put on a hat" has a lot of truth to it.

It is hard to emphasize enough the importance of drinking plenty of fluids. When you are dehydrated, your blood becomes thicker and peripheral circulation decreases. This is compounded at high altitudes by an increase in red blood cells, which further thicken the blood. Remember that the sensation of thirst occurs only after it is too late—if your pee is yellow instead of clear, you aren't drinking enough.

A hydration system with a drinking hose is one of the best accessories a mountaineer can carry because it encourages you to sip frequently. A good stainless-steel vacuum bottle allows a hot drink late in the day when it is needed most.

If you have crampons with vertical side rails, attach an anti-balling plate to the bottom. Then fill in the empty spaces between the rails with closed-cell foam for extra ground insulation.

Some climbers use chemical heat packs in their boots or supergaiters. One model contains packets that stick to the inside of your boots and which generate heat for about 5 hours. Another is a bit bigger and lasts up to 12 hours. These require oxygen for the thermal reaction, so place them on the inside of your calf at boot height where there is more airflow.

CHAPTER 19

SKI MOUNTAINEERING

DREAM THE FANTASY.

You crest out on a ridge after a long, gradual climb through the silent forest. Though the sun shines bright, the wind chills as your group dons shell gear and removes climbing skins. Below is 5000 ft. (1500 m) of fresh, untracked powder. At the top, it's *fantastic*—waist-deep champagne fluff with constant face shots. Dropping through the trees, you float effortlessly on a white cloud. Whoops of joy resound through the woods.

Know the reality.

You just finished rapping off an ice climb with your partner—you had a great time but are cold and tired. It's now midafternoon and several miles back to your car. Above tree line, the wind has blasted the snow into boilerplate and hideous *sastrugi* that breaks unpredictably and drops you into 2 ft. (60 cm) of sugarlike depth hoar. After struggling through this dreck and the willows that grab at your skis, you finally enter the trees. The summer hiking trail allows easier going, but it is so steep and narrow that turning is a nightmare (and not doing so is worse), with no help from that 40 lb. (18 kg) climbing pack. As you near the bottom, the snow has turned to mashed potatoes that suck what little energy is left from your legs. Cries of anguish accompany grunts of exertion.

In fantasy conditions, you can have fun with almost any ski equipment—even old Fischer Europa 99s and Asolo Snowfields. But in the real world of heavy crud, boilerplate ice, breakable crust, frozen corn, and big packs, alpine touring (AT) equipment means the difference between fun and endless face plants.

Also called ski mountaineering and *randonnée,* this hybrid alpine/nordic equipment is specifically designed for the worst, and best, backcountry conditions. The alpine-like, fat skis are designed to be used in shorter lengths. The bindings allow you to free your heels for flat and uphill sections and to lock your heels down, with release capability, for downhill runs. The boots resemble downhill models except they have Vibram soles and a hinged cuff that can be unlocked for walking.

Don't get me wrong, I'm a telemark (tele) fanatic—it's a graceful and powerful turn. But the telemark technique is harder to master and requires more energy than the parallel turn. Tele equipment makes little sense for alpinists: The square toe and flexible ball of the boot are terrible for rock climbing; the relatively long skis make tight turns harder and are more of a nuisance to carry on your pack; and a full-blown tele package is frequently heavier than, and just as expensive as, a modern AT package.

ALPINE TOURING SKIS

When you first look at AT skis, they appear to just be alpine models with holes in the tips. Looks can be deceiving—although they use similar materials and construction techniques (perhaps even the same molds), these are very different creatures.

Because they are intended for *off-piste,* meaning no ski trails, the AT ski must handle a wider range of snow conditions than even "extreme" or "all mountain" alpine skis. Remember, 80 percent of the time you are going up or on flat terrain.

Shorter skis are more maneuverable, lighter weight, and easier to carry [Photo 19.1]. The only advantages long skis offer are a bit more flotation and stability at high speeds—the latter should not be a consideration when you are miles from the trailhead. If in doubt, choose the shorter ski even if you've been alpine skiing since age 3.

The holes in the ski tips, and sometimes the tails too, allow you to clip a carabiner to the skis for hauling them up a cliff. They also allow you to rig

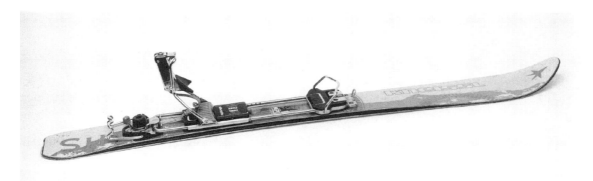

Photo 19.1 Miniature alpine touring skis (100 cm) can be ideal for approaches to climbs and for summer glacier travel. Longer skis (up to 190 cm) are better for deep, soft snow.

an emergency sled for evacuations. Many skis have a notch in the tail protector, which keeps the tail hook on some climbing skins from slipping off. If your skis lack this, it is easy to add with a hand file.

These days, most skis are made with cap construction, which uses the outer skin as a structural part of the ski. Although they are sometimes lighter than laminated skis (the traditional construction), other performance claims are highly debatable.

It is possible to make either great or lousy skis with any particular construction, so don't fret this detail. Furthermore, while all skis can bend or break given sufficient force, AT skis necessarily trade some strength for less weight. Wood cores tend to be more durable than foam, but if you are planning gonzo cliff jumping or mogul bashing, stick with alpine boards.

The greater side cut of shaped skis makes them easier and more fun to turn. However, very wide tips (over 100 mm) or narrow waists (under 70 mm) can make touring more difficult.

Skis with beveled sidewalls slice through heavy crud noticeably better than skis with vertical walls. In any other condition, these make very minimal difference.

An even bigger factor in wet, heavy snow is the weight of the skis. Very light skis tend to get pushed around, while heavier skis can power right through the glop.

Traditionally, alpine touring skis were made in garish fluorescent colors to aid in the rescue of avalanche victims, but most companies have now gone with more subtle graphics. All things being equal, lighter-colored skis are a better choice than dark skis because they are less prone to ice buildup on the deck. Waxing your top deck also helps minimize buildup.

The P-Tex of bases can be made by extruding the material, squeezing the molten material into sheets, or by sintering, where pellets are bonded by heat and pressure. Extruded bases are cheaper to produce and somewhat easier to repair, and a dry extruded base (all the wax worn off) has slightly better glide than a dry sintered base. Sintered bases are more durable, and their porous nature allows them to absorb and hold wax much better.

A properly tuned ski (stone-ground base, beveled edges, and hot wax) gives maximum performance. On the other hand, the very nature of alpine touring dictates that these are "rock skis" from day one. Thanks to improved manufacturing and tuning processes, most skis are coming off the rack in pretty good shape these days. Unless you know exactly what you are doing, I would recommend simply detuning (dulling) the tips and the tails, and hot waxing with an all-around alpine wax (no, it won't contaminate the adhesive on your climbing skins). While I do maintain my skis, it is not a bad idea to learn how to ski on dull edges without wax (again, real-world conditions).

APPROXIMATE SKI LENGTHS

Figures are based on a 175 lb. (80 kg) skier with gear; add or subtract 10 cm for each 25 lbs. (11 kg):

Backcountry touring	210 cm
Backcountry telemark	200 cm
Alpine touring with AT boots	190 cm
Approaches with mountaineering boots	180 cm
Summer glacier skiing	80–120 cm

BOOTS

If downhill turns are your primary goal, boots are the most important part of the package. Good boots can make up for bad skis, but great skis can't compensate for inadequate boots. Mountaineering boots are fine for flat and uphill terrain but leave a *lot* to be desired when skiing down with a pack.

Unfortunately, many people focus on getting skis and bindings first and "making do" with whatever boots they have. Bad idea—if you can afford only one part of the package and want downhill performance, put your money into good AT boots first and rent skis. Your feet will be happy and you will get a more accurate feel for the performance of different skis and bindings.

Boots designed for alpine touring have rectangular toes and heels that are compatible with AT bindings [Photo 19.2]. They should not be used in regular downhill bindings. These boots have a lugged hiking sole, with built-in rocker, and hinged cuffs that allow comfortable walking. When clamped down, with the cuffs locked into a forward lean, they provide roughly as much support as a soft alpine boot.

When comparing AT boots, there are several truths: (a) fit comes first; (b) lighter boots are softer; (c) softer boots are more comfortable; (d) stiffer boots provide more control. Notice that b and c conflict with d, which means you have to decide which is more important to you.

The most important characteristics of an AT boot are forward, backward, and lateral flex. When touring, a great deal of forward flex is desirable for maximum comfort. Some people prefer boots with a stiff forward flex for downhill skiing because it allows them to drive the tips through a turn. However, softer boots are more forgiving in rough terrain and generally more comfortable.

A lot of backward flex is desirable when walking downhill on trails and touring on the flats. On downhill runs, however, backward flex translates into crash and burn unless you have a lot of practice, so all AT boots have a method of locking and unlocking the backward flex. A few models have multiple forward-lean settings, which also lock the forward flex; these boots can provide a steeper, more aggressive stance but tend to be less forgiving.

AT boots can be remarkably good for moderate vertical ice- and rock-climbing and are fairly comfortable for walking on trails. However, since they have minimal lateral flex, they leave a lot to be desired on much of the ground in between. If your emphasis is on alpine climbs or very technical ice, stick with regular mountaineering boots.

All AT boots have removable inners with a traction sole for walking around huts and camps. Beware models that use sticky rubber rands because this makes it difficult to put the boots back together. If you have a hard time putting boots on in the store, think of what it will be like when the boots, and you, are frozen.

When walking and touring, you will want to leave the top buckle(s) attached but not closed. If the buckle flops around, it is likely to get broken. Other than by this operator error, buckles rarely break these days. However, those that rely on springs are more prone to freezing or jamming.

For AT boots that lack them, a power strap (a simple adjustable webbing loop that tightens the

Photo 19.2 Alpine touring boots with square toes and notches for the Dynafit binding. These ice- and rock-climb reasonably well and give far better skiing performance than mountaineering boots.

boot top) for downhill runs can add a great deal of support, weighs almost nothing, and costs less than $10.

BOOT ALTERNATIVES

Of course, climbers want to know whether they can use their plastic mountaineering boots with AT bindings. These boots do fit several (but not all) bindings and are adequate for getting into climbs and back again. However, they don't ski very well because they have too much backward and lateral flex. Plastic spoilers for mountaineering boots do very little except add weight. With practice, you can successfully use a modified fixed-heel telemark turn to regain some fore-aft control. If your goal is great ski runs, however, use appropriate AT boots.

Likewise, anyone with an expensive pair of downhill boots wants to know how they work for alpine touring. They do fit most of the bindings and give you maximum control but are heavy and not very comfortable on approaches.

BINDINGS

First and foremost, the binding has to hold your foot securely to the ski and transfer all of your actions directly into it [Photo 19.3]. Then, without

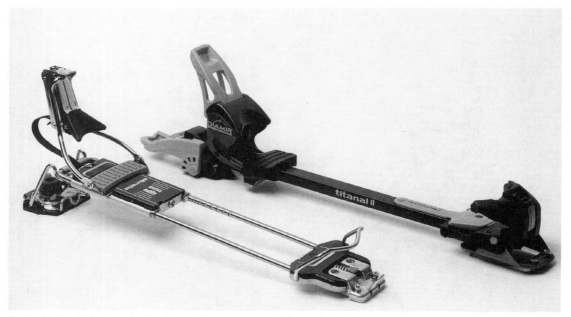

Photo 19.3   Alpine touring bindings offer touring capability with locked-heel downhill performance.

ever doing so prematurely, it has to release your foot in the right direction and at the right time. The binding must also provide complete touring freedom, both uphill and on flat terrain, under all conditions. Throw in the need for light weight and maximum durability, and you quickly realize that compromises have to be made.

It is important to realize that no AT binding offers the release performance of a modern downhill binding. As any lawyer can tell you, there is no such thing as a "safety" binding. The release function of AT bindings is directly related to your weight, size, and skiing ability, and the boots you are using. Soft mountaineering boots do not transmit the full force of a fall into the binding, so a lighter release setting is required.

There really is no such thing as a "prerelease," only a binding coming off when the forces exceed the settings. If you come out of your bindings more than once a day, assuming you're not taking major eggbeaters, then gradually tighten them until you stop releasing. Better yet, mellow a bit and

learn to ski less aggressively—a safer policy in the backcountry.

All AT bindings have heel elevators, stops that keeps your heels from going all the way down when climbing steep slopes. These save a great deal of energy and prevent calf strain, although some could be taller.

The mechanism by which the binding switches from touring to downhill mode is important. The nicest are pole-actuated so that you can switch on the fly. Others require you to bend over and flip a lever, no easy task with a full pack on your back. Some models make you step off the ski—not a problem if you are just going up, taking your skins off, and going down, but this can be a real nuisance in rolling terrain.

A unique accessory available for most AT bindings is detachable ski crampons, known as *harscheisen* [Photo 19.4]. These are very useful when climbing and traversing long sections of frozen snow. Arguments about the performance of crampon styles (those that raise with your foot versus those that are

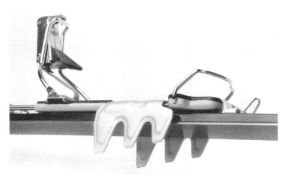

Photo 19.4 Ski crampons (*harscheisen*) are indispensable when ascending or traversing frozen slopes.

fixed to the ski) are pointless since the binding manufacturer makes that decision for you—and after all, any style is better than none when traversing a steep, icy slope.

All bindings have runaway straps available, some of which are poorly designed. These are required at ski resorts, and they are essential to prevent lost skis in deep powder (care to excavate an entire slope with a shovel?) or in a crevass.

A few bindings have optional ski brakes, which are great for firm snow because they prevent a windmilling ski from whacking you in the head. When crossing avalanche terrain (where you must detach runaway straps), brakes can prevent a lost ski after a crash. In powder, some people use brakes with ski flags, 15 ft. (5 m) pieces of fluorescent tape that tuck into pouches on the boots.

All bindings work more reliably if you maintain them. Clean them after a trip and lubricate them occasionally. Spraying the whole binding with silicone will help minimize icing and corrosion problems.

SKI POLES

For touring on relatively flat terrain, poles that are long enough to fit snugly under the armpit give the most power for forward momentum. On long tours,

this can increase your efficiency and save you energy. However, touring-length poles are not only a nuisance and more prone to breakage when skiing downhill, but they actually hinder your technique. A shorter, elbow-length pole helps get your body in position faster for the next turn. When touring in especially bitter weather, a shorter pole keeps your hands below your heart and thus noticeably warmer.

For all of these reasons, many backcountry skiers prefer using adjustable-length poles [Photo 19.5]. These tubes-within-tubes use a camming or clamping mechanism to lock their height. The durability, reliability, and comfort of these poles have steadily improved over the years. They are available in two- and three-section models; the only advantage of the latter is that they collapse smaller for travel. In general, I recommend the two-section models because there are fewer things to go wrong.

The most commonly seen pole-adjusting mechanism is the twist-lock, which uses an internal plastic piece that cams when tightened. Most problems with these poles can be traced to user error. People frequently don't tighten them enough, causing them to slip unexpectedly, or they overtighten them to the point that the lock cannot be loosened without a major struggle—simply tighten the pole until it is snug and then give it an extra half-twist (but no more).

It is important to keep these poles clean and dry inside for maximum holding power and to prevent corrosion. (Do *not* spray the insides with lubricant.) Some people use a few inches of friction tape or heat-shrink on the upper and lower sections to provide extra grip with wet gloves on. Warming the joint with bare hands or warm breath can help unstick frozen poles.

The cams can eventually wear out (try roughening them with a coarse sandpaper), so it is not a bad idea to get a few extras when you buy the poles. They are cheap and it is not uncommon for these parts to no longer be available after a few years. Pull the poles apart and check for cracks or

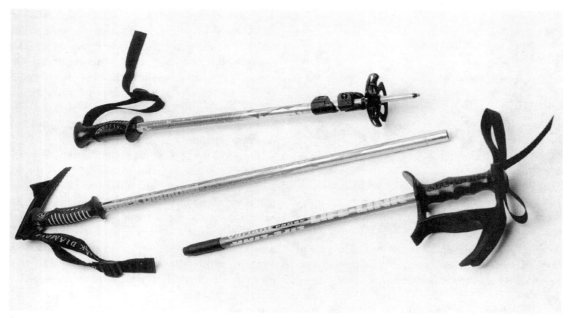

Photo 19.5   Three-section pole and two styles of self-arrest grips

loosening of the connection prior to big trips.

Many poles convert to avalanche probes if you remove the grips and join the shafts together. On some models, an optional connector can be carried for greater extension. Most of these poles do not work as well as a true avalanche probe because of the large diameter and protruding parts (some carbon-fiber poles are the exceptions). Probe poles are not a replacement for avalanche transceivers and good judgment!

The grips of most poles are now made of soft rubber, which is noticeably more comfortable than the older hard plastic or leather. Some have a corrective angle built in for improved downhill performance—a nice feature. Since I sometimes put my hands on top of the pole to push my way up a hill (which gives a lot more power), I prefer grips that have a large, smooth platform on top.

For skiers who enjoy steep terrain, some companies offer optional self-arrest grips that have a pick like that of an ice ax. I don't recommend these most of the time, but they can be real lifesavers if you fall on a chute or glacier with rocks or crevasses at the bottom.

(If you use self-arrest grips, then you probably need a ski helmet too! They have improved greatly in the past few years. Most climbing helmets are inadequate because of minimal side-impact protection.)

Many poles have straps that break away or release your hand when pulled from above, such as when a basket gets snagged. This is a good feature that *might* prevent a dislocated shoulder. Unfortunately, some of these come undone too easily, which can mean a lost pole in a crevassed region or when hauling up a cliff. It is not uncommon for the plastic piece on breakaways to just break, which can render a pole nearly useless on tours.

For touring, your hand enters the strap from below and wraps over the top. There is a left and a right—you can tell because the lower half of the strap goes to the thumb side. Adjust the strap so that it is snug, with your hand at the pivot point. Some poles have straps with large buckles that are uncomfortable when you're skiing bare-handed. When downhill skiing, just put your hand through the strap from above and grab the pole. The strap does not support the load.

All poles have removable baskets, and many models have different sizes or styles (which rarely are interchangeable between brands). The 3½ in. (9 cm) snowflake basket is the standard and works reasonably well for most conditions. Larger baskets may be desirable for deep powder but are more prone to breaking and snagging things.

Using poles on rocks wears down the tips; they are also prone to getting broken by levering in a crack. Therefore a replaceable tip is desirable if you will use them for hiking. (Be sure to carry a spare or two on long trips.) Carbide points are more durable and provide better bite on ice than do the standard steel points.

One final consideration is vibration. Some models really shake, rattle, and roll when whapped against a hard surface. This is irritating, and transmits more vibration into your hands.

The new generation of carbon-fiber poles are lighter and narrower for improved swing weight and less wind drag. They have a great feel and are remarkably durable. Once you try them, and get over the sticker shock, it is hard to go back to tapered aluminum poles.

CLIMBING SKINS

Climbing skins, or "Colorado black wax," save you a tremendous amount of energy on a tour with any substantial elevation gain. These strips of wool mohair (woven from mountain-goat fur), nylon plush, or plastic are strapped or glued onto ski bases. They allow the ski to glide forward but prevent slipping backward on slopes as steep as 35°. When removed, they fold up and fit in a small pouch [Photo 19.6].

There is little reason to buy mohair skins anymore. Nylon skins are less prone to icing, are more durable, and have only slightly less glide in dry powder snow.

In side-by-side comparisons, I could not detect any real difference in climbing power of mohair, blended mohair-nylon, and nylon skins. Plastic skins have great grip in soft snow, are rugged and cheap, but slip on icy tracks and have zero glide. Avoid them.

Strap-on skins are the easiest to attach and remove, but snow can build up between the skin and the ski, the straps interfere with edging on a traverse, and they will eventually be cut by the skis' steel edges. Adhesive skins are finicky, but they give superior performance.

Adhesive skins typically use solvent-based glues that work quite well at first but eventually lose their stickiness. Touch-ups are easy, but after a while they must be fully stripped (use a hair dryer, to warm the adhesive, and a plastic scraper) and the glue must be reapplied. Some older adhesives stick poorly in low temperatures, especially when they and the ski are cold (try warming the skins inside your parka).

For maximum climbing power, which is generally what you want skins for, they should be nearly as wide as the skis (the edges need to stick out for traverses) and almost as long. Unfortunately, some telemark-width skins are too narrow and do not have sufficient grip when used on a short, fat alpine touring ski, especially when traversing. Short "kicker" skins are great for lighter backcountry

Photo 19.6 Adhesive climbing skin with basic tip ring

touring setups but do not give adequate traction for climbing steep hills with a pack.

It is a good idea to use a tail hook and tip ring with a stretchable connector, particularly when yo-yo skiing (multiple runs on the same slope). Tip-tail fix kits minimize problems with adhesive skins and provide a backup system of attachment. If you really dislike tail hooks, just trim the skin so that it is 2 in. (5 cm) short of the tail. Get rid of the standard tip ring and get one with a rubber stretcher; that way you can remove the skin from the front instead of trying to peel up the tail end (which contaminates the adhesive in a critical area). Whatever you do, don't fold the skin over the tail of the ski; this guarantees they will peel off.

To apply adhesive skins, it is not necessary to remove touring wax unless it is softer than blue and really gobbed on. In that case, just use a scraper briefly to remove the excess. When removing an adhesive skin, pull off half and fold it together, glue to glue, and then repeat with the second half. With practice, you can also remove adhesive skins without taking off your skis.

When fresh from the factory, skins are treated for water repellency but this eventually wears off. If you are having problems with icing, rub climbing skin wax with the grain to improve glide and reduce water absorption.

Depending how much (and how) you ski, your climbing skins should hold up for several years. With care, which includes diligently avoiding rocks and renewing adhesive or replacing straps, they can last much longer. Keep your skins in a cool, dry place when they're not in use.

AVALANCHE TRANSCEIVERS

Avalanche transceivers, though expensive, are the cheapest life insurance you can buy. There is no substitute for *everyone* wearing them in potential avalanche country . . . and knowing how to use them.

All modern beacons are dramatically better than those manufactured just a few years ago [Photo 19.7]. Dual-frequency beacons served a purpose during the transition years, when the United States was switching frequencies to the international standard of 457 megahertz (MHz). However they are now obsolete, and it's time to retire them. Their range is poor, the electronics are ancient, and the earphones are inferior to external speakers and lights.

BEACON TIPS

- Prevention is infinitely better than victim detection. There is no substitute for good judgment and proper caution!
- Install fresh alkaline batteries at the start of every season. Do not use nicads or lithiums because their power output drops off rapidly, and the battery-life indicators are not calibrated properly for these batteries.
- Always wear your beacon next to your body (not in your pack) where it will stay warm and not get swept away in a slide. The best location is low and slightly off to one side (not on the center of your chest) with one strap over your head and shoulder and the other around your waist.
- Turn your beacon on at the trailhead, and don't turn it off until you get back to the car. Start each excursion by testing all the units in the group. This also reminds the group to adopt the mind-set that they are entering a danger zone.
- When searching, beware of tunnel vision—the tendency to stare at the flashing lights instead of looking around for visual clues (such as a hand sticking out of the snow!). Once a signal is acquired, the remaining rescuers should assemble probe poles and shovels while one searcher homes in. Start probing likely areas right away; you may get lucky and get a hit before the beacon arrives.

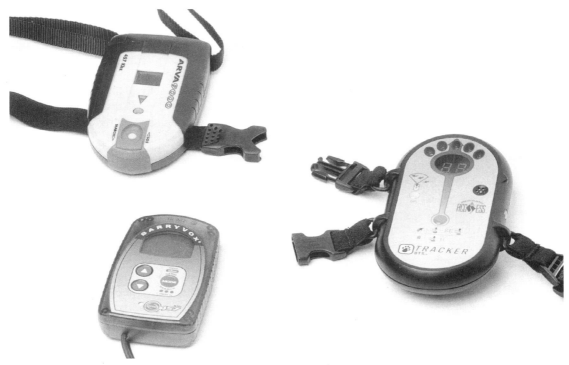

Photo 19.7   Avalanche beacons require practice every season!

Until recently, all avalanche transceivers used an analog signal translated into an audible beep that became louder as the signal strength increased. Old-style beacons with earphones generally require a grid search method that is reliable but slow. Models that have LEDs and external speakers make the tangent- (or induction-) line technique faster and more intuitive.

New digital transceivers interpret the buried beacon's signal with a computer and then present the information in a more user-friendly format, thus shortening search time further. In the hands of inexperienced users, digital beacons can yield significantly faster searches than other beacons.

No matter how simple beacons may become, that will not even slightly diminish the need for avalanche training and rescue practice. Failure to practice is the same as going climbing without learning to belay.

With all beacons, the primary stage of a search remains the same—the objective is just to detect a signal. When a lone climber is trying to search a large avalanche swath, a higher maximum range for a beacon can be advantageous. You want to cover a lot of terrain as quickly as possible and should never have to re-search an area, especially if it means climbing back up a slope.

However, maximum range is not everything. While a distant signal may prove very useful for well-trained rescuers who practice every year, less-experienced searchers tend to slow significantly once they pick up a distant signal. This can actually result in greater search times, compared with units that have less range.

Don't let price be the only consideration when choosing avalanche transceivers. Worthwhile features include bright lights for low-light operation, an external speaker, a visual transmit indicator, a battery check, and a waterproof case. The buttons or switches must be easy to operate with a gloved hand, and the on-off switch must be foolproof.

Try on the beacon and see how it rides. The harness should be easy to put on in the dark and comfortable to wear all day long. Some beacons tend to bounce around too much or get in the way of a climbing rack.

SNOW SHOVELS

A shovel is the most basic winter survival equipment you can carry [Photo 19.8]. Everyone in a group should have one. Not carrying one is risking someone else's life!

A snow shovel's most vital function is to excavate an avalanche victim in a hurry. Ever try digging avalanche debris with a ski tip or a pot? Not possible. A shovel is also needed to dig pits for snow study, to make snow shelters, and to unbury your car after a big dump. If you sleep in a snow cave, you are well advised to bring a shovel inside with you so you can get out in the morning. The blade of some shovels makes a good stove platform too.

Aluminum blades can be tough and are effective attacking avalanche debris because of their stiffness. It is helpful if they have a coating to minimize snow sticking to the blade. Composite material blades are new entries on the market that promise great strength and durability—but it's too early to tell how they'll perform.

Lexan-bladed shovels are remarkably strong, but they are not as stiff as aluminum blades, which makes them less effective when digging concrete-hard snow. Keeping the blade sharp with a flat file helps a lot. You can also use transparent blades as windows in a snow cave.

There is a persistent myth that metal blades are more durable than plastic. The reality is, many aluminum blades break because of stress fractures and abuse. If you stick any shovel blade in hard snow and lever hard on the handle, the blade *will*

Photo 19.8   A large blade with a telescoping handle and a D-shaped grip is the best choice for moving a lot of snow in a hurry. When weight is critical, an ice ax can be used as a handle on some shovels.

break. If the snow is very hard, it's better to chop at it with the blade.

Most people will want a shovel with an extendable handle. The increases in price and weight are minor compared with the benefits of increased power and reduced back strain. Although they're slightly bulkier, I also recommend D-shaped grips because they are more comfortable, especially if you wear mittens. A little insulating material around the lower part of the handle is a nice touch that you can add yourself. Some handles hold a snow saw inside.

It should be obvious that the bigger and deeper the blade, the more snow it can move in a hurry. Think of it this way: If you are buried under 3 ft. (1 m) of snow, do you want your friend using a teaspoon or a bulldozer? In some informal tests I conducted, the difference in time to fill a 55 gal. trashcan using a small versus large blade was more than two to one. The smaller blades are certainly more compact (and infinitely better than none), but it is a good idea to carry at least two big blades in a large group.

Keep your shovel readily accessible at all times, not buried at the bottom of your pack. Many packs now have shovel flaps that are ideal for this (as well as for carrying frozen ropes). If you must detach the handle, make sure there is no possibility of it getting lost. Out-of-bounds skiers and patrollers often carry the shovel like a pack, using a piece of webbing that goes from the holes in the blade tip to the handle as shoulder straps.

SNOW ACCESSORIES

A snow saw can also save you a lot of energy when digging a snow cave and is invaluable for making an igloo [Photo 19.9]. A snow saw that attaches to

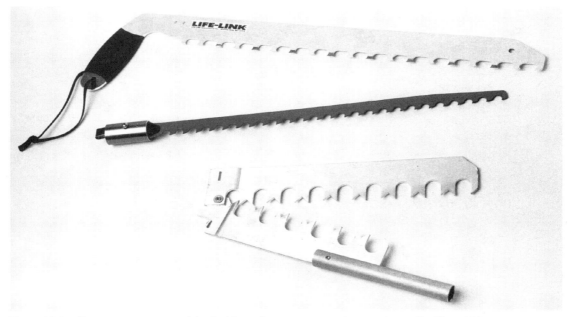

Photo 19.9   Snow saws can speed the building of snow caves and protective walls. The middle saw stows inside a shovel handle, which then becomes the saw handle. The bottom saw attaches to the end of a ski pole, which makes it much easier to cut a *rutschblock* for testing avalanche slopes.

the end of your probe pole is very helpful for performing a *rutschblock* (sliding block) test to check snowpack stability. There should be a saw in any group heading out on an extended trip.

True avalanche probe poles [Photo 19.10] are faster to assemble, longer, and easier to probe with than convertible ski poles. They resemble a tent pole but have a steel cable inside, a locking mechanism, and a pointed tip.

Tools for studying snow structure can be helpful for determining avalanche conditions [Photo 19.11]. You can never know too much about the snowpack. For day trips, I carry a small mister bottle filled with water and food coloring. When it's spritzed on the wall of a snow pit, different layers are clearly visible—a great teaching tool.

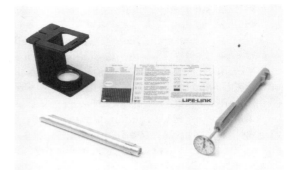

Photo 19.11   Tools for studying snow structure: Magnifiers and crystal card for looking at snow grains; dial-stem thermometer for checking temperature of snow near the surface and ground

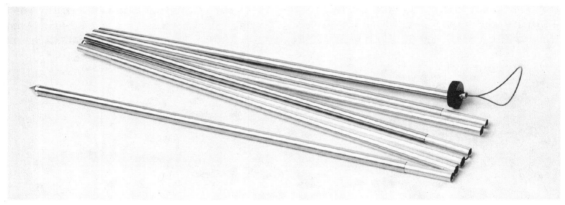

Photo 19.10   In dense avalanche debris, a good probe pole is superior to ski poles with tapered shafts.

CHAPTER 20

SNOWSHOES AND SLEDS

I WOULD RATHER SKI THAN SNOWSHOE any day. But there are times when snowshoes make more sense. Compared with alpine-touring skis, snowshoes are at least 5 lbs. (2.3 kg) lighter, more compact, more maneuverable, and less expensive.

In recent years, recreational snowshoeing has exploded in popularity, for three reasons: It's easy, fun, and cheap. Anybody can strap on a pair of basic snowshoes and have a good time tromping around without fear of injury. However, although numerous snowshoes are available on the market, most make poor choices for mountaineering, with its heavy loads, steep slopes, and often icy snow.

SNOWSHOE DESIGN

Right off the bat, you can rule out any radically asymmetric designs for climbing snowshoes. These allow a more natural stride than traditional snowshoes, making them well suited to casual walking and racing, but they sacrifice flotation and do not perform well when traversing steep slopes.

For the same reasons, snowshoes with parallel (or nearly parallel) sides are significantly better than those with radically flared sides. Similarly, long, pointed tails, while not an automatic disqualification for backcountry use, don't give the same performance as oval or blunt tails. Elongated oval snowshoes, sometimes called Western or Green Mountain styles, offer climbers the best combination of flotation, downhill control, and sidehill prowess [Photo 20.1].

The flatter a snowshoe's tip, the better it climbs steep terrain, yet the more prone it is to submarining during descents. Most mountaineering snowshoes compromise with 3 to 4 in. (8 to 10 cm) of gradual rise on the tips.

Some companies offer folding snowshoes. These may pack a bit easier, but they also add weight, complexity, and potential for breakage—three major strikes.

FLOTATION

What size to choose? The answer depends on how much you weigh, how much you normally carry, and what kind of terrain you most often travel.

As a 180 lb. (80 kg) kid who plays in the Colorado Rockies, I find relatively small, 8 by 25 in. (20 by 64 cm) snowshoes to be ideal for approaching ice climbs or for alpine day trips. I like this size because they are compact and maneuverable, but they lack sufficient flotation for breaking trail in deep powder or carrying an overnight pack. However, a significantly lighter person, or climbers in maritime climates with denser snow, should have no problems with heavy packs using this size.

By the time someone my size is fully decked out for a couple of days or longer in winter conditions, the payload can easily exceed 250 lbs. (115 kg). At this weight, or when traveling any distance in soft snow, you'll want the standard, midsize snowshoes that most companies offer: 9 x 30 in. (23 x 76 cm). For all-around use, this offers a good compromise size that still straps to a pack easily.

The next common size, 10 x 36 in. (25 x 91 cm), is too unwieldy for all but the biggest guys. The buoyancy would probably be nice if you often carried a heavy pack through flat or gently rolling terrain, but even pro football players will do fine on smaller shoes if they wait a few days after a storm for the snow to consolidate.

By the way, I've tried snowshoes both with lacing

Photo 20.1   Solid-deck snowshoe with fixed-toe cord, buckle binding

and with solid decks, and I could detect no notice-able difference in flotation.

CONSTRUCTION

If your snowshoe breaks far from the trailhead, you're in deep snow without a paddle. Therefore it pays to make some weight and price concessions in favor of durability.

Wooden snowshoes first appeared in Central Asia about 6000 years ago, but Native Americans developed the classic wood-framed snowshoe with rawhide lacing. Aesthetics aside, wooden shoes are no longer worth consideration for the serious snowshoer. Since Black Forest introduced aluminum frames in 1962 and Sherpa developed solid decking in 1971, virtually all mountaineer-ing snowshoes have incorporated these basic components.

The diameter and grade of the aluminum-alloy tubing is one of the key factors that separates in-expensive recreational snowshoes from the pricier mountaineering models. They may all look the same (especially when the frame is painted), and the marketing people are quick to point out they use "aircraft aluminum," but there are big differ-ences in strength and longevity among the various models.

Even when it is suspended between rocks by its tip and tail, a mountaineering snowshoe must re-peatedly withstand the lurching footfalls of a heavily laden climber. Beware of tubing frames that have holes drilled anywhere near the midsec-tion; this weakens the metal in a high-stress area.

The main reason companies use solid decks on snowshoes is cheaper production costs. Lacing re-quires more labor—driving up the cost—but also offers much better traction and can be replaced after heavy abuse [Photo 20.2].

Hypalon (rubber-coated nylon) is a popular choice for decking at many companies. While strong, Hypalon tends to wear out where it's tensioned over the metal frame. Snowshoes with replaceable decking attachments make sense if you climb in a very rocky region, such as New England.

Plastic snowshoes are increasingly appearing on the market. While significantly less expensive, some are heavier and less durable (rocks really chew them up) than sturdy metal-frame snowshoes. Still, plastic snowshoes are a good choice for the occasional user.

BINDINGS

The snowshoe's bindings are very important to climbers who frequent rugged terrain. A great snowshoe with a mediocre binding is little more than a toy, while a mediocre snowshoe with a great binding can be a serviceable tool.

The pivot, or hinge point, of the binding takes the full stress of snowshoeing, so it must be bombproof. Pivots usually are either "free rotating" (often around a pivot rod) or "fixed," typically using a heavy band as a hinge that forces the snowshoe to slap back to your heel after each step. Some bindings share characteristics of both.

In my experience, free-rotation bindings are better for breaking trail, especially in deep powder, because the tail dips with each stride and dumps snow off the back. When climbing steep, hard snow, the tip flips out of the way, allowing better purchase with the crampons underfoot. However, if you try to run with this style of pivot, the tips of the snowshoe will whap your shins—rather painfully, I might add.

Fixed-binding users can often be spotted because their backsides are covered with snow thrown up in a roostertail by the snowshoes. This design works well for running (the original intent), but is prone to diving in deep snow and forces you to lift your feet higher. Fixed-rotation bindings allow you to back up easily, and in soft snow, they make it easier to kick the snowshoe into steep slopes for climbing.

Photo 20.2   Lace-deck snowshoe with free-rotating, step-in binding

No matter which style of binding you choose, the critical feature is the lateral stability it provides. When traversing a steep slope, your heel should stay centered over the snowshoe for good edge control. Although most snowshoes have heel plates with teeth, these cannot overcome the deficiencies of a poor binding.

Many companies have ignored the needs of mountaineers in favor of snowboarders and hikers wearing soft boots. The result is cumbersome bindings whose straps, when cranked tight enough to hold you securely on steep terrain, tend to impede circulation in leather boots.

There is no way I will ever again use bindings that have nylon webbing or neoprene straps; my fingers have frozen enough, thank you very much. The new plastic straps are a huge improvement—they are strong, won't freeze, don't slip, and can be adjusted while wearing mittens.

Even more convenient are the buckle bindings adapted from the snowboard world. These typically require a bit of futzing, but are secure once they are on, and getting out of them is a breeze. Some of the buckles appear fragile, so spare parts may be a good idea for remote areas.

Speed tip: Once you adjust the position on the binding's heel strap to fit your boots, tape the buckle closed to prevent slipping. Next time you put the snowshoes on, just slide the boot back into position and then secure the front buckle or straps.

Since most mountaineers now wear boots compatible with clip-on crampons, a toe bail and heel lever is the optimal system for snowshoes as well. The best of these offers excellent lateral stability—nothing else even comes close if you do a lot of backcountry snowshoeing.

A few companies have developed snowshoes that incorporate your regular climbing crampons into the snowshoe binding [Photo 20.3]. However, these can be more tiring on a long approach since

Photo 20.3   Adjustable-length plastic snowshoe with a strap-on binding that accepts most crampons

the combined weight can be greater than a standard snowshoe and binding.

SNOWSHOE CRAMPONS

When you're hiking in the alpine zone, snow conditions can vary tremendously through the course of a day. Aggressive, built-in snowshoe crampons are often necessary to climb steep slopes, provide traction on traverses, and brake on downhills. The best systems have long claws under the rotating part of the binding, as well as additional teeth under the heel or near the snowshoe edges [Photo 20.4].

These crampons need to be durable enough to withstand walking on rocks. Heat-treated aluminum is okay, but snow will stick to it unless it's covered with plastic. In wet snow, you can spray WD-40 or Pam onto the crampon to temporarily prevent sticking.

Beginners often want maximum traction when going downhill, but advanced snowshoers appreciate less grip and more glide. Some models actually glissade quite well on steep slopes—a technique that is faster and a lot more fun than plodding along. If this appeals to you, make sure the crampons won't brake too hard.

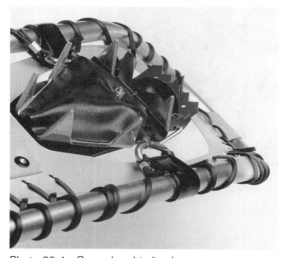

Photo 20.4   Snowshoe binding/crampon

ACCESSORIES

Ski poles are essential for any serious backcountry snowshoeing. Poles provide a huge advantage when negotiating obstacles, traversing slopes, and attacking hills. Using a long ice ax with a snow basket (if you can even find one) is a poor alternative, but it is better than no pole at all.

Ski poles don't need to be fancy—a $5 pair from a garage sale is fine—but make sure they have wrist straps and large baskets. Cross-country ski poles are too long. To size them correctly for snowshoeing, flip a pole upside down and grab the shaft just under the basket; your lower arm should rise no more than 30° from horizontal.

If you have them, poles that convert to avalanche probes are nice. However, spend the money on a shovel and beacon before paying extra for probe poles.

Heel elevators are de rigueur on backcountry skis to prevent calf burn, and these lifts can also be helpful with snowshoes if you have lots of long, steep hills to climb.

EXPEDITION SLEDS

Whether you're traveling on skis or snowshoes, towing a sled allows you to haul far more gear, with greater comfort and less energy, than you could carry in the largest expedition pack.

My practical weight limit for skiing with a pack is about 45 lbs. (20 kg) (a bit more with snowshoes). Though it is physically possible to carry more, the exertion increases exponentially with the load. Believe me, you feel pretty helpless upside-down in deep snow underneath an 80 lb. (36 kg) pack.

With a standard-sized sled, however, one person can reasonably haul as much as 90 lbs. (40 kg) in moderately steep snow country. If your idea of fun is crossing Greenland on skis, fiberglass expedition sleds can handle up to 400 lbs. (180 kg).

Nearly all backcountry sleds have optional kid-seat attachments, complete with harnesses to keep the youngsters in place. A windshield is mandatory to keep flying snow and branches from hitting your kids, and don't use fixed-binding snowshoes to tow the sled, or you'll bury the little ones in the snow kicked up behind you.

HOMEMADE RIGS

Before we talk about commercial sleds, it's well worth considering less expensive alternatives. If you are looking at a onetime use, such as a trip to Denali, spending $300 or more on a sled probably doesn't make sense. (Renting may be an option in some places.)

More than two-thirds of the sleds used on the West Buttress of Denali, for example, are simple kids' plastic jobs, sometimes beefed up with hardware-store materials for a total cost of less than $50. For basic hauling without much sidehilling, these are lighter and much cheaper than the commercial rigs.

If you decide to rig your own sled, or are picking a kiddie sled out of the pile at Kahiltna Basecamp,

consider bolting on a pair of keels made from aluminum angle stock to stiffen the hull and minimize sideslipping. Be careful not to rip the plastic when you punch holes for your towline, and reinforce the holes with duct tape and/or washers. Bamboo or PVC pipe for stiff traces give much more control than a towrope.

Another sledding alternative is the drag bag, which is simply a horizontal haul bag—about as low-tech (though not low price) as can be. Because they have greater friction, drag bags aren't as prone to running you over on downhills as a sled on a towrope, but on sidehills they still tend to find their own way. Use a swivel to prevent the rope from kinking.

COMMERCIAL SLED DESIGNS

Personally, I like having maximum control of a heavy load that seems determined to pull me off my feet. That's where commercial backcountry sleds have the real advantage over homemade ones.

The standard backcountry sled is roughly 3½ ft.

SNOWSHOE OPTIONS

With many ice climbs, the long uphill approaches are tedious to descend by snowshoe, but too narrow or steep to ski. That is unless you pack mini-skis. Woo-hoo, you're back at the car in 30 minutes with a huge grin on your face.

Mini-skis are not just toys for ski resorts but also useful backcountry tools. Light and compact, these strap easily to a pack. They work well for descending packed snowshoe trails, supersteep powder, and summer glaciers, but they bog down in low-angle soft stuff and don't tour well.

Climbing snowshoes represent another category of backcountry gear that falls outside the normal definitions because they are so small and have no pivoting binding [Photo 20.5]. Resembling overgrown pie tins, they are made for climbing steep snow without switchbacking. For really

steep snow, going from standard snowshoes to climbing snowshoes is like changing from approach shoes to good rock shoes.

Photo 20.5   Climbing snowshoes are great for steep terrain but don't work well on the flats.

(1.1 m) long and has about twice the volume of an expedition pack, yet retains a modicum of maneuverability and meets airline requirements. The commercial sleds all have runners or keels, spaced to fit in ski tracks, to improve tracking and side-hilling performance.

If you need to carry your gear over rocky stretches or very steep terrain, be sure there are internal straps to hold your pack in place with the suspension facing up. Then when it's time to hoof it, you can open the sled cover, stow the traces, and wear the shell and pack as a unit. This is easier if the hull has a truncated end (like a square-stern canoe) that won't interfere with your legs. Longer sleds often have tapered sterns, so they'll slide over snow humps instead of dropping with a thud.

The hulls on all standard-sized sleds are made of molded polyethylene plastic that won't crack down to –100°F (–73°C). Larger sleds are made of fiberglass for greater stiffness and reduced weight. Although none of these materials will hold wax like a sintered ski base, a rub-on glide treatment can help reduce your workload.

The attached waterproof covers on commercial sleds protect equipment yet still allow easy access during the day. I prefer full-length zippers to folding closures, but the latter type is better than a simple tarp. Compression straps with quick-release buckles are important to hold gear in place when—not if—the sled overturns. Surprisingly, few sleds have handles at the bow, stern, and sides to allow quick lifts over obstacles.

To prevent the sled from picking up too much speed on downhills, make a simple brake by tying a bunch of overhand knots in a rope and running it under the sled from bow to stern.

Perhaps the best accessory for a backcountry sled is the Mountainsmith Rear Brake/Rudder Kit. With a little creativity, the kit can be fitted to most sleds that have a truncated stern. When climbing steep hills, the brake allows you to take a breather without fear of backsliding. On steep traverses, you can lower the rudder 6 in. (15 cm) for much better tracking.

HARNESS

For skiing, the sled's traces (the poles linking the sled to the harness) need to be about 7 ft. (2.1 m) long; shorter lengths work better for snowshoeing. Traces are usually parallel to each other and spaced far apart on the sled for maximum control. Traces that cross (form an X) allow a tighter turning radius and better tracking.

Most of the commercial sleds come with nicely padded hipbelts, suitable for moderate loads. It is important that the hipbelt adjust in circumference, so its anchors are on your sides no matter your waist size. When you approach maximum capacity, especially with expedition sleds, a shoulder harness helps distribute the load.

You can rig the traces to your pack's suspension system (sternum strap required), but be sure to choose very sturdy attachment points and confirm that detachment is easy. Some companies also offer a snowmobile hitch and a dog harness—now we're talking!

CHAPTER 21

EYEWEAR

FEW THINGS ARE MORE PRECIOUS THAN eyesight. Yet climbers, especially those venturing to high elevations, subject their eyes to incredibly severe conditions, including drying winds and burning ultraviolet rays. Without adequate protection, we risk severe pain and, possibly, eventual blindness.

When you see a rainbow, the visible segment of the electromagnetic spectrum—380 to 760 nanometers (nm)—is beautifully displayed, with a deep purple on the inside and a bright red on the outside [Illustration 21.1]. However, it's the stuff just beyond our perception—the remaining 55 percent of the sun's energy that reaches the earth's surface—that can hurt us.

UV RADIATION

The most damaging of these rays is ultraviolet (UV) radiation. Long-term exposure to UV radiation has been shown to cause cataracts, a clouding of the lens. Furthermore, UV radiation has also been implicated in the onset of presbyopia (the need for reading glasses) and age-related macular degeneration (ARMD), one of the leading causes of blindness in adults.

UV radiation is subdivided into three types: UVA (320 to 380 nm), UVB (290 to 320 nm), and UVC (200 to 290 nm). The last is filtered out entirely by the ozone layer, many miles above the earth's surface, so it is of no concern, even on high-altitude peaks. Companies hyping UVC protection are simply preying on unfounded fears. This is also true for claims about protection against infrared radiation, at the other end of the visual spectrum. Although they may cause minor discomfort from heat buildup (often interpreted as eyestrain), infrared rays appear to be harmless to the body and are mostly blocked by average tinted lenses.

The best-known UV threat to our health comes from UVB waves, which are absorbed by the cornea, the outer surface of the eye. These are the so-called burning rays that fry our skin and cause snow blindness (technically called photokerititis), essentially a sunburn on the surface of the eye. Patients' descriptions of this condition include "sandpaper rubbing my eyeballs," "burning sand poured into my eyes," and "red-hot pokers massaging my eye sockets." In severe cases, ulceration of the cornea can cause permanent damage. Clearly, this isn't something to be taken lightly. Fortunately for victims, the cornea is the fastest-healing organ in the body (often taking less than 48 hours to heal).

A more insidious threat comes from UVA rays,

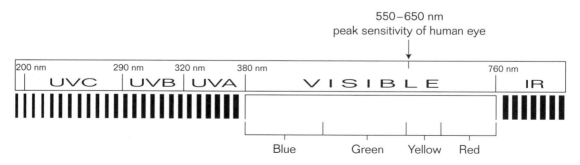

Illustration 21.1   The spectrum of light

often mistakenly called tanning rays. These wavelengths were once thought to be relatively benign because UVA is one thousand times less effective than UVB at reddening the skin. However, there is a great deal of evidence that UVA rays, which penetrate deeper into the skin and are absorbed by the slow-healing lens of the eye, cause significant long-term damage. One percent of the UVA reaches the retina, the inner surface of the eye, which has no healing ability. Furthermore, we are bombarded by ten to one thousand times as much UVA as UVB because the atmosphere does not filter it as effectively (20 percent of a sunburn comes from UVA). And although we are frequently warned that 10 A.M. to 2 P.M. is the most dangerous part of the day for sunburns, early morning and late afternoon still contain significant UVA levels.

Mountaineers need to be extra careful about their choice of eyewear because UV intensity increases by 4 percent with every 1000 ft. (300 m) of elevation gain. At around 10,000 ft. (3050 m), there is nearly 50 percent more UV radiation than at sea level; at 18,000 ft. (5500 m), there is twice as much; and at 28,000 ft. (8500 m), there is three times the amount.

The intensity of UV radiation also increases the closer you get to the equator because of the solar rays' steeper angle through the atmosphere. So you will burn three times faster at 14,000 ft. on Chimborazo in Ecuador than at the same altitude on Denali in Alaska. For the same reason, UV radiation is more intense in the summer than in the winter.

Finally, remember that snow is an excellent reflector. About 85 percent of UV radiation is bounced

FULL-PROTECTION SUNSCREENS

While a bronzed body may be gorgeous, dermatologists agree there is no such thing as a "healthy tan"—some refer to tanning booths as "death boxes."

Unfortunately, most sunscreens and lip balms do not give true protection. In fact, they may foster a false sense of security. Both the sun protection factor (SPF) for sunscreens and the UV Index issued by the National Weather Service are based solely upon UVB; neither takes into account UVA. While protecting our skin from quick sunburns, we may be inadvertently increasing our odds of long-term problems.

Just because a sunscreen has a very high SPF doesn't mean it protects against UVA. Even the term "broad spectrum" has little meaning because a sunscreen can claim protection against UVA even if it filters only 1 percent of the UVA rays. To get protection against UVA, look for products containing Parasol (avobenzone), an ingredient recently approved by the FDA. This provides superior UVA protection.

Currently, you can buy SPF 45 sunscreens.

However, they'll cost significantly more than SPF 30 and offer minimal extra protection. In May 2001, the FDA will require that numerical ratings be replaced with terms: minimum (SPF 2 to 11), moderate (SPF 12 to 29), and high (SPF 30 and above).

Zinc oxide, the old standby for mountain sun protection, responsible for thousands of white-nosed climbers, does not offer full protection against UVA. For maximum protection, make sure your zinc oxide or other sunblock contains titanium dioxide.

Always reapply sunscreen several times a day because even "bonding," "waterproof," or "sweatproof" varieties will rub off. And wear a full-brimmed hat, as opposed to the ubiquitous baseball cap. This reduces UV radiation to the eyes by about 50 percent and gives much better protection to the ears, neck, and cheeks.

Many prescription drugs can cause photosensitivity; be sure to heed warning stickers. Even some nonprescription drugs, including ibuprofen, antihistamines, and dandruff shampoos, can increase sensitivity to sunlight.

back at us by snow, versus 17 to 25 percent by sand and rock. Don't be deceived by cloud cover, either; scattered clouds allow roughly 89 percent of the UV through, and even overcast skies transmit 31 percent. The nasty thing is, you can sizzle your eyes without knowing it. The searing pain sets in several hours after the fact.

SUNGLASSES

For basic recreational use, the choice of frame and lenses in sunglasses hardly matters. Virtually all sunglasses, even the cheapies sold at convenience stores, provide adequate protection against UVB radiation. However, when selecting sunglasses for outdoor sports, particularly those performed at high altitudes, you should be more careful. Lens shape and tint are far more important than fashion.

You don't need to spend a fortune to get glasses with sufficient protection. That said, there is a noticeable difference between the inexpensive models and the high-end varieties. Now that I've been spoiled by good sunglasses, I could never again be content with budget shades—quality glasses truly enhance the outdoor experience.

FRAMES

Your first consideration should be frame style: traditional glacier glasses with side shields or contoured sunglasses (called sport shields). Without a doubt, if you plan to spend multiple days on a snowfield at high altitude, you should get a pair of properly fitting glacier glasses [Photo 21.1].

Resist the temptation to buy glacier glasses until you have tried on at least four or five different frame styles. It is extremely important to choose a frame and side shields that fit your face closely, especially between your cheek and the bottom of the frame. Look to the extreme edges of your vision to spot light leaks. People with smaller faces may need to find frames made for children to get a good fit.

Most glacier glasses now come with detachable side shields of varying quality. These frames often have a prominent inside edge, used for mounting the side shields, that can cut your face and eyebrow during a face plant. On cheaper brands, the attachment pins for the side shields tend to break easily. Nearly every company uses side shields made of leather, which tends to shrivel up after a few weeks of sun and sweat; boot wax can protect or restore leather side shields.

Glacier glasses often suffer from poor ventilation, making them prone to fogging when you trudge up a long snow slope on a hot day. Look for side shields that have vent holes; the best glasses also have vents in the bridge over the nose.

For ultrabright conditions, especially when wearing mirrored lenses, consider a nose shield for extra protection. Typically made of leather (or duct tape for do-it-yourselfers), these attach to the bridge of the frame and should extend past the tip of the nose. The nicest ones have a moldable wire mesh inside.

While glacier glasses are really the only option

Photo 21.1   Glacier glasses come in many shapes. Find the ones that fit your face the best.

for extended periods on snow, they leave a lot to be desired the rest of the time. For high-speed activities, such as mountain biking, *on-piste* skiing, and driving, contoured sunglasses offer better peripheral vision. The new generation of wraparound sunglasses and sport shields also provide more sun and wind protection than poorly fitting glacier glasses, as well as superior ventilation and comfort. Most of the better sport shields and a few of the newer glasses offer interchangeable lenses, which let you replace thrashed lenses easily and customize your shades to match conditions.

In my experience, the better sport sunglasses and shields work nearly as well as glacier glasses in all but the brightest conditions. As long as I'm not on snow, they give good protection even at 15,000 ft. (4500 m). Traditional sunglass styles, such as cat-eyes or aviators, with relatively flat lenses, are not as effective.

Frame Features

No matter the frame style, the glasses' wearing comfort is determined largely at the points of contact: earpieces and nose pads. Look for temples and earpieces that adjust in length and are bendable. Some glasses come with interchangeable earpieces (straight or hooked around the ear). However, if you're like me, you'll just end up losing the ones not in use. Nose pads should be adjustable and fairly large; the best are made of soft silicone or synthetic rubber, which hold better than hard plastic when your face gets sweaty.

The choice of metal or plastic frames is much less important than the overall fit. Virtually any frame can break if sat upon or crushed in a pack, and will last forever if stored in a safe place (such as in a sturdy case).

A good-quality metal frame has thick welds, sturdy hinges, and adjustable nose pads. Metal frames are often more adjustable than plastic models. Some claim that metal frames are more likely to frostbite your cheeks; however, if it's that cold, you're better off with goggles.

Plastic frames are generally made of either nylon (a.k.a. polyamide and Grilamid) or cellulose acetate (Zylonite); the latter is more common in designer glasses. The quality of nylon can vary tremendously, and the cheap stuff will become brittle with age. Better frames have strong hinges and are free of sharp edges and burrs.

LENSES FOR PROTECTION

Among quality sunglasses, there are two basic choices of lens materials: glass or polycarbonate. Each material has its pros and cons.

Glass (a.k.a. mineral) lenses provide the least distortion and are the most scratch-resistant. However, they are about twice the weight of most plastics and may shatter when struck hard, even after they are chemically or thermally treated for impact-resistance. Raw glass does not block enough UV radiation, so a filtering agent is melted in (better) or a coating applied to the lenses.

Virtually all "sport" glasses and many glacier glasses now have lenses made of polycarbonate. This lightweight material is the most impact-resistant available—an important feature that could save your sight should a falling stone or windmilling ski tip catch you in the face.

The material has a higher refractive index than glass, so lenses made from polycarbonate can be thinner. The lenses also filter out nearly all UV radiation. However, polycarbonate leaves a bit to be desired optically, so more complex lens shapes (read: expensive) are necessary for prime viewing. The distortion of cheap lenses can give you headaches and eyestrain. Polycarbonate also scratches fairly easily as compared to glass.

The cheapest lenses use acrylic. This has neither the impact resistance nor scratch resistance of polycarbonate. If you just want "disposable" glasses, acrylic lenses are adequate; they still meet minimum standards for UV and impact resistance.

Scratch-resistant polymer coatings are often applied to the outside and inside surface of plastic lenses; these resist but do not prevent scratches.

The best lenses have multilayer anti-reflection coatings on their inside surface. (Single-layer coatings are less effective.) These dramatically reduce distracting internal reflections and also improve scratch resistance on the inside. A hydrophilic coating can also be applied to the inside of the lenses. This absorbs moisture and reduces fogging. However, it rubs off easily.

Make your lenses last longer by cleaning them only with a special lens cloth (often supplied with the glasses). Cleaning them with your tee shirt, as we are all wont to do, inevitably leads to numerous small scratches.

Tints

Sunglasses come in a huge range of lens tints. The choice depends mainly on your personal preference and, to an extent, on your favorite activities.

The amount of visible light transmitted through lenses can vary from as much as 88 percent for a light yellow lens to as little as 3 percent for the darkest glacier glasses. Most people find that 5 to 10 percent transmission is sufficient for climbing on glaciers at high altitude. If your lenses are too dark, it's as if somebody turned the lights out when a cloud comes along. (Dark lenses can also make traffic signals hard to recognize.) Lenses in the 10 to 30 percent light-transmission range are fine for general outdoor activities and driving.

Some people like photochromic lenses, which darken as UV intensity increases. However, I find these lenses are often dark when I don't want them to be, not dark enough when I need protection, and slow to change.

Polarized lenses work something like a venetian blind, by only allowing light waves that vibrate in a specific direction to pass through. They are great for reducing glare from roads, snow, and water (fishermen love them), but I don't care for them because they tend to "deaden" the view.

The performance of any lens can be enhanced by the application of different coatings. Mirror coatings (a.k.a. flash coatings) are effective at blocking glare and can cut visible light transmission by an additional 4 to 9 percent. For the most protection, lenses have a full silver mirror coat; colored mirrors are less effective. However, be aware that mirrored lenses can fry your nose. Double-gradient lenses are dark on the top and bottom but leave the center section lighter; I find the banding annoying.

COLOR YOUR WORLD

Although the choice of tints for sunglasses is largely a matter of personal preference, each tint has different characteristics. You may want to choose lenses based on their suitability for your favorite outdoor sports.

- Yellow lenses will literally clear things up because they filter out vision-blurring blue light. This makes them the best choice for skiing in flat light. However, yellow lenses distort other colors significantly.
- Green tint gives neutral color rendition (because it matches the eye's sensitivity), has exceptional clarity, and naturally filters UV and infrared.
- Gray lenses give the least color distortion but tend to "flatten" the view because they do not enhance contrast; they are a popular choice for very bright conditions.
- Rose-colored lenses offer a comfortable way to view the world and they enhance contrast in flat light. Compared to yellow, rose isn't quite as good in low light but is better in bright conditions, and the color shift is less objectionable.
- Orange lenses fall in between rose and yellow—great for flat light.
- Brown or amber is perhaps the best all-around tint, as long as you don't mind a little color distortion. These lenses minimize eyestrain on blue-sky days and increase contrast and definition when the clouds come out.

GOGGLES

If you've ever had to defrost your eyelids with your bare hands, you understand the need for goggles

Photo 21.2   Good goggles have dual lenses that can bend, a flexible frame that conforms to your face, and good venting.

in full conditions. Goggles are also indispensable on bright, sunny days when the wind is howling and it's bitterly cold. My subjective experience is that goggles make you feel 20°F (11 °C) warmer. Quite simply, good goggles are essential for the mountaineer and skier [Photo 21.2]. The newer, low-profile designs of goggles also offer better peripheral vision and fit inside a parka hood more easily than bulky older models.

This is one item not to skimp on. Cheap goggles are almost worse than none because they lack UV protection and fog up when you need them most—not to mention their terrible optics.

Goggles with rigid lenses are optically superior to ones with flexible lenses, but they are prone to

cracking. I prefer a goggle that conforms to the face and can be bent in half without breaking. Do not even consider goggles without a double-pane lens; the air pocket between the panes forms a thermal barrier that greatly reduces fogging, the bane of all goggles. Another key factor in preventing fogging is the ventilation system. Better goggles direct airflow across the inside of the lens; look for vents on top and bottom. Many people who wear prescription glasses swear by goggles with built-in, battery-operated fans that pull the moisture out.

No matter which type of goggles you own, an anti-fog solution can really help prevent fogging, especially after the factory coating wears off. In many cases, the best way to prevent goggles from fogging is to put them on when they're warm (pre-heat inside your parka) and leave them on. When you take them off, remove them completely. Putting goggles on your snow-covered or sweaty forehead is bound to cause problems when you pull them back over your eyes.

As with sunglasses, the fit of the goggles is crucial to their performance. They need to seal around your face, yet still provide good peripheral vision. I find that many goggle frames press on my nasal passages, making it harder to breathe. Try on several different models and brands to find the ones that work best for you.

When choosing goggles to fit over prescription glasses, select a low-profile model that has plenty of ventilation and cutouts in the sides for glasses' temples. Don't buy goggles from a catalog if they are meant to fit over glasses; you need to try them on over your frames. Large goggles fit most frames, but the bulk makes them a nuisance with a hood.

Light amber is the most versatile color for goggle lenses because it improves vision in flat light and snowy conditions. Anything less than 100 percent UV filtration is unacceptable. Although I don't like photochromic lenses on sunglasses, I like them on goggles because goggles are often used in such highly variable conditions.

A new generation of hybrid eye protection combines sunglasses styling with goggle performance. These goggles typically have two contoured, double-pane lenses with foam seals around each eyepiece and an elastic strap or earpieces. They are great for contact-lens wearers who suffer from dry eyes when wearing normal sunglasses. I find them a bit hot; watch out for models with poor ventilation or single-layer lenses.

PRESCRIPTION PROTECTION

Eyeglass wearers, I feel your pain—I am one of you. Prescription glasses always get dirty in the mountains and they are prone to fogging at the worst times. And switching back and forth between regular and tinted glasses is a nuisance.

CONTACT LENSES

For climbers who can wear them, contact lenses solve most of the problems of glasses, although they come with their own set of headaches. Personally, I cannot deal with the hassle of daily-wear contacts, especially on multiday excursions where cleanliness is nigh impossible. I prefer extended-wear soft contacts. They are large in diameter, so they stay in place well, and they have fairly good oxygen permeability. This is a concern at altitude because the cornea is the only part of the body that does not obtain oxygen from the blood; a less-permeable lens can reduce the oxygen supply, possibly resulting in infections or permanent scarring of the eye.

I have worn extended-wear disposables with great success—from 50 m (165 ft.) underwater to 8035 m (26,360 ft.) above sea level. When camping at high altitudes above 6000 m (20,000 ft.), it's important that the lenses be clean or fresh; otherwise, I wake up with sore eyes from lack of oxygen. It's a good idea to carry rewetting drops (not standard eyedrops) on overnight adventures.

Daily-wear disposables do not seem to breathe as well as extended-wear models, and they are less comfortable for me—your mileage may vary. Disposable toric contact lenses, for those with astigmatism, are now available.

Contact wearers should still carry prescription glasses and sunglasses as a backup on extended trips, to rest the eyes or in case contacts become unwearable or get lost.

PRESCRIPTION SUNGLASSES

Prescription sunglasses can be made from glass, plastic (CR-39), or polycarbonate. Glass lenses provide the best optics and are the most scratch-resistant. However, the weight makes them rather uncomfortable for those with moderate to strong vision correction, especially in the relatively large lenses of many glacier glasses. Glass also seems to fog more easily than plastic and can shatter if struck by a rock.

The standard plastic used in prescription lenses also has good optics, but it scratches easily and the lenses must be slightly thicker than glass. CR-39 plastic lenses are prone to dropping out of metal frames in extreme cold due to different contraction rates. Polycarbonate is slightly lighter than plastic and allows for thinner lenses, but it also has the worst optics.

Weight is the enemy of long-term comfort, so thinner and lighter lenses are desirable. In the past decade, glass and plastic have become available with higher indexes of refraction, which allows for much thinner and less-curved lenses. The trade-offs are reduced optical performance and significantly higher cost. For stronger prescriptions, you might consider aspheric lenses (which are flatter).

You can have lenses tinted to virtually any color and darkness. Dark tints applied to plastic lenses will fade and may need to be reapplied. Optional coatings (all of which I recommend) include scratch resistance, UV, and anti-reflection.

While some eyeglass outlets carry a few glacier frames, you may get a better fit by buying the sunglasses you want and replacing the lenses. You don't have to go to the manufacturer to custom-order prescription sunglass lenses. Even the "fast-food" eyewear places in malls can make what you need if you provide a frame and give them the right specifications. However, prescription sunglass specialists will be more aware of a climber's needs and can provide better service.

An option to expensive prescription sunglasses is relatively cheap prescription inserts that can be used with sport shields. These create a modular system that has interchangeable lenses and can be used with or without contacts. Depending on the system you choose (read: how much you spend), the performance can range from mediocre to good.

CORRECTIVE SURGERY

Sooner or later, any outdoor athlete with poor eyesight is going to wonder about refractive surgery, which ostensibly can eliminate one's dependency on glasses or contacts. The first procedure to gain wide acceptance was radial keratotomy (RK), in which the cornea is reshaped with four or eight starlike cuts. By today's standards, this is an outdated, imprecise technique that weakens the structural integrity of the eye.

Recently, laser surgery has gained a lot of attention. Photo-refractive keratectomy (PRK), the first such technique approved in the United States, blasts away the surface of the cornea with a broad-beam excimer laser. Newer, focusing lasers with eye-tracking features promise better results, but they are not yet widely available. Numerous side effects are associated with PRK, including permanent haze and poor night vision.

A newer technique called laser-assisted intra-stroma keratomileusis (LASIK) seems to offer more promising results. However, the success of the surgery depends greatly on the skill of the surgeon. In LASIK surgery, a paper-thin flap is cut from the cornea, the exposed material is sculpted, and the flap is then precisely replaced (you hope).

Consult your ophthalmologist about the risks and benefits of surgery for your particular correction needs. (Make sure to get an opinion from a doctor with no vested interest in the procedure.) The long-term and high-altitude effects of laser surgery are still in question, and newer techniques and more sophisticated machines are constantly being developed.

Many people who have had their eyesight corrected are happy with the results, but there are others who are sorry they had it done. Holding off on laser eye surgery is prudent since prices are expected to drop radically in the next few years while the technology improves.

CHAPTER 22

NAVIGATION

IT ISN'T ALWAYS EASY STAYING FOUND. Predawn approaches, lousy guidebooks, post-sunset escapes, and whiteout conditions all conspire against the mountaineer. And you should never count on actually being able to see where you are.

COMPASS

The basic requirements of a good compass are a jeweled bearing for the needle inside a liquid-dampened capsule, with a rotating bezel on a clear base plate [Photo 22.1]. Highly desirable features include declination adjustment for magnetic north (so you don't have to make mental calculations), a sighting mirror (for more accurate readings, and for shaving and changing contact lenses), and a clinometer (for measuring the angle of potential avalanche slopes).

For all of North America and Europe, your normal compass will work fine. However, if you are going to southern latitudes (such as Chile, Australia, or Antarctica), the needle will dip so much, because of the curvature of the earth's magnetic field, that it does not rotate properly. Purchase a compass made for southern magnetic zones or a "global" compass that is made to work anywhere.

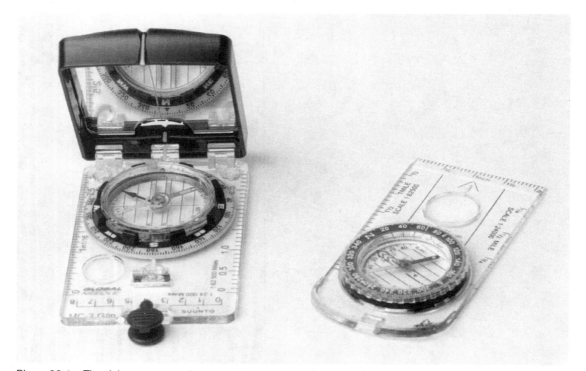

Photo 22.1   The deluxe compass has a sighting mirror, declination adjustment, and clinometer, and it works anywhere on the planet.

Be aware that magnetic declination (the variation between true north and magnetic north) changes with time. If you are using old topographic maps, the declination marked on the map can be off by several degrees. This probably won't affect short-distance calculations, but it could throw you off significantly over the long haul. Check the United States Geological Survey (USGS) website *(www.usgs.gov)* for updated declination adjustments.

ALTIMETER

Some people consider them a gadget, but an altimeter is an important navigation tool in the alpine world [Photo 22.2]. Aside from all the trivia it generates (feet climbed, descent rate, etc.), an altimeter can help you pinpoint your position on a map, even in the dark or a complete whiteout. They are also helpful for predicting changes in the weather, giving you advanced notice of when the storm is about to break.

An altimeter and a barometer are in fact the same thing—they simply read in different units. These devices are in effect very sensitive scales that weigh the column of air over your head. As you move higher, there is less air above you and the scale moves to indicate a gain in altitude.

The atmosphere above us is actually an ocean of air, complete with waves. If you were a scuba diver sitting on the sea bottom and a large wave

Photo 22.2   An analog or a digital altimeter can be an invaluable tool in the mountains.

moved overhead, your depth gauge would indicate that you had descended, even though you hadn't moved. As the trough of the wave moves by, the gauge would show you had gone up.

The same thing happens when high pressure (the wave) or low pressure (the trough) passes overhead. Your altitude appears to decrease or increase when you have not changed position. This is a fact of life for *all* altimeters—none are immune to weather fluctuations.

Therefore, if you want accurate readings, you must frequently calibrate your altimeter at known positions. Usually, this needs to be done only once or twice a day, but you may want to do it more often if you're experiencing wild weather—fluctuations of 500 ft. (150 m) in a day are not uncommon.

Although I like the simplicity and craftsmanship of a good analog altimeter, such as a Thommen, it's hard to recommend purchasing one anymore. (Cheap analogs are just toys.) Modern digital wrist altimeters provide equal accuracy and far greater convenience, along with a few bells and whistles.

When selecting an altimeter, be sure that it reads in 10 ft. and 5 m increments and is temperature-compensated for consistent readings. Since these are all good alarm watches as well, a backlight is essential for checking the time in the dark. User-replaceable batteries will save you a lot of headaches. A built-in compass, while probably not very accurate, can be convenient for quick bearing checks.

GPS

While far from a necessity, a global positioning system (GPS) receiver can sure be handy at times [Photo 22.3]. An array of twenty-four Department of Defense satellites allows you to find your position anywhere on the planet in any weather condition.

You need a wide-open sky for the best readings because the calculations are made by triangulation (a few satellites right overhead don't help much). Even under ideal circumstances, such as standing in the middle of a big clearing, you will get an

Photo 22.3 GPS receivers are getting smaller and more affordable. This one is at least five years old and obsolete.

accuracy of only about 50 ft. (15 m). Altitude readings on your GPS will be off by several times this amount, so they're pretty much worthless as altimeters.

At present, civilian GPS receivers are still rather heavy (6 oz., 170 g) and bulky, so they often aren't practical for climbers to carry unless you're a gear freak or have a specific application—crossing icefields or locating food caches, for example.

HEADLAMP

Pity the fool without a headlamp when the lights go out. Holding a flashlight in one hand, or clamped in your teeth, is simply not an option for many climbing situations.

It's worth carrying a mini-headlamp that uses only two AA-batteries (or even two AAAs) on longer day climbs in case you are benighted [Photo 22.4]. These are very compact and lightweight, but they don't put out much light and they can have limited battery life.

If you intend to climb or approach at night, a lamp that uses four AA-batteries (or one 4.5-volt flat battery) is much more serviceable. These put out a lot more light, even with their standard bulbs,

and often have acceptable battery life with halogen bulbs. Remote battery packs, which can be worn inside a parka to keep batteries warm, are a good choice for very cold temperatures.

Headlamps that fail are the stuff epics are made of. There's never really a good time for your light to crap out on you, but there are occasions when it can precipitate disaster. The electronics should be highly water-resistant, or fully waterproof, and solidly constructed so that wires or contacts cannot loosen from vibration.

Without question, the leading cause of nonworking headlamps is a switch that accidentally gets turned on inside a pack. Even switches tucked inside a recessed cavity can get activated mysteriously unless there is some sort of lock. Rotating switches work well as long as you snug them down firmly. If your headlamp lacks a locking switch, either flip the batteries over or disconnect a wire when it's not in use.

Try on the headlamp to be sure it stays in place when you shake your head; some models with heavier battery packs need constant readjustment. The headlamp should also be comfortable on your forehead because you may end up wearing it for hours at a time.

Whether or not one is provided, it's a good idea

Photo 22.4   Good headlamps are water-resistant, stay in place, are comfortable to wear for hours at a time, and don't turn on accidentally.

to carry a spare bulb inside the headlamp so it's always available. Stock up ahead of time; you never find them when you need them. LED bulbs are an emerging alternative that use little energy and last a long time.

BATTERIES

These days, the weak link in the system is most often the batteries. For most general applications, alkaline batteries remain the best choice because of the amount of energy they hold and their reasonable weight and cost. Their main drawbacks are a negative environmental impact and a dramatic 80 to 90 percent loss of performance in cold temperatures.

Rechargeable batteries are a good choice for use on expeditions and those who use their lights on a daily basis. The basecamps of the world's major peaks are littered with decaying alkaline batteries discarded by thoughtless climbers.

Using solar chargers will keep your headlamp, radios, and other "niceties" running without harming the mountains. There are many chargers available, ranging from inexpensive toys barely adequate for a few AAs to giant arrays capable of running notebook computers. The big ones aren't cheap but are much faster and can handle more batteries [Photo 22.5]. Smaller ones can be strapped to the top of your pack so you have fresh juice at the end of the day's trek.

Although nickel-cadmium (nicad) batteries have better cold-weather performance than alkalines, they have other drawbacks. Nickel–metal hydride (NiMH) batteries cost more but charge faster, hold about 25 percent more juice, and do not have problems with memory.

Lithium batteries are the best solution for working in extreme cold, but the very high cost makes them unacceptable for everyday use. A set of four AAs also saves nearly 2 oz. (55 g) compared to alkalines. However, since some lithiums have twice the voltage, you may have to swap lightbulbs.

Photo 22.5   A large solar charger for expeditions

CHAPTER 23

COMMUNICATION

YOUR PARTNER IS LEADING THE SIXTH pitch on the classic South Face of the Petit Grepon in Rocky Mountain National Park. It's a beautiful weekday with no one else around. Suddenly you hear a cry of *"Falling!"* followed by a massive pull on the rope and a few rocks whizzing by. The ensuing silence is eerie. Shouts to your partner go unanswered.

After escaping the belay, you prusik the rope and reach your unconscious partner. A cursory check reveals a severely fractured ankle, but of greater concern is the large dent on her helmet, clear fluid in her ears, and a dilated pupil. Lowering her to a ledge, you stabilize her as best you can and plan your next course of action.

At a minimum, it will take 4 hours to get off the climb and run to the trailhead. By the time a rescue team is mobilized, it will be well after dark. The winds have picked up, which rules out a helicopter. Will your partner survive the night alone?

This nightmare scenario is one we all should be prepared to handle. Any climber who leaves the relative safety of indoor gyms and bolted sport routes should know how to deal with an emergency. You are simply fooling yourself if you think it'll never happen to you. As you venture farther into the wilderness, preparation may include bringing communications equipment.

Although some people are morally opposed to them, radios and cell phones have already been credited with saving the lives of numerous climbers, skiers, and other backcountry users. As the technology advances and prices come down, more and more people will be carrying a means of calling for help from a remote location. However, radios and cell phones should not be a replacement for self-sufficiency—you must always have a plan for getting out on your own.

CELL PHONES

Cell phones are easy to use and portable, can be inexpensive to purchase (or even free), and provide private conversations. On the minus side, they have poor coverage in the mountains, don't work well for groups, are not usable in Europe or Asia (unless you have special models), and are expensive to operate.

If you know how to use a telephone, you know how to use a cell phone—as long as you remember to press the *send* key. Cell phones are little more than ultrahigh frequency (UHF) radio transceivers, 842 to 894 megahertz (MHz), using a system of repeaters. All handheld phones have a maximum output of 0.6 watt; the much-larger transportables and car phones generate 3 watts of power.

The standard, no-frills flip phones, sold even in grocery stores, are a bit bulky and weigh about 11 oz. (310 g). A standard nicad battery pack has about 8 hours of standby time or 35 minutes of talk time when new. Of course, the more money you spend on the unit, the better the feature-set. High-end cell phones weigh only 3 oz. (85 g), are incredibly small, and have prolonged talk times.

Because of their low power and frequency range, portable cell phones are more dependent upon line-of-sight transmission than ham radios. If you can get to high ground or are in a heavily populated area, then you have a good chance of making a connection. But even in areas with good cell coverage, you may have difficulty getting connections in canyons and valleys. Changing position just a few feet can mean a dropped call.

Despite this limitation, many lives have been saved as a result of quick rescues made possible by cell phones—and there is also something to be said for being able to call in your takeout order of

Szechuan on the way back from the crag. On the other hand, rescue groups are experiencing more frivolous requests for help from people who might otherwise have taken care of themselves.

That $20 phone will cost you a bare minimum of $280 the first year. And if you exceed your monthly airtime allotment, the cash register really starts racing—roaming charges and long-distance rates can make your monthly bill soar. Over three years, a cell phone with basic service can easily cost you close to $1500. However, a deactivated cell phone can still call 911 for free, just nothing else.

Satellite phones that many heavily sponsored expeditions carry are ridiculously expensive and bulky at present. New satellite-based phone service from anywhere on the planet is becoming available, although you may have to sell your first-born to pay for a call.

RADIOS

Sooner or later, every climber will encounter situations in which voice communication with his or her partner is problematic at best. High winds, noisy rivers, routes that traverse arêtes, and highway traffic can steal the shouted word.

When the voice system fails, most climbers resort to a system of tugs on a rope. However, on a long, winding pitch—especially when using a 60 m (196 ft.) rope—this may not work. Assuming a rope that stops running for a while and then is taken in quickly means the leader is off belay is risky—you may find yourself simul-climbing.

In Alaska and Canada, climbers often need to communicate with bush pilots. On expeditions to big Himalayan peaks, radios are invaluable for keeping the team together and handling logistics.

When considering radios, be aware of the following: the shorter the wave, the better it bounces; the longer the wave, the better it propagates (spreads out); the more power it puts out, the farther the sig-

nal will go. And regulations vary from country to country.

SHORT RANGE

Don't waste your money on the cheap walkie-talkies sold at electronics stores. They're just low-powered FM radios that broadcast and receive on a frequency of 49 MHz. Most are poorly built and have very limited range.

The new Family Radio Service (FRS) band UHF-FM radios (462 to 467 MHz) have become very popular and are available in many outdoors stores [Photo 23.1]. These are compact, lightweight—about 6 oz. (170 g)—rugged, and reasonably affordable. Speaker mikes are available for some, but they tend to decrease range considerably because the antennas end up in packs or pockets.

The maximum range of all FRS radios is around 2 miles (3 km). (Up to 10 miles or 16 km is possible if you have line-of-sight between the two radios.) This decreases to 1 mile (1.6 km) in areas with gentle intervening hills, to about a ½ mile (0.8 km) in heavy forests, and to as little as a ¼ mile (400 m) (or less)

Photo 23.1   Family Radio Service radios are compact and affordable but have fairly limited range. All brands use the same channels.

with large obstructions blocking the "view."

You do not need a license from the Federal Communications Commission (FCC), but these radios are presently illegal in Canada, Mexico, and many other countries. A similar radio service, called PMR-446, is available in Europe, but the frequencies are not the same.

The FRS radios have fourteen channels (each of which has thirty-eight "privacy codes"). They are limited by law from putting out more than 0.5 watt, and most have a nonreplaceable stubby antennae. They typically use four AAA batteries.

If you want a heads-up on incoming weather, some models of CB and FRS radios can also receive National Weather Service broadcasts (161 to 163 MHz).

MIDRANGE

Handheld citizens band (CB) radios offer up to forty AM channels (27 MHz), one of which (channel 9) is for emergencies. However, CBs are rather bulky and heavy (six to ten AA batteries), static noise and skip can be a nuisance, and the inexpensive models don't have enough range for most backcountry rescues.

The most powerful models (generating 5 watts) have a range of about 5 miles under ideal circumstances, and this can be severely hampered by sunspot activity. The antennas used by portable CBs are very inefficient—they need to be 35 ft. (10 m) long for best performance.

Because of these limitations, CBs are probably the least useful communication devices for climbers. But because they are favored by bush pilots in Alaska, you may need to use one up there.

LONG RANGE

The next step toward greater range requires an FCC license. You can buy ham radios without a license, but transmitting without one can result in a very hefty fine. (The exception would be a legitimate, life-threatening emergency, for which you may use any means of communication available.) Originally developed for emergency use in times

of war and natural disasters (still an important use), amateur radio is now a hobby for more than 600,000 people throughout the United States and 2 million people worldwide.

You no longer need to learn Morse code for the entry-level Technician Class license. Most anybody can learn the material in less than 2 weeks, and the license is good in the United States and Canada for ten years.

Once you jump through the hoop, you'll have access to 90 percent of the amateur radio bands, the most popular of which are 2-meter VHF-FM (144 to 148 MHz) and 70 cm UHF-FM (420 to 450 MHz). The nationwide network of 2-meter-band repeaters is so extensive that there are relatively few places from which you cannot reach out and touch someone. If your signal can reach a repeater, it's possible to talk to people hundreds of miles away. A network of 70 cm repeaters exists, but these don't have as much range. The greater bounce of the signal makes them better for urban areas.

Connections to the phone system are possible with either band. I know of one climber who, at 13,000 ft. (4000 m) on the East Ridge of Mount Logan in Canada, talked with his wife in California via a phone patch through a ham in Yakutat, 100 miles (160 km) away. Be aware, however, that your phone conversation can be overheard by anyone with a ham radio.

Although many are too bulky and heavy for backcountry use, quite a few new radios are the size of a compact cell phone and use only four AA batteries. You can purchase a handheld transceiver for either band for between $200 and $400; a dual-band model offers more flexibility and costs between $350 and $500.

Handheld transceivers are good for both short- and long-range communication, especially if you replace the standard rubber-whip-style antenna with a longer, telescoping one [Photo 23.2]. Some radios allow you to use a compact 2 watt back for short trips or a bulkier 5 watt back for when you need greater range.

Although doing so is illegal, it is possible to

Photo 23.2 A ham radio system offers great range and customizability. Modular backs allow smaller size or greater range. The standard flexible antenna is compact but the telescoping antenna significantly boosts range. For a basecamp, the 10-foot cable antenna gives a huge range increase.

modify many dual-band radios for "out-of-band" transmission (140 to 174 MHz and 420 to 470 MHz). This gives you the ability to transmit on police, rescue, forest, and park service frequencies. In a real emergency, this could be invaluable, and using it for that purpose probably would not get you into trouble. However, calling the police if your car breaks down or the ranger if you sprain an ankle will result in *severe* penalties.

A dual-band radio with this extended CAPS/MARS modification will also transmit on marine VHF frequencies (156 to 162 MHz) and FRS UHF (462 to 467 MHz). However, the aviation band (118 to 137 MHz) requires a different radio. You may

need to find a sympathetic "Elmer" (an experienced ham) to do the modification.

One drawback of ham radios is that they are quite complicated. Someone who is unfamiliar with how they work would probably not be able to use the radio in an emergency.

POWER

The big bugaboo of all electronic gadgets is the power they need to work. The same climber who called his wife from Mount Logan went on to add:

"The sadder news was that our batteries were all dead on the descent, so we weren't able to alert our pilot that we had summited a week early, and we had to wait out that week in a storm. Remembering the boredom still causes nausea."

Most radios and cell phones normally operate off of nicad batteries, which are fine for day or weekend trips. For longer excursions, take AA-battery packs that accept alkalines and nicads (see chapter 22, Navigation). In cold weather, keep spare batteries inside your parka or use expensive lithium AAs.

SIGNALING ALTERNATIVES

Other options are available for calling for help. The 1986 tragedy on Oregon's Mount Hood, in which nine people died, prompted the local rescue services to devise a system for finding victims. They came up with a small radio beacon, called the Mount Hood Locator Unit (MLU), which climbers can rent for a few dollars from local stores. When in distress, the climber is supposed to activate the beacon . . . assuming he or she is conscious. It only works on the south side of the mountain, and a friend must alert authorities that somebody is overdue.

A system that's very popular in Europe is starting to show up in the United States. Known as Recco, which means "reflect" in Swedish, it consists of a small reflector, about the size of a quarter, that climbers or skiers attach to their boots or clothing. If a person is reported missing, helicopters equipped with a special transmitter can home in on the victim. Because the reflectors never wear out and cost only about $10 for a pack of two, and the victim has no responsibilities, the Recco system has a lot going for it.

Many ships and planes carry an Emergency Position Indicating Radio Beacon (EPIRB), which transmits a signal to a satellite when activated. These are not intended for use by outdoors people, but it's unlikely you would be prosecuted if you relied upon one during a life-threatening emergency. However, it takes several passes of the satellite for an accurate fix—within 10.8 miles (17 km)—on the most-portable EPIRBs (Class B), so rescue is likely to take at least 36 hours. The high number of false alarms from EPIRBs (because there is no voice communication) can slow rescues further. Although these are perhaps a good thing if you are planning an Arctic crossing or exploring the Amazon, they are not suitable for all-around use.

A signaling device is another option for someone stuck in the backcountry. This can be simple and low-tech, such as a signaling mirror (about $10) that reflects sunlight at would-be rescuers. If you carry a better compass, the built-in mirror can serve that purpose.

Because mirrors only work on sunny days, a portable strobe has definite advantages. Some of the small ones are waterproof to 200 ft. (60 m) and nearly indestructible. Using two AA batteries, they blast a 250,000-lumen light over 360° for 8 hours. If a search team is looking for you, this is sure to get its attention . . . again, assuming you can activate it.

Portable aerial flares have little value for backcountry users because they burn out quickly, don't tell rescuers where you are, and cost almost $10 a shot. They're also dangerous in dry forests.

Probably the most useful signaling item is a simple whistle. The human voice does not carry very far, and it's extremely difficult to make a loud noise for hours on end. If you balk at everything else—and even if you carry a radio or cell phone—there's no excuse for not carrying a whistle. Don't bother with the metal coaches' whistles (or any that use a ball inside); these can freeze. Get a real survival whistle. Buy several whistles and spread them throughout your outdoor gear (some make good zipper pulls), just as you should do with lighters.

And don't forget the most basic communication device: pencil and paper. Especially when heading out alone, leave a note for a friend, or on your car's dashboard, with your destination and estimated return time. It can prevent headaches for a lot of people.

CHAPTER 24

FIRST AID

FACT OF LIFE: THE MORE YOU PLAY, THE more you bleed. Most injuries are minor, but there is no way to prevent them entirely without giving up our games and growing up (never!). Given this reality, the smart thing to do is to be prepared.

There seems to be a prevailing attitude among many climbers that it's uncool to be prepared for an emergency. Somehow it is more macho to never carry a first-aid kit or to bother learning minimal skills for treating injuries. In a word . . . wrong. You are fooling yourself if you think accidents will never happen to you or your partners.

Even minor problems, such as blisters or scrapes, can make a climbing trip miserable or possibly force a retreat unless you have the means to treat them.

FIRST-AID SUPPLIES

No single first-aid kit is suitable for every type of climbing trip, from sport climbs to mountaineering expeditions, just as no single boot is. Depending on the activity, the duration of the trip, and the number in your party, you will need to tailor your existing kit or, better yet, have multiple sport-specific kits.

When comparing first-aid kits, there are three general components to look at: consumables (the items you use up over time), tools (hard goods), and the carrying case. Be prepared for sticker shock. Quality supplies and well-designed kits are expensive, but they are worth it. To add insult to injury, there isn't a single commercial kit on the market that can't benefit from a few additions.

There are no cut-and-dried rules on how comprehensive your first-aid kit needs to be. Part of this is based on your level of paranoia and training; kits invariably grow after you've completed a good first-aid course.

The size of the first-aid kit should correspond to the size of the pack you are using: in a fanny or day pack, carry an extra-small kit; in an alpine pack, carry a small kit; in an internal-frame pack, carry a medium kit; in an expedition pack, carry a large kit; when you have porters, carry an expedition kit.

CONSUMABLES

Since consumables make up nearly two-thirds of the overall cost, these are what you should check out first. The first clue to the overall quality of any first-aid kit is what gets used most: adhesive bandages. If they are the generic plastic ones, which don't breathe and fall off easily, it's an indication the company is skimping. If you see the pricier stretch fabric ones such as Curad Acti-flex (these conform to the body, apply mild pressure to the wound, last for days, and stay on when wet), it's a good sign that the kit contains better components overall.

For larger wounds, the kit should include non-stick sterile pads, as well as gauze sponges and stretch-roller gauze (better than regular roller gauze) for holding things in place. The latest, greatest dressing is 3M Tegaderm, a clear, breathable film that protects the wound while keeping scabs from forming (which speeds healing)—pricey, but it helps keep you playing. Another new dressing that works well for a variety of applications is Spyroflex, a flexible adhesive foam that breathes and absorbs exudate, or wound weepage. Crack climbers especially appreciate a few stretch knuckle bandages.

Butterfly bandages are inexpensive and useful for closing gashes, though you can make reasonable facsimiles from adhesive tape. Cover-Strip II wound closures are far superior. They are clear and very flexible, hold better, and can be repositioned. Tincture of benzoin, either in a bottle or individually packaged swabs, helps any adhesive bandage stick to wet or damp skin.

Most kits contain individually packaged pain-killers that may require supplementing—especially if you are of the Vitamin I (ibuprofen) generation (aging baby boomers). Although it doesn't matter whether these analgesics are brand names (like Tylenol or Advil) or generic, the dosage does matter. The active-ingredient content in a pill can range from 200 mg to 1000 mg—a difference the kits' lists of contents don't reveal. Once the pills provided are used up or outlive their expiration dates, I buy them in bulk and carry them in small zip-lock bags.

Blister supplies are also oft-used consumables. The chintzier kits contain a few pieces of generic Moleskin only slightly better than adhesive, or even duct tape. Better kits include Spenco 2nd Skin (also good for abrasions and burns), adhesive knit (a tapelike loose fabric patch) that holds dressings in place, and adhesive foam for padding. None of the kits included the best blister product I have used, Compeed (a.k.a. Band-Aid Blister Block). Tincture of benzoin can also toughen the skin to prevent blisters.

Antiseptic towelettes for cleaning wounds and double or triple antibiotic ointment (a few people are allergic to the latter) for preventing infections are also important to carry. Both sunscreen and sunburn cream should be in all but the smallest kits. Something to soothe insect bites is also helpful. Other medications to look for are antihistamines, decongestants, throat lozenges, antacids, and anti-diarrheals.

TOOLS

Among the most basic supplies in any first-aid kit are pencil and paper, preferably in the form of an accident report. The form developed by The Mountaineers helps you keep track of vital information during the excitement of an emergency. Make a few enlarged copies of it because most commercial kits have only one.

All but the smallest kits contain scissors in one of three styles: surgical, bandaging, and EMT (Emergency Medical Technician) shears. Sharp points on the surgical scissors are good for removing bits of flesh and sutures but otherwise are a hazard. The blunt-nosed, angled bandaging scissors work well on cloth and tape but not webbing or heavy winter fabrics. EMT shears are versatile utility scissors that can cut heavy clothing and webbing yet weigh no more than the others [Photo 24.1]. The last is my preference since my Swiss

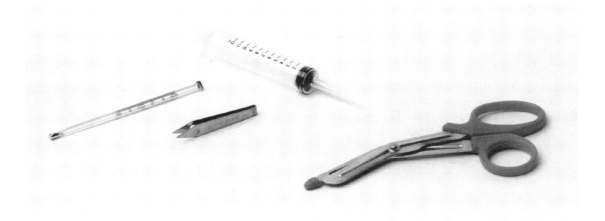

Photo 24.1 Fever thermometer, tweezers, lavage syringe, EMT shears

Army knife has decent small scissors for smaller trims.

Speaking of which, a sharp blade is a good idea. (Most people don't keep their Swiss Army knife sharp enough.) Disposable scalpels (with #11 blade) are best, but a one-sided razor blade suffices. You can never have too many safety pins. Add more of various sizes to any kit; you will find dozens of uses for them.

A pair of tweezers is essential for removing splinters and cactus spines. Long, needle-nosed models work well, but I prefer the little stubby ones that don't get bent, are easy to hold, and work well for removing ticks. Remarkably, few kits contain a hemostat; this small, lightweight clamp is useful for a variety of tasks (including retrieving a lens cap from narrow cracks).

For rock (or road) rash, it really helps to have a 20 cubic centimeter (cc) syringe with an irrigation tip to flush wounds with water or antiseptic. This generates the force required to remove particles without abrasion. (Debridement could earn you a black eye from a screaming patient, but may still be necessary to remove dirt in severe cases.)

Some of the larger kits contain glass hyperthermia (fever) thermometers. These typically go down to only 95°F (35°C), the point at which mild hypothermia sets in. To diagnose profound hypothermia, with body temperatures below 90°F (32°C), you need a special low-reading—86° to 100°F (30° to 38°C)—glass thermometer. Having crushed a few glass thermometers over the years, I've switched to an inexpensive digital model that is lightweight and reads from 90°F to 107°F (32° to 42°C).

Beware of some of the useless things, many of which are packaged in cute little boxes, found in a few commercial first-aid kits. These include suction-cup snakebite kits, tick removers, wire splints, bandage compresses, and even triangular bandages. These take up space, add weight, and can often be improvised from things in your pack.

Your first-aid kit needs to survive being crushed in the bottom of a pack for weeks, dropped from great heights, and soaked in downpours. Once sterile supplies get wet, they must be replaced. Rest assured that towelette packs, tubes of gels, and containers of liquids *will* rupture and leak unless you take precautions. Pill bottles take up space even when empty and can get crushed; small, heavy-duty zip-lock bags work better.

Infectious Disease

Welcome to the new millennium. All first-aid kits should include at least one pair of surgical gloves and, ideally, a cardiopulmonary resuscitation (CPR) microshield [Photo 24.2]. The risk of infection by serious blood-borne diseases, such as hepatitis B and AIDS, dictates that all caregivers must protect themselves. Don't take this danger lightly—it's real and possibly fatal! Latex gloves deteriorate with exposure to air (but block viruses, unlike the more durable vinyl), so store gloves in a zip-lock bag and replace them annually; otherwise, they will tear when you really need them. Dispose of used gloves and other contaminated supplies in sturdy zip-lock bags.

The CPR microshield is very compact (the size of a box of matches), weighs only ½ oz., and helps to keep good Samaritans alive. Its plastic shield covers the victim's mouth area, and a one-way valve keeps the victim's fluids out of your mouth. (Carry a large CPR mask in your car because highway accidents are more common than climbing accidents, and facial trauma can be messy.)

CASES

The organized pouches that the commercial kits come in are a huge improvement over tossing everything into a stuff sack [Photo 24.3]. Even if you build your own kit, I encourage you to buy one of the empty organizers. The best designs open up neatly and display the contents, while keeping them protected from the wet ground. Being able to hang the kit vertically without dumping the contents is a definite plus for climbers. A carrying handle that accommodates a gloved hand is helpful when dashing over a boulderfield; some of the larger organizers have hide-away waist belts too.

The best cases have removable subkits (small

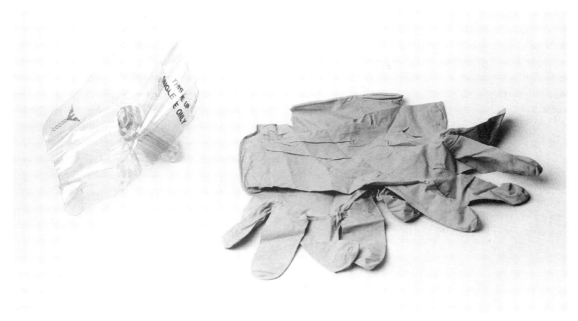

Photo 24.2   CPR mask and gloves. The first rule of rescue is "Protect yourself."

pouches) that can be unfastened for shorter excursions or special needs. However, it's important that subkits also protect the contents from dirt and moisture. It's a good idea to build a little redundancy into the mother-and-daughter kits, in case one is not available.

Color of the kit pouch doesn't truly matter, but brightly colored kits are easier to find in the dark bottom of a big pack. Reflective trim makes it easier to spot the kit by headlamp.

Regarding internal pockets: I am a big fan of clear vinyl versus white netting. Clear vinyl makes it easier to view contents and keeps snow and rain off the contents while the kit is laid open. If higher-grade plastics are used, these pockets will remain flexible in very cold conditions. However, if you live in a humid area, leave zippers partly open to prevent condensation and mildew.

SUPPLEMENT KITS

Several companies offer preassembled first-aid modules (without cases) that can be used to replace supplies or to supplement your kit. These are excellent alternatives to buying individual components when starting from scratch.

Although the large and extra-large commercial first-aid kits are quite comprehensive, there are some situations they cannot handle. You can do a lot to close a large wound with adhesive strips and tincture of benzoin. But in some cases further measures may be needed.

A skin stapler and removal tool are very compact and simple to operate. For very deep wounds or those over a joint or on the face, it is preferable to suture. This is a tricky procedure (definitely not as easy as a skilled surgeon makes it look) that really needs to be practiced ahead of time if you are contemplating bringing the supplies necessary to do it. Some companies offer well-designed, preassembled suture kits. These contain all the necessary supplies (except lidocaine).

When climbing in remote parts of Third World countries, where medical clinics are often very poorly supplied, it's a good idea to carry your own suture/syringe kit [Photo 24.4]. Even if you don't know how to use it, you'll have sterile supplies available to be used on you.

Another supplementary kit for extended trips is a dental repair kit, which helps with common dental problems, including the replacement of lost fillings.

GAMOW BAG

Many high-altitude expeditions now carry a portable hyperbaric chamber, designed by Igor Gamow, used for treating pulmonary and cerebral edema. Inflation using a foot pump causes an increase in internal pressure that can artificially lower the atmosphere inside by up to 7000 ft. (2130 m).

This device has already been credited with saving many lives. Its main drawbacks are its size—

22 x 15 x 9 in. (55 x 38 x 23 cm), rolled up—and weight—14½ lbs. (6.6 kg)—not to mention that it really helps to have medical oxygen along, another 15 lbs. (7 kg) or so.

The Gamow Bag is expensive, but that won't matter if you are the one inside it. Fortunately, you can rent them for a reasonable price—pretty cheap insurance.

PRESCRIPTION MEDICATIONS

While over-the-counter drugs in commercial first-aid kits are adequate for minor complaints, you are going to need prescription drugs to manage more serious problems. Anyone who tells you strong

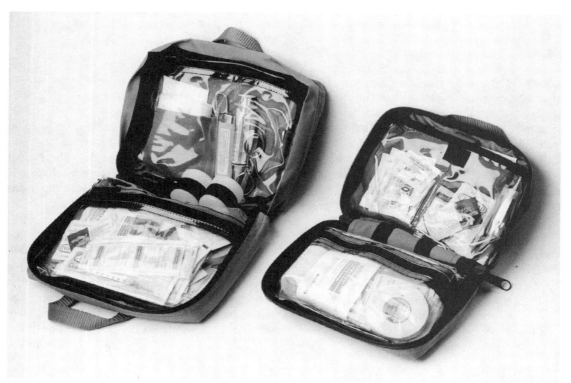

Photo 24.3 First-aid kit cases should make the contents easily accessible while protecting them from dirt and moisture, even when open.

Photo 24.4   In remote regions, supplement your first-aid kit with suture and dental supplies.

painkillers are unnecessary and shouldn't be carried has never suffered a dislocated shoulder miles from the trailhead. Trust me, a few Advil won't do it—been there, done that, hurt like hell.

When an injury occurs days away from medical care, infections are also a major (and, possibly, life-threatening) concern. Likewise, anaphylaxis (allergic shock) can kill long before help arrives. In putting together your kit, it's important to know the allergies of everyone in your group—to medications, foods, and insects.

Finding a sympathetic doctor to stock your kit with prescription drugs isn't easy; even your family physician may balk at giving you narcotics. Understand that if you give drugs to someone else, you are legally practicing medicine without a license. Screwups on your part (such as giving Augmentin to a person allergic to penicillin, or narcotics to someone with a head injury) can come back to haunt the doctor who originally prescribed the medicine.

If you go into your doctor's office well informed, you are more likely to get the necessary prescription. Read up on the indications (pros) and contraindications (cons) of the various medications before asking for them. Any pharmacy has a Physicians Desk Reference (PDR).

If your general practitioner can't help you, try doctors in an emergency room—they can relate to your dilemma more easily because they understand emergency situations (and some are climbers too).

A discussion of prescription medicines likely to be needed by climbers is beyond the scope of this book. However, there are several that you should be aware of and discuss with your doctor. These include hydrocodeine (Vicodin), hydroxyzine (Atarax), botorphanol tartrate (Stadol NS), prochlorperazine (Compazine), Lomotil, erythromycin, azithromycin (Zithromax), ciprofloxacin (Cipro), cephalexin (Keflex), dexamethasone (Decadron), acetazolamide (Diamox), nifedipene (Procardia), epinephrine (Ana-Guard), and prednisone.

HOMEMADE KITS

Many people are surprised to learn that buying a premade first-aid kit is often cheaper than building one from scratch. It's a matter of economies of scale. Quality health supplies are expensive—unless you are a company that buys in bulk.

The key to building your own kit is to make several sport-specific kits or modules. For example, make a day-climbing kit that will live in your pack, a mountain-biking kit that stays with the Camelbak, a backpacking kit for extended trips, a trauma kit for the car, etc. This will keep the overall price of each to a reasonable level and increase the likelihood that you will have a kit when it's needed.

You can save money by substituting some medical supplies with products that work as well or better. Carry duct tape rather than cloth tape, maxi-pads as blood stoppers for wounds instead of absorbent bandages, a tube of cake icing instead of a tube of Glutose (for hypoglycemia), and Vet-rap (animal bandage) instead of stretch gauze since it's cheaper and comes in fashionable colors.

EXTRA SUPPLIES

There are a number of extra items that you may want to consider adding to your first-aid kits, whether they're commercial or homemade. An emergency space blanket can be very helpful in managing shock and mild hypothermia. A small whistle attached to a zipper pull for attracting help, a miniature flashlight, and a spare lighter can be lifesavers.

One of the more useful medical accessories is a SAM splint, a piece of foam-padded, malleable

SECOND AID: INSURANCE

It goes without saying that you should have health insurance to cover the costs of a climbing accident. Getting injured is bad enough—paying for the rest of your life is even worse. However, your standard medical policy often doesn't cover the costs of rescue and evacuation.

When you join the American Alpine Club, the benefits include a rescue insurance policy that pays up to $5000, with a $200 deductible, anywhere in the world when climbing up to 6000 m (19,685 ft.). For trips to bigger peaks, you have to pay additionally for the period of time from trailhead to trailhead: peaks up to 7000 m (20,000 ft.) cost $25 per week; those between 7000 and 8000 m (20,000 and 26,240 ft.) cost $50 per week; those over 8000 m (26,240 ft.) cost $75 per week. It doesn't matter that many peaks under 8000 m are much more dangerous than peaks that are higher.

If you will be traveling to climb, one of the best deals going is the Diver's Alert Network membership—even if you are not a scuba diver. For only $25 a year, you get $100,000 of evacuation coverage for all medical emergencies anywhere more than 50 miles (80 km) from home. The major catch is that they must arrange the evacuation. You must call their 24-hour, toll-free domestic or international number. If you call from the chopper, you will not be reimbursed.

For that trip of a lifetime, you might consider a vacation protection plan. Your premium depends on the cost and duration of your trip (roughly $500 for a 2-month excursion) for trip-cancellation, emergency-medical, and transportation insurance and a pittance for baggage coverage. Some credit cards include variations on this coverage, as a matter of course, and your gear may be covered by homeowner's or renter's insurance. For all of these, read the fine print; there are a **lot** of exclusions.

aluminum that can be used for everything from a wrist splint to a cervical collar, to a patch for a broken tent pole. These are available either rolled or folded; the folded SAM splint is easier to store. Wire and ladder splints are a waste; don't bother with them.

Household items are useful too. Super Glue (cyanoacrylate) is great for closing small facial and hand wounds (after disinfecting), but it burns and could be toxic on large wounds. Dental floss can be used to remove a fishhook or a ring from a swollen finger (if you know the tricks); it also provides a strong thread for repairs. Duct tape has a thousand purposes (gaffers tape and black tape are even better but cost more).

If you are climbing away from snow, a disposable chemical cold pack for treating sprains is recommended. In snake country, it's a good idea to carry a Sawyer Extractor, a powerful pump that can remove 30 percent of the venom if used within 3 minutes of the bite. The rubber suction cups sold in "snakebite" kits do not work (neither does your mouth).

Those who are allergic to poison ivy and oak will be relieved to know there are at least two products on the market (Stokogard and IvyBlock) that are supposed to protect you from exposure. If you do manage to get covered, try Tecnu Cleanser to remove the oils before the rash develops.

When climbing at high altitudes, it is a very good idea to carry a stethoscope to help in detecting and diagnosing lung problems as early as possible. In a situation where you must leave an unconscious patient unattended (such as when you have to run for help), a large oral airway will prevent the tongue from closing the trachea.

TRAINING

A first-aid kit is only as good as the person using it. Listening to your partner gasping for air is *not*

the time to read a manual about how to treat a sucking chest wound. At an absolute minimum, as a human being, you should take a basic first-aid and CPR course.

However, basic first aid is inadequate training if you will be going into areas where help is more than 2 hours away. Unfortunately, the courses offered by the American Red Cross are poorly suited to wilderness situations—as a former Advanced First Aid instructor, I no longer recommend them unless there is no good alternative.

Several schools throughout the country offer specialized courses on wilderness care. These cover prolonged treatment of the patient using limited equipment in difficult environments.

A basic-level Wilderness First Aid class is only about 16 hours long—too little, in my opinion, to be of much value. You really need more time to learn about medical conditions and practice the skills. Though I wouldn't call it a waste of time, this class does not prepare you for the wilderness.

Best-suited to most climbers is Wilderness Advanced First Aid—a 36-hour class that will give you essential information for backcountry emergencies. It includes more time for practicing scenarios.

I strongly recommend taking the Wilderness First Responder class, before going on extended trips, leading groups, or volunteering with a rescue squad. This 80-hour curriculum meets the standards of the U.S. Department of Transportation (which licenses all EMTs and paramedics in the United States) and has an emphasis on problems encountered in the backcountry. The most advanced level of certification, Wilderness EMT, requires about 160 hours of training. This is superb for professional guides and members of search-and-rescue teams and is more than most climbers need, not that it's possible to be overtrained.

You should also be aware that many volunteer mountain-rescue teams offer free practice sessions one or two weekends each month. You can truly learn a lot from these people, and you may get to actually help someone in need.

CHAPTER 25

PHOTOGRAPHY

IT'S DIFFICULT TO IMAGINE GOING ON A scenic climb without a camera of some type. Perhaps you aren't shooting for National Geographic, but it's always great to bring home memories to share with friends.

No matter which format or camera you choose, the main concerns for climbing photography are durability, minimal weight, lens quality, and exposure control. Other features, such as a motor drive and even autofocus, are secondary in importance and often are not desirable for climbers.

DIGITAL

Digital photography is advancing at a phenomenal rate and already offers some real advantages over film. Nonetheless, I've good reason to believe film won't be obsolete for many years to come.

Currently, the better consumer digital cameras can record around 2.5 megapixels (million pixels) [Photo 25.1]. This compares with about 25 megapixels achievable from a good 35 mm film image (high-end lens, tripod, fine-grain film). A handheld shot with a cheap lens or point-and-shoot (P&S) camera on average film delivers only about 4 million pixels.

Although the resolution is getting fairly close, the current digital cameras are still limited by the amount of color they perceive. Each pixel gets only 8 bits of data, while good film scanners go to 36 bits, allowing much more accurate color rendition, better shadow detail, and greater contrast. To surpass 35 mm film at present, you need to use large-format digital cameras, but these are absurdly expensive and not at all portable.

Consumer digital cameras over 2 megapixels

Photo 25.1　Digital cameras are rapidly improving but still have a long way to go before replacing film.

allow you to make good images for the Web and decent 8 x 10 in. (20 x 25 cm) prints (without cropping) on a home computer system. But a good 35 mm film image can be enlarged up to 16 x 20 in. (40 x 50 cm) without too much grain, and can be shown in slide shows and submitted to magazines for publication.

In the long run, digital photography is *much* more expensive, even though you no longer have to buy film and processing. Assuming you already have a powerful computer and color printer (so that cost isn't factored in), you still need a lot of storage for large photo files, both in the field and at home. Photo-quality paper and ink for printers is surprisingly costly. And digital cameras eat batteries like we eat potato chips.

Without exception, the 2 meg cameras are far more expensive than equivalent 35 mm cameras. As predicted by Moore's Law (chip density doubles every 18 months), you can look forward to the digital camera being obsolete three years after you buy it—with minimal resale value. You will also have to deal with transferring your digital files to new media and formats as computer technology advances.

Lest you think this is an anti-digital rant, I'm actually a big fan of the technology. The wonderful thing about digital cameras is the immediacy of being able to view and edit images. This fact alone makes digital more *fun* than conventional photography for many people.

Should you decide to buy a digital camera, follow the guidelines for P&S cameras. Start with the lens, then investigate other features.

---

35 mm

For the vast majority of climbing photographers, 35 mm camera systems still make the most sense. Compared to other formats, these cameras offer the best combination of compactness, durability, and performance.

POINT-AND-SHOOT

The small size and minimal weight of point-and-shoot (P&S) cameras makes them very attractive for climbers [Photo 25.2]. However, the majority are

Photo 25.2   Fixed-focal-length point-and-shoot cameras can go anywhere and give excellent performance. Those with zoom lenses will disappoint unless you spend a lot.

also PHD ("push here, dummy") cameras that have no exposure control and insufficient brain power to handle tricky lighting.

The lens quality of many P&S cameras is also unsuitable for a lot of climbers, both in terms of optical quality and speed. Since a lot of climbing takes place in shade or low light levels, faster lenses are extremely useful.

The wide-range zoom lenses are the worst offenders. All the compact cameras with lenses that extend beyond 100 mm are dreadfully slow. When the camera lens is listed as 38 to 140 mm, f/4.8 to f/12, that means its widest aperture when zoomed out is f/12, making it usable with only very fast (ISO 400), grainy film. About all you can expect with better ISO 100 film is blurred natural-light images and black backgrounds in shots with flash.

If price is a major consideration, your best bet for a good, compact climbing camera is one with a fixed lens. These usually have a focal length between 28 and 35 mm with an aperture between f/2.8 and f/3.5. Many have autofocus, auto-advance, fill-flash, and (possibly) exposure compensation or a spot meter.

If you really need that zoom lens, it's worth spending the money on one of the high-end P&S cameras (Contax, Leica, Rollei). For around $1000, you get a fairly fast (under f/5.6), sharp lens with lots of exposure control and elegant design. Just don't drop it.

Weatherized cameras help keep dirt and moisture from jamming things—a really good feature. However, many P&S cameras were apparently designed by people with very small hands who never wear gloves.

Don't waste money on a camera with a "panorama" feature. These simply crop the image in the camera when you can do the same thing at home. Worse, you can accidentally crop your images without even knowing it.

The meters on some P&S cameras are optimized for print film and will consistently overexpose slide film. Before you buy, find out whether the meter can be adjusted.

Finally, don't rule out the "disposable" cameras. They can make some astonishingly good prints (slides are not an option), and the parts are actually recycled. You certainly don't have to worry about dropping one.

RANGEFINDER

The next step up in size and performance is rangefinder cameras. These are still a lot smaller than single lens reflex (SLR) cameras because there is no bulky prism to allow you to look through the lens. Rangefinders also have much better lenses (sharper, more contrast, faster) than any of the P&S cameras.

The legendary Leica M cameras are the epitome of this design and have corresponding prices. However, Contax, Konica, and Voigtländer make somewhat more affordable models that are quite good.

While wonderful cameras, rangefinders are more complex to use and thus really aren't practical for most climbers. They are ideal for the advanced photographer who travels a lot, but the casual user is better off looking through the lens.

SLR SYSTEMS

The main drawback of P&S and rangefinder cameras is that you cannot see through the lens while composing. Single lens reflex (SLR) cameras permit the photographer to see the results of changing lens focal length or using filters. Most SLR cameras are part of a large system of bodies, lenses, and accessories that give greater flexibility than any other format.

If you haven't invested in one brand yet, give careful consideration to your present and future needs. Once you have a body and a few lenses, it becomes *very* expensive to switch to a different system. When you're shopping for a camera, the ergonomics plays a subtle yet important role. Spend time holding the body in your hands, operating the function buttons, and considering how it will be used. Many cameras only work well for horizontal images—they are literally a pain in the wrist if you shoot a lot of verticals. Some are almost unusable if you have large hands or are wearing gloves. Consider the balance of the lens/body combinations as well; some systems just "feel" better.

Compare the image area of the viewfinder on various cameras. The difference can be astounding—some have 25 percent more ground glass for composing your images. How information is presented in the viewfinder is also important; cluttered screens are distracting.

Ultrafast shutter speeds (1/4000th and up) are great for sports like skiing . . . if you have hyperexpensive lenses. Faster flash syncs (1/250th and up) are wonderful for daylight fill . . . if you buy and carry the dedicated flash and aren't using a slow zoom lens. Otherwise, you'll rarely need more than 1/1000th or 1/125th for flash.

If you have to prioritize your funds, put your money into better glass instead of a fancier camera body. Perfect exposures are for naught if the lens (and photographer) can't deliver.

Just Say "No" to Auto

Many camera stores and magazines would like you to believe that the latest gadgetry is essential for taking good photos. Never mind that all these features add weight and bulk, often while decreasing reliability and lens performance. Cameras from thirty years ago are just as capable of taking excellent images as today's wünderbricks.

For the working professional photographer, autofocus and quality lenses are indispensable assets in many, but not all, cases. However, the average consumer has been sold a lot of promises that cannot be delivered by the "affordable" cameras and lenses.

The dirty secret of autofocus (AF), even on state-of-the-art pro cameras, is that maximum lens resolution is reduced by over 30 percent due to the limitations of sensors. Even the "in-focus" indicators of AF cameras in manual mode are significantly less accurate (12 percent on average) than focusing with a good manual camera. Thus, if you go to the trouble to shoot fine-grain film using a tripod, you will never achieve the true potential of your lens.

You can't just turn off autofocus and get manual performance either. The majority of auto-everything cameras do not have interchangeable view screens, so you are stuck with what they give you. View screens optimized for autofocus are bright but have poor contrast, which makes them lousy for manual focus—things don't snap into sharpness as with a good ground glass.

These AF obstacles are evident in good light, and the situation gets worse in dim or low-contrast lighting often encountered while climbing. The human eye is over thirty-two times more sensitive for focusing in low light than consumer AF systems. In bad light, unless you have fast glass, you get to experience the frustration of shutter lag (the delay between pressing the button and making the exposure) while the lens tries to lock on to something.

For ultrawide lenses (14 to 21 mm), there is no need for AF since they have such huge depth of field, even wide open. Other situations in which AF is a real detriment include macro work and close portraiture.

Even with a great lens, shutter lag on good AF cameras is about five times longer than when in manual mode (rangefinders are even faster). The continuous-guess (predictive) focusing of the most expensive cameras is required for professional results in fast-action photography. Without it, manual focusing beats auto every time for sports and nature images.

Compositions resulting from AF cameras are often tediously boring because the sensors are centered (even cameras with multiple sensor points concentrate them near the center). Using a tripod becomes a hassle since it requires focusing and then recomposing.

Along with all the "convenience" of auto-everything comes a computer programming manual that you must memorize. Unless you are a pro using the camera every day, the odds are that you won't recall how to use all the gee-whiz functions of your camera.

Many autofocus cameras do not have a depth-of-field preview button, so you cannot check composition or use split-density filters. The lenses rarely have depth-of-field markings or distance scales, so hyperfocal focusing is difficult. And consumer cameras often lack mirror-lockup, needed for sharp images with exposures between 1/30th and 1 second, and don't accept a cable release.

When taking pictures in a Buddhist temple, a Catholic cathedral, or even a quiet canyon, some AF cameras have all the subtlety of a firecracker. The noise of motors focusing, film advancing, and the long whir of rewind can be disturbing, even rude.

If you still insist on going auto-everything, then spend the money on a pro-level camera body (Nikon F100 or Canon EOS3) that has the least drawbacks and is built for hard use. Or plan on carrying two amateur bodies on trips-of-a-lifetime so you have a backup.

You can look forward to more frequent and expensive repairs either way. For example, even if they aren't used, LCD panels wear out after five to ten years. If the part is no longer available, you get to buy a new camera.

The Manual Alternative

For climbers—mountaineers in particular—and serious photographers, there is a lot to be said for manual bodies and lenses. They are often lighter, smaller, and more rugged than AF photo gear. And you are less dependent on batteries, a blessing in extreme cold or very humid conditions. AF cameras often use four AA-batteries (which are never listed with the body's weight) that get sucked dry in a hurry.

Excellent manual SLR cameras are still made by Contax, Nikon, and Olympus—the latter remains a top choice for climbers because of compactness, durability, and superior optics [Photo 25.3]. Equally important, these systems offer a good selection of fine-quality lenses that are often better than their AF counterparts.

Many of these bodies have sophisticated auto-

Photo 25.3   Fully mechanical 35 mm single-lens reflex (SLR) systems give better performance and are more reliable than all but pro-level autofocus systems. Spend your money on good glass.

exposure functions that do a good job most of the time. However, also look for manual override so you can take control when necessary. Fully manual cameras will operate at all shutter speeds without any batteries at all.

If you shop carefully, there are many good deals available on the used market, but do your homework first so you don't get a lemon. Some of the older cameras use a mercury battery that is no longer sold in North America or Europe (though there are workarounds).

Lenses

The huge selection of lenses available is the big advantage of 35 mm systems. Some systems shine above the rest in particular areas (e.g., Canon for long telephoto and Olympus for macro), but most of the major brands offer a good assortment. Third-party lenses (Sigma, Tamron, Tokina), once derided by serious photographers, are now very competitive with the "majors."

Try to buy the fastest glass (f/2.0 to f/2.8) that you can afford and are willing to carry. These are optically superior in normal light and give you a vital edge in low-light conditions. Used manual-focus lenses can be great values that offer excellent performance. However, older zooms and many early autofocus lenses are real dogs that should be avoided. Modern zoom lenses can deliver optical performance equal to fixed-focal-length lenses. But the ones of that caliber are universally heavy, bulky, and expensive.

The inexpensive zooms, from any manufacturer, have slow f/stops, flimsy construction, and mediocre optics. Their design is often compromised with smaller lens elements and lighter parts to allow the motors to work more efficiently. These may be fine for your application, but realize that you will never get "pro" results from them. In general, a three-to-one zoom range (e.g., 28–80 mm, or 70–210 mm) is the maximum for decent performance (unless you spend major bucks).

Unfortunately, cheap zooms have replaced the 50 mm/f1.8 lens as the standard option when a new camera is purchased. Thus most people end up

with a lens that is far slower (two to three stops), less sharp, heavier, and bulkier. In the "available darkness" photography that climbers encounter, these zooms just can't deliver.

Although less convenient, fixed-focal-length lenses are often more compact and better built, and have the extra speed that comes in handy. For climbing and other mountain photography, three lenses—20 mm, 35 mm, and 105 mm—will cover the vast majority of situations. You can even get by with a 28 mm and 85 mm and still come home with better images than you'd get with a budget zoom.

FILM

Photographers tend to get very dogmatic about film selection, though often they don't really understand or keep up with the subject. Although lots of people ballyhoo certain films (and the speed they rate them), they rarely test them against others under the conditions for which they'll typically be used. Personal prejudice either for or against Agfa, Fuji, or Kodak tends to extend long after emulsions have changed.

Because it is the medium for slide shows and publication in books and magazines, color transparency (positive) film is the clear choice for many climbers. Processing slides is generally less expensive than color print film, and you can view the results directly. You may want to purchase plastic sheet holders for easy archiving.

With the new emulsions available, there are few reasons to shoot slow films (ISO 50 and below) anymore. They are arguably better for landscape but still can't compete with larger film formats, and they are too slow for many climbing situations.

The current generations of ISO 100 slide films are remarkably fine-grained, with good color saturation and contrast. Many of the emulsions are available in a "pro" version and an "amateur" version—the main difference is price, not quality. Some film is made in the United States or overseas, but in this case, it's worth the extra money for the consistency of the local variety.

These ISO 100 films often push quite well for

an extra stop (ISO 200), though many labs charge a lot more. Faster ISO 200 or 400 films cost more but are cheaper to process, so they may be a better choice if you really need the speed.

Unless prints are your final goal, it's best to avoid color negative film. The exposure latitude is more forgiving (the reason it's found in disposable cameras), and it's easier and cheaper to make good (not necessarily better) prints than with slide film. But even small proof prints are expensive, and not many photographers can read a color negative without them.

More power to you if you choose to shoot black-and-white film. The creative possibilities are extraordinary, while far fewer people are up to the challenge.

OTHER FORMATS

For the majority of climbers and skiers, the 35 mm film format makes the most sense—it's a great all-around compromise. However, there are valid reasons that other formats are still thriving.

APS

The Advance Photo System (APS) is the newest film format intended for snapshots. While it offers some conveniences, such as drop-in film cartridges, APS inevitably will be replaced by digital photography—probably sooner than later.

The cute little APS cameras are fairly inexpensive and the better ones are capable of surprisingly good, small color prints. However, APS film (17 x 30 mm) is 42 percent smaller than 35 mm (24 x 36 mm), so big enlargements just don't compare. Although black-and-white and color slide films are available, they are not practical to use with standard enlargers or slide projectors.

An even bigger concern is the long-term availability of film and processing. My guess is that owners of APS cameras will be out of luck in a decade (remember 110 or disk film?). Many digital scanners don't accept the format either, so getting prints made in twenty years might be impossible.

MEDIUM

If you are really serious about producing quality images, then you need to consider larger film sizes. When cropped to the dimensions to make a standard 8 x 10 in. (20 x 25 cm) print, a 35 mm negative has a usable image area of 24 x 30 mm. A 6 x 4.5 cm negative has 1.7 times more information, a 6 x 6 cm neg gives 1.9 times more, and a 6 x 7 cm neg has 2.3 times the info of the little neg. This translates to greater sharpness and less grain in large prints. Equally important but more subtle is far greater tonal information that contributes to a sense of depth (and better scans). A slide show of medium-format images can be absolutely stunning!

The trade-off is bulkier, heavier cameras with a limited selection of lenses that have less depth of field. With 220 film, you get only thirty shots on 6 x 4.5, 24 shots on 6 x 6, or twenty shots on 6 x 7 —and it's far less convenient to load during a snowstorm.

Despite the drawbacks, I carried a Mamiya 6 medium-format rangefinder, with three lenses, to the summit of Gasherbrum II, 26,362 ft. (8035 m). This system (a Leica with a thyroid problem) is well suited to climbing and travel because of its relative compactness and tolerable weight (comparable to a high-end 35 mm system) [Photo 25.4].

Most of the boxy medium-format systems (Bronica, Hasselblad, Mamiya, Rollei) are better off used in the studio or near the parking lot. However, climbers might consider some of the rangefinder cameras that have an attached lens (Fuji). The Pentax 67 system, which looks like a giant 35 mm SLR, is also popular with dedicated outdoor photographers.

PANORAMA

As climbers, we get to enjoy some of the best views on the planet. However, even with ultrawide lenses, it is difficult to convey the scope of the land-

Photo 25.4   A medium-format rangefinder is about the same size and weight as a 35 mm pro SLR, but the larger film allows far greater detail and tonal gradation.

scape in conventional formats with an aspect ratio (height to width) of less than 1 to 1.5 (24 x 36 mm), in a 35 mm image. Conveying the best "feel" of what it's like to be in some locations calls for a much more elongated panorama format with aspect ratios greater than 1 to 2.

Although some 35 mm cameras claim to offer "panoramic" images, in reality these are just wide-angle views with the top and bottom cropped off (12 x 36 mm). These pseudo-panoramas offer no advantages over a normal camera, but do increase complexity and cost.

There are two styles of real panorama cameras—rotational and nonrotational—but the former is more practical for climbers [Photo 25.5]. Available for either 35 mm or 120/220 film, these use a lens that swings across an arc of more than 120°.

The 35 mm swing-lens cameras (Horizon, Noblex) are about the same size and weight as a regular SLR with a lens. Most don't have niceties like a light meter, or even focus, and changing film takes some dexterity. But the large negative (24 x 56 mm) and minimal distortion (compared to a fisheye lens) makes them well worth the effort if you are going into spectacular country.

A nonrotational 35 mm panorama from Hasselblad/Fuji is also an alternative that is reasonably compact. This is a much more sophisticated camera system with many advanced features and a choice of three lenses.

While some of the medium-format panorama cameras (6 x 12 cm to 6 x 17 cm) produce glorious images, they are monstrous beasts to carry and can't be handheld. Even the swing-lens models are big and weigh over 4 lbs. (1.8 kg).

LARGE

Moving up to even larger sheet film is best reserved for the truly dedicated (some might say fanatic). Yet the most practical size, 4 x 5 in. (10 x 13 cm), can be surprisingly compact, lightweight, and even affordable [Photo 25.6].

I've used my 4 x 5 field camera up to basecamp on Ama Dablam in Nepal—but no higher. It's certainly a labor of love, but the rewards were worth it . . . to me. The availability of inexpensive porters and pack animals makes carrying large-format cameras feasible in some parts of the world.

If you want the ultimate in photographic prints, nothing comes close to rivaling platinum contact

Photo 25.5   A swing-lens panorama camera makes images that offer a greater sense of "being there."

prints from ultraformat (8 x 10 in. and larger) negatives. My 7 x 17 in. (17 x 43 cm) banquet camera isn't practical to carry on trips longer than day hikes. But within that range, it delivers images that you have to see to comprehend.

TRIPODS

Although impractical on many climbs, a tripod is essential if you are serious about capturing good images. Even the cheapest tripod is better than none in low light.

What the more expensive aluminum tripods give you is greater stability and reliability. If you can afford one, the carbon-fiber tripods offer the least vibration for the least weight [Photo 25.7].

Tripods are rated for how much weight they can carry. In practice, I find you can extend these ratings by almost 50 percent if you are very careful to minimize vibration.

Tripod heads are often sold separately, so you can mix and match with the legs. For most outdoor situations, a sturdy ball head is more convenient than three-way heads. The Arca Swiss B-1 ball head sets the standard against which others are judged. Consider a quick-release system if you anticipate using your tripod a lot.

Clamps with ball sockets are occasionally sold to fit ice axes and ski poles, but these are rare now and weren't particularly steady to begin with (adequate for point-and-shoots though). Some of the mini-pods available can be set on a boulder or braced on a wall and are sturdy enough for an SLR.

One surprisingly effective trick for steadying a camera is the "string-pod." Simply fit an eyebolt to the camera's mounting hole, attach a couple of feet of cord, step on the dangling end, and pull up while you shoot—it's good for an extra stop.

CASES

Camera cases come in every conceivable size and shape, and which you choose is largely dependent on your system and personal preference. It's likely that you will end up owning several cases, each suited to a different need.

For climbing or skiing, you often want a small case that holds just a body and lens. Be sure it is easy to operate with one hand yet is secure and keeps out water, spindrift, and dust. Some have a harness that holds the case on your chest—good for hiking or skiing, but it gets in the way when climbing.

Padded fanny packs are popular for somewhat larger systems, although the bigger ones attempt to hold too much. Take note that you could have over $1,000 worth of equipment relying on a $3 plastic buckle. While big cases with lots of padded pockets are nice at times, I find a modular system with several smaller cases more versatile.

ACCESSORIES

Your three most valuable photo accessories are a light table, a good-quality loupe, and a large trashcan. Edit ruthlessly and never show *anybody* subpar work!

Photo 25.6 A 7 x 17 in. view camera gives the ultimate mountain landscape images. When compactness and weight are concerns, a 4 x 5 in. field camera is a good compromise.

When traveling light and fast, you don't want to carry a lot of unnecessary extras. Here are some items that often are indispensable: cable release, marking pen (for film canisters), Lens Pen (a great cleaning tool), spare batteries, and a coin that fits the battery slot.

FILTERS

If you have high-quality optics, it's worth paying extra for multicoated filters for the least possible contrast degradation of your images. On the other hand, most photographers can't tell the difference between these and the less-expensive un-coated filters that are easier to clean.

The most noticeable difference between high-end and cheap filters is the quality of the mount. The good ones are solidly built with brass rings and thread on and off much easier. Cheap filters often jam or cross-thread.

Many photographers like to compensate for the coolness of shade and high altitude with a warming filter, such as an 81B, that neutralizes excessive blue. Be wary, as this can have an unnatural effect, particularly with snow. UV filters are good for protecting your lens but aren't vital, even at altitude. Skylight filters should be avoided because they add a slight pink cast to your images.

Probably the most widely abused filter is the polarizer—these harm more shots (they look "dead") than they help and should not be used indiscriminately (and very rarely with lenses wider than 28 mm). For most modern SLR cameras, you need a circular polarizer so that the meter will work properly. Less-expensive linear polarizers are fine for any camera without through-the-lens metering (and some older ones with it).

Rectangular split-density filters that are gray fading to clear are invaluable for landscapes with varying amounts of light. These are a bit tricky to use because the fade zone moves when the lens stops down for exposure. Push the depth-of-field preview button to position the filter. Be sure the filter is a true neutral gray or you will get odd-looking skies.

Photo 25.7 A carbon-fiber tripod is expensive but gives the best weight-to-performance ratio. A tabletop tripod can be braced against a wall or propped on a rock.

FLASH

An auxiliary flash unit ranks up there with a tripod as one of the first things to be left behind on many climbing trips. However, it can be very useful in many situations and may be worth the hassle.

While many P&S and amateur SLR cameras have built-in flash, these have very limited range and drain batteries. In-camera flashes are near the lens, which results in portraits with devilish red eyes (the light bouncing off the back of the eyeball). Although many now have pre-flash to minimize this effect, the subject often moves be-

Photo 25.8   A reflector attached to a portable flash can make more pleasing portraits.

tween the time you press the shutter release and when the exposure is actually made a few seconds later.

Extending the flash away from the camera eliminates red-eye and allows more pleasing portraits (the shadow location can be controlled). Dedicated flash units work with the camera's electronics to greatly simplify exposure control and achieve nice effects, such as daylight fill-flash and rear-curtain sync. A cable that allows extending the flash is useful for portraits and macro.

Simple, lightweight attachments allow you to modify the otherwise harsh quality of the typical flash unit [Photo 25.8]. These either bounce the light or soften it with a diffuser, although you typically lose two stops.

Another option for daylight fill is a collapsible reflector with white on one side and metallic gold on the other; these are compact and lightweight. With an assistant to position the reflector, you can direct a very nice quality of fill light at your subjects.

TRAVEL TIPS

When traveling internationally, you will have to deal with dreaded X-ray machines and guards with guns. Never, ever send your film with checked baggage, because this is subjected to much higher intensities of radiation. Fogging caused by X-rays is cumulative, so the less exposure the better.

Before leaving, remove your film from all boxes. If the plastic canisters aren't transparent, you should transfer the film to ones that are (photo labs often have plenty of extras). This will save having to open them all up for a security guard.

Put all the film canisters in large zip-lock bags and request hand inspection at security checkpoints. Often the guards will comply because you've made it easy for them. If they insist on running it through the machine, a lead pouch will help reduce exposure of your precious film.

SUGGESTED ROCK RACK

Vary to suit your local area and personal tastes.

BASIC EQUIPMENT

- 1 Locking carabiner
- 1 Climbing harness
- 1 Belay device
- 1 Pair of climbing shoes
- 1 Chalk bag and belt
- 1 Climbing helmet
- 1 Large dollop of common sense
- 1 Day pack
- 1 Water bottle with carrying strap

BEGINNING LEAD RACK: BASIC EQUIPMENT, PLUS

- 1 10.5 or 11 mm dynamic climbing rope, 50 m (165 ft.)
- 5 Passive cams
- 10 Wired wedges
- 25 D-shaped or oval carabiners
- 2 Locking Ds
- 5 Quickdraws, 6 to 12 in. (15 to 30 cm) loops
- 5 Full-length runners, 24 in. (60 cm) loops
- 1 Nut tool

INTERMEDIATE LEAD RACK: BEGINNING RACK, PLUS

- 3 Micronuts (e.g., RPs 3 to 5)
- 3 Small camming nuts (e.g., Tricams 0.5, 1, 1.5)
- 2 Large nuts (e.g., Hexentrics 9 and 10)
- 3 Spring-loaded camming devices (SLCDs)
- 5 Quickdraws
- 5 Bent-gate carabiners
- 10 Lightweight D-shaped carabiners
- 1 Double-length runner, 48 in. (1.2 m) loop
- 1 Cordelette or webolette
- 2 Prusik loops, 18 in. (45 cm) loops of 6 mm accessory cord
- 2 Descending rings

ADVANCED LEAD RACK: INTERMEDIATE RACK, PLUS

- 3 Three-cam units (TCUs)
- 2 Small SLCDs
- 2 Additional SLCDs
- 2 Large SLCDs

GEAR LIST

This is a list of items that *may* be needed for a multiday trip or expedition—it is neither gospel nor all-inclusive. Adjust the list according to your needs and the demands of the trip. An asterisk (*) indicates equipment shared by a group.

THE TEN ESSENTIALS
Map of area
Compass
Sun protection (glasses, hat, and sunscreen)
Water bottle or hydration system
Extra food (energy bars are excellent)
Extra clothing
First-aid kit
Knife
Headlamp (with extra batteries and bulbs)
Waterproof matches and candle

CLOTHING
  Base Layer
Synthetic underwear
Synthetic long underwear (top and bottoms)
Wool socks (two pairs)
Liner gloves
Shorts
Tee shirts
  Insulating Layer
Long-sleeved shirts
Long pants
Belt or suspenders
Pile jacket
Synthetic vest
Down or synthetic parka
Down booties and mukluks
Gloves or mittens
Warm hat or balaclava (wool or pile)
Headband
Neck gaiter or scarf
  Outer Layer
Boots
Extra boot wax (for long trips) *

Camp shoes or sandals
Gaiters
Supergaiters or overboots
Overmitts
Wind shirt
Rain/wind jacket
Rain/wind pants
Sun hat with wide brim or neck cape
Face mask
Goggles (with spare lens)

CAMPING GEAR
  Packs
Day pack or fanny pack
Alpine or expedition pack
Pack rain cover
Hydration system (for water only)
Stuff sacks (for organizing gear)
Sled
Travel duffel
  Sleeping
Sleeping bag
Sleeping bag liner or overbag
Insulated pad (two in winter)
Stuff sack (stuff with parka to make a pillow)
Ear plugs (invaluable when the tent's flapping and
    in noisy cities)
Eye mask (a night shade helps you to rest when
    you need to)
  Shelter
Bivouac sack
Tent (with rain fly, poles, and stakes) *
Tent groundsheet *
Sponge or brush (to keep tent clean) *
Snow stakes for tent *

Basecamp Gear

Camp chair
Basecamp tent*
Portable shower*
Lantern*
Cutting board*
Clothesline and pins*

Kitchen Gear

Water bottle (1 liter, wide mouth for carbohydrate
  drinks)
Pee bottle (widemouth but a different shape)
Cup
Bowl
Spoon
Fork
Lighters
Stove (and spare parts)*
Windscreen*
Fuel*
Fuel funnel (if necessary)*
Cook set*
Extra pot (for melting snow)*
French press for coffee*
Stove pad*
Pot grips*
50 ft. (15 m) 3 mm cord (to hang food in bear
  country, rig tarps, etc.)*
Bear canister for food (to save a lot of trouble)*
Spice kit*
Zip-lock freezer bags*
Biodegradable soap*
Pot scrubber*
Water sack*
Water filter, purifier, or treatment*
Thermos bottle*
Trash bag*

WINTER AND GLACIER GEAR

Mountaineering ice ax
Alpine crampons
9 mm dry rope*
Bamboo wands with flagging*
Snow flukes*
Snow pickets

Ice screws
Sit harness
Slings
Carabiners
Ascenders or prusiks
Small pulley
Climbing helmet
Snowshoes
Skis
Ski boots
Ski poles
Ski helmet
Wax kit (waxes, cork, scraper)
Climbing skins (and extra adhesive for long trips)
Snow shovel
Snow saw*
Avalanche transceiver
Avalanche probe pole
Snow kit for avalanche analysis (slope meter, pit
  card, magnifier, etc.)*

ADDITIONAL GEAR

Spare glasses or contact lenses
Personal medications
Lip balm
Insect repellent (50 percent or more DEET)
Mosquito net hat (for severe bug country)
Foot powder
Feminine napkins
Bandanna
Toilet paper (in plastic bag with matches)
Trowel
Birth control (avoid the Pill at high altitude)
Toothbrush and toothpaste
Watch (with alarm)
Altimeter
Thermometer*
Wind speed indicator*
GPS receiver*
FRS or ham radios*
Solar charger
Umbrella (for sun and rain protection)
Hand warmers
Trekking poles

Parachute cord*
Candles or lantern*
Towel
Fishing equipment and license
Binoculars or spotting scope*
Field guides*
Notepad and pen
Reading material
Games (cards, backgammon, Frisbee, etc.)*
Cash (including coins for a pay phone)

Repair Kit

Tools (vise grip, file, screwdrivers, Allen wrenches, etc.)
Baling wire
Duct tape
Seam Grip
Fabric repair tape
Safety pins
Zip ties
Sewing needle and thread
Tent pole splint
Binding and crampon screws
Epoxy and steel wool
Spare cables or bails
Ski pole patch kit
Spare ski pole basket and tip

First-Aid Kit (basic supplies, expand for remote trips)

Aspirin/pain reliever
Band-Aids
Blister kit (Second Skin, foam, etc.)
Adhesive tape (1 in.)
Gauze pads (4 x 4 in.)
Stretch roller gauze
Ace bandage
Soap or cleanser
Antibacterial ointment
Sawyer Extractor snakebite kit
Tweezers and scissors
Whistle
Emergency blanket
First-aid booklet

Camera Equipment

Camera bodies
Lenses
Filters
Flash
Flash cable
Flash modifier
Tripod
Cable release
Spare batteries
Lens cleaner and brush
Coin for changing batteries
Film
Film X-ray shield
Camcorder

INTERNATIONAL TRAVEL

Passport (make sure it hasn't expired!)
Visas
Health documentation (vaccinations, personal medical information, copies of prescriptions)
Passport/money carrier
Inflatable pillow (for long flights and train rides)
Notarized list of camera equipment serial numbers
Extra passport photos
Airline tickets and itinerary
Hotel reservations
Youth hostel card
International student ID
Travelers checks
Credit cards
Dress clothes (because soirees happen)
Calculator
Address book
Guidebooks and maps
Language dictionaries
Travel alarm
Voltage converter/adapters
Combination locks for luggage zippers
Cable bike lock (to secure luggage)
Toiletries (comb, shampoo, shaving supplies, nail clippers, etc.)

Diarrhea medicine

Sink stopper

Mesh bag (for dirty laundry)

Clothesline and pins

Travel packages of laundry soap

Sleep sack (for youth hostels)

Photos of family, friends, and home

Gifts for exchanging

Polaroid camera

THINGS TO DO BEFORE LEAVING

Get backcountry permits.

Get in shape (allow more than 2 weeks).

Take a first-aid course.

Take an avalanche course.

Get vaccinations (plan 6 months ahead).

Research destination in guidebooks.

Notify relative or friend of destination and itinerary.

Get someone to feed the pets and water the plants.

Repack food into zip-lock bags.

Fuel and prep the car.

Stop the newspaper and mail.

Empty the refrigerator.

Take out the trash.

GLOSSARY

Abseil British equivalent of rappel. Abseil is from the German and means "to rope down."

Aid climbing Climbing in which the climber ascends or rests by making use of the rope or gear to support his or her weight.

Alpine style An approach to climbing peaks in which the ascent is made in one push, usually by traveling as light as possible.

Anchor Any tree, block, nut, bolt, or other protection device that holds a climber or team to a wall, slope, or cliff with rope, slings, and carabiners.

Ascender A piece of gear (e.g., Jumar) that enables a climber to ascend a rope. Attached to the rope, it will grip in one direction (down) and slide in the other (up).

Back-clean Removing protection from a section of a pitch that has already been climbed, for use on the upper section of the pitch.

Back-clip Improper method of clipping rope into a carabiner in such a way that the rope could more easily unclip itself.

Belay An old sailing term meaning "to secure." The use of a rope to stop a climber's fall.

Bergschrund The uppermost crevasse on a glacier, where the glacier separates and flows away from the snow/ice field that feeds it. Often just called a "schrund."

Big wall Extremely long, multipitch routes, which usually are climbed over several days.

Bight A bend in a rope.

'Biner Short for carabiner.

Bivy To bivouac. Camping with little protection from the elements. Climbers often bivouac on summit days, when it is impractical to carry full camping gear.

Bomber An anchor system or placement that is very solid and can be completely trusted.

Bong A very large angle piton once made for cracks 3 to 6 in. (7 to 15 cm) wide. When hammered upon, the piton made a *bong, bong* sound instead of the *ping, ping* of smaller pitons.

Brain bucket Slang for a helmet.

Bucket A very large, in-cut hold that a climber can wrap his or her fingers over.

Butterfly or backpack coil Quick method of coiling a rope, in two sets of bights of doubled rope, so that it may be easily transported, worn on the back like a pack.

Cam Any protection that widens as it rotates. Usually refers to a spring-loaded camming device (SLCD).

Carabiner An aluminum, steel, or titanium snap-link used for holding the rope and connecting it to gear.

CEN *Comité Européen de Normalisation,* the body that sets standards for products sold in Europe.

Chalk Made from magnesium carbonate. For decades gymnasts, weight lifters, and climbers have used chalk to counteract sweaty hands and improve grip.

Chickenhead A protrusion of rock, so-named because of its resemblance to the head of a chicken. These holds sometimes make good anchors to girth-hitch with a sling.

Chimney A crack wide enough to fit a climber's entire body inside. Also the technique used to ascend the crack.

Chock An artificial chockstone wedged into a crack for protection by hand without the use of a hammer. Synonymous with "nut."

Cleaning Removing protection while seconding or rappelling.

Cold shut Steel rod bent into a loop and usually welded shut. Used for bolt hangers.

Copperhead A cylinder of copper alloy swaged to a wire loop and pounded into shallow cracks or depressions for body-weight aid placements.

Cordelette A 20 ft. (60 m) length of kernmantle cord tied in a loop and used to equalize several belay anchors.

Couloir Snow- or ice-filled gully.

Crevasse A deep crack in a glacier.

Crux The hardest part of a climb or pitch.

Daisy chain A series of loops sewn into a piece of webbing so that there are many places to clip into it.

Deck When a falling climber hits the ground.

Denier The weight in grams of 9000 meters of fiber. Commonly used to denote the fineness of the material (larger numbers are coarser).

Draw Short for "quickdraw."

Edging Technique in which the climber places his or her feet on narrowly protruding edges.

Epic Slang term for a climbing adventure that was long, arduous, or somehow much more than was expected.

Equalized Usually used in reference to anchors set in such a way that the weight of the climbing team and/or the force of a fall is distributed equally among all the pieces that are part of the anchor.

Expedition style An approach to climbing big peaks in which the ascent is made by shuttling gear and establishing a series of camps that eventually puts the climbers in a position to make a summit bid.

Face climbing Using the features that protrude from a rock face (rather than cracks in the face) to climb.

Fixed line A rope left attached to an anchor so it can be readily used for ascending or descending. Used to avoid releading part of a climb or to enable a relatively quick, safe descent during a storm or darkness.

Flash A successful lead of a climb on the first attempt.

Follow After one climber leads a pitch, a second (or third, or fourth, and so on) will climb it—follow—while the leader belays them from above.

Free climbing Using only natural features to support the climber's weight during an ascent.

Free-solo To free-climb without a rope and therefore without needing a partner.

Friend The original spring-loaded camming device with a trigger to retract the cams.

Full conditions High wind and heavy snow, as in a "full-on storm."

Gaposis Slang for gaps in clothing layers resulting from poor design.

Geature A "feature" added to a product for the sole purpose of appealing to gear freaks.

Glacier travel In order to prevent a fall into a crevasse, partners must walk roped together. Prusik knots are attached to the rope so that the climber can climb out of a crevasse or set up a pulley system to haul out an injured victim.

Glissade A quick method of descending a snowfield in which the climber sits, crouches, or stands, with an ice ax ready for self-arrest, and slides down the slope. In the sitting or crouching position, the tail of the ax can be used as a rudder to control direction and speed.

Goldline The brand name of a laid (twisted), sheathless nylon rope. It was the most widely used climbing rope in the United States in the 1960s.

Grade The difficulty rating attached to a climb.

Gripped Scared.

Hanging belay To belay hanging from bolts or gear placed in cracks, without a substantial ledge on which to stand or sit.

Hex Short for Hexentric. A hollow, nutlike, hexagonal-shaped type of protection.

Hueco A Spanish word meaning a hole or pocket in the wall/rock.

Icefall The fractured, tumultuous, unstable part of a glacier, where it flows over a relatively steep drop. Analogous to a river rapid.

Jug A large hold. "To jug" means to jumar.

Jumar A mechanical rope ascender. "To jumar" means to ascend a fixed rope with any brand of mechanical ascender.

Krab British slang for carabiner.

Lead climbing The first climber (the leader) places protection as he or she climbs and is belayed from below.

Lost Arrow A solid steel piton that works well

for horizontal cracks. Also a famous spire in Yosemite.

Nut A chock. The first artificial chockstones were threaded hexagonal nuts picked up along railroad tracks on the way to British crags. A sling was put through the hole and a krab (karabiner) attached to the sling.

Offwidth A crack that is too large for fist jams yet too small to accommodate the whole body and be climbed like a chimney.

Onsight A flash ascent made without prior knowledge of the climb.

Pin A piton.

Pinkpoint A redpoint ascent made using preplaced gear.

Pitch One rope length, from the ground or one belay station to the next belay.

Protection The gear that a climber attaches the rope to as he or she climbs. Often called just "pro."

Prusik knot A loop of cord or webbing that is wound around a rope of larger diameter. When the knot is properly tied and weighted, it should not slip; when unweighted, it can slide up or down the rope.

Pumped The condition in which lactate-filled muscles can no longer perform well.

Quickdraw A short piece of webbing and two carabiners.

Rack The collection of gear a lead climber takes up the climb, usually on a gear sling and/or attached to his or her harness.

Rappel To self-lower from the top of a climb using a rope. Rappel is a French word meaning "to recall." Often shortened to "rap" or "rapping."

Redpoint An ascent, usually after multiple attempts, of a difficult climb that is made while placing all the gear or clipping all the bolts and without ever hanging on the rope.

Runners Traditionally a "running belay," so-called because it extends the belay to each piece of protection (as long as the protection doesn't fail). American climbers often refer to any sling they carry for protection (or extending protection) as a "runner."

Runout A description of a climb, or section of a climb, in which protection is spread out far enough to make the prospect of a long fall especially frightening or dangerous.

Screamer A long fall. Also a load-limiting device for marginal protection.

Second After the leader, the next person to climb a pitch. "To second" means to follow a pitch.

Serac Building-size blocks of glacial ice, such as those found in an icefall. Seracs can collapse spontaneously and wipe out anything below.

Sewed-up A reference to a climb in which the leader has placed protection very close together, usually every 5 ft. (1.5 m) or less.

Sharp end Slang for the end of the rope that the leader ties into.

Simul-climb When both the leader and the second are a rope-length apart (with pro in between) and climbing at the same time, very fast on easy ground.

Slack Extra rope.

Sling A loop of nylon or Spectra/nylon, webbing, or cord. Often carried over the climber's shoulder—single, doubled, or tripled, depending on the length of the sling.

Smearing A technique in which the climber gains purchase on the rock using friction from the sole of the shoe.

Spectra A very strong fiber used in cord or webbing.

Sport climbing Climbing routes on which preplaced bolts are used for protection.

Spot To protect a boulderer by preparing to prevent his or her head from hitting the ground if he or she were to fall.

Static rope A kernmantle rope with very little stretch, e.g., a haul line.

Stick-clip Using a device to attach the rope to the first bolt of a climb from the ground. Doing so protects the climber from hitting the ground if he or she should fall before the first bolt.

Swinging leads On a multipitch route, the

pattern of alternating the roles of leader and follower. "Climbing in blocks" refers to the same climber leading several pitches in a row before his or her partner takes over (sometimes faster on alpine or big wall climbs).

TCU Any three-cam protection device.

Tension To hold the climber tightly with the rope.

Top-rope Any situation in which the belay is above the climber. The most common form for practice climbs is a "redirect" or "slingshot" top-rope, where the belayer is on the ground and the rope runs up to an anchor and down to the climber.

Trad Common term for traditional climbing.

Traditional climbing Climbing routes on which removable gear is placed for protection by the leader as he or she ascends. The second removes the gear.

UIAA *Union Internationale des Associations d'Alpinisme*, the international climbing organization that sets standards for equipment.

Unit Slang for any camming device.

Webbing Flat-profile nylon.

Whipper A long lead fall in which the leader is jerked about on the end of the rope.

Wire A nut slung on steel cable. Also used as a verb meaning to memorize a sequence of moves.

Zipper A series of protection placements that pop out in sequence when the leader falls. Best avoided.

SUGGESTED READING

TECHNIQUE

Cliff, Peter. *Ski Mountaineering*. Seattle: Pacific Search Press, 1987. Ignore the gear discussions; the rest is very informative.

Daffern, Tony. *Avalanche Safety for Skiers and Climbers*, second edition. Seattle: The Mountaineers, 1999. A must-read for anyone heading into snow country.

Fasulo, David. *Self-Rescue*. Evergreen, Colorado: Chockstone Press, 1996. This is stuff all climbers should know and practice.

Graydon, Don, and Kurt Hanson, editors. *Mountaineering: Freedom of the Hills*, sixth edition. Seattle: The Mountaineers, 1997. The bible for neophyte mountaineers.

Long, John. *Climbing Anchors*. Evergreen, Colorado: Chockstone Press, 1993. Lots of valuable info here.

Long, John. *How To Rock Climb!*, third edition. Evergreen, Colorado: Chockstone Press, 1998. One of the better introductions to the sport.

Long, John and Craig Leubben. *Advanced Rock Climbing*. Conifer, Colorado: Chockstone Press, 1997. Read this one too.

Long, John and John Middendorf. *Big Walls*. Evergreen, Colorado: Chockstone Press, 1994. Essential reading before tackling the big stone.

Lowe, Jeff. *Ice World: Techniques and Experiences of Modern Ice Climbing*. Seattle: The Mountaineers, 1996. A master tells it like it was and is.

Parker, Paul. *Free-Heel Skiing: Telemark and Parallel Techniques for all Conditions*. Seattle: The Mountaineers, 1995. We all wish we could ski like Paul.

Selters, Andy. *Glacier Travel and Crevasse Rescue*, second edition. Seattle: The Mountaineers, 1999. Very important info that must be learned and practiced.

Twight, Mark and James Martin. *Extreme Alpinism: Climbing Light, Fast, & High*. Seattle: The Mountaineers, 1999. An excellent reference for wannabe hardcore climbers.

TRAINING

Aaberg, Everett. *Muscle Mechanics*. Champaign, IL: Human Kinetics, 1998. One of the best references for learning about weight training.

Burns, Bob and Mike Burns. *Wilderness Navigation*. Seattle: The Mountaineers, 1999. Learn to use the technology and stay found.

Clark, Nandy. *Sports Nutrition Guidebook*, second edition. Champaign, IL: Human Kinetics, 1997. A good starting point for healthier eating.

Forgey, William. *Wilderness Medicine*, fourth edition. Merrillville, IN: ICS Books, 1994. A good, fairly advanced reference.

Goddard, Dale and Udo Neumann. *Performance Rock Climbing*. Mechanicsburg, PA: Stackpole Books, 1993. Mostly for sport climbers.

Hodgson, Michael. *Weather Forecasting*, second edition. Globe Pequot Press, 1999. Some useful info to help keep you out of trouble.

Hörst, Eric. *How to Climb 5.12*. Evergreen, Colorado: Chockstone Press, 1997. Another good training book if you just want to climb rock.

Houston, Charles S. *Going Higher: The Story of Man and Altitude*, fourth edition. Seattle: The Mountaineers, 1998. A complicated subject put into laypeople's terms.

Musnick, David and Mark Pierce. *Conditioning for Outdoor Fitness*. Seattle: The Mountaineers, 1999. A fairly good introduction to training.

Reifsnyder, William. *Weathering the Wilderness*.

San Francisco: Sierra Club Books, 1980. Great info on U.S. weather patterns.

Wilkerson, James. *Medicine for Mountaineering and Other Wilderness Activities*, fourth edition. Seattle: The Mountaineers, 1992. The standard reference.

Williamson, Jed, editor. *Accidents in North American Mountaineering*. Golden: American Alpine Club Press, annual. Learn from other people's mistakes.

PERSPECTIVE (THE TOP PICKS OF BOOKS ON CLIMBING)

Benuzzi, Felice. *No Picnic on Mount Kenya*. New York: The Lyons Press, 1999. An incredible ascent by escaped prisoners in WW II.

Bonatti, Walter. *On the Heights*. London: Rupert Hart-Davis, 1964. One of the alpine greats.

Buhl, Hermann. *Nanga Parbat Pilgrimage*. Seattle: The Mountaineers, 1998. Reinhold Messner considers Buhl one of the best.

Diemberger, Kurt. *Summits and Secrets*. Included in *The Kurt Diemberger Omnibus* with *The Endless Knot* and *Spirits of the Air*. Seattle: The Mountaineers, 1999. Diemberger was one of two men who made first ascents of two 8000 m peaks (Buhl was the other).

Harrer, Heinrich. *The White Spider*. New York: Penguin USA, 1998. Great history of the Eiger's North Face.

Hornbein, Tom. *Everest: The West Ridge*. Seattle: The Mountaineers, 1998. First traverse of Everest, in 1963.

Houston, Charles S. *K2: The Savage Mountain*. New York: The Lyons Press, 2000. Near disaster in 1953.

Maraini, Fosco. *Karakoram: The Ascent of Gasherbrum IV*. New York: Viking Press, 1961. Incredibly difficult climb in 1958.

Mummery, Albert Frederick. *My Climbs in the Alps and Caucasus*. Oxford: Basil Blackwell Oxford, 1936. A mountaineering classic first published in 1895.

Simpson, Joe. *Touching the Void*. New York: HarperCollins, 1990. Epic survival in the Peruvian Alps.

Terray, Lionel. *Conquistadors of the Useless*. Seattle: The Mountaineers, 2001 (new edition to be released in paperback). Best book title ever and a good read.

INDEX

ABOUT THE AUTHOR

Clyde Soles is a senior contributing editor of *Rock & Ice* and *Trail Runner* magazines. For the past six years, his primary job has been testing climbing gear and writing product reviews for *Rock & Ice*. He also edited the Performance section (techniques, training, nutrition) of the magazine.

Soles got an early start in the outdoors while growing up in Washington, DC. The afternoon sports he took in high school were rock climbing and whitewater kayaking instead of football and baseball. His summers were spent as a whitewater raft guide and canoe instructor in West Virginia, and he adventured all over the East Coast.

Since 1980, Soles has been involved in the outdoor industry, in a variety of capacities from salesperson to store manager. He has visited nearly two dozen manufacturers around the world to see how gear is produced and tested, and he has spent well over 75 days in trade shows listening to sales pitches. He is also a founding member of the International Mountaineering History Association.

Soles has climbed throughout much of the United States and in Europe, Mexico, and Nepal. In 1997, he climbed Gasherbrum II 26,365 ft. (8,035 m) in Pakistan. Among other things, he has skied the Haute Route in Switzerland (Chamonix to Saas Fee), road- and mountain-biked extensively in Colorado and Utah, and scuba dived in many of the oceans of the world (he is a PADI Dive Master).

Soles is also a freelance photographer, writer, editor, and project consultant. He lives and plays in Boulder, Colorado.

THE MOUNTAINEERS, founded in 1906, is a non-profit outdoor activity and conservation club, whose mission is "to explore, study, preserve, and enjoy the natural beauty of the outdoors. . . . " Based in Seattle, Washington, the club is now the third-largest such organization in the United States, with 15,000 members and five branches throughout Washington State.

The Mountaineers sponsors both classes and year-round outdoor activities in the Pacific Northwest, which include hiking, mountain climbing, ski-touring, snowshoeing, bicycling, camping, kayaking and canoeing, nature study, sailing, and adventure travel. The club's conservation division supports environmental causes through educational activities, sponsoring legislation, and presenting informational programs. All club activities are led by skilled, experienced volunteers, who are dedicated to promoting safe and responsible enjoyment and preservation of the outdoors.

If you would like to participate in these organized outdoor activities or the club's programs, consider a membership in The Mountaineers. For information and an application, write or call The Mountaineers, Club Headquarters, 300 Third Avenue West, Seattle, Washington 98119; 206-284-6310.

The Mountaineers Books, an active, nonprofit publishing program of the club, produces guide-books, instructional texts, historical works, natural history guides, and works on environmental conservation. All books produced by The Mountaineers are aimed at fulfilling the club's mission.

Send or call for our catalog of more than 450 outdoor titles:

The Mountaineers Books
1001 SW Klickitat Way, Suite 201
Seattle, WA 98134
800-553-4453

mbooks@mountaineers.org
www.mountaineersbooks.org

ROCK&ICE
THE CLIMBER'S MAGAZINE

Rock & Ice is a grassroots magazine for passionate climbers of all styles and abilities. In eight issues a year, *Rock & Ice* celebrates the climbing spirit with articles and photographs that are as bold, funny, independent, diverse, and surprising as the climbers it covers.

To subscribe, call toll-free 1-877-ROCKICE, or visit us online at www.rockandice.com.

Other titles you may enjoy from The Mountaineers:

MOUNTAINEERING: The Freedom of the Hills, 6th Edition, *The Mountaineers*
The completely revised and expanded edition of the best-selling mountaineering "how-to" book of all time—required reading for all climbers.

A LIFE ON THE EDGE: Memoirs of Everest and Beyond, *Jim Whittaker*
Whittaker, the first American to summit Everest, tells the story behind the many stunning successes of his career in this extraordinary memoir. CEO of Recreational Equipment, Inc.; confidante of Bobby Kennedy; leader of the 1990 International Peace Climb; explorer and sailor who is circumnavigating the world with his family: here is an American hero revealed.

THE BURGESS BOOK OF LIES, *Adrian & Alan Burgess*
The tall tales, edge-of-your-seat adventures, and poignant stories from identical twins and accomplished mountaineers Adrian and Alan Burgess. Full of stories from major climbs all over the world, this is a great read for climbers and armchair adventurers alike.

SHERMAN EXPOSED: Slightly Censored Climbing Stories, *John Sherman*
A hilarious and irreverent collection including the best of Sherman's "Verm's World" columns for *Climbing* magazine, plus profiles of prominent climbers and previously unpublished essays.

DARK SHADOWS FALLING, *Joe Simpson*
Troubled by the 1996 events on Mount Everest, veteran mountaineer Simpson boldly speaks out on declining ethical standards in mountaineering.

POSTCARDS FROM THE LEDGE: Collected Mountaineering Writings of Greg Child, *Greg Child*
Sharp, incisive, and irreverent, this masterful storyteller entertains even as he plumbs the art and culture of the sport of mountaineering.

ERIC SHIPTON: Everest and Beyond, *Peter Steele*
Steele draws upon scores of personal interviews as well as Shipton's own correspondence to draw a complete portrait of the self-effacing explorer, with new information about his public and private life.

REINHOLD MESSNER, FREE SPIRIT: A Climber's Life, *Reinhold Messner*
One of history's greatest Himalayan mountaineers, Messner reveals the forces and events that have shaped him as an individual and as a climber in this classic autobiography.

ICE WORLD: Techniques and Experiences of Modern Ice Climbing, *Jeff Lowe*
Renowned climbing veteran Jeff Lowe shares personal stories and professional insight in this comprehensive book, which offers a history of the fascinating sport and an overview of the world's best ice climbs.

THE BEST OF ROCK & ICE: An Anthology, *Dougald MacDonald, editor*
For more than 20 years, *Rock & Ice* magazine has published excellent writing from the world's best climbers. Now, for the first time, *Rock & Ice* editor Dougald MacDonald has gathered together a collection of the magazine's best essays.